RENEWABLE ENERGY: RESEARCH, DEVELOPMENT AND POLICIES

CLEAN ENERGY

AN EXPORTER'S GUIDE TO INDIA AND CHINA

RENEWABLE ENERGY: RESEARCH, DEVELOPMENT AND POLICIES

Additional books in this series can be found on Nova's website under the Series tab.

Additional E-books in this series can be found on Nova's website under the E-book tab.

RENEWABLE ENERGY: RESEARCH, DEVELOPMENT AND POLICIES

CLEAN ENERGY

AN EXPORTER'S GUIDE TO INDIA AND CHINA

ISAAC P. LUTTRELL

EDITOR

Nova Science Publishers, Inc.

New York

For permission to use material from this book please contact us:
Telephone 631-231-7269; Fax 631-231-8175
Web Site: http://www.novapublishers.com

NOTICE TO THE READER

The Publisher has taken reasonable care in the preparation of this book, but makes no expressed or implied warranty of any kind and assumes no responsibility for any errors or omissions. No liability is assumed for incidental or consequential damages in connection with or arising out of information contained in this book. The Publisher shall not be liable for any special, consequential, or exemplary damages resulting, in whole or in part, from the readers' use of, or reliance upon, this material. Any parts of this book based on government reports are so indicated and copyright is claimed for those parts to the extent applicable to compilations of such works.

Independent verification should be sought for any data, advice or recommendations contained in this book. In addition, no responsibility is assumed by the publisher for any injury and/or damage to persons or property arising from any methods, products, instructions, ideas or otherwise contained in this publication.

This publication is designed to provide accurate and authoritative information with regard to the subject matter covered herein. It is sold with the clear understanding that the Publisher is not engaged in rendering legal or any other professional services. If legal or any other expert assistance is required, the services of a competent person should be sought. FROM A DECLARATION OF PARTICIPANTS JOINTLY ADOPTED BY A COMMITTEE OF THE AMERICAN BAR ASSOCIATION AND A COMMITTEE OF PUBLISHERS.

Additional color graphics may be available in the e-book version of this book.

Library of Congress Cataloging-in-Publication Data

Clean energy : an exporter's guide to India and China / editors, Isaac P. Luttrell.
    p. cm.
 Includes bibliographical references and index.
 ISBN 978-1-60741-329-5 (alk. paper)
 1. Clean energy industries--United States. 2. Exports--India. 3. Exports--China. I. Luttrell, Isaac P.
 HD9502.5.C543U6 2009
 333.79--dc22
                                          2009032009

Published by Nova Science Publishers, Inc. † New York

CONTENTS

Preface   vii

Chapter 1   Clean Energy: An Exporter's Guide to India   1
                 United States Department of Commerce

Chapter 2   Clean Energy: An Exporter's Guide to China   145
                 United States Department of Commerce

Chapter Sources   275

Index   277

PREFACE

This book is a clean energy technology market overview for India and China with two primary objectives: (1) to analyze the clean energy markets in India and China and (2) to identify opportunities for trade and investment through 2020. Clean energy technologies include renewable energy, hybrid and co-generation, and energy efficiency technologies for power generation; alternative fuels; and advanced technologies for transportation. They produce power for a wide range of applications using no fuel or less fuel than fossil-fuel-based technologies, produce no or fewer pollutants than conventional technologies and can use renewable energy sources, which, unlike fossil fuels, are not depleted over time. The renewable energy technologies considered in this book are biomass and biofuels, waste-to-energy, solar power, wind power, geothermal, hydropower, and ocean power. This is an edited, excerpted and augmented edition of two U.S. Department of Commerce publications.

Chapter 1- After a short introduction, Section 1 addresses clean energy technologies for India, including information on India's overall energy status, both current and projected; a market overview; identification of clean energy policies; trade and investment opportunities for U.S. firms; and barriers to clean energy market entry, development, and commercialization. This chapter also includes annexes on Indian policy-makers with authority over clean energy technologies. Section 2 provides definitions of the clean energy technologies addressed in the report.

Chapter 2- After a short introduction, Section 1 addresses clean energy technologies for China, including information on China's overall energy status, both current and projected; a market overview; identification of clean energy policies; trade and investment opportunities for U.S. firms; and barriers to clean energy market entry, development, and commercialization. This chapter also includes annexes on Chinese policy-makers with authority over clean energy technologies and information on the renewable energy industry in China. Section 2 provides definitions of the clean energy technologies addressed in the report.

In: Clean Energy: An Exporter's Guide to India and China   ISBN: 978-1-60741-329-5
Editor: Isaac P. Luttrell   © 2011 Nova Science Publishers, Inc.

Chapter 1

CLEAN ENERGY: AN EXPORTER'S GUIDE TO INDIA

United States Department of Commerce

ACRONYMS

ABS	asset-backed securities
AC	alternating current
ACEEE	American Council for an Energy-Efficient Economy
ACORE	American Council on Renewable Energy
ADB	Asian Development Bank
AEE	Association of Energy Engineers
AESP	Association of Energy Services Professionals
AFV	alcohol fuel vehicle
ALM	asset liability management
ANERT	Agency for Non-Conventional Energy and Rural Technology
APEDA	Arunachal Pradesh Energy Development Agency
APM	administered pricing mechanism
APP	Asia–Pacific Partnership on Clean Development and Climate
ASE	Alliance to Save Energy
ASEAN	Association of Southeast Asian Nations
ASTAE	Asia Alternative and Sustainable Energy
ASTM	American Society for Testing and Materials
bcm	billion cubic meters
BEE	Bureau of Energy Efficiency (India)
BERC	Bihar Electricity Regulatory Commission
BHEL	Bharat Heavy Electricals, Ltd.
BIPV	building-integrated photovoltaics
BIS	Bureau of Indian Standards
BOO	build, own, operate
BOOT	build, own, operate, and transfer
BOV	battery-operated vehicle

BPL	below poverty line
BREDA	Bihar Renewable Energy Development Agency
BSES	Brihanmumbai Suburban Electrical Supply
BT	billion tons
CCF	City Challenge Fund
CCI	Controller of Capital Issues
CDM	Clean Development Mechanism
CE	European Conformity (French acronym)
CEA	Central Electricity Authority
CER	credits for emission reductions
CERC	Central Electricity Regulatory Commission
CET	clean energy technology
CFL	compact fluorescent lighting
CHCP	combined heat, cooling, and power
CH4	methane
CHP	combined heat and power
CII	Confederation of Indian Industry
CLASP	Collaborative Labeling and Appliance Standards Program
CNG	compressed natural gas
CO2	carbon dioxide
CPCB	Central Pollution Control Board
CREDA	Chhattisgarh State Renewable Energy Development
CVC	Central Vigilance Commission
DC	direct current
DFI	development financial institution
DISCOM	distribution company
DME	di-methyl ether
DOC	U.S. Department of Commerce
DOE	Department of Environment (India)
DOP	Department of Power (India)
DSM	demand-side management
EC	energy conservation
ECB	external commercial borrowing
ECBC	Energy Conservation Building Codes
ECO	Energy Efficiency Commercialization Project
EE	energy efficiency
EEB	Bureau of Economic, Energy and Business Affairs (United States)
EEI	energy efficiency indicator
EERE	Office of Energy Efficiency and Renewable Energy (United States)
EIB	European Investment Bank
EJ	exajoule
EMCO	energy management contract
EPC	equipment procurement and construction
ESCO	energy service company
ETC	evacuated tube collectors
EV	electric vehicle

EVA	solid phase crystallization of Evaporated silicon
Ex-Im	Export–Import Bank of the United States
FAS	Foreign Agricultural Service (United States)
FDI	foreign direct investment
FI	financial institution
FYP	Five-Year Plan
GATT	General Agreement on Tariffs and Trade
GB	Guojia Biaozhun
gce	gram of coal equivalent
GDP	gross domestic product
GEDA	Gujarat Energy Development Agency
GEF	Global Environment Facility
GENCO	generation company (India)
GERC	Gujarat Electricity Regulatory Commission
Gg	gigagram
GHG	greenhouse gas
GNP	gross national product
GOI	Government of India
GPV	gas-powered vehicle
GRP	glass fiber–reinforced plastic
GW	gigawatt
GWe	gigawatt electric
GWp	gigawatt peak
HAREDA	Haryana Renewal Energy Development Agency
HDFC	Housing Development Finance Corporation Limited
HFC	hydrofluorocarbon
HIT	heterojunction with intrinsic thin layer
HT	high-tension
HUDCO	Housing and Urban Development Corporation (India)
IBRD	International Bank for Reconstruction and Development
ICB	international competitive bidding
IDBI	Industrial Development Bank of India
IDFC	Infrastructure Development Finance Company (India)
IEA	International Energy Agency
IEC	International Electrotechnical Commission
IFC	International Finance Corporation
IFCI	Industrial Finance Corporation of India
IFI	international financing institution
IGCC	integrated gasification combined cycle
IIFCL	India Infrastructure Finance Company Limited
IL&FS	Infrastructure Leasing & Financial Services Limited (India)
INR	Indian National Rupees
IP	intellectual property
IPA	Indian Patent Act
IPP	independent power producer
IPR	intellectual property rights

IREDA	Indian Renewable Energy Development Agency
ITA	U.S. International Trade Administration
JAKEDA	Jammu and Kashmir Energy Development Agency
JBIC	Japan Bank for International Cooperation
JCF	Japan Carbon Finance, Limited
JV	joint venture
kgce	kilogram of coal equivalent
kha	kilohectare
KREDL	Karnataka Renewal Energy Development Limited
kT	kiloton
kV	kilovolt
kW	kilowatt
kWe	kilowatt electric
kWh	kilowatt hour
kWp	kilowatt peak
LC	letter of credit
LED	light-emitting diode
LIC	Life Insurance Corporation (India)
LNG	liquefied natural gas
LOLP	loss of load probability
LPG	liquefied petroleum gas (Propane)
MANIREDA	Manipur Renewable Energy Development Agency
mb/d	millions of barrels per day
MEDA	Maharashtra Energy Development Agency
MIGA	Multilateral Investment Guarantee Agency
MJ	megajoule
MMSCM	million standard cubic meter
MNES	Ministry of Non-conventional Energy Sources (India)
MNRE	Ministry of New and Renewable Energy (India)
MoEF	Ministry of Environment and Forests (India)
MoF	Ministry of Finance (India)
MOP	Ministry of Power (India)
MPUVNL	Madhya Pradesh Urja Vikas Nigam Limited
MSIHC	Manufacture, Storage, and Import of Hazardous Chemicals
Mt	million tons
MT	magnetotelluric
mToe	million tons of oil equivalent
MU	million units
MW	megawatt
MWe	megawatt electric
MWeq	megawatt equivalent
MWp	megawatt peak
NABARD	National Bank for Agriculture & Rural Development (India)
NAESCO	National Association of Energy Service Companies
NB	national competitive bidding
NBC	National Building Code (India)

NCE	non-conventional energy
NEDA	Non-conventional Energy Development Agency (India)
NEDCAP	Non-conventional Energy Development Corporation of Andhra Pradesh
NELP	New Exploration and Licensing Policy (India)
NHPC	National Hydroelectric Power Corporation (India)
N2O	nitrous oxide
NOx	nitrogen oxide
NREDA	Nagaland Renewable Energy Development Agency
NREL	National Renewable Energy Laboratory of the U.S. Department of Energy
NTPC	National Thermal Power Corporation (India)
NUTP	National Urban Transport Policy (India)
OECD	Organization for Economic Co-Operation and Development
OFAC	Office of Foreign Assets Control (United States)
OGL	open general license
O&M	operation and maintenance
OPIC	Overseas Private Investment Corporation (United States)
PCF	Prototype Carbon Fund
PDCOR	Project Development Corporation (India)
PDD	Project Design Documentation
PE	private equity
PECVD	plasma-enhanced chemical vapor deposition
PEMF	Private Energy Market Fund LP
PEMFC	proton exchange membrane fuel cell
PFC	Power Finance Corporation (India)
PFDF	Pooled Finance Development Fund (India)
PGC	Power Grid Corporation (India)
PHWR	pressurized heavy water reactor
PIS	Patent Information System (India)
PNB	Punjab National Bank
PPA	power purchase agreement
PPP	public–private partnership
PSU	public–sector undertaking
PTC	Power Trading Corporation (India)
PV	photovoltaic
RBI	Reserve Bank of India
R&D	research and development
RE	renewable energy
REC	Rural Electrical Corporation (India)
REPS	renewable energy portfolio standard
RGGVY	Rajiv Gandhi Grameen Vidhyutikaran Yojana
RPS	reserve energy portfolio standard
RSPM	respirable suspended particulate matter
RTI	Right to Information Act (India)
RVE	Remote Village Electrification
SBA	Small Business Administration (United States)

SBI	State Bank of India
SEBI	Securities and Exchange Board of India
SEFI	Sustainable Energy Finance Initiative
SEK	Svensk Exportkredit
SERC	State Energy Regulatory Commission (India)
SHP	small hydropower
SHS	solar home system
SI	solar ingot
SICLIP	Swedish International Climate Investment Program
SIDBI	Small Industries Development Bank (India)
SME	small and medium enterprise
SO2	sulphur dioxide
SOE	state-owned enterprise
SPCB	State Pollution Control Board (India)
SPV	solar photovoltaics
SRDA	State Renewable Development Agency (India)
SWH	solar water heating
TC-88	Technical Committee 88 of the IEC
tce	tons of coal equivalent
TEDA	Tamil Nadu Energy Development Agency
TERI	Tata Energy Research Institute
toe	tons of oil equivalent
TPES	total primary energy supply
TRIPS	Trade-related Aspects of Intellectual Property Rights
TüV	Technische Überwachungsvereine (Germany standards/testing company)
TWh	terawatt hour
UL	Underwriters Laboratories
ULB	urban local body
UNDP	United Nations Development Program
UNICITRAL	United Nations Commission on International Trade
UPS	uninterruptible power supply
UREDA	Uttranchal Renewable Energy Development Agency
URIF	Urban Reform Incentive Fund
USAID	U.S. Agency for International Development
USDA	U.S. Department of Agriculture
USDOE	U.S. Department of Energy
USTDA	U.S. Trade and Development Agency
USTR	U.S. Trade Representative
VAT	value-added tax
VER	Verified Emission Reduction
VSD	variable-speed drive
W	watt
WEEA	World Energy Efficiency Association
WOFE	wholly-owned foreign enterprise
Wp	watt peak

| **WTG** | wind turbine generator |
| **WTO** | World Trade Organization |

Executive Summary

Introduction

This report is intended as a clean energy technology market overview for India, with two primary objectives: (1) to analyze the clean energy markets in India and (2) to identify opportunities for trade and investment through 2020. The report provides the following:

- An analysis of the existing infrastructure of clean energy technologies and market opportunities in India through 2020 including market forecasts, market drivers, cost data, and market segment analysis.
- A review of government policies for clean energy development in India.
- A detailed analysis of barriers and obstacles to clean energy technologies trade and investment in India.
- A definition of clean energy technologies for India.
- A review of resources available to U.S. businesses that wish to enter the Indian clean energy markets.

After a short introduction, Section 1 addresses clean energy technologies for India, including information on India's overall energy status, both current and projected; a market overview; identification of clean energy policies; trade and investment opportunities for U.S. firms; and barriers to clean energy market entry, development, and commercialization. This chapter also includes annexes on Indian policy-makers with authority over clean energy technologies. Section 2 provides definitions of the clean energy technologies addressed in the report.

Clean Energy Technology Defined

Clean energy technologies include renewable energy, hybrid and co-generation, and energy efficiency technologies for power generation; alternative fuels; and advanced technologies for transportation. They produce power for a wide range of applications using no fuel or less fuel than fossil-fuel-based technologies, produce no or fewer pollutants than conventional technologies and can use renewable energy sources, which, unlike fossil fuels, are not depleted over time. The renewable energy technologies considered in this report are biomass and biofuels, waste-to-energy, solar power, wind power, geothermal, hydropower, and ocean power.

Biomass consists of plant and plant-derived material. Sources include agricultural residues such as rice hulls, straw, bagasse from sugarcane production, wood chips, and coconut shells and energy crops such as sugarcane or switch grass. Biomass can be used directly for energy production or processed into fuels. Waste-to-energy technology converts energy from a waste source, such as a city's municipal waste system, farms, and other agricultural operations, or waste from commercial and industrial operations. Large-scale waste-to-energy systems can supply heat or electricity in utility-based electric power plants or district heating systems. Small-scale systems can provide heating or cooking fuel and electricity to individual farms, homes, and businesses.

Solar technologies convert light and heat from the sun into useful energy. Photovoltaic (PV) systems convert sunlight into electricity, and thermal systems collect and store solar heat for air and water heating applications. *Wind* power technology converts energy in the wind into useful power; the primary market for wind power technology is for wind turbines, which convert wind energy into electricity. *Geothermal* power is generated using thermal energy from underground sources, including steam, hot water, and heat stored in rock formations; various technologies are used to generate electricity. *Hydropower* is the conversion of energy embodied in moving water into useful power. Today, hydropower supplies about 19 percent of the world's electricity. Finally, *ocean power* technology makes use of energy in the ocean by converting it into electricity. This technology is still in the development phase,

Hybrid and co-generation power systems take advantage of the benefits of multiple technologies in a single, integrated system for power generation. Renewable-based hybrid power systems use combinations of wind turbines, PV panels, and small hydropower generators to generate electricity. Hybrid power systems typically include a diesel or other fuel-based generator (including biofuels) and may include batteries or other storage technology.

Co-generation systems, also called combined heat and power (CHP) systems, generate both electricity and useful heat. Conventional fossil-fuel-based electric power plants generate heat as a byproduct that is emitted into the environment; co-generation power plants collect this heat for use in thermal applications, thereby converting a higher percentage of the energy in the fuel into useful power. The most efficient conventional power plants have a typical fuelto-electricity conversion factor of about 50 percent, while cogeneration plants can achieve efficiencies of over 75 percent. Examples of thermal loads that can be served by a co-generation plant are: district heating systems that provide heat for towns and neighborhoods; industrial processes that require heat, such as paper mills; institutions such as prisons and hospitals; and wastewater treatment plants.

Energy efficiency (EE) involves replacing existing technologies and processes with new ones that provide equivalent or better service using less energy. EE results in energy savings at the time that the energy service is provided. Energy service providers can also use load management to change the time that an energy service is delivered in order to reduce peak loads on an energy distribution system. Demand-side management uses both load management and EE to save the amount of primary energy required to deliver the energy service.

Almost half a billion vehicles on the world's roads contribute to half of the global oil consumption and generate about 20 percent of the world's greenhouse gases, including carbon monoxide, nitrous oxides, and particulates. *Transportation technologies* can help address these issues through the use of alternative fuels and advanced technologies. Alternative fuels for transportation include biodiesel, ethanol, natural gas, and propane. Advanced vehicle technologies include electric vehicles and hybrid electric vehicles, which offer air pollution improvements over average fossil fuel vehicles. Finally, mobile idle reduction systems and diesel engine retrofits can reduce the emissions of heavy-duty vehicles.

India: Energy Overview

Clean energy technologies have received unprecedented attention in the last few years in India as its energy demand grows every year. This is largely a result of India's economy, which has steadily advanced over the last 30 years, averaging a 7 percent per year growth since 2000. During 2004 and 2005, only China's economy grew faster. With 1.1 billion people, India is the world's second most populous country behind China and is expected to have the world's largest population by 2030. Further population increases and the country's continued economic growth are expected to increase India's energy demand from 537 million tons of oil equivalent (Mtoe) in 2005 to 770 Mtoe in 2015 and to 1,299 Mtoe by 2030.

Coal is the dominant fuel in India's energy mix, a condition that is expected to persist for at least the next 25 years. India has vast coal resources, but most are of low quality. Indigenous oil and gas reserves are in short supply while demand for oil almost quadrupled from 1980 to 2005. Oil imports are projected to increase even more going forward, leaving the country more vulnerable to international price spikes and potentially unreliable supplies. In 2005 India ranked fourth in energy consumption, after the United States, China, and Russia. By 2030, India is expected to surpass Russia and be the third-largest energy consumer.

Energy demand grew by 3.5 percent per year during the period 1990–2005. Supply has not kept up, and a deficit of 11,463 megawatt (MW), equivalent to 12.3 percent of peak demand, was recorded in peak hours in India during 2006. The states of Gujarat, Maharashtra, Meghalaya, Jammu and Kashmir, Punjab, and Madhya Pradesh recorded more than a 20 percent deficit in the availability of power during peak hours – a deficit that is expected to increase in the future. India has an installed base of about 124,287 MW of electricity as of the year 2006, which includes about 66 percent thermal energy (85 percent of which is coal based) followed by hydro with 26 percent, nuclear with 3 percent, and renewable energy with 5 percent. Of the current total installed renewable energy base, wind constitutes 69 percent, followed by small hydro (19 percent), biomass (co-generation, 11.5 percent), waste-toenergy (0.42 percent), and solar (0.03 percent).

Market assessments indicate that India could eventually be the largest renewable market in the world, given its abundance of renewable energy resources. The country has already developed electricity from small hydro, wind, and biomass (co-generation), but the contribution of waste-to-energy and solar energy is very small, while electricity generation from solar thermal, geothermal, and ocean power is non-existent. This is an indicator of the opportunity that is available in harnessing the full potential of these sectors.

Renewable Resources, Capacity, and Potential

India's renewable energy resource potential is significant, with wind energy, biomass, and small hydropower representing the technologies with the largest potential. Wind has been the most successful renewable resource to date and has the most potential going forward. Currently however only nine states use wind energy and they represent over 99 percent of the nation's total wind capacity. Assuming 20 percent grid penetration in the future and an increase in the availability of wind resources in certain provinces – most notably Maharashtra, Andhra Pradesha, Tamil Nadu, and Gujarat – wind could potentially account for up to 45,000 MW of energy per year. Since the total installed wind capacity in 2006 was only 5,341 MW, this represents a significant opportunity for American companies. The majority of wind resources are found in coastal states, where geographic and climatic conditions are favorable for wind farms.

The approximate potential for biomass utilization (largely co-generation) is estimated at about 22,000 MW. Waste-to-energy potential is approximately 2,700 MW. It has been estimated that India produces 139 million tons of surplus biomass every year, which can produce about 16,000 MW of electricity. Rajasthan, Punjab, Uttar Pradesh, Maharashtra, Madhya Pradesh, Haryana, and Gujarat account for 76 percent of the projected potential, and Rajasthan alone accounts for 25 percent of the total projected potential. The installed capacity of biomass power/co-generation increased from 381 MW in 2002 to 1,253 MW through September 2007. Andhra Pradesh, Karnataka, Tamil Nadu, and Uttar Pradesh account for 77 percent of the total installed capacity in the country. This trend is due to the availability of biomass and bagasse, which is used as raw material for electricity generation. Maharashtra and Uttar Pradesh are the two major bagasse-producing states, accounting for 57 percent of India's projected bagasse potential (3,500 MW total). About 166 MW of renewable energy can be found in distributed non-grid connected generation in India

Ethanol and biodiesel have been identified as key focus areas by the Indian Government, though currently both are in the early stages of commercialization. In 2004, the government mandated a 5 percent blending of gasoline with ethanol, subject to certain conditions. In addition, an autonomous National Biodiesel Board was created to promote, finance, and support organizations that are engaged in oilseed cultivation and oil processing leading to biodiesel production. The state governments of Andhra Pradesh, Chhattisgarh, Gujarat, and Tamil Nadu have even created state biodiesel boards and are implementing buy-back schemes with farmers to promote additional biodiesel development. Private players are participating in the plantation phase of the biodiesel production chain in Tamil Nadu. In Gujarat, private companies are producing quality biodiesel that meets the American Society for Testing and Materials (ASTM) 16750 standard.

India has an estimated hydropower potential of 84,000 MW, of which 15,000 MW is from small hydropower (SHP). The Ministry of New and Renewable Energy (MNRE) has identified 4,227 potential SHP sites, which could account for 10,324 MW of potential energy. India had only 1,748 MW of installed SHP capacity in 2006, meaning the market for SHP is expected to increase substantially. The potential of this sector is however dependent on the availability of water resources, which are thus far abundant in a majority of states. In fact, of the 135,000 MW capacity addition requirement anticipated by the government, 35,500 MW are expected to come from hydropower. Toward this end, a 50,000-MW hydroelectric initiative was launched in 2003.

India also receives abundant solar radiation equivalent to over 5,000 trillion kilowatt hours (kWh) per year. The government has had a PV program in place for over two decades, yet the current installed capacity is just 3 MW, only a small proportion of the overall energy mix. PV systems are promoted primarily for rural and off-grid applications, consisting mainly of mini-grids, solar home systems, solar lanterns, and solar street lights. The overall solar water heater potential in India is estimated to be 140 million m^2 of collector area, of which about 1.9 million m^2 have been installed in buildings and in industry.

Energy Efficiency, Co-Generation, and Transportation

India's energy efficiency potential mostly comes from supply side high-efficiency, low-emission coal, thermal, or electric power generation. Transmission and distribution losses have been recorded to exceed 25 percent, indicating a potential market for firms able to reduce these inefficiencies. Industry has been a major target of the energy efficiency effort, as it accounts for 50 percent of the total commercial energy use in India. Six key industries—aluminum, cement, fertilizers, pulp and paper, petrochemicals, and steel—account for about two-thirds of total industrial energy use. The energy intensity in these industries is higher than in developed countries, mainly owing to obsolete and energy inefficient technologies. Nonetheless, energy efficiency in Indian industry has increased steadily. In cement, steel, aluminum, and fertilizers, the average energy consumption has been declining as a result of energy conservation in existing units and the development of efficient technologies. Energy efficiency in building and construction has not been the beneficiary of a concerted energy efficiency effort and needs to be assessed and targeted.

As of 2006, India had an installed capacity of 582 MW of bagasse co-generation, including grid and off-grid installations. By 2012, a total of 1,200 MW of installed cogeneration from bagasse is projected.

In transportation, the rapid growth in motor vehicle activity in India is contributing to high levels of urban air pollution, among other adverse socioeconomic, environmental, health, and welfare impacts. The demand for transport increased by 1.9 percent per year from 2000–2005, but is projected to double by 2015 and more than quadruple by 2030. The slow growth in demand for diesel to date may be due to improved effi ciency of new cars and trucks and switching to compressed natural gas vehicles for public transportation in some major cities. However, like many developing countries, India lacks mandatory vehicle fuel effi ciency standards. The Ministry of New and Renewable Energy is promoting several research, development, and demonstration projects including a demonstration project in batteryoperated vehicles (BOVs), which help in conserving oil and curbing environmental pollutions. In addition, fuel cell–battery hybrid vehicles with domestically developed exchange membrane fuel cells of 10 kW have undergone field performance evaluation, which could lead to domestic production and wider applications of fuel cell systems across the country. Hydrogen fuel is expected to be a major alternative to fossil fuels for India's transport sector by 2020. Various laboratories in the country are developing different technologies for production, storage, and transportation.

Market Analysis

In India's 11th Five-Year Plan, the government aims to achieve a GDP growth rate of 10 percent and maintain an average growth of about 8 percent during the next 15 years. This growth will be highly dependent on the expansion of the country's energy consumption. Due to rapidly expanding demand for power, a capacity addition of over 100,000 MW is planned through 2011 and 2012. Though this is largely based on growth of thermal generation, the contribution of electricity from renewable sources is expected to increase, with wind energy continuing to lead the way. As Table A shows, India needs 347,000 additional megawatts of energy through 2020, of which renewables can account for 24 percent of the needed capacity. One of the major requirements for developing this sector is the availability of cost-effective technologies and successful demonstrations.

Table A also shows the renewable energy targets in the 11th Five-Year Plan—which goes through 2012. These targets correspond to a need for massive investment in the clean energy sector in India. In fact, the projected addition of 15,000 MW from renewable energy could lead to $21 billion in investment over the next ten years.

Table A. India's Renewable Energy Potential and Targets

	Potential (MW)	Installed Capacity as of March 2007 (MW)	Target of 11th five year Plan (MW)
Small hydro	15,000	1,976	1,400
Wind	45,000	7,092	10,500
Solid biomass	19,500	569	500
Bagasse CHP	3,500	615	1,200
Waste-to-energy	1,700	43 400	
Solar	3	50	
Distributed RE power Systems	950		
Total	**84,700**	**10,298**	**15,000**

Source: Report of the Working Group on New and Renewable Energy for 11th Five-Year Plan.

The current capital cost of small hydro and wind in India is similar and ranges from $900–1300/kW and $950–1100/kW, respectively. Biomass is slightly less, at $800–1000/kW. Bagasse co-generation and biomass gasification range from $600–800/kW. PV is by far the highest at $5000–6500/kW. The delivery cost for all the above except for PV ranges from $0.045–7/kWh, with co-generation at the bottom of the range and wind at the top; PV is in the range of $0.19–40/kWh.

India currently manufactures wind generators with up to 1,650 kW of per unit capacity. To harness the projected wind potential, however, new technologies with higher capacities are needed in the country. India has a fairly developed capacity and technology for designing, constructing, and operating small hydropower plants. There has been continuous improvement with time in India's small hydro technology, with increasingly efficient and reliable domestic equipment. In addition, India has manufacturing facilities for equipment and components used in solar PV systems, though there is a need for megawatt-scale PV power-generating systems. A number of solar thermal applications have also been developed in India, which include water/air heating, cooking, drying of agricultural and food products, water purification, detoxification of wastes, cooling and refrigeration, heat for industrial processes, and electric power generation. Most of the solar thermal devices and systems are manufactured in India.

Manufacturing capability also exists in India for the equipment/machinery required in biomass projects. Biomass co-generation combustion technology is already in operation as well as atmospheric gasifiers, in which the country has significant experience and expertise. Thus, except for critical control equipment and high-effi ciency turbines, most of the equipment can be procured from indigenous sources. India has limited local capacity for waste-to-energy technology, however, and large-scale operation of biomethanation, combustion/incineration, pyrolysis/ gasification, landfill gas recovery, and other technologies requires import of design, engineering, and equipment.

Three major drivers exist for clean energy demand in India. First, the gap between existing electricity supply and demand is large and expected to grow. Second, the need to strengthen energy security has caused India to invest in wind, biomass, and hydropower generation as a way to diversify their energy portfolio. Third, fossil fuels imports are increasingly susceptible to price fluctuations and leave India vulnerable to supply insecurity;

increasing dependence on indigenous and renewable resources is thus an attractive countermeasure.

India's environmental, social, and health concerns are serious—India is a top greenhouse gas (GHG) emitter in the world, with corresponding costs in health and productivity. Indoor air pollution in rural areas from reliance on biomass for cooking, for instance, causes serious health issues for women and children. Nonetheless, India enjoys significant resources for clean energy development including both human and ecological resources, and strong government support. These factors in themselves are important indicators of India's energy future.

Energy Policy

India's energy sector has undergone a significant renaissance over the last decade as a number of new policies have created both the institutions to promote clean technology development but also the momentum and government support needed to see projects through to completion. New policies include the National Environment Policy, which provides guidance on air pollution reduction, climate change, and GHG mitigation; promotion of clean technologies; and the measurement of effi ciency per unit of economic output. The National Tariff Policy establishes power purchase tariffs for the State Electricity Regulatory Commissions. India's Ministry of New and Renewable Energy has issued a draft renewable energy policy that identifies the strategies for increased deployment of grid-connected renewable energy technologies. The country's Rural Electrification Policy goals include provision of access to electricity to all households by the year 2009.

The National Electricity Policy of 2005 stipulated that the energy intensity of GDP growth must be lowered through higher energy efficiency, and merged the Petroleum Conservation Research Association and the Bureau of Energy Efficiency to form an agency capable of moving energy efficiency investments forward. The newly created board set standards for labeling energy-intensive equipment created financial penalties for equipment that fails to meet minimum standards, and mandated the purchase of renewable-energy-based through competitive bidding.

As of March 2007, the conduct of energy audits has been made mandatory in large energy-consuming units in nine industrial sectors. These units, indicated as "designated consumers," are also required to employ "certified energy managers" and report energy consumption and energy conservation data annually. To achieve the potential of 15,000 MW of renewable energy within the 11th Five-Year Plan period, the proposed energy efficiency measures include forming industry-specific task forces, conducting energy audits among designated consumers, recording and publishing best practices per sector, developing energy consumption norms, and monitoring compliance with mandated provision by designated consumers. The program includes capacity building to train key personnel in energy efficiency measures and management.

Among the fiscal policies already in place are income tax holidays, accelerated depreciation, duty-free import of renewable energy equipment, capital subsidies and concessionary financing from the Indian Renewable Energy Development Agency, requirements for energy purchases by distribution companies, and exemptions from electricity taxes and sales taxes. In addition to these financial incentives, wind energy projects and equipment used in biomass/bagasse power generation can claim accelerated depreciation in the first year of the project. There is also a liberalized foreign investment approval regime to facilitate foreign investment and transfer of technology through joint ventures.

Opportunities for U.S. Clean Technology Firms in India

Opportunities for U.S. clean tech firms are numerous in India thanks to the scope of energy demand and the government's warm response to energy efficiency and renewable technologies. According to India's integrated energy policy, in order to deliver a sustained growth of 8 percent through 2031, India will need to expand its primary energy supply by at least three to four times and electricity supply by five to seven times its current consumption. As such, the power sector is expected to add over 150,000 MW over the next 15 years, of which at least 10 percent is expected to come from renewable energy technologies. Different states are in the process of issuing tariff orders for renewable energy electricity generation and specifying quotas for power from renewable energy in accordance with the Electricity Act of 2003. This government push can translate into major opportunities for foreign firms.

Other major government initiatives include an installment of 1 million household solar water heating (SWH) systems, rural electrification of 24,000 villages using renewable mini-grids, and deployment of 5 million solar lanterns and 2 million solar home lighting systems throughout the countryside. Investment opportunities are available for corporate users of power, long-term investors in power, promoters of clean power, and trading credits for emission reductions. Private-sector companies can set up enterprises to operate as licensee or generating companies. A foreign investor can enter into a joint venture not only for renewable energy devices/products but also for manufacturing renewable-energy-based power generation projects on a build, own, and operate basis.

At the sector level, small hydropower (SHP), wind, and solar energy offer the maximum scope for clean energy development. However, these sectors are relatively mature with significant local capacity; therefore, U.S. companies may face competition in these sectors. Geothermal and tidal energy sectors offer the advantages of early entry into the Indian market. Opportunities for U.S. firms include products, equipment, demonstrated technology, and project development in these sectors. There is a need to assess the potential of geothermal resources in India and to harness these resources for power generation and for direct heat applications for space heating, greenhouse cultivation, and cooking. The potential of tidal energy and harnessing it for power generation also needs to be assessed.

In general, a lack of technical expertise exists in installation, operations, maintenance, troubleshooting, and other aspects of clean energy implementation. Technological needs in the SHP sector include technology for directdrive low-speed generators for low-head sources, technology for submersible turbo-generators, and technology for variable-speed operation. There is also a need for proven high capacity wind turbines, generally greater than 1-2 MW. In addition, there is a need for turbines adapted to low-wind regimes and improved design for rotor blades, gear boxes, and control systems. In the PV sector, there is demand for thin-film solar cell technology, technology for megawatt-scale power generation, and improvements in crystalline silicon solar cell/module technology. Building integration for PV and solar thermal systems is also an area of opportunity.

In bioenergy, opportunities are many and include development of megawatt-scale fluidized bed biomass gasifiers; development of poly-generation facilities for the production of liquid fuels, a variety of chemicals, and hydrogen in addition to power production; development of more efficient kilns for charcoal production and pyrolysis of biomass; and raising the system efficiency of small (up to 1 MW) combustion and turbine technologies. Biofuel needs include engine modifications for using more than 20 percent biodiesel as a diesel blend. There is a need for waste-to-energy technological development across the board, including the successful demonstration of biomethanation, combustion/incineration, pyrolysis/gasification, landfill gas recovery, densification, and pelletization. In the nascent geothermal and ocean power sectors, there is a need for technology suppliers, equipment manufacturers, and project developers. Finally, energy-efficiency service companies and energy efficiency equipment suppliers for buildings and industries could be extremely profitable.

Barriers for U.S. Firms

Given the existing market conditions in India, U.S. firms may encounter challenges in the areas of competition from local suppliers and equipment manufacturers in the SHP, wind, and solar energy sectors. In addition, there appears to be a lack of coordination and integration of renewable energy and energy efficiency policies across broader development issues, including a disconnect between Indian government ministries, states, and sub-sectors. Policies are often unclear and inconsistent and distortions may arise because of uneven price settings across and within sub-sectors. The enforcement of the legal restrictions has also been a significant barrier to participation in the renewable energy market. Issues include informal governance based on social relationships and reciprocity that arises from a complex legal process and the lack of legal enforcement. Regulatory issues such as time delays, complexity in the permitting and sitting of projects pose, and the lack of monitoring of legal and financial disclosures are present additional barriers.

Conclusion

Clean energy technologies have moved to the forefront of India's energy infrastructure and investments opportunities. This is driven by the need to enhance energy security and fuel diversity, meet increasing energy needs in an environmentally sustainable manner, and advance economic and social development, all while reducing poverty and sustaining economic growth. Though barriers exist from a technology, policy, and investment perspective, India promises to be one of the largest markets for clean energy, and U.S. companies have a significant role to play in both trade and investment. The advantages of the Indian clean energy technology market include a strong industrial base and fast-growing economy; availability of skilled, relatively cheap labor; one of the world's largest renewable energy programs; the world's only dedicated federal ministry to support renewable energy (MNRE) and the only government financial institution exclusively supporting renewable energy and energy efficiency (Indian Renewable Energy Development Agency—IREDA). These are buttressed by a favorable government policy environment, low inflation and moderate tax rates, and a strong and growing carbon finance market.

By 2012—the completion of the 11th Five-Year Plan—the Indian Government has set a goal for at least 10 percent of power generation to come from renewable energy sources, with a 4–5 percent share in the electricity mix. Presently at over 10,000 MW of installed capacity, renewable energy is projected to reach over 24,000 MW by 2012. India's rich renewable energy resource endowment provides opportunities across a spectrum of technologies—

biomass, solar PV, solar thermal, wind, hydropower, solid and industrial waste-to-energy, geothermal, and tidal energy. The prospects for U.S. firms are encouraging, including research, development, and demonstration; technical collaborations; product and equipment sales; project design, development, and promotion; power generation and production; operational and maintenance (O&M); project monitoring; carbon finance/trading; and consulting services. U.S. firms should find ample opportunity to enhance their competitive market position in this rapidly expanding marketplace.

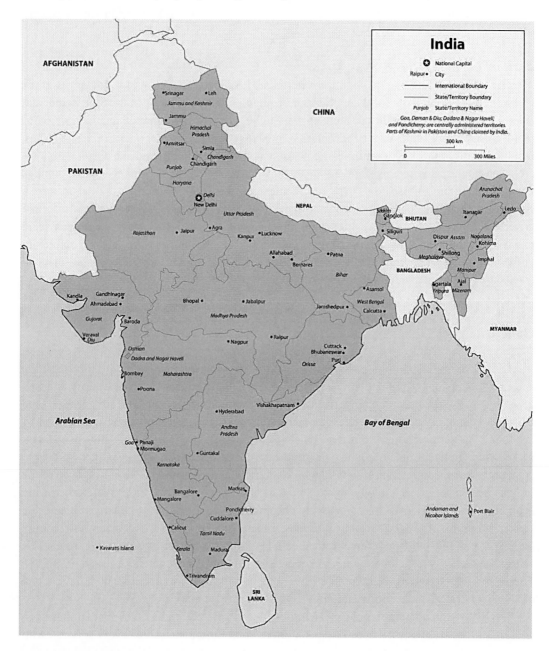

INTRODUCTION

Purpose

The report's objectives are twofold: (1) to analyze the clean energy market in India and (2) to identify opportunities for trade and investment through 2020.

Approach

The report provides the following:

- An analysis of the existing infrastructure of clean energy technologies and market opportunities in India through 2020. This includes market forecasts, market drivers, cost data, and market segment analysis.
- A review of government policies for clean energy development in India.
- A detailed analysis of barriers and obstacles to clean energy technologies trade and investment in India.
- A definition of clean energy technologies for India.
- A review of resources available to U.S. businesses that wish to engage in clean energy trade and investment in India.

Methodology

Both primary and secondary data sources were used in the preparation of this report. These included:

India Resources

- Annual reports from relevant ministries at the national level and, where available, at the state levels;
- List of relevant agencies, areas of operation, and contact details;
- Policy documents (e.g., India's Electricity Act 2003, India's New and Renewable Energy Policy Statement 2005) as well as documents stating quotas, tax requirements, procurement requirements, foreign investment policy, and master plans for technology development in different sectors;
- Statistical documents containing installed capacity, energy balance, consumption, etc.;
- Five-Year Plans and ministerial long-term development plans; Annual Reports of relevant corporations;
- Data related to financial markets in India.

U.S. Government Sources

- U.S. Department of Commerce;
- U.S. Department of Energy, including the National Renewable Energy Laboratory, Energy Information Agency, and Office of Energy Efficiency and Renewable Energy;
- U.S. Agency for International Development (India);
- U.S. Trade and Development Administration;
- Export–Import Bank of the United States;
- Asia–Pacific Partnership on Clean Development and Climate.

International Institutions

- Asian Development Bank;
- World Bank;
- International Energy Agency.

Trade, Industry, and Sector Associations; Business Counsels

- Interviews conducted with key trade associations, including the Indian Confederation of Indian Industry (CII);
- Interviews with the United States–India Business Council;
- Documents from the American Council on Renewable Energy (ACORE).

Transmission and Distribution Agencies, Manufacturers, Generators

- Annual Reports from various industry leaders operating in India;
- Annual Reports of major electricity generators in India.

Organization of the Report

The remainder of this report is organized as follows:

- Section 1 provides a market overview for India. This chapter includes information on India's overall energy status, both current and projected; a market overview; identification of clean energy policies; trade and investment opportunities for U.S. firms; and barriers to clean energy market entry, development, and commercialization. The chapter also includes annexes on key Indian policy-makers with authority over clean energy technologies and information on the renewable energy industry in India.
- Section 2 provides a definition of clean energy technologies addressed in the report. This chapter includes energy efficiency, distributed generation, combined heat and power, wind, solar photovoltaics, solar thermal, small hydropower, biomass, biofuels, waste-to-energy, geothermal, and ocean energy technologies.

- Appendix A provides a compendium of trade and investment resources for U.S. clean technology firms. Contact information for individual organizations is also included.
- Appendix B provides a directory of sustainable energy-financing sources. This directory is synthesized from the on-line resource available at www.sef-directory.net/, which is maintained by the Sustainable Energy Finance Initiative, a joint initiative of the United Nations Environment Program and the Basel Agency for Sustainable Energy.

SECTION 1: INDIA

1. India's Energy Status

India is the world's fourth-largest economy, after the United States, China, and Japan. India's economy has grown steadily over the last 30 years, averaging 7 percent annually since 2000. During 2004 and 2005, only China's economy grew faster.[1] India is now home to approximately 1.1 billion people—constituting roughly 17 percent of the world's population—and is the world's second most populous country. By 2030, India is expected to overtake China and have the world's largest population.

Energy Supply and Demand

Due primarily to the projected increase in population and the country's continued economic growth, primary energy demand in India is expected to increase from 537 Mtoe in 2005 to 770 Mtoe in 2015 and to 1,299 Mtoe by 2030 (see Table 1.1). Over the period 1990–2005, demand grew by 3.5 percent per year.

As indicated by the above table, coal is expected to remain the dominant fuel in India's energy mix over the next 25 years. Demand for oil will steadily increase to a projected 328 mToe by the year 2030, still one-half the projected demand for coal. Other renewables, mostly wind power, are projected to grow 12 percent per year, albeit from a relatively low baseline. Nuclear and hydropower supplies grow in absolute terms, but they make only a minor contribution to primary energy demand in 2030—3 percent in the case of nuclear and 2 percent for hydropower.

Table 1.1. Indian Primary Energy Demand in the Reference Scenario (mToe)

	1990	2000	2005	2015	2030	2005–2030*
Coal	106	164	208	330	620	4.5%
Oil	63	114	129	188	328	3.8%
Gas	10	21	29	48	93	4.8%
Nuclear	2	4	5	16	33	8.3%
Hydro	6	6	9	13	22	3.9%
Biomass	133	149	158	171	194	0.8%
Other renewables	0	0	1	4	9	11.7%
Total	**320**	**459**	**537**	**770**	**1299**	**3.6%**
Total excluding biomass	*186*	*311*	*379*	*599*	*1105*	*4.4%*

Source: International Energy Agency, World Energy Outlook 2007: China and India Insights (Paris, France: OCED/IEA, 2007).

Table 1.2. Key Energy Indicators for India

	1980	1990	2000	2005
Total primary energy demand (Mtoe)	209	320	459	537
Oil demand (mb/d)	0.7	1.2	2.3	2.6
Coal demand (Mtoe)	75	152	235	297
Gas demand (bcm)	1.4	11.9	25.4	34.8
Biomass and waste (Mtoe)	116	133	149	158
Electricity output (TWh)	119	289	562	699
TPES/GDP (index, 2005 = 100)	163	142	120	100
Total primary energy demand per capita (toe)	0.30	0.38	0.45	0.49
CO2 emissions per capita (tonne)	0.43	0.69	0.95	1.05
Oil imports	0.5	0.6	1.6	1.8
Electricity demand per capita (kWh)	174	341	553	639

Source: International Energy Agency, World Energy Outlook 2007: China and India Insights (Paris, France: OCED/IEA, 2007, p. 444).

As shown in Table 1.2, demand for oil in India almost quadrupled from 1980 to 2005, with consumption in 1980 in the amount of 0.7 mb/d, increasing to 2.6 mb/d in 2005.[2] These increasing oil imports have left the country more vulnerable to international price spurts and potentially unreliable supplies. Likewise, gasoline demand spiked from 1.4 bcm in 1980 to 34.8 bcm in 2005, a growth of over 2,000 percent.

Figure 1.1 shows in 2005 India ranked fourth in world energy consumption, after the United States, China, and Russia. By 2030, however, India is expected to surpass Russia and become the third-largest energy consumer in the world, after China and the United States.

As of 2006, India had an installed 124,287 MW base of electricity. Thermal energy (coal, oil, and diesel) contributes 66 percent of the total, followed by hydro (26 percent), renewable energy (5 percent), and nuclear (3 percent). The regional split is roughly equal. Southern India contributes 29 percent of the country's installed capacity, the western region 28 percent, northern India 27 percent, and eastern India 16 percent. The installed electricity generation capacity in India by state is listed in Table 1.3.

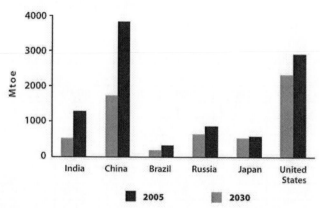

Source: International Energy Agency, *World Energy Outlook 2007: China and India Insights* (Paris, France: OCED/IEA, 2007).

Figure 1.1. Primary Energy Demand in Selected Countries in the Reference Scenario

Table 1.3. Installed Electricity Generation Capacity (MW) in India during 2006

STATE/ UNION TERRITORY / CENTRAL SECTOR	HYDRO	%	COAL	%	GAS	%	OIL	%	TOTAL THERMAL	%	NUCLEAR	%	RENEWABLE ENERGY SOURCES	%	TOTAL
Northern region															
Chandigarh	0	0	0	0	0	0	2	100	2	100	0	0	0	0	2
Delhi	0	0	320	34.32	612.4	65.68	0	0	932.4	100	0	0	0	0	932.4
Haryana	946.64	37.07	1602.50	62.76	0	0	3.92	0.15	1606.42	62.91	0	0	30	0.01	2553.36
Himachal Pradesh	323.00	86.78	0	0	0	0	0.13	0	0.13	0.03	0	0	49.08	13.19	372.21
Jammu and Kashmir	309.15	61.38	0	0	175.00	34.74	8.94	1.77	183.94	36.52	0	0	10.59	2.10	503.68
Punjab	2470.52	52.39	2130.00	45.17	0	0	0	0	2130.00	47.03	0	0	115.25	2.44	4715.77
Rajasthan	1008.84	26.72	2420.00	64.09	113.80	3.01	0	0	2533.80	67.10	0	0	233.29	6.18	3775.93
Uttar Pradesh	518.60	10.78	4280.00	88.98	0	0	0	0	4280.00	88.98	0	0	11.40	0.24	4810.00
Uttarakhand	986.93	96.79	0	0	0	0	0	0	0	0	0	0	32.77	3.21	1019.70
Central sector	4108.00	28.45	6840.00	47.37	2311.99	16.01	0	0	9151.99	63.38	1180.00	8.17	0	0	14439.99
Private sector	390.30	61.73	0	0	0	0	0	0	0	0	0	0	241.91	38.27	632.11
Subtotal	11061.88	32.77	17592.50	52.11	3213.19	9.52	14.99	0.04	20820.68	61.68	1180.00	3.50	694.59	2.06	33757.15
Western region															
Chhattisgarh	125.00	8.86	1280.00	90.72	0	0	0	0	1280.00	90.90	0	0	6.00	0.43	1411.00
Dadra and Nagar Haveli	0	0	0	0	0	0	0	0	0	0	0	0	0	0	0
Daman and Diu	0	0	0	0	0	0	0	0	0	0	0	0	0	0	0
Goa	0	0	0	0	0	0	0	0	0	0	0	0	0.05	100.00	0.05
Gujarat	745.00	12.91	4429.00	76.76	478.72	8.30	17.28	0.30	4925.00	85.36	0	0	99.73	1.71	5769.73
Madhya Pradesh	1573.17	42.01	2157.50	57.61	0	0	0	0	2157.50	57.61	0	0	14.51	0.39	3745.18
Maharashtra	2777.66	27.26	6425.00	63.06	912.00	8.95	0	0	7337.00	72.01	0	0	74.76	0.73	10189.42
Central sector	1000.00	12.58	4360.00	54.83	1292.00	16.25	0	0	5652.00	71.08	1300.00	16.35	0	0	7952.00
Private sector	460.50	7.61	2290.00	37.84	2398.00	39.62	0.20	0	4688.20	77.46	0	0	903.78	14.93	6052.43
Subtotal	6681.33	19.02	20941.50	59.63	5080.72	14.47	17.48	0.05	26039.70	74.15	1300.00	3.7	1098.83	3.13	35119.86
Southern region															
Andhra Pradesh	3582.61	51.63	2952.50	42.55	272.30	3.92	0	0	3224.80	46.47	0	0	131.46	1.89	6938.87
Karnataka	3376.20	61.50	1470.00	26.78	0	0	127.92	2.33	1597.92	29.11	0	0	515.31	9.39	5489.43
Kerala	1807.60	86.47	0	0	0	0	234.60	11.22	234.60	11.22	0	0	48.12	2.30	2090.32
Puducherry	0	0	0	0	32.50	100.00	0	0	32.50	100.00	0	0	0	0	32.50
Tamil Nadu	2145.85	32.43	2970.00	44.89	431.00	6.51	0	0	3401.00	51.40	0	0	1069.85	16.17	6616.70
Central sector	0	0	8090.00	86.80	350.00	3.76	0	0	8440.00	90.56	880.00	9.44	0	0	9320.00
Private sector	55.45	0.93	510.00	8.56	2348.70	39.41	576.80	9.68	3435.50	57.65	0	0	2468.75	41.42	5959.70
Subtotal	10967.71	30.09	15992.50	43.88	3434.50	9.42	393.32	2.58	20366.32	55.88	880.00	2.41	4233.49	11.62	36447.52
Eastern region															
Bihar	44.90	7.14	553.50	88.02	0	0	0	0	553.50	88.02	0	0	30.40	4.83	628.80
Jharkhand	130.00	9.33	1260.00	90.38	0	0	0	0	1260.00	90.38	0	0	4.05	0.29	1394.05
Orissa	1921.93	82.04	420.00	17.91	0	0	0	0	420.00	17.91	0	0	1.30	0.06	2345.23
Sikkim	32.00	69.41	0	0	0	0	5.00	10.85	5.00	13.19	0	0	9.10	19.74	46.10
West Bengal	161.70	4.44	3305.00	90.84	101.00	2.75	12.06	0.31	3417.06	93.92	0	0	59.70	1.64	3638.46
Private sector	0	0	1441.36	99.50	0	0	0.14	0.01	1441.52	99.51	0	0	7.12	0.49	1448.64
Central sector	204.00	2.92	6682.50	95.79	90.00	1.29	0	0	6772.50	97.08	0	0	0	0	6976.50
Subtotal	2496.53	15.15	13662.38	82.91	190.00	1.15	17.20	0.10	13869.58	84.17	0	0	111.67	0.68	16477.78
Northeastern region															
Arunachal Pradesh	18.50	30.74	0	0	0	0	15.88	26.19	15.88	26.39	0	0	25.80	42.87	60.18
Assam	2.00	0.33	330.00	55.25	2444.50	40.93	20.69	3.46	595.19	99.65	0	0	0.11	0.02	597.30
Manipur	1.50	2.95	0	0	0	0	45.41	89.28	45.41	89.28	0	0	3.95	7.77	50.86
Meghalaya	185.52	98.12	0	0	0	0	2.05	1.08	2.05	1.09	0	0	1.51	0.80	189.08
Nagaland	25.50	83.14	0	0	0	0	2.00	6.52	2.00	6.52	0	0	3.17	10.34	30.67
Tripura	16.00	10.78	0	0	127.50	85.94	4.85	3.27	132.35	89.21	0	0	0.01	0.01	148.36
Mizoram	4.05	6.08	0	0	0	0	51.86	77.86	51.86	77.84	0	0	10.71	16.08	66.62
Central sector	860.00	69.64	0	0	375.00	30.36	0	0	375.00	30.36	0	0	0	0	1235.00
Private sector	0	0	0	0	24.50	93.87	0	0	24.50	93.87	0	0	1.60	6.13	26.10
Subtotal	1113.07	46.30	330.00	13.73	771.50	32.09	142.74	5.94	1244.24	51.75	0	0	46.86	1.95	2404.17
Islands															
Andaman and Nicobar Islands	5.25	10.39	0	0	0	0	40.05	79.23	40.05	79.23	0	0	5.25	10.39	50.55
Lakshadweep	0	0	0	0	0	0	9.97	100.00	9.97	100.00	0	0	0	0	9.97
Private sector	0	0	0	0	0	0	20.00	99.16	20.00	99.16	0	0	0.17	0.84	20.17
Subtotal	5.25	6.51	0	0	0	0	70.02	86.78	70.02	86.78	0	0	5.42	6.72	80.69
All India	32325.77	26.01	68518.88	55.13	12689.91	10.21	1201.75	0.97	82410.54	66.31	3360.00	2.70	6190.86	4.98	124287.17

Source: TERI Energy Data and Yearbook 2006.

India's Energy Deficit

The state-by-state peak demand, supply, and deficit for 2006 are shown in Table 1.4. As the table indicates, a 11,463 MW deficit was recorded in 2006, equivalent to 12.3 percent of peak demand. Gujarat, Maharashtra, Meghalaya, Jammu and Kashmir, Punjab, and Madhya Pradesh recorded more than a 20 percent deficit in availability of power during peak hours. Goa, Daman and Diu, Chandigarh, Dadra and Nagar Haveli, Puducherry, and Damodar Valley Corporation recorded negligible peak-hour deficits in electricity. However, all other states also noted electricity deficits during peak hours. At the regional level, the eastern region recorded the least peakhour deficits, while the western region recorded most.

Electricity supply and demand scenarios for national, regional, and state levels are summarized in Table 1.5. This table indicates that a deficit of 52,938 million units (MU), equivalent to 8.4 percent of demand, was recorded in 2006. Maharashtra, Meghalaya, Jammu and Kashmir, and Uttar Pradesh each recorded more than a 15 percent deficit in availability of power during 2006. Except for Puducherry, all states and union territories recorded overall deficits in availability of electricity. At the regional level, the southern region recorded the least deficit, while the western region recorded the least deficit, while the western region recorded the highest. The deficit is expected to increase in the future considering the future demand scenarios described in subsequent sections.

Table 1.4. Peak Supply and Demand Scenario over 2006

State/System/Region	Peak Demand (Mw)	Peak Met (Mw)	Surplus/Deficit (Mw)	(%)
Chandigarh	240	240	0	0
Delhi	3722	3600	-122	-3.3
Haryana	4333	3931	-402	-9.3
Himachal Pradesh	788	749	-39	-4.9
Jammu and Kashmir	1600	1225	-375	-23.4
Punjab	7731	6158	-1573	-20.3
Rajasthan	5588	4850	-738	-13.2
Uttar Pradesh	8175	6588	-1587	-19.4
Uttarakhand	991	857	-134	-13.5
northern region	**28154**	**25200**	**-2954**	**-10.5**
Chhattisgarh	2133	1857	-276	-12.9
Gujarat	9783	7610	-2173	-22.2
Madhya Pradesh	6558	5136	-1422	-21.7
Maharashtra	116069	12360	-3709	-23.1
Daman and Diu	223	223	0	0
Dadra and Nagar Haveli	387	387	0	0
Goa	368	368	0	0
Western region	**31772**	**25257**	**-6515**	**-20.5**
Andhra Pradesh	8999	8542	-457	-5.1
Karnataka	5949	5558	-391	-6.6
Kerala	2623	2578	-45	-1.7
Tamil Nadu	9375	8297	-1078	-11.5
Puducherry	251	251	0	0.00
Southern region	**24889**	**23,372**	**-1517**	**-6.1**
Bihar	1314	1116	-198	-15.1
Damodar Valley Corporation	1531	1531	0	0.00
Jharkhand	669	623	-46	-6.9
Orissa	2437	2396	-41	-1.7
West Bengal and Sikkim	4790	4644	-146	-3
Eastern region	**10161**	**9677**	**-484**	**-4.8**
Arunachal Pradesh	75	73	-2	-2.7
Assam	733	679	-54	-7.4
Manipur	113	109	-4	-3.5
Meghalaya	280	205	-75	-26.8
Mizoram	76	72	-4	-5.3
Nagaland	90	87	-3	-3.3
Tripura	171	155	-16	-9.4
Northeastern region	**1385**	**1192**	**-193**	**-13.9**
All India	**93255**	**81792**	**-11463**	**-12.3**

Source: www.cea.nic.in/power sec-reports/executive summary/2006 04/22-23.pdf

Table 1.5. Overall Supply and Demand Scenario Over 2006

Region	Requirement (MU)	Availability (MU)	Surplus/ Deficit (MU)	Deficit (%)
Chandigarh	1260	1258	-2	-0.2
Delhi	21602	21281	-321	-1.5
Haryana	23791	21631	-2160	-9.1
Himachal Pradesh	4302	4258	-44	-1
Jammu and Kashmir	9268	7672	-1596	-17.2
Punjab	35682	32591	-3091	-8.7
Rajasthan	32052	30879	-1173	-3.7
Uttar Pradesh	55682	44033	-11649	-20.9
Uttarakhand	5155	5008	-147	-2.9
Northern region	**188794**	**168611**	**-20183**	**-10.7**
Chhattisgarh	13012	12540	-472	-3.6
Gujarat	57137	52436	-4701	-8.2
Madhya Pradesh	36846	31619	-5227	-14.2
Maharashtra	102765	84117	-18648	-18.1
Daman and Diu	1346	1323	-23	-1.7
Dadra and Nagar Haveli	2539	2531	-8	-0.3
Goa	2338	2338	0	0.00
Western region	**215983**	**186904**	**-29079**	**-13.5**
Andhra Pradesh	53030	52332	-698	-1.3
Karnataka	34601	34349	-252	-0.7
Kerala	13674	13578	-96	-0.7
Tamil Nadu	54194	53853	-341	-0.6
Puducherry	1678	1678	0	0.00
Southern region	**157177**	**155790**	**-1387**	**-0.9**
Bihar	7955	7218	-737	-9.3
Damodar Valley Corporation	10003	9891	-112	-1.1
Jharkhand	4033	3868	-165	-4.1
Orissa	15208	15010	-198	-1.3
West Bengal and Sikkim	25148	24719	-429	-1.7
Eastern region	**62347**	**60706**	**-1641**	**-2.6**
Arunachal Pradesh	208	206	-2	-1
Assam	4051	3778	-273	-6.7
Manipur	510	489	-21	-4.1
Meghalaya	1382	1144	-238	-17.2
Mizoram	230	216	-14	-6.1
Nagaland	408	389	-19	-4.7
Tripura	745	666	-79	-10.6
Northeastern region	**7534**	**6888**	**-646**	**-8.6**
All India	**631757**	**578819**	**-52938**	**-8.4**

Source: www.cea.nic.in/power-sec-reports/executive-summary/2006 04/22-23.pdf Power Development
    Scenario in the 11th Five-Year Plan: 2007–20121
Note: MU is million unit, where one unit = 1 kWh.

> With GDP per capita rising by about 5.4% per year in 2000-2005 and expected to grow by 6.4% in 2005-2010, the potential for energy demand growth in India is enormous. But there are challenges. India has vast coal resources, but most of them are of low quality. Indigenous oil and gas reserves are in short supply. Energy imports are growing. Renewable energy holds promise, but, with the exception of traditional biomass and hydropower, its use is very limited today.
>
> World Energy Outlook, 2007

Power Development Scenario in the 11th Five-Year Plan: 2007–2012[3]

The Fifth National Power Plan (2007–2012) prepared by the Central Electricity Authority (CEA) reports that India needs an installed capacity of 212,000 MW and a system reliability level of less than 1 percent loss of load probability (LOLP) by the end of the 11th Five-Year Plan. The primary resources for electric power generation to meet this projected installed capacity have been identified as hydro, fossil fuel (coal, lignite, oil, and natural gas), and nuclear energy. It is predicted that the contribution from renewable sources such as wind, biomass, and tidal energy will increase to meet much of the projected increase in demand. The Working Group on Power, constituted by the Planning Commission, had planned a 41,110 MW capacity addition during the 10th Five-Year Plan, comprising 14,393-MW of hydro power, 25,417-MW of thermal, and 1,300-MW of nuclear. Out of the total thermal capacity of 25,417 MW, the contribution of coal/lignite-based capacity had been predicted to be 20,053 MW. For the 11th plan, CEA has identified a capacity addition requirement of 67,439 MW, comprising 23,358-MW hydro, 38,166-MW thermal, and 5,915-MW nuclear. Out of the total thermal capacity of 38,166 MW, the coal/lignite-based capacity had been predicted to be 30,411 MW.

Power Development Scenario Beyond the 11th Five-Year Plan: 2012–2020

CEA has estimated a capacity addition requirement of 135,000 MW for 2012–2020. The breakdown of this requirement has been estimated to be 35,500-MW hydro, 10,000-MW nuclear, and 89,500-MW thermal (including 6,500-MW gas-based plants). The coal-based capacity requirement has been projected at 83,000 MW during this period. Any shortfall in achieving the hydro capacity would be supplemented by additional coal projects. Keeping in view the huge power generation capacity requirement to be added during the 11th and 12th Five Year Plans, an urgent need has been identified to develop large-scale thermal power plants in an environmentally friendly manner. To achieve this mix and to accelerate hydropower development, a 50,000-MW hydroelectric initiative was launched in 2003 and the Nuclear Power Corporation has plans to add 20,000 MW of additional nuclear power between 2012–2020.

Power Development Scenario: 2020 and Beyond

It has been estimated that the primary energy intensity in India will fall 1.2 percent annually based on GDP estimates. By extrapolating historical electricity intensity through 2022 and accounting for the expected 1.2 percent annual reduction in primary energy intensity, the growth rates of the primary energy and electrical energy have been estimated in Table 1.6 and represent a significant challenge to Indian power generation.

Table 1.6. Annual Primary and Electricity growth Rate (%)

Period	Primary Energy	Electricity
2002–2022	4.6	6.3
2022–2032	4.5	4.9
2032–2042	4.5	4.5
2042–2052	3.9	3.9

Table 1.7. Renewable Energy Development Potential in India

Source	Potential
Small hydropower	15,000 MW
Wind power	45,195 MW
Biomass power/co-generation	21,881 MW
Solar	4-6 kWH/m2/day
Waste-to-energy	2,700 MW
Total	**84,776 MW (excluding solar)**

Source: Government of India Ministry of New and Renewable Energy http://mnes.nic.in/

Growth rates in per capita electricity generation should reach 5,300 kWh per year by 2052 and total about 8,000 TWh. This would correspond to an installed capacity of roughly 1,300 gigawatts (GWe). Given this, annual primary energy consumption should increase to 117 exajoules (EJ) by 2052.

Table 1.8. Total Installed Capacity Based on Different Renewable Energy Sources from 2001–2007

Renewable Energy Source	Total Installed Capacity (MW)						
	2001	2002	2003	2004	2005	2006	2007
Hydro	1,341	1,423	1,463	1,603	1,693	1,747	1,976
Wind	1,626	1,867	2,483	2,980	3,595	5,342	7,092
Solar PV	2	2	2	3	3	3	3
Solar Thermal	0	0	0	0	0	0	0
Biomass	273	358	468	613	727	797	1,184
Waste-To-Energy	15	17	25	42	47	35	43
Geothermal	0	0	0	0	0	0	0
Tidal/Ocean	0	0	0	0	0	0	0
Total	**3,241**	**3,650**	**4,441**	**5,240**	**6,065**	**7,995**	**10,297**

Source: Government of India, Annual Reports of Ministry of New and Renewable Energy, 2000–2001 to 2006–2007.

Current Status of Indian Clean Energy Technology

Renewable Energy

Renewable energy resources are abundant in India, including hydropower, solar, wind, biomass, and wasteto-energy. Table 1.7 presents the assessed potential for renewable energy development, estimated at 84,776 MW – this excludes solar and large hydropower. The breakdown indicates wind energy, biomass, and small hydropower constitute 97 percent of the total projected potential. Wind energy alone accounts for 54 percent followed by biomass/co-generation and small hydropower.

Table 1.8 provides a breakdown of installed renewable capacity by resource. As noted, the total installed capacity as of May 2007 was 10,297 MW, up from 3,241 MW in 2001. Wind constitutes 69 percent of the total, followed by small hydro (19 percent), biomass (co-generation, 11.5 percent), waste-to-energy (0.42 percent), and solar (0.03 percent).

Table 1.8 also demonstrates India's need to develop alternative forms of renewable energy and diversify its energy portfolio even further. The contributions of waste-to-energy and solar-energy, for instance are considerably less than their potential indicates. Solar thermal, geothermal, and tidal energy are virtually non-existent, an indicator of the significant potential these sectors have for development.

A breakdown of distributed renewable energy is provided in Table 1.9. As indicated, 166 MW equivalent renewable energy exists in distributed (non-grid-connected) sectors. Biomass-gasifier-based renewable energy contributes 52 percent, followed by 36 percent from biomass (co-generation) and 12.2 percent from waste-to-energy. These figures again indicate the lack of a mature market and demonstrate the potential opportunity for American firms.

Table 1.9. Breakout of Distributed Renewable Energy

Biomass Power/Co-Gen. (Non-Bagasse)	59.00 MW
Biomass gasifier	86.53 MWeq
Waste-to-energy	20.21 MWeq
Total	165.74 MWeq

Source: Government of India Ministry of New and Renewable Energy http://mnes.nic.in/

Table 1.10. Wind Power Potential in India, by State

State	Gross Potential (MW)	Technical Potential (MW)
Andhra Pradesh	8,257	2,110
Gujarat	9,675	1,900
Karnataka	6,620	1,310
Kerala	875	610
Madhya Pradesh	5,500	1,050
Maharashtra	3,650	3,060
Orissa	1,700	1,085
Rajasthan	5,400	1,050
Tamil Nadu	3,050	2,150
West Bengal	450	450
Total	45,177	14,775

Source: Confederation of Indian Industry, "Background Paper," 1st India Clean Tech Forum, August 3, 2007.

Wind

Statewide gross and technical wind power potential is given in Table 1.10. The technical potential has been estimated by assuming 20 percent grid penetration, which would increase with the augmentation of grid capacity in certain states. Table 1.10 indicates that Maharashtra, Andhra Pradesh, Tamil Nadu, and Gujarat are the leading states, with 62 percent of the projected "technical" potential.

Table 1.11 shows India had 5,341 MW of installed electricity capacity from wind energy as of March 2006. Nine states accounted for 99 percent of the installed capacity in the country. Tamil Nadu accounted for 54 percent of wind generation, while Maharashtra accounted for 18.7 percent of installed capacity in India. Most of states enjoying wind power generation – 70 percent -- are located in coastal areas with geographic and climatic conditions favorable for wind farms.

Solar PV and Solar Thermal

India receives abundant solar radiation equivalent to over 5,000 trillion kWh per year. The daily average solar energy incident varies from 4–7 kWh per square meter depending upon the location. A government-supported program for PV has existed for two decades, but the current installed capacity equals only 3 MW, a small proportion of the country's total energy mix. PV systems are promoted primarily for rural and off-grid applications, consisting largely of mini-grids, solar home systems, solar lanterns, and solar street lights.

The overall solar water heater potential in India is estimated to be 140 million square meters of collector area, of which about 1.9 million square meters have been installed in buildings and in industry – 99 percent of the potential is therefore undeveloped.

Table 1.11. Break-out of Installed Base of Electricity generation from Wind Energy, by State, in 2006

State	31 March 2006		
	Demonstration Projects	Private Projects	Total Capacity
Andhra Pradesh	5	116	121
Gujarat	17	322	338
Karnataka	7	578	586
Kerala	2	0	2
Madhya Pradesh	0.6	40	40
Maharashtra	8	993	1001
Rajasthan	6	352	358
Tamil Nadu	19	2873	2894
West Bengal	1	0	1
Others	2	0	3
Total	**69**	**5271**	**5341**

Source: TERI Energy Data and Yearbook 2006.
Note: Numbers may not add exactly owing to independent rounding.

Table 1.12. National Biomass Power Estimation, by State

State	Area (Kha)	Crop Production (Kt/Year)	Biomass Generation (Kt/Year)	Biomass Surplus (Kt/Year)	Power Potential (Mwe)
Andhra Pradesh	2,540.2	3,232.0	8,301.7	1,172.8	150.2
Assam	2,633.1	6,075.7	6,896.3	1,398.4	165.5
Bihar	5,833.1	13,817.8	20,441.8	4,286.2	530.3
Chhattisgarh	3,815.5	6,142.8	10,123.7	1,907.8	220.9
Goa	156.3	554.7	827.2	129.9	15.6
Gujarat	6,512.9	20,627.0	24,164.4	7,505.5	1,014.1
Haryana	4,890.2	13,520.0	26,160.9	9,796.1	1,261.0
Himachal Pradesh	710.3	1,329.2	2,668.2	988.3	128.0
Jammu and Kashmir	368.7	648.7	1,198.7	237.7	31.8
Jharkhand	1,299.8	1,509.0	2,191.2	567.7	66.8
Karnataka	7,277.3	38,638.5	23,766.8	6,400.6	843.4
Kerala	2,041.7	9,749.7	9,420.5	5,702.6	762.3
Madhya Pradesh	9,937.0	14,166.9	26,499.6	8,033.3	1,065.4
Maharashtra	15,278.3	51,343.3	36,804.4	11,803.9	1,585.0
Manipur	72.6	159.4	318.8	31.9	4.1
Meghalaya	0.8	14.0	42.0	8.4	1.1
Nagaland	27.1	87.6	149.2	27.2	3.1
Orissa	2,436.6	3,633.3	5,350.4	1,163.4	147.3
Punjab	6,693.5	27,813.7	46,339.8	21,267.0	2,674.6
Rajasthan	12,537.5	93,654.8	204,887.6	35,531.1	4,595.0
Tamil Nadu	2,454.0	24,544.6	15,976.6	6,658.7	863.7
Uttar Pradesh	12,628.2	46,800.8	50,416.7	11,725.9	1,477.9
Uttaranchal	66.4	135.8	159.9	51.6	6.6
West Bengal	5,575.6	21,062.8	23,316.0	2,959.7	368.3
Total	**105,786.8**	**399,262.1**	**546,422.6**	**139,355.8**	**17,981.8**

Source: Government of India Ministry of New and Renewable Energy http://mnes.nic.in/

Table 1.13. Bagasse-based Co-generation Potential in India, by State

State	Potential (MW)
Maharashtra	1000
Uttar Pradesh	1000
Tamil Nadu	350
Karnataka	300
Andhra Pradesh	200
Bihar	200
Gujarat	200
Punjab	150
Others	100
Total	**3500**

Source: Confederation of Indian Industry, "Background Paper," 1st India Clean Tech Forum, August 3, 2007.

Bioenergy

Statewide biomass potential is presented in Table 1.12. India produces 139 million tons of surplus biomass every year, amounting to 16,000 MW of electricity. Rajasthan, Punjab, Uttar Pradesh, Maharashtra, Madhya Pradesh, Haryana, and Gujarat account for 76 percent of the projected potential, with Rajasthan alone accounting for 25 percent of the total projected potential.

Bagasse-based co-generation potential is presented in Table 1.13. Maharashtra and Uttar Pradesh, the two major bagasse-producing states, account for 57 percent of the total projected potential. In 2006, India had 582 MW of installed bagasse co-generation (grid and off-grid); projections through 2012 call for 1,200 MW installed.

Table 1.14. Waste-to-Energy Potential in India, by State

State	Liquid Waste (MW)	Solid Waste (MW)	Total (MW)
Andhra Pradesh	16	107	123
Delhi	20	111	131
Gujarat	14	98	112
Karnataka	26	125	151
Maharashtra	37	250	287
Tamil Nadu	14	137	151
Uttar Pradesh	22	154	176
West Bengal	22	126	148
Other	55	349	404
Total	**226**	**1,457**	**1,683**

Source: Confederation of Indian Industry, "Background Paper," 1st India Clean Tech Forum, August 3, 2007.

Table 1.15. List of Commissioned Biomass Power/Co-generation Projects (MW), by State

State	Upto March 31, 2002	2002– 2003	2003– 2004	2004– 2005	2005– 2006	2006– 2007	2007– 2008	Total
Andhra Pradesh	101.20	58.85	37.70	69.50	12.00	22.00	33.00	334.25
Chhattisgarh	11.00	—	—	—	16.50	85.80	17.50	130.80
Gujarat	0.50	—	—	—	—	—	—	0.50
Haryana	4.00	—	—	2.00	—	—	—	6.00
Karnataka	75.60	33.78	26.00	16.60	72.50	29.80	8.00	262.28
Madhya Pradesh	0.00	—	1.00	—	—	—	—	1.00
Maharashtra	24.50	—	—	11.50	—	40.00	19.50	95.50
Punjab	12.00	10.00	—	—	6.00	—	—	28.00
Rajasthan	0.00	—	7.80	—	7.50	8.00	—	23.30
Tamil Nadu	106.00	—	44.50	22.50	—	42.50	12.00	227.50
Uttar Pradesh	46.50	—	12.50	14.00	48.50	—	22.00	143.50
Total	**381.30**	**102.63**	**129.50**	**136.10**	**163.00**	**228.10**	**112.00**	**1252.63**

Source: Ministry of Non-conventional Energy Sources, Annual Report 2005/06 (New Delhi, India).

Based on COGEN Europe[4] and Tata Energy Research Institute (TERI) estimates, the total combined heat and power (CHP) potential in India is over 10,000 MW, 61 percent from non-sugar-based industries. These estimates are based on internal heat-to-power ratios, which would meet the plant's energy requirements and still meet the production capacities of the various industry categories. The prominent industry categories are paper, cotton textile, caustic soda, fertilizers, iron and steel, refineries, rice mills, man-made fibers, cement, sulfuric acid, and aluminum.

State-based waste-to-energy potential is presented in Table 1.14. Maharashtra, Uttar Pradesh, Karnataka, Tamil Nadu, and West Bengal account for more than 53 percent of the projected waste-to-energy potential.

The statewide list of commissioned biomass power/co-generation projects as of September 30, 2007, is given in Table 1.15. As shown, the installed capacity of biomass power/co-generation has tripled from 381 MW in 2002 to 1,253 MW in 2007. Andhra Pradesh, Karnataka, Tamil Nadu, and Uttar Pradesh account for 77 percent of the total installed capacity, due to the availability of biomass and bagasse.

Small Hydro

Statewide small hydropower potential in India is provided in Table 1.16. India has an estimated hydropower potential of 84,000 MW, 15,000 MW from SHP. The Ministry of New and Renewable Energy (MNRE)[5] has identified 4,227 potential small hydropower sites accounting for 10,324 MW in potential projects amounting to 25 MW. The remaining potential sites are under study. Himachal Pradesh, Uttarakhand, Jammu and Kashmir, and Arunachal Pradesh have 52 percent of the projected SHP potential.

As Table 1.17 demonstrates, 1,748 MW of installed small hydropower (SHP) operated in India in 2006. Karnataka and Maharashtra accounted for 17 and 11 percent of the total, respectively. The states of Punjab, Andhra Pradesh, Himachal Pradesh, and Jammu and Kashmir together accounted for more than 17 percent of installed capacity. The potential of this sector is dependent on available water resources, which are abundant in the majority of states.

Since India needs 347,000 MW of additional capacity through 2020 of which renewable energy can contribute 24 percent. Major requirements for developing this sector include continued technology improvements, cost reductions, and successful demonstrations.

Energy Efficiency

The most important supply-side efficiency prospects are high-efficiency, low-emission coal thermal electric power generation and reductions in losses in electricity distribution. The National Thermal Power Corporation (NTPC), for example, envisions a 660-MW green-field project employing supercritical steam parameters. A USAID-funded feasibility study of an integrated gasification combined cycle (IGCC) demonstration project estimated a 200-MW demonstration plant could be constructed for $2,000/kW.

Table 1.16. Small Hydropower Potential in India, by State

State	Number of Sites	Technical Potential (MW)
Andhra Pradesh	286	255
Arunachal Pradesh	492	1,059
Himachal Pradesh	323	1,625
Jammu and Kashmir	201	1,207
Karnataka	230	653
Kerala	198	467
Madhya Pradesh	85	336
Maharashtra	234	599
Tamil Nadu	147	339
Uttarakhand	354	1,478
Uttar Pradesh	211	267
Other States	1,466	2,039
Total	**4,227**	**10,324**

Source: Confederation of Indian Industry, "Background Paper," 1st India Clean Tech Forum," August 3, 2007.

Currently, 25 percent of Indian power is lost through transmission and distribution losses alone. A reduction of 5 percent of these losses could result in significant augmentation of the electricity supply. Industry represents 50 percent of the total energy consumption and is a major target of the energy efficiency effort. Six key industries—aluminum, cement, fertilizers, pulp and paper, petrochemicals, and steel—account for two-thirds of the nation's total industrial energy use. The energy intensity in these industries is higher than in developed countries, mainly due to obsolete and energy inefficient technologies, which have not been retrofitted with higher efficiency products. Nonetheless, recently energy efficiency in Indian industry has increased steadily. In the cement, steel, aluminum, and fertilizer industries, average energy consumption has declined as these industries have placed a higher importance on conservation and the installation of state-of-the-art technology. Latent potential in the building and construction sectors however remains significant and should be addressed going forward.

Fuel-Based Energy Sources

Table 1.18 depicts the present status of fuel-based resources. The estimated domestic mineable coal resources are 38 billion tons (BT), and the estimated hydrocarbon reserves are 12 BT. These reserves together may provide 1,200 EJ of energy. To meet the projected demand, India needs to develop all options, including efficient use of known fossil reserves, competitive importation of energy, hydro potential both large and small, and non-fossil resources including both nuclear and non-conventional energy sources.

Table 1.17. Installed Base of Electricity Generation from Small Hydro, by State, in 2006

State/Union Territory	Potential		Existing Projects		Ongoing Projects	
	Number of Sites	Capacity (MW)	Number of Sites	Capacity (MW)	Number of Sites	Capacity (MW)
Andhra Pradesh	286	254.63	57	178.81	9	13.9
Arunachal Pradesh	492	1059.03	62	34.30	52	51.42
Assam	90	148.90	3	2.11	7	26.00
Bihar	92	194.02	5	45.90	9	14.00
Chhattisgarh	174	179.97	4	11.00	2	8.00
Goa	3	2.60	1	0.05	—	—
Gujarat	290	156.83	2	7.00	—	—
Haryana	22	30.05	5	62.70	—	—
Himachal Pradesh	323	1624.78	53	119.08	10	52.50
Jammu and Kashmir	201	1207.27	30	109.74	7	7.31
Jharkhand	89	170.05	6	4.05	8	34.85
Karnataka	230	625.61	53	300.63	22	112.74
Kerala	198	466.85	14	84.62	7	57.75
Madhya Pradesh	85	336.33	8	41.16	3	24.20
Manipur	96	105.63	8	5.45	3	2.75
Meghalaya	98	181.50	3	30.71	9	3.28
Mizoram	88	190.32	16	14.76	3	15.50
Nagaland	86	181.39	8	20.47	6	12.40
Orissa	161	156.76	6	7.30	7	40.92
Punjab	78	65.26	24	113.40	6	26.35
Rajasthan	49	27.26	10	23.85	—	—
Sikkim	68	202.75	12	35.60	5	15.20
Tamil Nadu	147	338.92	12	77.70	2	7.90
Tripura	8	9.85	3	16.01	—	—
Uttarakhand	354	1478.24	76	75.45	37	23.01
Uttar Pradesh	211	267.06	8	21.50	1	3.60
West Bengal	145	182.62	20	92.30	7	5.80
Andaman and Nicobar Islands	6	6.40	1	5.25	—	—
Total	**4404**	**10,450.35**	**537**	**1,747.98**	**227**	**585.13**

Source: Ministry of Non-conventional Energy Sources, Annual Report 2005/06 (New Delhi: MNES, Government of India, 2006).

Clean Transportation Technology

The rapid growth in motor vehicle activity in India is contributing to high levels of urban air pollution, among other adverse socioeconomic, environmental, health, and welfare impacts. The demand for transport increased by 1.9 percent per year from 2000 to 2005, but is projected to double by 2015 and more than quadruple by 2030. The slow growth in demand for diesel to date may be due to improved efficiency of new cars and trucks and switching to compressed natural gas vehicles for public transportation in some major cities. However, like many developing countries, India lacks mandatory vehicle fuel efficiency standards.[6]

Table 1.18. Fuel-based Energy and Electricity Resources

	Amount	Thermal Energy			Electricity Potential
		EJ	Twh	GW/Year	GWe/Year
Fossil					
Coal	38 BT	667	185,279	21,151	7,614
Hydrocarbon	12 BT	511	141,946	16,204	5,833
Non-fossil					
Nuclear					
Uraniummetal	61,000 T				
In PHWRs		28.9	7,992	913	328
In fast breeders		**3,699**	**1,027,616**	**117,308**	**42,231**
Thoriummetal	225,000 T				
In breeders		13,622	3,783,886	431,950	155,502

The Ministry of New and Renewable Energy is promoting several research, development, and demonstration projects including a demonstration project in battery-operated vehicles (BOVs). Under the program a central subsidy is provided for the purchase of the BOVs through renewable energy development agencies. In addition, fuel cell–battery hybrid vehicles with indigenously developed exchange membrane fuel cells of 10 kW have undergone field performance evaluation. Efforts made are expected to lead to the indigenous production and wider applications of fuel cell systems in the country. Various laboratories are developing different technologies for production, storage, and transportation including hydrogen fuel, which some argue has the potential to replace fossil fuels as early as 2020.[7]

2. Market Analysis

Clean energy technologies in India, including renewable energy and energy effi ciency, have received unprecedented attention in the last few years as the country's energy demand grows each year. Increased use of clean energy technologies will help mitigate concerns that often accompany rapid economic development in areas that are already resource constrained—such as poor air quality, desertification, dependence on imported fuel, and exponential growth in demand.

Renewable Energy

There is a need for massive investment in the Indian renewable energy sector. Table 1.19 provides the renewable energy targets under the 11th Five-Year Plan, as well as associated outlays for grid-connectivity and distributed power generation. The total investment required to meet the 15,000 MW goal would be about $19.5 billion, 19 times the proposed budgetary support. This includes 1,000 MW targeted from distributed renewable power systems with an outlay of $531.6 million and $6.3 million for performance testing. The detailed breakout is given below.

The Electricity Act of 2003 included a renewable portfolio standard, building on the precedent of those states that had already set targets of 5–10 percent to be realized by 2010.

These targets virtually ensure a guaranteed market for renewable energy technologies in the country. While the target set out in the 10th Five-Year Plan for installed capacity is 3,075 MW, the actual achievement is likely to be in excess of 6,000 MW.

Table 1.19. Potential Targets and Associated Investments Required to Meet the Targets

Program Component	Physical Target (MW)	Proposed Outlay ($ Million)	Investment Requirement ($ Million)
Wind power	10,500	18.9*	15,530
Small hydro	1,400	177.2	2,070
Co-generation	1,200	151.8	1,106
Biomass power	500	50.6	492
Urban waste-to-energy	200	37.9	295
Industrial waste-to-energy	200	18.9	
Subtotal (A)	14,000	455.6	
Solar power (grid-interactive/distributed generation)	50	50.6**	
Distributed RE power systems (excluding solar)	950	481	
Subtotal (B)	1,000	531.6	
Total (renewable power) (A+B)	15,000	987.3	
Performance testing	–	6.32	
Grand Total	**15,000**	**993.6**	**19,493**

Source: Report of the Working Group on New and Renewable Energy for 11th Five Year Plan.
   * For demonstration projects in states where there is sizable potential but where no commercial activity has commenced.
   **Subsidy limited to $265.8 per household. Investment required is dependent on subsidy, which varies during the annual budget of thegovernment of India.

Wind Energy

Individual wind turbine capacity has increased from 55 kW in the mid-1980s to 2,000 kW today. India already manufactures wind electric generators with up to 1,650 kW per unit capacity domestically and their expertise in the subject continues to grow. Enercon (India) Ltd., Vestas RRB India Ltd., and Suzlon Energy Ltd lead the industry, but a full list of electric generators installed through 2006, by manufacturer, is provided in Annex 1, as well as a listing of wind turbine manufacturers.

To harness the projected potential, new technologies with higher capacities are needed in the country. These technologies may include wind power systems greater than 1–2 MW, wind machines for low-wind regimes, and better designs for rotor blades, gear boxes, and control systems.

Small Hydro

India has a fairly developed capacity for designing, constructing, and operating small hydropower plants. A list of small hydropower turbine/equipment manufacturers in India is provided in Annex 1.

Small hydro technology has improved steadily over time and is now more efficient, reliable, and automatic compared with several years ago. Some of the new technological advances include the replacement of mechanical governing systems by electronic governors and analogue controls by digital systems. The projects are now completely automatic from start to grid synchronization. The concept of remotely operating projects and Supervisory Control and Data Acquisition systems have been introduced in this sector. Apart from improvement in equipment designs, there is a need to improve/standardize civil design and hydraulic structures to reduce construction time. The areas of technological interventions include development of direct-drive low-speed generators for water sources with low heads; standardized control and monitoring hardware packages; submersible turbo-generators; compact equipment, which requires the laying of few cofferdams; appropriate turbine design suitable to electrical output below 1 MW; variable-speed operation (optimal use of low- and variable-head sites); flexible small hydro turbines for very low heads (<2.5 m); and adaptation of high-pole permanent magnet excitation generators to SHP.

Solar Photovoltaics

India has manufacturing facilities for equipment and components used in solar photovoltaic (PV) technology. The list of solar cell and module manufacturers in India is provided in Annex 1. New technologies are still needed however. These include the development of polysilicon and other materials, device fabrication processes and improvements in crystalline silicon solar cell/module technology, and thin-film solar cell technology (based on amorphous silicon films; cadmium telluride films and copper indium diselenide thin films; and organic, dyesensitized, and carbon nano tubes). There is also a need for megawatt-scale solar PV power-generating systems.

Solar Thermal Technology

A number of solar thermal applications have been developed in India, which include water/air heating, cooking, drying of agricultural and food products, water purification, detoxification of wastes, cooling and refrigeration, heat for industrial processes, and electric power generation. Most of the solar thermal devices and systems are manufactured in India. Evacuated tube collectors (ETC) used in one of the configurations of solar water heating systems are imported and marketed in the country by the solar thermal industry.

Annex 1 provides a listing of solar cooker manufacturers, ETC suppliers and manufacturers, and Flat Plate Collector–based solar water heating systems, driers, air heating, and solar steam-generating systems in India. The major opportunities for American firms are solar thermal (high-temperature) power generation systems and energy effi cient buildings utilizing solar energy concepts.

Bioenergy

Manufacturing capability exists in India for the equipment/machinery required to establish and operate biomass projects. Biomass combustion technology using co-generation is in operation in industries throughout the country. India also has significant experience and technology in atmospheric gasifiers, where biomass is converted into producer gas via gasification. With the exception of some critical control equipment and high-efficiency turbines, most of the equipment can be procured from domestic sources. A number of large manufacturers have established capabilities for manufacturing spreader-stoker-fired, traveling grate/dumping grate boilers; atmospheric pressure fluidized bed boilers; and circulating fluidized bed boilers. Almost all combinations—condensing, single-extraction/double-extraction condensing, back pressure, etc.—are available in the country with full aftersales service guarantees. There is a well-established capability and capacity for the manufacture of related equipment in the bioenergy field, including harvesters, balers, briquetting equipment, handling and firing equipment, and pollution control systems. Annex 1 provides the list of companies in the areas of gasifier manufacturing, plasma arc technology, pyrolysis/gasification technology, and biogas burners.

Some of the new areas where technical expertise is required include:

- Development of megawatt-scale fluidized bed biomass gasifiers, hot-gas clean-up systems, and optimum integration of the system following the principles of IGCC.
- Development of poly-generation facilities for the production of liquid fuels, development of a variety of chemicals and hydrogen in addition to power production through IGCC, and establishment of the concept of a biorefinery.
- Increase in the efficiency of atmospheric gasification to 25–30 percent along with cooling systems, complete tar decomposition, and safe disposal of wastes in commercial production.
- Increase in the system efficiency of small (up to 1 MW) combustion and turbine technologies to 20 percent or more.
- Design and development of high-rate anaerobic co-digestion systems for biogas and synthetic gas production.
- Development of gasifier systems based on charcoal/ pyrolysized biomass.
- Development of efficient kilns/systems for charcoal production/pyrolysation of biomass.
- Design and development of engines, Stirling engines, and micro-turbines for biogas, producer gas, and biosyngas.
- Design and development of direct gas-fired absorptive chillers, driers, stoves, etc., and improvement in biomass furnaces, boilers, etc.
- Engine modifications for using more than 20 percent biodiesel as a blend with diesel.
- Development of second-generation bioliquid fuels and related applications.
- Diversification of feedstocks to utilize alternate biomass wastes along with cattle dung for setting up household biogas plants.
- Methods for sustaining biogas production during winter months.
- Development of biogas micro-turbines and engines.
- Local power grids compatible with dual fuel engines and gas engines/turbines.
- Removal of hydrogen sulfide from biogas produced in night soil-based biogas plants.
- Additional treatment methods for effluent from night soil-based biogas plants.

Waste-to-Energy

The technological options available for waste-to-energy projects include biomethanation, combustion/incineration, pyrolysis/gasification, landfill gas recovery, densification, and pelletization. However, India has limited local capacity in these technology areas. The large-scale operations of any of these technologies require import of design, engineering, and equipment. There is also a need to demonstrate the usefulness of these technology options throughout the country.

The list of suppliers of these waste-to-energy technologies in India is given in Annex 1. It should be noted, however, that the majority of these suppliers are dealers, franchisees, and/or licensees of technology suppliers outside India.

Geothermal Energy

There is a need to assess the potential of geothermal resources in India and to harness these resources for power generation to be used in space heating, greenhouse cultivation, and cooking. Past projects undertaken by the MNRE have demonstrated the applications of geothermal fluids for small-scale power generation and in poultry farming and greenhouse cultivation. Magnetotelluric (MT) investigations to delineate sub-surface, geo-electric structures and evaluate their geothermal significance have been carried out by the National Geophysical Research Institute in the Tatapani geothermal area in Chhattisgarh, the Puga geothermal area, and the Ladakh region of Jammu and Kashmir. Similar studies are in progress for geothermal fields in the states of Surajkund in Jharkhand and Badrinath-Tapovan in Uttarakhand and in the Satluj-Beas and Parvati Valleys in Himachal Pradesh. The National Hydroelectric Power Corporation (NHPC), with the support from the Indian Government, prepared a feasibility report for development of geothermal fields in Puga, the Ladakh region of Jammu and Kashmir, and the Tatapani geothermal field in the Surguja district of Chhattisgarh. Currently, there is no technology supplier for geothermal energy harnessing/ equipment manufacturing in India.

Ocean Energy

The potential of ocean and tidal energy for power generation in India has yet to be assessed. Some potential sites for tapping tidal energy have been identified in the Gulf of Kuchch and Gulf of Cambay in Gujarat and the Delta of the Ganga in the Sunderbans region in West Bengal. A detailed project report for the proposed 3.65-MW tidal power project at Durgaduani/Sunderbans, West Bengal, has been prepared by the West Bengal Renewable Energy Development Agency and is being updated by the NHPC. Currently, there is no technology supplier for tidal energy harnessing/equipment manufacturing in India.

Key Market Drivers

A number of market drivers are spurring the development of clean energy markets in India. These include:

- Existing and projected gaps in the electricity supply.
- Increasing fuel importation to augment the electricity supply, thereby increasing dependence on imported resources.
- Rising prices of fossil-fuel-based energy delivery (prices reached $100/barrel in January 2008).
- Projected potential of locally available renewable energy resources and the need for energy portfolio diversity.
- Favorable policy environment to promote the use of clean energy technologies (national, state, local) and improved investment climate.

- Expanded financial support for renewable energy and energy efficiency from local and international financial institutions, multilateral agencies, donor organizations, and others.
- Growing carbon credit markets, including the Clean Development Mechanism (CDM) and voluntary markets.
- Existence of local capacities/capabilities to harness the clean energy sector and relatively inexpensive local labor supplies.
- Growing environmental, social, and health concerns over fossil fuel development.

At present, India is the fourth-largest greenhouse gas (GHG) emitter in the world, ranking second only to China as the fastest growing GHG emitter.[8] India is also a major emitter of methane and nitrous oxide, and has exceeded its national ambient air quality standards in eight major cities. There is thus a major need for the development of clean energy options in the country.

Policy Drivers

According to India's integrated energy policy, sustained growth of 8 percent through 2030 will require primary energy supply to increase three to four times and electricity supply by five to seven times compared to current consumption. If no alternative arrangements are made to reduce the consumption of coal, an annual coal requirement is expected to be 2,040 mt by 2010, which will lead to a substantial increase in GHG emissions. The power sector is expected to add over 150,000 MW in the next 15 years, of which at least 10 percent is expected to come from renewable energy technologies.

Implementation of Section 86(1)(e) of the Electricity Act of 2003 and Section 6.4(1) of the National Tariff Policy is underway. Different states are in the process of issuing tariff orders for renewable energy-based electricity generation and specifying quotas/shares for power from renewable energy in accordance with the provisions of the Electricity Act. For example, the Maharashtra Electricity Regulatory Commission (MERC) has stipulated the minimum percentage targets (3 percent for FY 2006–2007, 4 percent for FY 2007–2008, 5 percent for FY 2008–2009, and 6 percent for FY 2009–2010) for procuring electricity generated from eligible renewable energy sources. Similar orders have been issued by other states, based on the potential resources available in their respective states.

Other major renewable energy initiatives include: (1) installation of 1 million household solar water heating systems, (2) electrification by renewable mini-grids of 24,000 villages without electricity, (3) deployment of 5 million solar lanterns and 2 million solar home lighting systems, and (4) establishment of an additional 3 million small biogas plants.

The integrated Indian energy policy set the ambitious goal of a 25 percent reduction in energy intensity from current levels. Within mining, electricity generation, transmission and distribution, water pumping, industrial production processes, building design, construction, heating, ventilation, air conditioning, lighting, and household appliances, energy efficiency can play a key role. Nearly 25,000 MW of capacity creation through energy efficiency in the electricity sector alone have been estimated in India. The energy conservation potential for the economy as a whole has been assessed at 23 percent, with maximum potential in the industrial and agricultural sectors. The target areas identified by the Board of Energy Efficiency (BEE) in which to achieve energy efficiency include:

- Indian industry program for energy conservation;
- Demand-side management;
- Standards and labeling program;
- Energy efficiency in buildings and establishments;
- Energy conservation building codes;
- Professional certification and accreditation;
- Manuals and codes;
- Energy efficiency policy research program;
- School education;
- Delivery mechanisms for energy efficiency services.

A financial requirement of about $162 million has been projected for the 11th Five-Year Plan for energy-efficiencyrelated initiatives. A number of pilot and demonstration projects have been taken up for load management and energy conservation through reduction of transmission and distribution losses in the system. In the area of building energy efficiency, building plans will not be approved by local authorities unless they comply with the Energy Conservation Building Codes (ECBCs) after 2009. The ECBCs will make it mandatory for buildings not to exceed 140 kilowatt/hour per square meter annually.

Ethanol and biodiesel have likewise been identified as key focus areas, with both at the early stages of commercialization. In 2004, the government of India (GOI) mandated a 5 percent blending of petrol with ethanol, subject to certain conditions. An autonomous National Biodiesel Board is being created to promote, finance, and support organizations that are engaged in the field of oilseed cultivation and oil processing leading to biodiesel production.

Cost Analysis

Tables 1.20 and 1.21 below provide the current costs of renewable energy technologies in India, as well as their market value—derived from the current costs—as of March 2007.

The existing market figure of $13,366 million given in Table 1.21 is based on estimating the value of the total investments in the installed capacity in each subsector, which has been estimated at today's costs per megawatt of installed capacity. It must be noted that these capacities have been installed over the last two decades, and, thus, this is a reflection of the value of investment in renewable energy at today's cost. At least 60 to 70 percent of the installed assets would have been depreciated by over 60–80 percent, and some would also have been upgraded with refurbishments or even replaced. If one assumes 80 percent depreciation, then the true value of the market is about $4 to $5 billion at the end of 2007. By 2012—the completion of the 11th Five-Year Plan—the GOI has mandated that 10 percent of the nation's power supply comes from renewable energy sources, resulting in a 4–5 percent share of the electricity mix. As a result, the current 10,000 MW of installed renewable capacity is projected to reach 24,000 MW by 2012. This should translate from the current CET market size to more than $21 billion by 2012, in a best case scenario. Even under the realistic assumption of just a 50 percent capacity addition in the renewable and energy efficiency sub-sectors by 2012, the estimated market size would be $11 billion by 2012.

No figures for export of CET are available for India as of early 2008. However, according to Indian Government sources, only solar photovoltaic components are exported from India. Wind energy equipment manufactured in India is not exported as it supplies the domestic market. Domestic SHP turbines and biomass gasifiers manufactured in India are also used in-country.

Table 1.20. Cost of Clean Energy Technologies in India

Technology	Capital Costs (Million $/MW)	Unit Costs ($/Kwh)
Small hydropower	1.27–1.53	0.038–0.064
Wind power	1.02–1.27	0.051–0.076
Biomass power	1.02	0.064–0.089
Bagasse co-generation	0.89	0.064–0.076
Biomass gasifier	0.48–0.51	0.064–0.089
Solar photovoltaics	0.66–0.69	0.382–0.509
Waste-to-energy	0.64–2.55	0.064–0.191

Source: Planning Commission (Integrated Energy Policy; http://planningcommission.nic.in/reports/genrep/intengpol.pdf)

Table 1.21. Market value of CETs as of March 2007

	Installed Capacity March 2007 (MW)	Value of Investment (Million $)
Small hydro	1,976	2,964
Wind power	7,092	8,865
Solar PV (home lighting)	86	366
Solid biomass	569	569
Bagasse CHP	615	538
Waste-to-energy	43	65
Total		**13,366**

Source: Based on government projections and reports of the GOI's Planning Commission.

3. Clean Energy Policies

The market potential of clean energy technologies, including renewable energy and energy efficiency, can be realized by enabling policy and regulatory frameworks supported by an adequate institutional structure. Over the last decade, the government of India (GOI) has prepared a road map for economic development by opening up different sectors of the economy. In particular, the energy sector has witnessed substantial regulatory reforms, liberalization, and a number of new policy initiatives, followed by the creation of new institutions to support these developments. In this context, the following sections describe the key policies, laws, decrees, plans, institutional structure, and policy drivers impacting U.S. energy companies wishing to do business in India, as well as potential opportunities posed by policy interventions.

Key Policies, Laws, Decrees, and Plans

India's policy framework and developmental plans are formulated by the national government. The state governments align their policies and development plans as the national policy framework and action plans mandate. In the area of clean energy, there is no single over arching policy of the government of India and thus state governments are forced to develop often ad hoc policies based on patchwork policies, laws, decrees, and plans. Many of these are shown Table 1.22.

Salient features of the above policies, in the context of renewable energy and energy efficiency, are outlined below.

Rural Electrification Policy

- Goals of the Rural Electrification Policy include provision of access to electricity to all households by the year 2009, quality and reliable power supply at reasonable rates, and minimum lifeline consumption of one unit per household per day by 2012.
- For villages/habitations where grid connectivity would not be feasible or cost effective, off-grid solutions based on stand-alone systems may be taken up for the supply of electricity. Where these also are not feasible, and if the only alternative is to use isolated lighting technologies, solar photovoltaics may be adopted.

Table 1.22. Summary of India's Clean Energy–related Policies

Year	Title	Main Thrust
Major Policies		
2006	Rural Electrification Policy	Establishes a national goal for universal access, assigns responsibilities for implementation, and creates new financing arrangements.
2006	National Environment Policy	Provides guidance on air pollution reduction, climate change and GHG mitigation, and CDM; promotes clean technologies, environmental resource usage, and efficiency per unit of economic output.
2006	National Urban Transport Policy	Encourages integrated land use and transportation planning in cities.
2006	National Tariff Policy	Provides guidance on establishing power purchase tariffs by State Electricity Regulatory Commissions.
2006	MNRE (Draft) R&D Policy	Establishes resource requirements for the 11th Five-Year Plan.
2006	MNRE (Draft) Renewable Energy Policy	Identifies the strategies for increased deployment of grid-interactive RE technologies.
2005	National Electricity Policy	Provides guidelines for accelerated development of the power sector.
Major Acts		
2003	Electricity Act	Legislates a comprehensive reform and liberalization process for the power sector.
2001	Energy Conservation Act	Provides the legal framework and institutional arrangements for embarking on a national energy efficiency drive.
1986	Environment (Protection) Act	Provides broad objectives, goals, and guidance for environmental compliance.

National Electricity Policy of 2005

Lowering the energy intensity of GDP growth through higher energy efficiency is critical to meeting India's energy challenge and ensuring its energy security. Some of the key provisions are provided below:

- Policy measures for improving energy efficiency include:
- Merging the Petroleum Conservation Research Association and the Bureau of Energy Efficiency (BEE) into an autonomous statutory body under the Energy Conservation Act, independent of other energy ministries and separately funded by the government of India.
- Making the expanded BEE responsible for accelerating efficiency improvements in energy-consuming appliances, equipment, and vehicles through schemes such as the "Golden Carrot" incentives.
- Implementing energy effi ciency standards and labeling of energy-using equipment, using financial penalties if equipment fails to meet minimum energy performance standards.
- Establishing benchmarks for energy consumption in energy-intensive sectors.
- Increasing gross efficiency in power generation, including improvements of 10 percent in existing generation and 5–10 percent in new plants, and promoting urban mass transport, energy efficient vehicles, and freight movement by railways.
- Progressively increasing the share of electricity from non-conventional sources. This requires that each state regulatory authority create a renewable energy portfolio standard (RPS) for the transmission and distribution companies serving their jurisdictions.
- Distribution companies are directed to purchase power from renewable energy sources through a competitive bidding process at a preferential price fixed by the regulatory commission.

Tariff Policy of 2006

Salient features of the tariff policy include:

- As per Section 86(1)(e) of the act, the appropriate commission shall fix a minimum percentage for purchase of energy from renewable sources, taking into account availability of such resources in the region and its impact on retail tariffs.
- It will take some time before non-conventional technologies can compete with conventional sources in terms of cost of electricity. Therefore, procurement by distribution companies shall be done at preferential tariffs determined by the appropriate commission. This procurement should be done using competitive bidding. In the long term, these technologies will need to compete with other sources in terms of full costs.
- The Central Commission should lay down guidelines within three months for pricing non-firm power,[9] especially from non-conventional sources, to be followed in cases where such procurement is not through competitive bidding.

National Urban Transport Policy

The National Urban Transport Policy (NUTP) of the Ministry of Urban Development promotes integrated land use and transport planning in cities. It focuses on greater use of public transport and non-motorized modes of transportation by offering central financial assistance. The policy incorporates urban transportation as an important parameter at the urban planning stage.

Renewable Energy Policy

The Ministry of New and Renewable Energy has prepared a draft R&D policy (December 12, 2006)[10] based on resource requirements estimated for the 11th Five-Year Plan. The MNRE has also prepared a draft renewable energy policy, which identifies the strategies for increased deployment of grid-connected RE technologies. The renewable energy policy statement is available in Annex 3. These policies have yet to be approved.

The Electricity Act of 2003

The Electricity Act of 2003 combines the various provisions of: (a) The Indian Electricity Act, 1910; (b) The Electricity (Supply) Act, 1948; and (c) The Electricity Regulatory Commissions Act, 1998. This was necessitated by the rapid developments in the electricity sector mainly in the areas of reforms, regulation, and technology development. The act recognizes the role of renewable energy technologies for supplying power to the utility grid as well as in stand-alone systems. Some of the important provisions in the act in this regard include:

- As per Section 3(1), the central government shall from time to time prepare the national electricity policy and tariff policy, in consultation with the state governments and the authority for development of the power system, based on optimal utilization of resources, such as coal, natural gas, nuclear substances or materials, hydro, and other renewable sources of energy.
- As per 1.0.2.2 Section 4, the central government shall, after consultation with state governments, prepare a national policy permitting stand-alone systems (including those based on renewable energy and other nonconventional energy sources for rural areas).
- As per Section 61(h), the appropriate commission shall, subject to the provisions of this act, specify the terms and conditions for the determination of tariffs and, in so doing, shall be guided by the promotion of co-generation and generation of electricity from renewable sources of energy.
- As per Section 86(1)(e), one of the functions of the state regulatory commission is to promote co-generation and generation of electricity through renewable sources of energy by providing suitable measures for connectivity with the grid and sale of electricity to any persons and also specify, for purchase of electricity from such sources, a percentage of the total consumption of electricity in the area of a distribution licensee. Section 86(1)(e) also makes it mandatory for distribution companies to buy a certain percentage of the total energy consumption from renewable sources of energy. The State Energy Regulatory Commissions (SERCs) have been given the responsibility of determining this percentage or a quota for renewable power.

- As per Section 6, appropriate government endeavors are required to extend the electricity supply to villages and hamlets.
- As per Section 14, there is no requirement for a license if a person intends to generate and distribute electricity in rural areas.

The Energy Conservation Act of 2001

The Energy Conservation Act of 2001 includes the promotion of energy efficiency and energy conservation in the country to make power available to all Indian citizens by 2012. In this context, the Energy Conservation Act of 2001 was passed and BEE set up to carry out the various functions it envisioned. The act provides the legal framework, institutional arrangement, and a regulatory mechanism necessary to promote energy efficiency in the country.

Legal Framework for Environmental Compliance

The legal framework required for ensuring environmental compliance for a clean energy project has been briefly described in terms of "basic" requirements and "others." The basic requirements need to be met in order to obtain "Consent to Establish" and "Consent to Operate." Other requirements refer to with the use of hazardous chemicals for storage as well as planning, construction, and implementation of a project.

Plans, Guidelines, Codes, and Other Policies

The National Building Code of India (NBC) provides guidelines for regulating building construction across the country and serves as a model code for all agencies involved in building. It contains administrative regulations; development control rules and general building requirements; fire safety requirements; stipulations regarding materials, structural design, and construction (including safety); and building and plumbing services.

In March 2007, the conduct of energy audits was made mandatory in large energy-consuming units in nine industrial sectors. These units, indicated as "designated consumers," are also required to employ "certified energy managers" and report energy consumption and energy conservation data annually. Energy Conservation Building Codes (ECBCs) have been prepared for each of the six climatic zones of India. The ECBCs provide minimum requirements for energy efficient design and construction of commercial buildings, including air conditioning, lighting, electric power and distribution, and service water heating and pumping. Some of the short/long-term measures undertaken and/or proposed by BEE to catalyze energy efficiency are given below:

- Energy conservation—complete pilot phase of program for energy efficiency in government buildings and prepare action plan for wider dissemination and implementation.
- Energy audit of government buildings including complete energy audits for nine government buildings. Legal performance contract agreements, payment security mechanisms, bid selection, and evaluation criteria are provided to all building owners to support implementation.
- Capacity building among departments to upgrade energy efficiency programs—BEE will train core group members to implement energy efficiency in buildings.

- Priority measures including forming industry-specific task forces, specifying more industries as designated consumers, conducting energy audits among designated consumers, recording and publicizing best practices (sector-wise), developing energy consumption norms, and monitoring compliance with mandated provisions by designated consumers.

Over 700 CDM projects have been approved by the India CDM National Designated Authority, and about 240 of these have been registered by the CDM Executive Board. The registered projects have already resulted in over 27 million tons of certified CO_2 emissions reductions and have directed investment in renewable energy projects by reducing the perceived risks and uncertainties of these new technologies, thereby accelerating their adoption.

The MNRE has prepared a renewable energy plan and a national master plan for development of waste-toenergy. In addition, the government of India adopted the Biodiesel Purchase Policy in 2005. This policy mandates oil marketing companies to purchase biodiesel from registered suppliers at a uniform price to be reviewed every six months. Some public sector oil companies are already experimenting with various mixes of biodiesel in state transport buses and are in discussions with the automobile industry to share results.

The National Auto Fuel Policy of 2003 provides a road map for achieving various vehicular emission norms over a period of time and the corresponding requirements for upgrading fuel quality. While it does not recommend any particular fuel or technology for achieving the desired emission norms, it suggests that liquid fuels should remain the primary auto fuels throughout the country and that the use of CNG/LPG should be encouraged in cities affected by higher pollution levels so as to enable vehicle owners to have the choice of the fuel and technology combination.

The Working Group for the 11th Five-Year Plan on Coal[11] has identified the need for energy efficiency and demand-side management. This has emerged from the various supply scenarios and is underlined by rising energy prices. The average gross efficiency of generation from coal power plants is 30.5 percent. The best plants in the world operate with supercritical boilers and obtain gross efficiencies of 42 percent. It should be possible to get gross efficiency of 38–40 percent at an economically attractive cost for all new coal-based plants. This alone could reduce the coal requirement by 111 mToe of coal (278 mt of Indian coal). The working group therefore has prioritized the development of high-efficiency coal-fired technologies, stating that all new thermal power plants should be commissioned with a certified fuel conversion efficiency of at least 38–40 percent. Power plants operating at a smaller plant load factor are required to undertake comprehensive renovation and modernization of units/technology and, wherever possible, old plants should be replaced by higher-capacity ultra-mega power plants with supercritical technology.

The Department of Electronics and Telecommunication has proposed a special incentive package scheme to encourage investments in semi-conductor fabrication and other micro- and nano- technology manufacturing industries in India. In addition, the national and state-level industry associations have been working with the central and state governments to promote a range of policies for sustainable participation in the country's economic development.

In April 2005, the Ministry of Power introduced the Rajiv Gandhi Grameen Vidhyutikaran Yojana (RGGVY) Program, which aims at providing electricity in all villages and habitations by 2009. Under RGGVY, the electricity distribution infrastructure establishes a Rural Electricity Distribution Backbone with at least a 33/11-kilovolt (kV) sub-station, a Village Electrification Infrastructure with at least a distribution transformer in a village or hamlet, and stand-alone grids where grid supply is not feasible. This infrastructure should cater to the requirements of agriculture and other activities in rural areas including irrigation pump sets, small and medium industries, khadi and village industries, cold chains, healthcare and education, and communication technologies. This would facilitate overall rural development, employment generation, and poverty alleviation. Up to 90 percent of the subsidies toward capital expenditure will be provided through the Rural Electrification Corporation Limited (REC), which is a nodal agency for implementation of this program. Electrification of unelectrified below-poverty-line households will be financed with 100 percent capital subsidies at $38.00 per connection in all rural habitations. The Management of Rural Distribution is mandated through franchises, but the services of the Central Public Sector Undertakings are available to assist states in executing rural electrification projects.

4. Opportunities for U.S. Firms in India

The geographical region, type of opportunity, and policy drivers associated with each technology are identified below. At the sector level, small hydropower, wind, and solar energy offer maximum scope for clean energy development. These sectors are relatively mature and significant local industries already exist. On the other hand, geothermal and tidal energy technologies are nascent and offer important early entry advantages to U.S. companies.

Renewable Energy Technology

Geographically, major opportunities by sector are provided in Table 1.24 below.

Specific subsectors, which offer opportunities for U.S. companies, are listed in Table 1.25.

Table 1.24. Clean Technology Opportunities by Sector

Sector	Geographic Opportunity
Small hydropower	Himachal Pradesh, Uttarakhand, Jammu and Kashmir, and Arunachal Pradesh
Wind energy	Maharashtra, Andhra Pradesh, Tamil Nadu, and Gujarat
Solar	All over India
Bioenergy	Rajasthan, Punjab, Uttar Pradesh, Maharashtra, Madhya Pradesh, Haryana, and Gujarat
Waste-to-energy	Maharashtra, Uttar Pradesh, Karnataka, Tamil Nadu, and West Bengal
Geothermal	Jammu and Kashmir, Himachal Pradesh, Uttarakhand, and Chhattisgarh
Tidal	Gulf of Kuchch and Gulf of Cambay in Gujarat and the Delta of the Ganga in the Sunderbans region in West Bengal.
Energy efficiency	All over India

Table 1.25. Specific Technology Opportunities for U.S. Firms in India

Sector	Technology Opportunity
Small hydropower	• Technology for adaptation of high-pole permanent magnet excitation generators to SHP. • Technology for low-speed generators (direct-drive low-speed generators for low heads). • Technology for submersible turbo-generators. • Technology for appropriate turbine designs suitable to electrical output below 1 MW. • Technology for variable-speed operation (optimal use of low-and variable-head sites). • Technology/projects for flexible small hydro turbines for very low head (<2.5 m).
Wind energy	• Latest technologies with higher capacities are needed. These technologies may include wind power systems greater than 1–2 MW. • Wind machines for low-wind regimes and better designed rotor blades, gear boxes, and control systems.
Solar	• Technology for polysilicon and other materials. • Technology for device fabrication processes and improvements in crystal-line silicon solar cell/module technology. • Thin-film solar cell technology (based on amorphous silicon films; cadmi-um telluride films and copper indium diselenide thin films; organic, dye-sensitized, and carbon nano tubes). • Technology for megawatt-scale solar photovoltaic power-generating systems. • Technology for solar thermal (high-temperature) power generation sys-tems and energy efficient buildings utilizing solar energy concepts.
Bioenergy	• Development of megawatt-scale fluidized bed biomass gasifiers, hot-gas clean-up system, and optimum integration of the system following the principles of IGCC. • Development of poly-generation facilities for the production of liquid fuels, variety of chemicals and hydrogen in addition to power production through the IGCC route, and establishing the concept of a biorefinery. • Raising efficiency of atmospheric gasification to 25–30% along with cooling systems, complete tar decomposition, and safe disposal of wastes in commercial production. • Raising system efficiency of small (up to 1 MW) combustion and turbine technologies to 20% plus. • Design and development of high-rate anaerobic co-digestion systems for biogas/synthetic gas production. • Development of gasifier systems based on charcoal/ pyrolyzed biomass. • Development of efficient kilns/systems for charcoal production/pyrolyzation of biomass. • Design and development of engines, Stirling engines, and micro-turbines for biogas/producer gas/biosyngas. • Design and development of direct gas-fired absorptive chillers, driers, stoves, etc., and improvement in biomass furnaces, boilers, etc. • Engine modifications for using more than 20% biodiesel as a blend with diesel.
	• Development of second-generation bioliquid fuels and related applications. • Diversification of feed stocks to utilize alternate biomass wastes along with cattle dung for setting up household biogas plants. • Methods for sustaining biogas production during winter months. • Development of biogas micro-turbines and engines. • Local power grids compatible with dual fuel engines and gas engines/ turbines. • Removal of hydrogen sulfide from biogas produced in night soil-based biogas plants. • Additional treatment methods for effluent from night soil- based biogas plants.
Waste-to-energy	• Technology and successful demonstration of biomethanation, combustion/ incineration, pyrolysis/gasification, landfill gas recovery, densification, and pelletization.
Geothermal	• Technology supplier/equipment manufacturer/project developer for geo-thermal energy harnessing.
Tidal	• Technology supplier/equipment manufacturer/project developer for harne-ssing tidal energy.
Energy efficiency	• ESCOs, energy efficiency equipment for buildings/ industries.

Table 1.26. Energy Efficiency Opportunities

Attributes	Geographical Area/States
Agricultural DSM	National level
Municipal DSM	
Building energy efficiency	
Policy implementation (budget/organization set-up/action plans)	Haryana, Gujarat, Maharashtra, Tamil Nadu, Kerala, Karnataka, Delhi

Energy Efficiency

Opportunities for U.S.-based organizations (based on proposals by the BEE) include:

- About $12 million has been allocated by BEE for development of five-year energy efficiency action plans by state-level agencies. These plans will propose interventions, which will be implemented using national/statelevel funding, as well as funds from the private sector.
- BEE has requested proposals from national/international consulting organizations to assist the agency in the preparation of bankable proposals in the area of agricultural demand-side management (DSM) (pumping efficiency) for all the states within two years.
- BEE has requested proposals from national/international consulting organizations to assist the agency in the preparation of bankable proposals and to develop projects in the area of municipal DSM for all the states within two years.
- BEE has requested proposals from national and international consulting organizations to assist in the promotion of compact fluorescent lighting (CFL) and to claim certified emission reduction credits (CERs) through CDM projects.
- The State of Uttar Pradesh has solicited an expression of interest from agencies to implement CFL usage under a public–private partnership (PPP) model, where the operator can claim benefits from CERs.
- The State of Gujarat has solicited proposals for implementing municipal DSM by ESCOs.

Table 1.26 is an energy efficiency opportunity matrix prepared on the basis of policy-level attributes and geographical area of implementation.

Other Opportunities

The state governments of Andhra Pradesh, Chhattisgarh, Gujarat, and Tamil Nadu are promoting biodiesel production, including the development of state biodiesel boards and farmer buy-back schemes. In both Tanil Nadu and Gujarat, private companies are producing quality biodiesel that meets the American Society for Testing and Materials (ASTM) 16750 standard.

Table 1.27. Incentives for the Promotion of CETs

No.	Sector	Incentives/ Subsidies/Tariffs/Quotas
1.	All RE projects	Customs duty for RE projects under 50 MW fixed at 20% ad valorem.
		Central sales tax exemption. Minimum purchase rates of $0.057 per unit of electricity.
2.	SHP	10.75% interest rates (interest rate subsidy).
		Fifteen states—Andhra Pradesh, Haryana, Himachal Pradesh, Jam-mu and Kashmir, Karnataka, Kerala, Madhya Pradesh, Maharash-tra, Orissa, Punjab, Rajasthan, Tamil Nadu, Uttar Pradesh, Uttara-khand, and West Bengal—have declared buy-back tariffs from SHPs.
		Thirteen states—Andhra Pradesh, Gujarat, Haryana, Himachal Pradesh, Karnataka, Kerala, Madhya Pradesh, Maharashtra, Orissa, Rajasthan, Tamil Nadu, Uttar Pradesh, and West Bengal —have declared quotas for purchase of power from SHP.
3.	Wind power	10.25% interest rates (interest rate subsidy).
		Eight states—Andhra Pradesh, Gujarat, Karnataka, Kerala,
		Madhya Pradesh, Maharashtra, Rajasthan, and Tamil Nadu—have declared buy-back tariffs.
		80% accelerated depreciation on the equipment during the first year. Concessions on customs and excise duties. Liberalized foreign investment procedures. Preferential tariffs for wind power.
4.	Biomass/bagasse/ co-generation	10.75% interest rate (interest rate subsidy) for biomass.
		11.25% interest rate (interest rate subsidy) for bagasse.
		Twelve states—Andhra Pradesh, Chhattisgarh, Gujarat, Haryana, Karnataka, Kerala, Madhya Pradesh, Maharashtra, Punjab, Raja-sthan, Tamil Nadu, and Uttar Pradesh—have declared buy-back tariffs for bagasse.
		MNRE provides interest subsidies for co-generation projects. In addition, it provides capital subsidies to bagasse-based co-genera-tion projects in cooperative with public sector sugar mills. State governments also provide various fiscal and financial incentives.
		MNRE provides subsidies for installation of biomass gasifier sys-tems. Financial incentives valued at $30,000 per 100 kWe are pro-vided for 100% producer gas engines, with biomass gasifier sys-tems for both off-grid and grid interactive applications. 80% depre-ciation on equipment during first year.
		Five-year tax break with 30% exemption for projects with power purchase agreement.
5.	Energy from urban and Industrial waste	The 12th Finance Commission has recommended that at least 50% of the grants provided to ULBs through states should be utilized to support the cost of collection, segregation, and transportation of waste.
6.	Solar PV systems	Implementation of the water pumping program was continued through the state nodal agencies and IREDA. A subsidy is pro-vided under the scheme at $75 per watt of SPV array used, subject to a maximum of about $1,200 per system.
	Solar water heating systems	GOI, through MNRE, has provided various interventions in terms of subsidies and other fiscal benefits to promote solar water heating systems.
7.	Renewable ener-gy technologies for distributed generation	MNRE provides financial assistance for meeting up to 90% of the project costs and for comprehensive maintenance for periods up to 10 years.

Table 1.28. Status of Specified quotas for Renewable Energy Procurement, by State

State	Quota/Renewable Purchase Obligation	Time Period
Andhra Pradesh	Minimum 5% of total energy consumption (of this, 0.5% is to be reserved for wind)	2005–2006, 2006–2007, & 2007–2008
Gujarat Minimum	Minimum 1% of total energy consumption	2006–2007
	Minimum 1% of total energy consumption	2007–2008
	Minimum 1% of total energy consumption	2008–2009
Himachal Pradesh	Minimum 20% of total energy consumption	2007–2010
Haryana	Up to 2% of total energy consumption	2006–2007
	Up to 2% of total energy consumption	2007–2008
	Up to 2% of total energy consumption	2008–2009
	Up to 2% of total energy consumption	2009–2010
Karnataka	Minimum 5% and maximum of 10% of total energy consumption	
Kerala	Minimum 5% of total energy consumption (of this, 2% from SHP, 2% from wind, and 1% from all other nonconventional (NCE) sources)	2006–2009
Madhya Pradesh	Minimum 0.5% of total energy consumption includ-ing third-party sales from wind energy	2004–2009
Maharashtra	Minimum 3% of total energy consumption	2006–2007
	Minimum 5% of total energy consumption	2007–2008
	Minimum 5% of total energy consumption	2008–2009
	Minimum 5% of total energy consumption	2009–2010
Orissa	3% (for wind and SHP)	2007–2008
Rajasthan	Minimum 4.88% of total energy consumption	2007–2008
	Minimum 6.25% of total energy consumption	2008–2009
	Minimum 7.45% of total energy consumption	2009–2010
	Minimum 8.50% of total energy consumption	2010–2011
	Minimum 9.50% of total energy consumption	2011–2012
Tamil Nadu	Minimum 10% of total energy consumption	2006–2009
Uttar Pradesh	5% of total energy consumption	—
West Bengal	Minimum: 1.9%	2006–2007
	Minimum: 3.8%	2007–2008

Source: Regulations of different State Electricity Regulatory Commissions.

Incentives

An addition of 15,000 renewable MW over the next decade most likely equates to a $21 billion Indian market for renewable technologies. Renewable energy is already often competitive with conventional power sources due to fiscal policies and incentives and has been strengthened recently with the creation of a renewable portfolio standard. Income tax holidays, accelerated depreciation, duty-free imports, capital subsidies, and concessionary financing, and exemptions from electricity taxes and sales taxes all bolster this emerging market. Table 1.27 provides a summary of these incentives.

Table 1.29. Purchase Tariffs for Renewable Energy Projects by State (in dollars)

State/Union Territory	Wind Power	Small Hydropower	Biomass Power
Andhra Pradesh	0.085 Fixed for 5 years	0.068 (2004–2005)	0.066 (2005–2006) Esc. at 0.01 for 5 years
Arunachal Pradesh	—	—	—
Assam	—	—	—
Bihar	—	—	—
Chhattisgarh	—	—	0.068 (2005–2006)
Gujarat	0.085 Fixed for 20 years	—	0.075 No esc.
Haryana	—	0.056 (1994–1995)	0.101 biomass 0.094—co-generation Esc. at 0.02 (base 2007–2008)
Himachal Pradesh	—	0.063	—
Jammu and Kashmir	—	—	—
Jharkhand	—	—	—
Karnataka	0.086 Fixed for 10 years	0.073	0.069—co-generation 0.072—biomass Esc. at 0.01 for 10 years (base year 2004–2005)
Kerala	0.079 Fixed for 20 years	—	0.0708 (2000–2001) Esc. at 0.05 for 5 years
Madhya Pradesh	0.100–0.083	0.056	0.084–0.130 Esc. at 0.03–0.08 for 20 years
Maharashtra	0.088 Esc. at 0.15 per year	0.0569 (1999–2000)	0.077—co-generation 0.077–0.086—biomass Esc. at 0.01 for 13 years
Manipur	—	—	—
Meghalaya	—	—	—
Mizoram	—	—	—
Nagaland	—	—	—
Orissa	—	—	—
Punjab	—	0.069 (1998–1999)	0.076 (2001-2002) Esc. at 0.03 for 5 years limited to 0.0348
Rajasthan	0.073 Esc. at 0.05 for 10 years	0.069 (1998–1999)	0.091–0.100 Water—air cooled
Sikkim	—	—	—
Tamil Nadu	0.068 (fixed)	—	0.069 (2000–2001)* Esc. at 0.05 for 9 years
Tripura	—	—	—
Uttar Pradesh	—	0.056	0.072—existing plants 0.075—new plants Esc. at 0.04 per year

Source: Government of India Ministry of New and Renewable Energy www.mnes.nic.in

Notes: * Rs. 2.48 per unit at 0.05 escalation for nine years (2000–2001) for off-season power generation using coal/lignite (subject to ceiling of 0.90 of high-tension (HT) tariff).

Policies for wheeling/ banking/ third-party sale vary from state to state.

Esc. = Escalation.

Table 1.30. Interest Rates of IREDA for Different Power generation Technologies

Renewable Energy Source	Interest Rate (%)
Biomass	10.75
Bagasse Co-Generation	11.25
Small Hydro	10.75
Wind	10.25

Source: Financing guidelines, IREDA. www.ireda.in

The National Electricity Policy of 2005 and Electricity Act of 2003 have given a clear mandate to the State Electricity Regulatory Commissions to promote renewable energy, including fixing a share for renewable energy–based electricity. Presently the investment decisions from a policy perspective are based on the following: buy-back tariffs, wheeling charges, whether banking of power is allowed or not, and whether thirdparty sales are allowed or not. The present status of issuing tariff orders and specifying quotas for renewable energy procurement in major Indian states is summarized in Table 1.28. This table also shows the attractiveness of the various states for renewable energy.

Most of these states have also specified the purchase tariff for procurement of power from different renewable energy–based projects. These tariffs have been designed on the basis of cost of generation, assuming 14–16 percent returns on equity by investors. Yet because the resource, generation, and costs of a given project vary by state, purchase tariffs also vary. The purchase tariffs for renewable energy projects in different states are presented in Table 1.29.

Fiscal and Financial Incentives

There are no direct financial incentives or subsidies for grid-connected power generation projects based on renewable energy sources. However, an interest subsidy is provided through IREDA. Present applicable interest rates for grid-connected renewable energy power generation are shown in Table 1.30.

In addition, wind energy projects and the equipment used in biomass/bagasse power generation can claim accelerated depreciation benefits in the first year of the project, providing a tax benefit for investors.

5. Investment and Financing of Clean Energy

Investment and financing of clean energy technologies including renewable energy and energy efficiency can occur through a favorable investment and business environment supported by an adequate institutional structure. In the case of India, the business and investment climate has improved significantly in the last decade. The following section describes these changes.

Foreign Investment Policy for Renewables

Foreign investors can enter joint ventures with an Indian partner for financial and/or technical collaboration and also for the establishment of renewable energy projects. There is a liberalized foreign investment approval regime to facilitate foreign investment and transfer technology through joint ventures. Proposals with up to 74 percent foreign equity participation qualify for automatic approval and full foreign investment as equity is permissible with the approval of the Foreign Investment Promotion Board but the GOI encourages foreign investors to create renewable energy–based power generation projects on a public–private partnership basis.

Funding and Financial Mechanisms, Capital Markets and Financial Institutions

Currently, government funding drives the financing of clean energy projects at three levels—national, state, and local (municipal). Other sources of finance include capital markets, financial institutions (national and international), and private sector finance.

Central Government

The government is responsible for policy and regulatory frameworks related to financing. The Ministry of Finance (MoF), with the help of the planning commission, is responsible for planning the budget and allocating funds to the various ministries. It provides equity for project agencies, offers guarantee mechanisms, funds programs for capacity building, promotes fiscal incentives, and fuels bond markets with government borrowing. The budgets of the line ministries have been growing during the past few years. For example, MNRE's budget increased from $39 million in 2005–2006 to $75 million in 2006–2007. These line ministries are providing financial assistance for states and districts (and organizations within them), both directly and through various programs.

State Government

The central government, together with multilateral agencies, is funding a large number of environmental projects at the state level. In many cases the states are expected to match contributions with state funding.

Local Government

Municipalities are often funded through grants, funding from the central government via state governments, state government grants, and local revenues generated through local taxes. Urban Local Bodies (ULBs) traditionally suffer from a lack of funds; typically, they receive only about 40 percent of their state funding share. This is due to deductions by state governments for items such as overdue power charges and loan payments, which result from a general lack of revenue generation. In addition, ULBs lack a system to identify and track income and expenditures.

Access to capital markets is an important way to bolster the finances of ULBs. Some of the key features in this type of financing are shown below:

- Municipal development funds have been established to enhance the viability of local development projects. Funds are often created through collaborations between an international firm a local counterpart, and the local government.
- Establishment of the City Challenge Fund (CCF), the Urban Reform Incentive Fund (URIF), and the Pooled Finance Development Fund. Presently, URIF targets selected reforms but does not finance specific infrastructure investments. CCF was designed to provide investment funding coupled with specific city-level reforms. Discussions

are underway concerning integration of URIF and CCF into an Urban Infrastructure Development Fund, a much bigger fund that could provide funding to states to support large infrastructure projects. The flow of funds to the states would be linked with reforms.

- Resources have been mobilized through taxable bonds and tax-free bonds. However, only financially strong, large municipalities are in a position to directly access capital markets. For smaller ones, pooled financing is an option. The Tamil Nadu Urban Development Fund in an example of pooled financing, the objective is to fund urban infrastructure projects including water supply, sewage, and solid waste management.

Capital Markets

A vibrant, well-developed capital market has been shown to facilitate investment and economic growth. India's debt and equity markets were equivalent to 130 percent of the GDP at the end of 2005. This impressive growth, starting from just 75 percent in 1995, suggests growing confidence in market-based financing. At nearly 40 percent of GDP, the size of India's government bond segment is comparable to many other emerging market economies, and India boasts a dynamic equity market. The sharp rise in India's stock markets since 2003 reflects its improving macroeconomic fundamentals.

India's debt markets are divided into two segments: corporate and government. The government bond segment is the larger and more active of the two, with issuers comprising the central government (which accounts for 90 percent of the total) with the remainder from state governments. The corporate bond market consists of Public Sector Undertakings (PSUs), corporate bodies, financial institutions, and banks. PSU bonds far outweigh the size of private corporate bonds, reflecting a number of factors, including regulatory requirements for private issues.

India's financial market began its transformative path in the early 1990s. The banking sector witnessed sweeping changes, including the elimination of interest rate controls, reductions in reserve and liquidity requirements, and an overhaul in priority sector lending. Its market infrastructure has advanced while corporate governance has progressed faster than in many other emerging market economies. The seamless move toward shorter settlement periods has been enabled by a number of innovations. The introduction of electronic transfer of securities brought down settlement costs markedly and ushered in greater transparency, while "dematerialization" instituted a paper-free securities market. Innovative products such as securitized debt and fund products based on alternative assets are starting to break ground. Asset-backed securities (ABSs) are the predominant asset class in India's securitized segment. The ABS market has risen exponentially since 2002, in tune with the sharp growth in credit since that time. In 2005, India's ABS market volume was roughly $5 billion, making it the fourth largest in the Asia–Pacific region.

At the institutional level, the Securities and Exchange Board of India (SEBI) was established in 1992 with a mandate to protect investors and improve the micro-structure of capital markets. The repeal of the Controller of Capital Issues (CCI) in 1992 removed the administrative controls over pricing of new equity issues. Competition in the markets increased with the establishment of the National Stock Exchange in 1994, leading to a significant rise in the volume of transactions and to the emergence of new important instruments in financial intermediation. The Reserve Bank of India (RBI) has maintained its role as the government's debt manager and regulator of governmentissued papers.

Development Financial Institutions and Commercial Banks

Development financial institutions (DFIs) at central, state, and municipal levels; provident funds; commercial banks; and export credit agencies provide funding for infrastructure projects. These agencies provide loans, work as financial intermediaries, arrange loans from other sources, provide guarantees, and assume advisory roles. DFIs usually provide the greatest portion of financing for large-scale projects.

Apart from debt, some of the DFIs also invest in equity. Among the types of financing available, project financing dominates the sector because of the capital-intensive nature and long gestation periods. Corporate financing is generally provided in low-risk projects with prominent corporate entities. Hybrid finance through equity/quasiequity is occasionally provided. Bond financing is used by established infrastructure companies or authorities with the backing of central and state governments.

The major domestic DFIs operating in the clean energy sector in India are:

- Industrial Finance Corporation of India (IFCI);
- Industrial Development Bank of India (IDBI);
- Life Insurance Corporation (LIC);
- Small Industries Development Bank (SIDBI);
- Infrastructure Development Finance Company (IDFC);
- Housing and Urban Development Corporation (HUDCO);
- India Infrastructure Finance Company Ltd (IIFCL);
- L&T Finance;
- Infrastructure Leasing & Financial Services Limited (IL&FS);
- Indian Renewable Energy Development Agency Ltd (IREDA);
- National Bank for Agriculture & Rural Development (NABARD).

FINANCING RENEWABLE ENERGY AND ENERGY EFFICIENCY IN INDIA

The potential offered by Indian capital markets for the financing of renewable energy and energy efficiency projects is enormous. In contrast to the government bond market, the size of the corporate bond market (i.e., corporate issuers plus financial institutions) remains very small, amounting to just $16.8 billion, or less than 2 percent of GDP at the end of June 2006. A welldeveloped corporate bond market would give companies greater flexibility to define their optimum capital structure. Structured finance offers immense potential. Securitization is an attractive growth segment in India's debt markets. The market is still in its nascent stages, where current activities primarily occur between banks, non-bank financial institutions, and asset reconstruction companies through private placements. Paving the way for a secondary market is the implementation of the proposed changes to the Securities Contracts Regulation Act, which would reclassify securitized debt as true marketable securities.

The power sector is the preferred investment for infrastructure financers, followed by roads and ports. In the waste management sector, active players are HUDCO, L&T Finance, and IL&FS. The majority of DFIs are gearing to become universal banks, which allows them to access low-cost savings and offer more flexibility in terms of loan types and tenors. IREDA is a specialized DFI providing soft loans for renewable energy and energy efficiency projects. IREDA has been a major funder of wind projects since its inception. However, due to depreciation allowances and other incentives, wind power projects have become viable investments by commercial banks. Currently, IREDA's focus has shifted mostly to financing small hydropower projects, an area that is currently financed by just two commercial banks. IREDA provides financing for projects, equipment, and manufacture of equipment.

Commercial banks are increasing their exposure to infrastructure. The major banks are the State Bank of India (SBI) and its associates, ICICI Bank, Punjab National Bank (PNB), Canara Bank, Union Bank of India, Allahabad Bank, and Corporation Bank. Due to the increased involvement of commercial banks, the need for DFIs is likely to diminish. The contribution of mutual funds and pension funds in lending for renewable energy projects has yet to mature.

International Financial Institutions (IFIs)

Major financial institutions that are involved in clean energy and related activities are shown in Table 1.31.

International Finance Corporation (IFC). The IFC is a private sector lending division of the World Bank Group, which fosters sustainable economic growth in developing countries by financing private sector investment, mobilizing capital in international markets, and providing advisory services to businesses and governments. Infrastructure projects are central to IFC's investment strategy with investments in power generation (including renewable energy), distribution, transmission, and energy efficiency projects. Additionally, IFC is associated with green-field projects, corporate loans, acquisition finance, and refinancing.[12]

IFC South Asia has a $1.6 billion lending portfolio covering India, Sri Lanka, the Maldives, Bhutan, and Nepal. India alone accounts for three-fourths of this portfolio. IFC's South Asia portfolio includes:

- One-third in financial markets [ICICI, Housing Development Finance Corporation (HDFC), Shrey International];
- One-third in general manufacturing (medium and large enterprises);
- One-third in infrastructure and agribusiness (power transmission and water utilities).

Table 1.31. Summary of Major Donors' Clean Development Activities

	Demand-Side EE	Supply-Side EE	Renewable Energy	Clean Fossil Fuels	Clean Transport
IFC	√				√
ADB	√	√	√		√
USAID	√	√	√	√	√
World Bank	√	√	√		√
Ex-Im		√	√	√	√

Source: USAID ECO–Asia Clean Development and Climate Program, 2006.

IFC has recently ventured into development-based lending focused on sub-national lending to municipalities for purposes of improving energy, water, and solid waste management by municipal corporations. This represents a new and risky area for IFC, where there is no sovereign guarantee.

Asian Development Bank (ADB). According to the ADB, the bank "extends loans and provides technical assistance to its developing member countries for a broad range of development projects and programs. It also promotes and facilitates investment of public and private capital for economic and social development."[13] ADB emphasizes the acceleration of renewable energy and energy efficiency in its developing member countries, including India. In the clean energy area, ADB supports capacity building, institutional development, policy and regulatory activities, and project development. The ADB has committed $1 billion per year for renewable energy and energy efficiency over the next few years. Of special note are its efforts to catalyze local financing institutions and the private sector to participate in the delivery of clean energy services and to include modern energy access. ADB's private sector operations department has also made equity investments in several funds targeting clean energy. ADB is financing a number of clean energy–related projects in India, including energy efficiency, CDM projects on the supply and demand sides, urban infrastructure projects, hydro-electric projects, and transportation services.

USAID. USAID's work on energy development in India dates back to the 1980s and focuses on three areas: building regulatory capacity at the state level in order to implement sector reform, asset-based reform and commercial capacity building focused on utilities, and relating public policy (e.g., the Electricity Act of 2003 and the Energy Conservation Act of 2001) to business policy via practical ways to overcome market and institutional barriers. USAID has promoted new concepts in energy efficiency in both industries and buildings. The major program on energy efficiency is the Energy Conservation and Commercialization ECO (Energy Efficiency Commercialization Project) III project.

World Bank. The World Bank has invested significant resources into energy efficiency projects including coal-fired power generation through rehabilitation [$45 million GEF, $157 million International Bank for Reconstruction and Development (IBRD)].[14] The World Bank is also supporting energy efficiency improvements in the urban sector. The Second Renewable Energy Project being implemented supports both renewable energy and energy efficiency. The project provides a financial intermediation loan of $200 million to IREDA, which will be lent to private companies to finance numerous small renewable energy projects. Sub-projects will be primarily for electricity generation and will include biomass power generation; co-generation at sugar refineries; and small hydropower, windmill power, solar PV power, and solar thermal projects. The project also includes a technical assistance component, which involves training and capacity building of energy managers, bankers, and the building sector. Further, it supports demonstration projects in the building sector. A new programmatic CDM effort with $75 million in GEF financing for India has also been launched by the World Bank.

Private-Sector Participation

The private sector is involved in implementation of Build, Own, Operate, and Transfer (BOOT) and Build, Own, and Operate (BOO) Projects. These models are actively followed in the small hydropower sector as evidenced in Uttarakhand, where clear guidelines have been defined by the government. The GOI is also promoting public–private partnerships (PPPs) in infrastructure development, including waste- to-energy and solid waste management. PPP projects with at least 51 percent private equity receive support from this facility through viability gap funding, reducing the capital cost of projects and making them attractive for private sector investment. Viability gap funding can take various forms, including capital grants, subordinated loans, O&M support grants, and interest subsidies. The total government support required by the project must not exceed 20 percent of the project cost. The projects may be proposed by any public agency at the central or state level, the ULB that owns the underlying assets, or a private agency, with sponsorship from the relevant central or state government agency. The government has also set up a special-purpose vehicle—India Infrastructure Finance Company Limited (IIFCL)—to meet the long-term financing requirement of potential investors involved in PPPs. The majority of companies involved in PPPs to date have been mostly domestic. This trend indicates the increasing participation of domestic companies and paves the way for foreign companies to enter through either joint ventures or equity participation.

Several development agencies and Indian financial institutions have already joined with state governments to promote environmental infrastructure development and facilitate private participation. Examples from the urban infrastructure sector include the Tamil Nadu Urban Development Fund, the Project Development Corporation (PDCOR) in Rajasthan, and iDeck in Karnataka. Fifty-Five ULBs have invited some form of private participation in solid waste management. Currently, most waste-to-energy projects are heavily dependent on subsidies provided by MNRE and financial institutions such as HUDCO.

Business Environment

The business environment in the context of clean energy can be explained in terms of subsidies and partially controlled regimes regulating the fossil-fuel-based energy supply.

Coal

Coal pricing has been decontrolled, but wholesale restructuring of the coal sector is still being debated. Coal continues to be included in the Essential Commodities Act of 1955 but can be freely imported under open general license (OGL). The pricing of coal was fully deregulated after the updated Colliery Control Order of 2000 went into effect on January 1, 2000. Since then, coal prices have been fixed on a cost-plus basis.

Oil, Gas, and Natural Gas

Crude oil prices have also been deregulated, allowing domestic exploration and production companies to negotiate with the refiners on the price of crude oil. The GOI has successfully implemented a new exploration licensing policy and now allots both national and international companies exploration blocks. With the dismantling of administered pricing mechanisms (APM) in April 2002, prices of petroleum products were linked to international markets. Since then, some of the trends that have emerged include:

- Petroleum products except diesel, kerosene, and liquefied petroleum gas (LPG) are governed by international prices.

- The government decreased the customs duty on petrol and diesel from 10 to 7.5 percent.
- The government has encouraged the import of liquefied natural gas (LNG) by placing it under the OGL list and permitting 100 percent foreign direct investment (FDI).
- There is no uniform method for determination of gas prices. With deregulation of the gas market, both market-determined and administered pricing coexist in the sector. Gas sold by national oil companies from the pre–New Exploration and Licensing Policy (NELP) blocks is under APM prices. In June 2006, under APM the revised prices for these categories were Rs 3840/million standard cubic meters (MMSCM) for general consumers and Rs 2304/MMSCM for northeast consumers. The gas produced under the NELP blocks can be sold at market-determined prices. These prices are decided on the basis of the production-sharing contracts and the gas sales agreement.

Biodiesel

Since January 1, 2006, public sector oil companies are mandated to purchase biodiesel. Twenty purchase centers have been identified where companies can purchase biodiesel that meets the standards prescribed by the Bureau of Indian Standards. The initial purchase price is about $6 per liter, which may be reviewed by the companies every six months.

Ethanol

The Indian Oil Corporation Ltd. has finalized a deal to source ethanol from sugar mills at $0.47 per liter ex-distillery, which was calculated on the basis of bids quoted.

Clean Energy

The broad policy framework for financing clean energy is formulated by the central government and is implemented at the state level by nodal agencies. Each state provides token or matching contributions to facilitate clean energy project development and implementation. The Electricity Act of 2003 mandates that the SERCs promote generation of electricity from non-conventional sources by providing suitable measures for connectivity with the grid and sale of electricity to any person and also by specifying, for purchase of electricity from such sources, a percentage of the total consumption of electricity in an area. Thirteen states have determined quotas for procurement of renewable energy as shown in Table 1.27. SERCs are now determining preferential tariffs for renewable electricity. Sixteen states have policies in place for private sector participation. The tariff policy has entrusted responsibility to the SERCs to lay down guidelines for pricing non-firm power, especially from non-conventional energy sources.

Tariffs

Fifteen states—Andhra Pradesh, Haryana, Himachal Pradesh, Jammu and Kashmir, Karnataka, Kerala, Madhya Pradesh, Maharashtra, Orissa, Punjab, Rajasthan, Tamil Nadu, Uttar Pradesh, Uttarakhand, and West Bengal—have declared buy-back tariffs from SHPs. Eight states—Andhra Pradesh, Gujarat, Karnataka, Kerala, Madhya Pradesh, Maharashtra, Rajasthan, and Tamil Nadu—have issued orders for determining tariffs from wind power. Finally, 12 states—Andhra Pradesh, Chhattisgarh, Gujarat, Haryana, Karnataka, Kerala,

Madhya Pradesh, Maharashtra, Punjab, Rajasthan, Tamil Nadu, and Uttar Pradesh—have issued orders for determining tariffs from biomass.

Financing and Subsidies

Financing and subsidies are available for all the sectors of clean energy. Descriptions for each sector of clean energy are given below.

Small Hydropower

Currently, most SHP capacity additions are being achieved through private investment. State Nodal Agencies for renewable energy provide assistance for obtaining necessary clearances in allotment of land and potential sites. The MNRE has been providing subsidies for public sector as well as private sector SHP. For the private sector, the subsidy is released to the participating financial institution after successful commissioning and commencement of commercial generation from the project. The subsidy is provided as an offset against the term loan provided to the developer. To ensure quality, equipment used in projects is required to meet international standards. Projects are also required to be tested for performance by an independent agency in order to receive the subsidy. Various financial institutions, namely, IREDA, Power Finance Corporation (PFC), and the REC, provide loan assistance for setting up small hydropower projects. In addition to these agencies, loans are also available from IDBI, IFCI, ICICI, and some nationalized banks.

Wind Energy Systems

Several financial and fiscal incentives are available to wind energy systems, including:

- Tax holidays for wind power generation projects;
- Eighty percent accelerated depreciation on the equipment during the first year;
- Concessions on customs and excise duties;
- Liberalized foreign investment procedures;
- Preferential tariffs for wind power.

Major national financial institutions such as IDBI, ICICI, REC, and PFC also finance wind power projects.

Bagasse-based Co-generation

MNRE provides interest subsidies for co-generation projects. In addition, it provides capital subsidies to bagassebased co-generation projects in cooperative with public sector sugar mills. State governments also provide various fiscal and financial incentives.

Biomass Gasifiers

MNRE provides subsidies for installation of biomass gasifier systems. Financial incentives valued at $30,000 per 100 kWe are provided for engines using 100 percent producer gas, with biomass gasifier systems for both off-grid and grid-interactive applications.

Energy from Urban and Industrial Waste

The 12th Finance Commission has recommended that at least 50 percent of the grants provided to ULBs through states should be utilized to support the cost of collection, segregation, and transportation of waste. This will facilitate operation of waste-to-energy projects.

Solar Photovoltaic Systems

Implementation of the water pumping program was continued through the state nodal agencies and IREDA. A subsidy is provided under the scheme at $75 per watt of solar PV (SPV) array used, subject to a maximum of about $1,200 per system.

Solar Water Heating Systems

Considering the vast potential and resource availability, the GOI, through MNRE, has provided various programs in terms of subsidies and other fiscal benefits to promote solar water heating systems.

Renewable Energy Technologies for Distributed Generation

To meet the electricity needs of villages, the Remote Village Electricification (RVE) Program utilizes solar, biomass, small hydro, wind, and hybrid combinations for decentralized and distributed generation of power and supply of electricity locally. Under the program, MNRE provides financial assistance for meeting up to 90 percent of the project costs and for comprehensive maintenance for periods up to 10 years. The Rural Electrification Corporation and the RVE Program of MNRE are the two national-level schemes that complement each other in achieving national electrification targets.

Effects of Financial Incentives of Clean Tech Costs

The effect of the incentives and tax regimes on the capital costs and delivered costs of renewable energy from various sources is provided in Table 1.32.

Table 1.33 below shows that, in general, the loan disbursements by IREDA have been declining since 2001, although in 2006–2007 there was an increase. Even in 2006, however, the share of IREDA financing was less than in 2001. This is an indicator that other mainstream financial institutions (FIs) have started financing renewable energy projects, and their share is increasing. This is the result of two factors: (1) interest rates now offered by IREDA at the same rate as those offered by other FIs meaning the market is beginning to decrease the risk associated with renewable projects, and (2) renewable power generation is now seen as a mature sector in India. These new FI loans are typically based on a number of traditional issues like strong project sponsorship, appropriate contractual structure, proven track record of equipment suppliers, appropriate fuel supply agreements, cost competitiveness and project viability on a stand-alone basis, and adequate mitigation of off-take, payment risk.

General financing trends of renewable energy and energy efficiency projects currently emerging from the commercial banks can be summarized as follows:

- High debt/equity ratio of about 2:1.
- Increasing trend of financing on a non-recourse/limited recourse basis. This is attributed to the evolution of the contractual framework in implementing renewable energy projects.

Table 1.32. Cost of Renewable Power generation, 2005

Type	Capital COST ($/KW)	Delivery COST (Cents/Kwh)
Small hydro	900–1300	5–6
Wind energy	950–1100	6–7
Biomass power	800–1000	5–6
Bagasse co-generation	600–800	4.5–5.5
Biomass gasification	600–800	5–6
Solar PV	5000–6500	19–40

Source: MNRE, 2005.

Table 1.33. Annual Loan Disbursements by IREDA (million $)

	2001	2002	2003	2004	2005	2006
Wind energy	75.4	31.3	30.9	24.1	14.0	73.9
Small hydro	20.4	19.9	31.4	19.1	17.5	20.7
Bagasse co-generation	41.9	28.9	37.2	6.6	6.5	1.7
Solid biomass	31.4	23.1	25.0	9.2	7.9	78.7
Waste-to-energy	0.2	2.7	7.5	0.5	0.5	0.00

Source: Government of India, Annual Reports of Ministry of New and Renewable Energy, 2000–2001 to 2006–2007.

- Long project implementation period of two to four years. This implies a delay in equity returns and a moratorium period for principal repayment.
- Longer repayment period (10–15 years) of maturity of debt.

The above trends indicate that, though commercial banks have started offering loans for renewable energy projects, the market for renewable energy investments must to continue to evolve.

Environment Related to Procurement and Contracts

Financing instruments facilitating export and import trade are quite developed at both the national and the state levels, where instruments such as letters of credit (LCs), security deposits, and bank guarantees are extensively used during export and import of services and products. Standard contractual guidelines formulated by the GOI have evolved over many years and have been modified since liberalization started in the early 1990s. These are also applicable for renewable energy and energy efficiency projects.

Procurement of services and products in specialized sectors follows open international and national competitive bidding (ICB/NB) procedures at both the national and the state levels. Increasing participation of international firms is an indicator of transparent procurement practices. Procurement by national and state governments through bidding procedures is subject to standard guidelines set by the Central Vigilance Commission (CVC), an independent national agency responsible for checking corruption in the procurement process. Recent implementation of the Right to Information (RTI) Act at both the national and the state levels has further assisted in ensuring transparency in procurement.

Increasing implementation of projects under public–private partnerships—with developed concession/revenue-sharing contractual agreements and securitization of payments through escrow accounts—is an indicator of the developing market. Standardization due to experience in developing and implementing power purchase agreements(PPAs) is another indicator. In addition, performance guarantees and liquidated damages are now being included in the standard contractual mechanism, as is an arbitration clause that takes recourse to the United Nations Commission on International Trade (UNICITRAL) or other international mechanisms, to provide a safeguard mechanism. ESCO financing is yet to emerge owing to scattered and unconsolidated energy efficiency markets. However, it is expected to evolve in future years as the efficiency market is more consolidated.

Increasing non-recourse financing through project financing is seen in the renewable energy sector. The major characteristics and stakeholders of this type of financing are given below:

- **Sponsors/Equity Investors:** Project sponsors generally hold at least 51 percent of the equity component either directly or indirectly. If the sponsor is holding less than 50 percent, then other investors are equipment procurement and construction (EPC)/O&M contractors/fuel suppliers and/or other investors seeking sufficient return.

- **Lenders:** Lenders often require project sponsors to have a strong track record in implementing similar renewable energy projects.

- **Power Off-taker/Purchaser:** The banks require a significant portion of power be tied up through a long-term PPA, while a certain portion is kept for merchant sale. This will further evolve as the recently constituted national-level power exchange starts functioning.

- **Fuel Supplier (not applicable in the case of wind energy and small hydropower projects):** The Fuel Supply Agreement provides the contractual basis for the supply of fuel to the power project. "Take or Pay" contracts provide a degree of comfort level to lenders for mitigating the risk of fuel supply and fluctuation in fuel prices.

- **Equipment Procurement and Construction (EPC) Contractor:** The lenders require EPC contracts to be awarded to reputable firms with successful track records to a more manageable risk.

- **Operation and Maintenance (O&M) Contractor:** The capability, capacity, and reputation of the O&M contractor are very important and will be evaluated by bankers.

Patent Enforcement

In India, patent legislation is governed by the Patent Act of 1970, which provides for the enforcement of patents by way of lawsuits for infringement. In dealing with these suits, the Indian courts follow the traditional principles and procedures of civil litigation. However, after enforcement of the Trade-related Aspects of Intellectual Property Rights (TRIPs) Agreement [the intellectual property component of the Uruguay round of the General

Agreement on Tariffs and Trade (GATT) Treaty] since 1995, various methods have been adopted to improve the enforcement measures with regard to patents. The differences between TRIPs and the Indian Patent (IPA) Act of 1970 are provided in Table 1.34.

- Subsequent to its obligations under the TRIPs Agreement, the Indian Parliament introduced various amendments in the Patent Act and the corresponding Patent Rules in 2002 (also in 2005 and 2006). According to the amendment, the defendant in a suit for infringement would be expected to prove his innocence rather than the plaintiff proving his guilt.

According to the amendment, the defendant in a suit for infringement would be expected to prove his innocence rather than the plaintiff proving his guilt.

Institutional Changes

The government is also revamping the Offices of the Controller General of Patents, Designs, and Trademarks. Modernization and computerization are being carried out in the patent offi ces, speeding up the legal process. The patent offi ces are being upgraded with the use of the Patent Information System (PIS), based in Nagpur. This new patent law has brought the Indian patent regime further in line with international norms. The changes provide new and powerful incentives for investment, both foreign and domestic. The operation of the patent offi ces in handling patent applications has also been improved. A patent can now be granted in less than three years, as opposed to an average of five to seven years just a few years ago.

Enforcement Measures Available under the Indian Law

The patentee may file an action for patent infringement in either a District Court or a High Court. Whenever a defendant counterclaims for revocation of the patent, the suit along with the counter claims is transferred to a High Court for the decision. Because defendants invariably counterclaim for revocation, patent infringement suits are typically heard by a High Court only. According to patent law in India, the High Court may allow the patentee to amend the application in order to preserve the validity of the patent. In such an event, the applicant must give notice to the Controller, who may be entitled to appear and be heard and shall appear if so directed by the High Court.

Table 1.34. Differences between TRIPs and the Indian Patent Act (IPA)

TRIPS	IPA
Grant of patent prescribes three conditions; if satisfied, both process and product patents to be granted in all industries. Duration of patent is uniform, a 20-year duration.	Only permits process patents for food, medicines, drugs, chemicals, micro-organisms, and seeds. Duration of patent is five years from date of sealing or seven years from date of patent.
For compulsory patents, license can be given only in the case of national emergency.	For compulsory patents, an application can be made after three years from grant of patent.
For life-form patents, patenting of micro-organisms and nonbiological, and micro-biological processes is required.	For life-form patents, patenting of life forms or farming techniques Is prohibited.
Onus of proof is on the infringer or the defendant.	Onus of proof lies on the patentee or applicant.

Table 1.35. Emerging Trends in Renewable Energy Financing

Existing Approach	Emerging Trends
Conventional lending through debt and equity	**Financing through:** Subordinated debt Private equity (PE) funds Insurance companies
Debt through rupee term loans	**Inflows through:** External commercial borrowings External credit agencies Multilateral lending agencies
Limited exit options for lenders	"Buy-out" clause in concession agreement
Difficult risk mitigation mechanism	Innovative financial engineering for risk mitigation

If a patentee is successful in proving its case of patent infringement and if the defendant does not comply with the judgment, a petition for contempt of court can be filed. Contempt of court is a criminal offense, while patent infringement is a civil offense. In the event of contempt of court, Indian law provides for imprisoning the authorized person(s) of the defendant. It is also possible to obtain a preliminary injunction, although the above-noted judicial backlog should be considered. The basis upon which a preliminary injunction will be granted is whether the plaintiff shows a prima facie case and also whether the balance of "convenience" is in the plaintiff's favor. However, an important consideration before enforcing a patent in India is to ensure the patentee has worked the invention directly or through its licensees in India.

Current Trends in Clean Energy Financing

Investment opportunities for renewable energy and energy efficiency are available for corporate users of power, longterm investors in power, promoters of clean power, and potential pollution traders or CER traders. Private sector companies can set up enterprises to operate as licensee or generating companies. A foreign investor can enter into a joint venture not only for renewable energy devices or products, but also for manufacturing renewable energy–based power generation projects on a build, own and operate basis. Investors are required to enter a power purchase agreement with the affected state. Various chambers of commerce and industry associations in India provide guidance to the investors in finding appropriate partners.

In addition, it is possible to set up a manufacturing plant as a 100 percent export-oriented unit (EOU). Generally, these are permitted import of raw materials and components duty free and are eligible to sell up to 20 percent of their production in domestic markets.

Table 1.35 above provides an overview of emerging trends in renewable energy financing. Other considerations in terms of investment opportunities include:

- The MNRE is promoting medium, small, mini-enterprises, and micro-enterprises for manufacturing various types of renewable energy systems and devices.
- No clearance is required from the Central Electricity Authority (CEA) for power generation projects up to $25 million.

- A five-year tax holiday is allowed for renewable energy power generation projects. A customs duty concession is available for renewable energy spare parts and equipment, including those for machinery required for renovation and modernization of power plants.
- Opportunities exist for enhancing manufacturing capacity of different end-use applications of renewable energy technologies through low-cost, proven devices and systems produced on a mass scale.
- Opportunities exist for Indian companies in joint ventures in the production and services related to wind electric equipment, particularly investment in power generation, as developers/project promoters and consultants and in O&M, monitoring, and inspection.
- Financial assistance exists for innovative demonstration projects for generation of power from municipal solid waste and for selected industrial waste.
- Financial assistance is available for up to 50 percent of the incremental cost for generation of power from biogas.
- A number of companies have entered into joint ventures with leading global PV manufacturers. There are no specific conditions laid down by MNRE for the formation of joint ventures. General conditions established by the Ministry of Industry, Secretariat for Industrial Approvals, and the RBI are applicable for this sector.

6. Barriers to Clean Energy Trade and Investment for U.S. Firms

Although clean energy technologies are a strong and growing industry in India, a number of barriers continue to stymie the competitiveness of American companies.

Policy Barriers

Perceived Lack of Coordination/Integration of Policy

India has a centralized energy sector that is dominated by state-owned enterprises. In this context, there appears a perceived lack of coordination/integration regarding renewable energy and energy efficiency policies that applies across Indian government ministries, states, and sub-sectors. Policies are often unclear and inconsistent between local and central government agencies and across line ministries charged with creating and implementing policies related to renewable energy, energy efficiency, power, and climate change. Further, there is a lack of clear and consistent long-term policy.

Market Distortions of Fossil Fuels versus Renewables

The major distortions are lack of accounting for externalities (both environmental and socioeconomic) in conventional fossil fuels, price distortions, uneven subsidies and tax structures, and capital cost accounting versus life-cycle accounting. Some distortions may arise due to uneven price setting across and within sub-sectors, lack of price level guarantees, and lack of price rationalization.

Weak or Unclear Legal/Regulatory Environment

The enforcement of the legal and regulatory environment in India is a significant barrier for private sector participation in the renewable energy market. Informal governance based on social relationships and reciprocity emerges from a long and complex legal process and lack of legal enforcement. Regulatory issues such as time delays and complexity in the permitting and sitting of projects pose additional legal and regulatory hurdles. The legal and financial disclosures made by firms are not monitored as there are few robust established or enforced systems for monitoring systems in place. This gap in monitoring systems creates a lack of credibility for potential joint ventures, mergers and acquisitions, and investment inflows. In general, renewable energy policy targets are not mandatory (and thus carry no penalty) and are not enforceable from a regulatory perspective.[15]

Confusion in Implementation of Renewable Energy Projects/Need for Standardization

There is considerable confusion at the state level regarding implementation of the Electricity Act and requirement for a renewable energy portfolio standard to be institutionalized by each SERC. In some states the RPS is higher, while in others there are preferences for specific types of renewable energy. In most states there are price differentials in the power purchase tariffs that each distribution licensee must follow when meeting their RPS. Given these differentials, there is a need for minimum standardization in setting the power purchase price.

Lack of Policy Guidelines for Waste-to-Energy Projects.

In waste-to-energy projects, there is lack of clear policy guidelines from state governments with respect to allotment of land, supply of garbage, power purchase arrangements, and evacuation facilities.

Lack of Strategic Review of Energy Efficiency at the National and State Levels

In the energy efficiency sector, there is a lack of strategic review to assess priorities for initiatives on energy efficiency development in the future. There thus appears to be a lack of focus for sustained, multi-year attention on the implementation of the policy initiatives and market-oriented investment mechanisms that can provide the most significant energy efficiency contributions. A long-term strategy with prioritized areas of intervention will lead to future investment pipelines. At the sub-national level, most of the state-designated agencies for energy efficiency have been formed fairly recently. They therefore lack capacity and infrastructure to develop state-level action plans for future implementation, and, as a result, no areas for energy efficiency interventions have been prioritized in the states.

Investment Barriers

Investment barriers include a general lack of access to affordable capital, the reasons for which are described below:

Payment Security

During the early to mid-1990s, a number of U.S. companies encountered difficulties recovering their costs of investment in power plants in India owing to non-payment. Most resulted in divestment and bankruptcy. At that time there was a sovereign guarantee in place by the government of India that in the event of default by any of the payees, the GOI would step in and ensure that the payments were made by the government. This policy is no longer in place. The act in force at the time was the Electricity Act of 1948. At the time the state electricity board was the sole purchaser of all electricity generated.

Since that time, regulatory commissions have been established through the Regulatory Commissions Act of 1998, which gave state and central regulatory commissions the power to set tariffs and make clear distinctions between the state (as the owner of the assets) and the companies (those who operated the assets). The states were requested to issue policy directions on tariffs, but the final tariff was set up by the regulatory commissions at the state and central levels.

The Electricity Act of 2003 deregulated the generation, transmission, and distribution of electricity and opened access universally. The act removed the obligation of power companies to sell all their electricity to monopolistic state-owned utilities and allowed them to sell power to any entity anywhere in India. Because there are now several generation and distribution entities at the central and state levels, the generators can also decide to sell the electricity to any of these entities.

Following the enactment of the Electricity Act, power trading companies and power exchanges have been created to sell excess power throughout the country. Credit rating agencies are now independently rating utilities and state electricity boards, on the basis of which financial institutions invest in the projects. The entire securitization is now based on market risk resulting in a more fluid, economically beneficial situation for the sale of electricity.

Project Developer Risks

Due to the higher ratio of initial capital costs to operating costs for many renewable energy projects, there is a need for longer-term financing instruments at affordable rates. As most of these projects are small scale, they often do not attract commercial financing structures for a number of reasons. First, projects are predominantly balance sheet funded based on the creditworthiness and strength of the borrower rather than on merits of the project. Second, borrowers are typically exposed to unlimited personal liability, if they are able to obtain the required financing. And third, renewable energy technologies are often new to project developers and sponsors, and this lack of experience can lead to higher completion and operational risk, further reducing the creditworthiness of the potential borrower, resulting in higher transaction costs.

Financiers' Unfamiliarity

Banks often provide funding to their existing customers on the basis of past relationships, trust, and credit history. They are typically hesitant to extend financing to new and unfamiliar clients. This occurs because of the weak regulatory environment and lack of legal enforcement, where they have no firm guarantee of legal recourse. Further, the type of projects tends to be newer to banks and financiers, leading to higher-risk perceptions and hesitation to extend debt to clients without a credible and established relationship.

Lack of Equity

Domestic and international venture capital and private equity investors have comparatively little expertise in investing in the Indian clean energy sector. Therefore, small-scale renewable energy project sponsors lack sufficient personal funds to invest as equity in the project or as collateral for banks to extend credit. Start-up and early-stage growth capital therefore often comes from project sponsors or developers and their acquaintances, limiting the amount of capital and creating informal governance mechanisms.

Lack of Long-term Loans

Long-term loans have not been made available to renewable energy projects because banks face a mismatch in asset liability management (ALM). Financial institutions such as insurance companies or pension funds that do not face ALM issues are not very active in the area of infrastructure financing thanks to limited institutional capabilities.

Limited Reach of Bond Market

Bond markets, which offer long-term loans at fixed rates, actively trade in government securities and AAA-rated companies. The secondary markets have very limited liquidity for other securities, thereby offering major constraints to finance projects through bonds.

Consumer Finance

On the consumer side, Indian retail finance and microfinance are in their infancy. The initial capital cost to install renewable energy systems is often prohibitive without tailored finance packages, which currently do not exist. Due to the distributed nature of endusers of distributed generation technologies, they often reside outside of the formal credit system, thus creating creditworthiness issues at the consumer level.

Constraints in External Commercial Borrowing (ECB) for Debt

The major constraints in availing ECBs include refinancing of rupee term loans by ECBs, absence of ECBs having tenor beyond five to seven years, inflexibility to prepay loans beyond $400 million, and the inability of Indian banks to act as financial intermediaries for ECB.

There are a number of financial risks and uncertainties associated with renewable energy, such as the intermittent nature of renewable energy generation, early-stage technology performance, reliable off-take, consistent policy, and expertise at the management and implementation levels. Due to insufficient returns on investment from gaps in policy implementation, immature market conditions, and uncompensated risks, there is a lack of appropriate and much needed risk management instruments to offset traditional project risks. Further, insurance is not currently offered for non-performance, technical failure, or indemnity, and no risk premium has yet been built into financial mechanisms or pricing structures.

Market distortions and uneven fiscal incentives are significant barriers to commercial viability of renewable energy adoption and development. The government continues to support fossil fuels with subsidies, regulations, and laws that benefit conventional energy generation. The major consumer of coal is the power sector, which is heavily regulated and cannot raise electricity tariffs in tune with increases in fuel costs. As a consequence, coal prices have not been allowed to change freely in order to protect the power sector from potential high fuel prices. The fear of rising electricity generation costs and a resultant hit to the economy has made deregulation difficult in practice. This situation highlights the inherent problems in the pricing and regulation of the coal sector in India, the complexities caused by a non-transparent subsidy to the power sector, and an imposed monopoly in the mining sector. At the time of dismantling of the APM, it was thought that subsidies on kerosene and LPG would be gradually phased out. However, after four years of dismantling, the subsidies on kerosene and LPG continue to exist.

Additional reasons for higher RE project costs include the following:

- Failure to account for environmental and socioeconomic externalities in the price of conventional fossil fuel energy sources.
- Non-recognition of RE portfolio value in price stability.
- Subsidies and tax structures on fossil fuels, which make energy portfolios heavily biased toward conventional forms of energy.
- Energy generation project costs are often viewed in cost-per-unit basis ($/MW installed) rather than on a life-cycle accounting basis, which includes initial cost, fuel cost, operation and maintenance cost, equipment lifetime, and decommissioning cost.

Carbon finance uncertainty also presents a barrier to American firms. Renewable energy projects have the *potential* to create a substantial revenue stream through Clean Development Mechanism (CDM) credits issued under the Kyoto Protocol. India has registered roughly 35 percent of all global CDM projects, a market that is very likely to grow. If a post-2012 agreement on climate change can be reached, carbon credits will become an even more financially rewarding venture.

Patent enforcement should also be considered a challenge for foreign firms, who generally lack the understanding of Indian legal structure and judicial precedent. These features include: no time frame prescribed for legal recourse; no criminal remedy available for infringement of patents, as opposed to that of copyrights, etc; and a backlog of patent applications.

Conclusion

Today, India is one of the fastest growing markets for clean energy technologies, offering a number of advantages that include:

- A strong industrial base and fast growing economy;
- Availability of skilled, relatively cheap labor;
- One of the world's largest renewable energy programs;
- A dedicated federal ministry to support renewable energy (MNRE) and the only government financial institution exclusively supporting renewable energy and energy efficiency (IREDA);
- A vast, untapped consumer base;
- Favorable government policy environment (national and state);

- Low inflation and moderate tax rates;
- Financial and fiscal incentives;
- Diversified domestic and international financing sources;
- A strong and growing carbon finance market.

By 2012—the completion of the 11th Five-Year Plan—the GOI has targeted 10 percent power generation from installed capacity to come from renewable energy sources, with a 4–5 percent share in the electricity mix. This should translate into a seven-fold market increase for renewable power generation – from $3 billion today to more than $21 billion by 2012. Even under the realistic assumption of 50 percent growth, the market would be $11 billion by 2012. India's rich renewable energy resource endowment provides opportunities across a spectrum of technologies—biomass, solar PV, solar thermal, wind, hydropower, solid and industrial waste-to-energy, geothermal, and tidal energy – that incentivize foreign investment and foreign expertise.

Further, a $2 billion market for energy efficiency technologies is anticipated, targeting energy-intensive industries such as cement, aluminum, fertilizers, pulp and paper, petrochemicals, and steel. India offers a number of prospects for U.S. firms, including research, development, and demonstration; technical collaborations; product and equipment sales; project design, development, and promotion; power generation and production; O&M; project monitoring; carbon finance/trading; and consulting services. Opportunities for foreign investors include equity participation in joint ventures with Indian partners, foreign direct investment, technology transfer, and establishment of manufacturing facilities or power projects.

Though barriers exist from technology, policy, and investment perspectives, India promises to be one of the largest markets for clean energy in the future, and U.S. companies have a significant role to play in both trade and investment in this rapidly expanding marketplace.

ANNEX 1. MAJOR MARKET PLAYERS IN INDIA

Wind Electric Generators Installed in India, by Manufacturer

Manufacturer	Rating (KW)	Numbers	Capacity (In MW)
ABAN–Kenetech	410	231	94.71
AMTL–Wind World	220	2	0.44
	250	328	82
	500	3	1.5
BHEL	55	16	0.88
	200	17	3.4
BHEL Nordex	200	79	15.8
	250	184	46
C-WEL	250	57	14.25
	600	2	1.2
Danish Windpower	150	12	1.8
Das Lagerwey	80	9	0.72
	250	284	71
Elecon	200	1	0.2
	300	51	15.3
	600	5	3
Enercon	230	451	103.73
	330	38	12.54
	600	681	408.6
	800	435	348
GE Wind Energy	1500	12	18
Himalaya	140	4	0.56
	200	24	4.8
JMP-Ecotecnia	225	10	2.25
Kirloskar–WEG	400	8	3.2
Micon (Pearl)	90	99	8.91
Mitsubishi	315	6	1.89
Nedwind-Windia	250	4	1
	500	20	10
	550	35	19.25
NEG Micon	750	674	505.5
	950	54	51.3
	1650	137	226.05

(Continued)

Manufacturer	Rating (KW)	Numbers	Capacity (In MW)
NEPC India	225	957	215.325
	250	16	4
	400	7	2.8
	750	12	9
NEPC-Micon	55	14	0.77
	110	2	0.22
	200	50	10
	225	589	132.53
	250	528	132
	400	121	48.4
	600	2	1.2
Pegasus	250	9	2.25
Pioneer Asia	850	35	29.75
Pioneer Wincon	110	10	1.1
	250	260	65
	755	1	0.76
REPL-Bonus	55	22	1.21
	100	1	0.1
	320	60	19.2
RES-Advanced Wind Turbine	250	80	20
Sangeeth–Carter	300	25	7.5
Suzlon	270	2	0.54
	350	836	292.6
	600	15	9
	1000	81	81
	1250	1255	1568.75
	2000	1	2
Tacke	250	4	1
	600	21	12.6
	750	1	0.75
Textool-Nordtank	300	65	19.5
	550	5	2.75
TTG/Shriram EPC	250	230	57.5
Vestas–RRB	55	31	1.71
	90	21	1.89
	100	5	0.5

(Continued)

Manufacturer	Rating (KW)	Numbers	Capacity (In MW)
	200	56	11.2
	225	735	165.375
	500	562	281
	600	65	
Wind Master	200	1	0.2
Windmatic	55	30	1.65
Wind Power	330	29	9.57
Total		**10825**	**5340.96**

Source: http://mnes.nic.in/

Hydropower Manufacturers

SHP Turbine/Equipment Manufacturers

Name and Address	Telephone	Fax
M/s Bharat Heavy Electricals Ltd. Piplani, Bhopal–462022	0755 546100, 540200	0755 540425
M/s Bharat Heavy Electricals Ltd. Hydropower Commercial Integrated Office Complex, Lodi Road New Delhi–100 003	011 4698167, 4618215	011 4626555, 4618837
M/s Boving Fouress (P) Ltd. Plot No. 7, KIADB, Industrial Area Bangalore–562114	08111 71263, 71455	08111 71399, 080 8395176
M/s VA Tech. Escher Wyss Flovel Ltd. 13/1, Mathura Road Faridabad–121 003	011 274319	0129 274320
M/s Jyoti Ltd. Industrial Area, P.O. Chemical Industries, Vadodara–390003	0265 380633, 380627, 381402	0265 380671, 381871
M/s Steel Industrials Kerala Ltd. Silk Nagar, Athani P.O., Trissur Kerala–680771	048795 7335, 7360, 7735	0487 40451 Public Call Office, 048795 7732
M/s The Triveni Engg. Works Ltd. D-196, Okhla Industrial Area, Phase-I New Delhi–110020	6811878, 6812930, 6819015	011 6819857, 6818216
M/s Kirloskar Bros. Ltd. Udyog Bhawan, Tilak Road, Pune–411002	0212 453455	0212- 32780, 434198, 431156
M/s HPP Energy (India) Pvt. Ltd. F-85 East of Kailash New Delhi–110 065	6289017/18/20/16	011 6289019, 6192787

(Continued)

Name and Address	Telephone	Fax
M/s Alstom Projects Pvt. Ltd. Chandiwala Estate, Maa Anand Mai Ashram Marg, Kalkagi New Delhi–110 019	011 251811100, 011 26826180	
Flovel Energy Private Ltd. 14/3, Mathura Road Faridabad–121 003	0129 4088800, 2252803	
Schneider Electric India Pvt. Ltd. A-29, Mohan Cooperative Indl. Estate Mathura Road, New Delhi–110 044	011 41590000, 41678011	
Voith Siemens Hydro Pvt. Ltd. Hydropower Generation, 201, 1st Floor, Okhla Industrial Estate, Phase-III New Delhi–110 020	011 51615385, 51615389	
Ushamil Hydro System (P) Ltd. A-292, Mahipalpur Extn., NH 8 New Delhi–110 037	011 30623740-47	

Wind Energy Manufacturers

Wind Turbine Manufacturers

Name and Address	Telephone	Fax
M/s Enercon (India) Ltd. "Enercon Tower" A-9, Veera Industrial Estate Veera Desai Road, Andheri–400053	022 66924848	022 67040473
M/s Pioneer Winco Private Ltd. 30/1A, Harrington Chambers, 2nd Floor, "B" Block Abdul Razaq, 1st Street, Saidapet Chennai–600095	044 24314790	044 24314789
M/s Shriram EPC Limited 9, Vanagaram Road, Ayanambakkam Chennai–600095	044 26533313	044 26532780
M/s Sothern Wind Farms Limited No. 15, Soundarapandian Salai, Ashok Nagar Chennai–600083		
M/s Pioneer Wincon Private Ltd. 30/1A, Harrington Chambers, 2nd Floor, "B" Block Abdul Razaq, 1st Street, Saidapet Chennai–600015	044 24314790	044 24314789
M/s Shriram EPC Limited 9, Vanagaram Road, Ayanambakkam Chennai–600095	044 2653313	044 6532780
M/s Southern Wind Farms Limited No. 15, Soundarapandian Salai, Ashok Nagar Chennai–600083	044 39182618	044 39182636

(Continued)

Name and Address	Telephone	Fax
M/s Suzlon Energy Ltd. 5th Floor, Godrej Millenium, 9, Koregaon Park Road Pune–411001	020 40122000	020 0122100
M/s Vestas RRB India Limited No. 17, Vembuliamman Koli Street, Kk. K. Nagar (West) Chennai–600078	044 23641111	044 23642222
M/s Vesta Wind Technology India Private Limited [formerly M/s NEG Micon (India) Private Ltd.] 289, Old Mahabalipuram Road, Sholinganallur Chennai–600119	044 24505100	044 24505101
M/s Vestas PRB India Limited No. 17, Vembuliamman Koli Street, Kk. K. Nagar (West) Chennai—600078	044 23641111	044 23642222

Solar Energy Manufacturers

Bureau of Indian Standard (BIS)–Certified Solar Cookers Manufacturers

Name and Address	Telephone	Fax
M/s Universal Engineers Enterprises Garg Bhavan, Prince Road, Gandhi Nagar, Moradabad (U. P.)	0591 2493619	0591 2499768
M/s Rural Engineering School Rojmal, Tal.: Gadhada (SN) District Bhavnagar–364750 Gujarat	02847 294127	02847 253535
Khadi Gramodhyog Prayog Samiti Gandhi Ashram Ahmedabad–380 027	Cell: 9825484275, 9879784255	079 27552469
Sayala Taluka Khadi Gramodyog Seva Mandal Motiram Building, below SBS Service Branch, Phulchhab Chowk Rajkot–360 001	Tel: 0281 2477226 Cell: 09825074591	

Other Known Manufacturers of Solar Cookers

Name and Address	Telephone	Fax
M/s J. N Enterprises F-12, Navin Shahdara, Delhi	Cell: 2350859119	
M/s Vishvakarma Solar Energy Co. G. T. Road, Phillour, District Jallandhar, Punjab	01826 22523, 01826 22217	

(Continued)

Name and Address	Telephone	Fax
M/s Fair Fabricators 142, Tilak Nagar, near Post Office Indore–452 018	Cell: 9425316707	0731 2491488
M/s Rohtas Electronics 15/268-B, Civil Lines, Kanpur–208001	0512 2305564	0512 2305390
M/s Rural Engineering School Rojmal, Tal.: Gadhada (SN), District Bhavnagar–364750, Gujarat	02847 294127	02847 253535
M/s Usha Engineering Works 40-A, Trunk Road, Madanur–635804 Vellore District, Tamilnadu	04174 73613	
M/s Geetanjali Solar Enterprises P/14, Kasba Industrial Estate, Phase-I, E. M. Bye Pass, P.O. East Kolkata Township Kolkata–700107	033 24420773, 24424027	033 24420773

List of Eligible Manufacturers/Suppliers Evacuated Tube Collector–Based Solar Water Heating Systems

Name and Address	Telephone	Fax
M/s Solar Hitech Geysers No. 4, Sri Krishna, Behind Bhima Jyothi LIC Colony, West of Chord Road Bangalore560 079		080 23223152, 23221511
M/s Photon Energy Systems Ltd. Plot No. 775-K, Road No. 45, Jubilee Hills Hyderabad–33	Cell: 9246333624	
M/s Sudarshan Saur Shakti Pvt. Ltd. 5, Rarak Colony, opposite Ramakrishna Mission Ashrama, Beed, By-pass, Aurangabad–431 005	2376610 Cell: 9225303600	0240 2376609
M/s Venus Home Appliances (P) Ltd. Mangammal Salai, 5/54 A, Senthilampannai Village Pudukottai P.O. Tuticorin District Tamil Nadu	0461 2271891	0461 2271890
M/s Twincity Sunlife 7, Ready Money Terrace, 167, Dr. A. B. Road, Worli, Mumbai–400 018	022 24954596, 24939644	022 24939644
M/s Kiran Lab Plast 23, Vallabh Nagar, Malegaon Road, Dhule–424001 (Maharashtra)	2562 233261	2562 233262
M/s Nutech Solar Systems Pvt. Ltd. #391/32, 12th Main, Dr. Rajkumar Road, 6th Block, Rajajinagar, Bangalore–560 010	080 23356789 Cell: 09448674998	080 23115802

(Continued)

Name and Address	Telephone	Fax
M/s G. P. Tronics Pvt. Ltd. 502, Kamalalaya Center (5th Floor) 156A Lenin Sarani Kolkata–700 013	033 22150301 Cell: 9831848002	
M/s Mamata Energy Plot No. 858, Kothari Industrial Estate, Behind Hutch Tower, Rakanpur Santej Road Santej–382 721 (Gujarat)	2764 394984	2764 268328
M/s Jay Industries D-64, Miraj MIDC Miraj–416 410 (Maharashtra), District Sangli		
M/s Hykon India (P) Ltd. Hykon House, Ikkanda Warrier Road Thrissur–1 (Kerala)	0487 2444163, 2444183	
M/s Tyche Peripheral Systems Ltd. Tyche House, 13-6-536/A/26, Lakshminagar Colony, Mehdipatnam Hyderabad–500028 (AP)	040 23525436, 23525437, 30903627	040 23525403
M/s EMMVEE Solar Systems Pvt. Ltd. #55, "Solar Tower," 6th Main, 11th Cross, Lakshmaiah Block, Ganganagar Bangalore–560 024	080 23337428	080 23332060
M/s Natural Energy Systems 5/51, Punjabi Bagh New Delhi–110 026	Cell: 9811104818	011 42463235
M/s ECON Appliances Pvt. Ltd. 85, MG Road, Camp, Pune–411 001	020 26331016/17	020 26331191
M/s Arsh Electronics (P) Ltd. 24, Surya Niketan, Vikas Marg Extn Delhi–110 092	011 22374859	011 22379973
M/s Bhambri Enterprises 794, Joshi Road, Karol Bagh New Delhi	011 23541114, 55388606 Cell: 9811759494	
M/s V. Guard Industries Pvt. Ltd. 44/875, Little Flower Church Road Kaloor, Cochin–682017 (Kerala)	0484 2539911, 2530912	0484 2539958
M/s Solanand Solar Systems Khera Chowk, Railway Road Ambala City–134 003	Cell: 9215627335	0171 556035
M/s Ados Electronics Pvt. Ltd. 1/30, Main Vikas Marg, Lalita Park Laxmi Nagar, Delhi–110 092	Tel: 011 22463701, Cell: 9811194519	
M/s Hiramrut Energies Pvt. Ltd. Plot No. 148 & 127, GIDC-II, Jamwadi, N.H. 8-B Gandal–360311, District Rajkot (Gujarat)	02825 224824, 224272	02825 240472
M/s Vijaya Industries Katapady–574 105, Udupi District, Karnataka	0820 2557127 Cell: 9448377327	0820 2557327

(Continued)

Name and Address	Telephone	Fax
M/s Phoenix Import & Exports 51, Deshmukh Colony, Sadar Bazar Satara–415 001 (Maharashtra)	02162 230383 Cell: 09422038284, 09423864592	
M/s Aurore Systems Auroshilpam, Auroville–605 101 (Tamil Nadu)	0413 2622749, 2622168, 2622277	0413 2622057
M/s Kraftwork Solar Pvt. Ltd. "Adithya" 29/2862 Near Gandhi Square, Poonithura Kochi–682 038	0484 2707339, 2707228	0484 2707228
M/s Shriram Green Tech 5th Floor, Akashdeep Bldg. 26A Barakhamba Road New Delhi–110 001	011 23312267	011 23313494
M/s Patory Export Import Pvt. Ltd. A-301, Ansal Chamber-1, 3, Bhikaji Cama Place New Delhi–100 066	011 51661341, 26175759	
M/s Marc Solar, Jyoti Stem Industries 5, Fatima, Nilayam, HASSS Building, Behind Arch- Bishop's House, S. D. Road Secunderabad–500 1003	040 27801293, 66311292	
M/s Savemax Solar Systems (P) Ltd. Jayprabha, Jadhavnagar, Vadgaon Bk. Pune–411 041	09822846201	020 24358613/8781
M/s Tata BP Solar India Ltd. 78, Electronics City Hosur Road, Bangalore–560 100	080 22358465, 51102577	
M/s K. S. Industries 195 R. M. T. Bunglow Road, Sai Nagar, Industrial Estate (post), Coimbatore–641 021 (Tamil Nadu)	0422 2673319, Cell: 9894111935	
M/s Rashmi Industries No. 60 & 61, Begur Road, Hongasandra, Bangalore–560 068	080 25734114/15	
M/s Hira Merica Industries Welcome Plaza, S-551, School Block-II, Shakarpur Delhi–110 092	011 22481802, 22483768	
M/s Kotak Urja 311, Lotus House, 33A V, Thackersey Marg, New Marine Lines Mumbai–400 020	022 22092139/41	
M/s Orange Impex No. 22, 1st Floor, Prestige Point, 283 ShukrawarPeth, behind Telephone Exchange Bajirao Road Pune–411 022	020 30421001	

List of Bureau of Indian Standards–Approved Manufacturers of Flat Plate Collector–Based Solar Water Heating Systems

Name and Address	Telephone	Fax
Andhra Pradesh		
Photon Energy Systems Limited Plot No. 46, Anrich Industrial Estate, IDA Bollarum, Medak Andhra Pradesh–502325	08458 279512	08458 279842
Sun-tech Solar Systems Plot No. 1-9-382/13/2, 26/06/2008, 1st Floor, Lalitha Complex, near Navkiran Industrial Estate, Kushaiguda Hyderabad–500062	040 32904766	040 27138634
Sri Sundaram Solar Solutions 8-2-70, Harshavardhan Colony, Old Bowenpally, Secunderabad Hyderabad District	040 27953661 Cell: 9949057469	
Shri Shakti Alternative Energy Limited F-8, Sie, 08/10/2008, City: Balanagar, Hyderabad Andhra Pradesh–500037	23770511 Cell: 9440409677	23770513
Sca GreenTtechnologies Plot No. 22 & 31, Survey No. 247, Subashnagar, Jeedimetla Hyderabad–500055	040 55996519	
Chandigarh		
Inter Solar Systems Pvt. Ltd. 901, Industrial Area Phase II Chandigarh–160002	0172 5085281	
Surya Shakti 739 Industrial Area, Phase II Chandigarh–160002	2653299	
Delhi		
Maharishi Solar Tecnology (P) Ltd. A-14, Mohan Co-operative Industrial Estate, Mathura Road New Delhi–110044	011 26959529, 30881700	011 26959669
Gujarat		
Sintex Industries Ltd. (Plastic Division), near Seven Garnala, Kalol, Gandhinagar District Gujarat–382721	02764 24301 to 24305	02764 20385
NRG Technologists Private Limited Plot No. 989/6, GIDC Industrial Estate, Makarpura Baroda, Gujarat–390010	0265 2642094, 2656167	0265 2642094, 2656167
Warm Stream Near Baroda Electric Meters Ltd., Vallabh Vidya Nagar, Anand, District: Kheda, Gujarat–388121	02692 232309, 231316	236478

(Continued)

Name and Address	Telephone	Fax
Solar Energy Service A/4/2, 02/08/2008 Operative Industrial Estate, B.I.D.C. Gorwa Vadodara–390016	02667 264239	
Himachal Pradesh		
Solchrome Systems India Limited 61, Sector-5, Parwanoo Solan District, Himachal Pradesh	01792 232572	
Karnataka		
Sundrop Solar Systems 44/2A, Industrial Estate, Opp Gangadhareshwara Kalyana Mantapa, NH 7, Bellary Road, Hebbal Bangalore–560024	23620077 Cell: 9844068721	
Sudhanva Industries 65/18, 1st Main, 0 7/08/2008, 1st Cross, Andrahalli Main Road, Hegganahalli Bangalore –560091	28366832 Cell: 9845313912	
Kinara Power Systems and Projects Pvt. Ltd. Unit 2, 10, 10th Cross, Patel Channappa Indl Estate, Andrahalli Main Road, Peenya 2nd Stage Viswaneedum Post Bangalore–560091	28365944	
Om Shakthi Industries No. 2 S. T. Narayana Gowda Industrial Estate, Sri Gandha Nagar, Doddanna Industrial Estate Near Peenya II Stage Bangalore–560091	28362967, 56982645 Cell: 9448062867	
Sabha Solar Energy 3/1 behind Balaji Petrol Bunk, 2nd Cross, Lakshmaiah Block, Ganganagar Bangalore–560032		
Velnet Non-conventional Energy Systems (P) Ltd. No. 120 Bhadrappa Layout Ring Road Nagashettyhalli Bangalore–560094	23418630, 23417940, 23512799 Cell: 9844050723	
Enolar Systems 45/29-1, Gubbanna Industrial Estate, 6th Block, Rajajinagar, Bangalore–560010	23355333, 23385500	23355333
Divya Industries No. 814, Chowdeshwari Nagar, Laggere Main Road Laggere, Peenya Post Bangalore–560058	8398471	
Shringar Egineering & Energy System Pvt. Ltd., No. 93, 7th Main, 3rd Phase, Peenya Industrial Area Bangalore–560058	28398197	
Perfect Solar Bangalore Pvt. Ltd. No. 16 Byraveshwara Industrial Estate, Andrahalli Main Road, Peenya 2nd Stage, Bangalore	28362515/1129 Cell: 9845106037	28362515

(Continued)

Name and Address	Telephone	Fax
Vijaya Industries 166/2 Katapady District Udupi, Karnataka Pin: 574105	0820 2557127, 2557327	2557700
Sunrise Solar Pvt. Ltd. B-4, Jayabharat Industrial Estate, Yeshwanthpur Bangalore–560022	23328533, 23523644	23425115
Sustainable Power Developers India Pvt. Ltd. 604/677, Magadi Road, P&T Layout Road, Sunkadakatte Bangalore–560079	23580066, 23581154	
Tata BP Solar India Ltd. Plot No. 78, Electronic City Phase–1, Hosur Road Bangalore–560100	080 56601300	080 28520972, 8520116
Emmvee Solar Systems Pvt. Ltd. Survey No. 13/1 Bellary Road, Jala Hobli Sonnapanahalli, Bettahalsur Post Bangalore–562157		
Kotak Urja Pvt. Ltd. 378 10th Cross, 4th Phase Peenya Industrial Area Bangalore–560058	28363330, 28362136	28362347
Sun Zone Solar Systems ¼, Balagangadhara Nagar, Mallathahalli, behind Sanford College Bangalore–560056	23282145, 23214777 Cell: 56979935	
Anu Solar Power Pvt. Ltd. 248 3rd Cross, 8th Main, 3rd Phase Peenya Industrial Area Bangalore–560058	28394259, 28393913, 28396001	
Nuetech Solar Systems Pvt. Ltd. P. B. No. 9167, B. M. Shankarappa Industrial Estate Sunkadakatte, Vishwaneedam Post, Magadi Main Road Bangalore–560091	080-23483766, 23481905	080 23281730
Vishwa Solar System Shed No. SM 19, KSSIDC Industrial Area, Manipal, District Udupi Karnataka–576119	0820 2522791, 2571323	
Dheemanth Industries 35, behind Check Post, Kamakshipalya Layout Bangalore–560079	23489377, 2342617	
Technomax Solar Devices Pvt. Ltd. No. 21/B, 4th Main, 1st Cross, Industrial Suburb Yeshwanthpur Bangalore–560022	3418723	
Digiflic Controls (India) Pvt. Ltd. SIT 2E8/03/2008, No. 9, 2nd Cross, Rajagopala Nagar Main Road Bangalore–560058	080 28366839	080 28362689

(Continued)

Name and Address	Telephone	Fax
Rashmi Industries 60 & 61 Begur Road, Hongasandra Village Bangalore–560068	25732309, 4114,4115	25732309
Solar Energizers P. Ltd. 36/3, 1st Cross, Pukhraj Layout, Bannerghatta Road, Adugodi Bangalore–560030	22245481	22225804
Navodaya Solaris No. 66, 2nd Main, Ramakrishnappa Building Ranganathpura, Magadi Road Bangalore–560079	23589736 Cell: 9448532177	
Nucifera Renewable Eergy System Raghavendranagar, behind Devanur, Church, Nalanda Convent Parallel Road Tumkur–572102	0816 290142	0816 254585
Maharashtra		
Bipin Engineers (P) Ltd. S. No. 143, Vadgaon Dhairy, Pune-Sinhagad Road Pune–411041		
Sudarshan Saur Shakti Pvt. Ltd. K-240, MIDC, Waluj, Aurangabad District Pin: 431136		
The Standard Products Mfg. Co. G-13/8, MIDC, Taloja Industrial Area, Taloja Raigarh District Pin: 410208	27402228	
Skylark Thermal Energy Systems Sr. No. 36/2, Dhandekar Estate, Kondhwa Budruk Pune Pin: 411048		
Solar Energie Technik Ltd. Urja Centre, Gat. No. 2329, Ganga Retreat Road, Wagholi Pune–412207	27052205/07	27052625
Jain Irrigation Systems Ltd. Jain Agri Park, Jain Hills, P.O. Box No. 72 Shirsoli Road Jalgaon Pin: 425001	0257 250011/22	0257 251111/22
Solar Product Company S. No. 166, Vadgaon Dhayari, Nanded Phata Pune––411041		
Kaushal Solar Equipments P. Ltd, S. No. 44 Warje Malewadi Pune–411029		
Solar Vision Agro Industries B-44/2, Gokul, Shirgaon MIDC, Kolhapur Pin: 416234	2672745	
Machinocraft S. No. 1, Ambegaon (BK) Katraj-Dehu Road Bypass Pune–411 046	020 24317400, 30910794, 9822441250	020 24317400

(Continued)

Name and Address	Telephone	Fax
Savemax Solar Systems Pvt. Ltd. S. No. 42/2B, Plot No. 26, Khadi Machine Road, Vadgaon Budruk Pune–411041		
Standard Engineering Company 131/7B, Hadapsar Indl Estate Pune–411013		
Akson`s Solar Equipments Pvt. Ltd. Gat. No. 213 (old 1005), Village Rajewadi, Taluka Khandala City: Satara		
Merloni Termosanitari (I) Ltd. 265/274-376, at Post Kharabwadi, Chakan, Taluka Khed, District Pune Pin: 410501		
Jay Industries Plot No. D-64 MIDC, Miraj Sangli–416410		
Tamilnadu		
Goodsun Industries SF. 206, Perks Campus Rajalakshmi Mills Road, Upplipalayam Coimbatore–641015	0422 2592171, 2592158, 2590937	0422 2590937
Sunlit Solar Energy (P) Ltd. SF. No. 5071, 2/08/2008, Pachapalayam Road Arasur, Coimbatore–641 407, Coimbatore District Tamil Nadu–641607	6571745 Cell: 9842216190	
Cascade Helio Termics Limited No. 355/2, Abbas Garden Road, Luna Nagar Coimbatore–641025	0422 2400254, 2401576	0422 2400347
Uttaranchal		
Bharat Heavy Electricals Limited Rudrapur–263153, District Udham Singh Nagar Uttaranchal–263153	05944 43415, 43724, 43725	05944- 3605

List of Known Manufacturers/Suppliers/Institutions Involved in Installation of Flat Plate Collector–Based Solar Driers/Air Heating Systems

Name and Address	Telephone	Fax
M/S Planters Energy Network (PEN) No. 5, Powerhouse Street, N.R.T. Nagar Theni–625531, Tamilnadu	04546 255272, 255271	04546 255271
M/S NRG Technologies 989/6, GIDC Estate, Makarpura Vadodara–390010	0265 2642094	0265 2642094
M/S Kotak Urja Pvt. Ltd. No. 378, 10th Cross, 4th Phase, Peenya Industrial Estate, Bangalore–560 058	080 23560456 7	23562233

(Continued)

Name and Address	Telephone	Fax
Sardar Patel Renewable Energy Research Institute Post Box No. 2, Vallabh Vidyanagar–388120 Gujarat	02692 231332, 235011	02692 37982
Northern India Textile Research Association Sector-23, Raj Nagar Ghaziabad–201002	91 4783586, 4783592	9 4783596

List of Known Manufacturers/Suppliers/Institutions Involved in Installation of Solar Steam Generating Systems

Name and Address	Telephone	Fax
M/s. Gadhia Solar Energy Systems (P) Ltd. Plot No. 86, OLD GIDC, Gundlav, Valsad–396 035, Gujarat		02632 236703
Project Co-ordinator Solar Steam Cooking System, Brahamakumari Ashram, Mount Abu, Rajasthan	02974 237049, 238788	02974 238951, 238952
M/s Solar Alternatives St. Mary's Church Compound, Phulwari Sharif, Patna–801505	0612 254487	227903
M/s Sharada Inventions 94/1, MIDC Satpur Nashik–422007	0253 2352444, 2353844	0253 2353853
M/s Supreme Rays Solar Systems 8, Kumbhar Building, behind Tekwade Petrol Pump, Opp. Akashwani, Hadapsar Pune–411028	020 26995588, 26996688	020 26980155
Unison Technologies Pvt. Ltd. No. 6, Ist Floor, Kodava Samaja Building, Ist Main, Vasanthnagar Bangalore–560052	080 2355238, 30909193	080 22289294

Solar Cell and Module Manufacturers in India

Name and Address	Telephone	Fax
Ammini Solar Pvt. Ltd. Plot No. 33–37, KINFRA Small Industries Park, St. Xaviers College PO Trivandrum–695 582	04712705588	04712705599
Bharat Electronics Limited 116/2, Race Course Road, Jalahalli, Bangalore–560015	080 25039300	080 25039305
Bharat Heavy Electricals Ltd. Electronics Division, Post Box No. 2606, Mysore Road Bangalore–560 026	08026998553	080 26744904, 26740137

(Continued)

Name and Address	Telephone	Fax
Central Electronics Ltd. 4, Industrial Area Sahibabad–201 010 U. P.	01202895151	01202 895148/42
EMMVEE Solar Systems Pvt. Ltd. 55, 6th Main, 11th Cross Lakshmaiah Block Ganganagar Bangalore–560024	080 23337427/28	080 23332060
Kotak Urja Pvt. Ltd. 378, 10th Cross 4th Phase, PIA, Bangalore 560058 Karnataka, India	08028363330	08028362347
Maharishi Solar Technology Pvt. Ltd. A-14, Mohan Cooperative Industrial Estate Mathura Road New Delhi–110 044	011 26959800, 26959701	011 26959 669
Microsol Power P Ltd. 605, 6th Floor Sapthagiri, SP Road Begumpet Hyderabad	04027766917	040 27730546, 04027766916
Moser Baer Photovoltaic Ltd. 43B, Okhla Industrial Estate New Delhi–110020	11 41635201 07, 91 11 26911570 74	11 41635211, 91 11 26911860
Photon Energy Systems Plot No. 775 –K, Road No. 45, Jublee Hills Hyderabad–560 033	04055661337/1338/1339	04055661340
Premier Solar Systems (P) Ltd. 41 & 42, Sri Venkateswara, Cooperative Indl. Estate, Balanagar Hyderabad–500 037		040 2271879
Rajasthan Electronics & Instruments Ltd. 2, Kanakpura, Industrial Area, Sirsi Road, Jaipur –302 012	01412203038	0141 2202701, 0141-2352841
M/s Sun Times E-3, Lajpat Nagar–II New Delhi–110 024		011-26839444
Tata BP Solar India Ltd. Plot No. 78, Electronic City, Hosur Road Bangalore–560100	08022358465	08028520972, 28520116
Titan Energy Systems Ltd. 16, Aruna Enclave Trimulgherry, Secunderabad– 500015 Andhra Pradesh, India	04027791085, 0402- 779-0751	040-2779 5629
USL Photovoltaics Pvt. Ltd. 1/473 Avinashi Road, Neelambur Coimbatore 641 014 India	04222627851	04222628504
Udhaya Energy Photovoltaics (P) Ltd. 1/279Z, Mudalipalayam, Arasur Post Coimbatore – 641 407		

(Continued)

Name and Address	Telephone	Fax
Webel SL Energy Systems Ltd. Plot No. N1, Block GP, Sector V, Salt Lake Electronic Complex Kolkata 700 091	03323578840	033-23573258
XL Telecom Ltd. 335 Chandralok Complex, SD Road, Secunderabad Andhra Pradesh 500003	04027849094	04027840081

Waste-to-Energy Technology Suppliers

Waste-to-Energy Technology Providers/Suppliers in India

Name and Address	Telephone	Fax
Biomethanation Technology		
M/s ENKEM Engineers Pvt. Ltd. 824, Poonamalle High Road, Kilpauk (near KMC) Chennai–600010	044 26411362, 26428992	044 26411788
M/s Mailhem Engineers Pvt. Ltd. 14, Vishrambag Society, Senapati Bapat Road Pune–411 016	020 24002285	020 25659857
M/s REVA Enviro Systems Pvt. Ltd. 3, Suyog Nagar, Ring Road, Nagpur–440 015	0712 2743123, 2743124	0712 2743120
M/s Linde Process Technologies India Ltd. 38, Nutan Bharat Society, Alkapuri Vadodara–390 007	0265 2336319, 2336196	0265 2335213, 2313629
M/s Hydroair Tectonoics Pvt. Ltd. 401, "Devavrata," Sector-17, Vashi, Navi Mumbai–400 705	022 27892813/68/95	022 27893892
M/s Chemtrols Engineering Ltd. Amar Hill, Saki Vihar Road, Powai, Mumbai–400 072	022 28575089, 28570557	022 28571913
M/s Degrimont India Ltd. Water and the Environment, D-43, South Extension - II New Delhi–110 049	011 26481191, 26481192	011 26228782
M/s Global Environmental Engg. Ltd. 1233/C, K. G. Mansion, Opp. Hotel Kohinoor Executive, Apte. Road, Pune–411 004	0212 2327876, 2328007	0212 2328441
M/s UEM India Limited D-19, Kalkaji New Delhi–110 019	011 26447825, 26421634	011 26239801
Plasma Arc Technology		

(Continued)

Name and Address	Telephone	Fax
M/s SELCO International H. No:1-10-74, R K Apartments, Ashok Nagar Hyderabad–550 020		040 27650114
M/s Shriram Energy Systems Ltd. 7-1-29, United Avenue (North End), G1 B–Block Ameerpet Hyderabad–500016, Andhra Pradesh	040 23739552	040 237 39551
Pyrolysis/Gasification Technology		
M/s Terrasafe Technologies (P) Ltd. J12 Basement, Saket New Delhi–110017	011 26533471/72, 26535062	011 26520514
M/s Global Enviro Plasma Technologies Dhruv International Pvt. Ltd. 306 Akashdeep Building, 26-A Barakhamba Road New Delhi–110001		
M/s Shri Damodar Synthetics Ltd. G-1, Nahar & Seth Industrial Premises, Near P&G Plaza, Chakala Road, Andheri (East) Mumbai–400 099	022 28366419, 28366420, 28365997	022 28252713
M/s Batliboi Environmental Engineering Ltd. Batliboi House, Govandi (W) Mumbai–400 043	022 25587421, 25583031	022 25566677, 25566949
Biogas Engine Supplier		
M/s Green Power International (P) Ltd. B-46, Ist Floor, Kalkaji New Delhi–110019	011 26447526, 26447527	011 26447525
M/s Guascor S.A. (Spain) M/s APE (India) Ltd. 19 Community Center, East of Kailash, New Delhi–110 065	011 26443889, 26420938	011 26470867
M/s Cogen India Engineering Pvt. Ltd. 5, Saraswati Heights, 759/39, Deccan Gymkhana Pune–411004	020 25676435/6	020 25675824
M/s. Greaves Ltd. Disel Engines Unit Chinchwad, Pune–411019		020 27472276

Biomass Technology Manufacturers

Manufacturers of Biogas Burners

Name and Address
M/s. Sunflame Industries (P) Ltd. Shed No. 2, Plot No. 58. P.O. Amar Nagar, Faridabad–121 003
Ms. Gas & Chemical Industries (P) Ltd. Works: 14/1 Mathura Road, Faridabad–121 003
M/s. Sweet Home Appliances Pvt. Ltd. 3-E/16, B. P. N. I. T., Faridabad–121 001
M/s. Associated Engineering Works Tanuku–534 211 (AP)
M/s. Agriculture Associates Station Road, Alwar (Rajasthan)
M/s. Rupak Enterprises 1/46 Vishwas Nagar, Shahdra, Delhi–110 032
M/s. Mech-Ci-Co. 1-7, GIDC Industrial Township, Vatwa, Ahmedabad–382 445

List of Gasifier Manufacturers in India

Name and Address	Telephone	Fax
M/s Ankur Scientific Energy Technologies Pvt. Ltd. Near Old Sama Jakat Naka Vadodara–390008	793098, 794021	0265 794042
M/s Cosmo Powertech Pvt. Ltd. Devpuri Near Jain Public School, Dhamtari Road Near Raipur–492015	0771 5011262	0771 5010190
M/s Netpro Renewable Energy (India) Ltd. 139/B, 10th Main, Rajmahal Vilas Extension Bangalore–560080	080 3613585, 3613457	080 3611584
Energreen Power Limited No. 1 Ashre 4B, 2nd Street, Nandanam Extension Chennai–600035	044 24321339, 52111348	044 24321339
Rishipooja Energy & Engineering Company M. G. College Road Gorakhpur–273001 (U. P.)	0551 340612, 339475	
Bioresidue Energy Technology Private Ltd. S-2, Dig Vijay Apartment, 1st Cross Ganesha Block , Sultanpalya R. T Nagar P.O. Bangalore–560032	080 3431533	080 3534503

ANNEX 2. INDIAN POLICY-MAKERS WITH AUTHORITY OVER CLEAN ENERGY TECHNOLOGIES

Institutional Structure at National and State Levels

At the national level, the government of India is assisted by the planning commission and line ministries to formulate policies related to clean energy. The institutional structure is shown in Figure 1.2.[16]

Among the line ministries, the Ministry of Power (MOP), MNRE, and Ministry of Environment and Forests (MoEF) are the major agencies for formulating policies and action plans related to clean energy. The Central Electricity Regulatory Commission (CERC), Central Electricity Authority (CEA), and BEE assist MOP to formulate policies and action plans. Utilities and public sector entities such as NTPC Ltd., the National Hydroelectric Power Corporation (NHPC), the Power Grid Corporation (PGC), the Power Finance Corporation (PFC), the Rural Electrification Corporation (REC), and the Power Trading Corporation (PTC) implement action plans at the national level. BEE implements action plans with the help of state nodal agencies. Statelevel renewable energy development agencies assist MNRE to implement policies and action plans at the state level. IREDA assists MNRE and state nodal agencies in project development and financing of renewable energy programs.

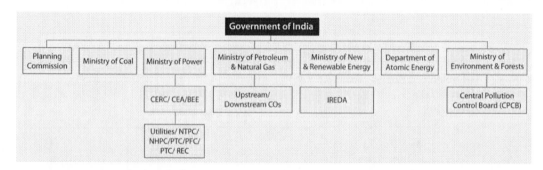

Figure 1.2. Institutional Framework at the National Level

The Central Pollution Control Board assists MoEF to formulate policies, rules, regulations, guidelines, and action plans related to the environment and pollution control at the national level. The State Pollution Control Boards (SPCBs) are responsible for ensuring compliance during project inception, construction, and implementation. MoEF also functions as a nodal ministry for CDM projects in India. Other line ministries such as the Ministry of Coal, Ministry of Petroleum and Natural Gas, and Department of Atomic Energy support clean energy programs peripherally. The Ministry of Petroleum and Natural Gas promotes clean energy through the promotion of CNG, LPG, and end-use energy efficiency in oil-fired equipment such as boilers and furnaces. The Ministry of Coal promotes clean technologies for coal production, coal gasification, and coal bed methane. A compendium of key government and state agencies is provided in Annex 2, which includes contact information.

The Ministry of Finance provides support for clean energy by determining tax benefits in the overall assessment of excise duties, central taxes, and provision of tax exemptions and fiscal incentives for clean technologies. The Department of Science and Technology provides support for clean energy by providing funds to technology development projects for clean energy. The Ministry of Rural Development is responsible for developing biodiesel projects across the country. The Ministry of Small-Scale Industries promotes clean technologies in small-scale industry sectors. Each of these ministries/departments has its own budget line for supporting clean technologies in its respective unit. Most of the funds pertain to demonstration units, with commercial funding for projects coming from the financial institutions as a part of the credit lines established for the purpose. In addition, there are individual ministries/departments dealing with steel, mines, pharmaceuticals and fertilizers, which have their own components of energy conservation and clean technologies as a part of their mandates.

At the state level, the policy and regulatory framework related to clean energy is implemented by the institutional structure shown in Figure 1.3. This consists of the State Electricity Regulatory Commission (SERC), the Department of Power (DOP), the State Renewable Development Agency (SRDA), and the Department of Environment (DOE). At the state level, the DOP implements policies and action plans through state utilities (generation, transmission, and distribution) and the electrical inspectorate, while the DOE implements policies and action plans for the environment and pollution control through the State Pollution Control Board (SPCB). SRDAs implement policies and action plans related to renewable energy. In some states and union territories, renewable energy falls under the jurisdiction of the DOP. The SRDAs also serve as nodal agencies for implementing energy efficiency policies and action plans as per the Energy Conservation Act.

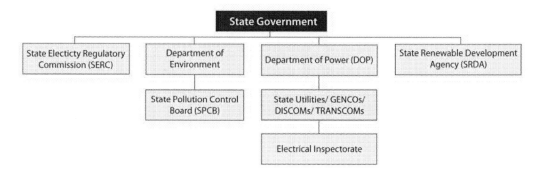

Figure 1.3. Institutional Framework at the State level

The institutional structure by state/union territory is provided in Table 1.36. This table shows the regulatory commissions, nodal agencies for energy efficiency, nodal agencies for renewable energy, and nodal agencies for pollution control in all the states that are implementing policies and action plans related to clean energy.

Table 1.36. Institutional Structure by State/Union Territory

	SERC	DOP	SRDA	Nodal Agency for Energy Efficiency	DOE/SPCB
Andhra Pradesh	√	√	√	√	√
Arunachal Pradesh	√	√	√	√	√
Assam	√	√	√	√	√
Bihar	√	√	√	√	√
Chhattisgarh	√	√	√	√	√
Goa		√			√
Gujarat	√	√	√	√	√
Haryana	√	√	√	√	√
Himachal Pradesh	√	√	√	√	√
Jammu and Kashmir	√	√	√	√	√
Jharkhand	√	√	√	√	√
Karnataka	√	√	√	√	√
Kerala	√	√	√	√	√
Madhya Pradesh	√	√	√	√	√
Maharashtra	√	√	√	√	√
Manipur		√	√		√
Meghalaya		√	√	√	√
Mizoram		√	√	√	√
Nagaland		√	√	√	√
Orissa	√	√	√	√	√
Punjab	√	√	√	√	√
Rajasthan	√	√	√	√	√
Sikkim		√	√	√	√
Tamil Nadu	√	√	√	√	√
Uttarakhand	√	√	√	√	√
Tripura	√	√	√	√	√
Uttar Pradesh	√	√	√	√	√
West Bengal	√	√	√	√	√
Union Territories					
Andman and Nicobar Islands		√			√
Chandigarh		√			√
Delhi	√	√	√	√	√
Lakshadweep		√			√
Puducherry		√	√	√	√

An Overview of Central Government Agencies

An overview of central government agencies is provided in Table 1.37. This compendium gives the names of respective ministries, agencies, and public sector undertakings that are responsible for implementation of policies and action plans at national levels. The three ministries covered are the Ministry of Power, Ministry of New and Renewable Energy, and Ministry of Environment and Forests. The Ministry of Power is supported by the Central Electricity Regulatory Commission, the Central Electricity Authority, and the Bureau of Energy Efficiency to draft and implement policies. NTPC Ltd. and the National Hydroelectric Power Corporation Ltd. are thermal and hydropower-generating utilities. The Power Finance Corporation Ltd. and the Rural Electrification Corporation Ltd. are the financial institutions operating under the Ministry of Power. The Indian Renewable Energy Development Agency is a financial institution under the Ministry of New and Renewable Energy with a mandate to finance renewable energy and energy efficiency projects in India. The Ministry of Environment and Forests is supported by the Central Pollution Control Board to frame environmental policies, guidelines, and standards in India.

Table 1.37. Compendium of Central government Agencies

Agency	Contact Details/ Address
Ministry of Power Government of India	Shram Shakti Bhavan, Ministry of Power, Government of India New Delhi–110001 Tel: 011 23710271, 23711316; fax: 011 23721487
Central Electricity Regulatory Commission	Central Electricity Regulatory Commission, Core 3, 6/7th Floors, SCOPE Complex, 7 Institutional Area, Lodi Road, New Delhi–110 003 Tel: 011 24361145, 24360216; Fax: 011 24360010
Central Electricity Authority	SEWA Bhawan, R. K. Puram, New Delhi–110 066 Tel: 011 26102583; fax: 011 26109212
Bureau of Energy Efficiency	4th Floor, SEWA Bhawan, R. K. Puram, New Delhi–110 066 Tel: 011 26179699; fax: 011 26178352
NTPC Ltd.	NTPC Limited, NTPC Bhawan, SCOPE Complex, 7 Institutional Area Lodhi Road, New Delhi–110003 Tel: 011 24360100; fax: 011 24361018
National Hydro-electric Power Corporation Ltd.	NHPC Office Complex, Sector 33, Faridabad–121 003, Haryana Tel: 91 129 2258331; Fax: 0129 2277941, 2278012
Power Finance Corporation Ltd.	Power Finance Corporation Ltd., "Urjanidhi," 1, Barakhamba Lane, Connaught Place, New Delhi–110 001 Tel: 11 23456000; fax: 011 23412545
Rural Electrification Corporation Ltd.	Core- 4, SCOPE Complex, 7, Lodhi Road, New Delhi–110003 Tel: 011 24365161; fax: 011 24360644
Ministry of New and Renewable Energy Government of India	Ministry of New and Renewable Energy, Block-14, CGO Complex, Lodhi Road, New Delhi–110 003 Tel: 011 24361298, 24360707; Fax: 011-24361830
Indian Renewable Energy Development Agency Limited	India Habitat Centre Complex, Core-4A, East Court, 1st Floor Lodi Road, New Delhi–110 003 Tel: 011 24682214 21; fax: 011 24682202
Ministry of Environment and Forests Government of India	Ministry of Environment and Forests, Paryavaran Bhavan CGO Complex, Lodhi Road, New Delhi–110 003 Tel: 011 24361669, 24360605, 24360570, 24360519, 24361147 Fax: 011 24362746
Central Pollution Control Board	Parivesh Bhawan, CBD-cum-Office Complex, East Arjun Nagar Delhi–110 032 Tel: 011 22307233; telefax 22304948

Overview of State/Union Territory Government Agencies

A compendium of state/union territory government agencies is provided in Table 1.38. This compendium provides the name of the state and the names of key agencies followed by the addresses of the ministry/department of power, electricity regulatory commission, utility, environment/pollution control agency, and the state nodal agency for renewable energy and energy efficiency.

Table 1.38. Compendium of State/Union Territory Government Agencies

State	Commission/Board/Agency	Contract Details
Andhra Pradesh	Principal Secretary (power)	Energy Department, Government of Andhra Pradesh, Hyderabad–500001 Telfax: 040 23455452, 23453305
	Andhra Pradesh Electricity Regulatory Commission	4th and 5th Floors 11-4-660, Singareni Bhavan Red Hills, Hyderabad–500 004 Tel: 23397381, 23397399, 23397556, 23397656, 23390970, 23390971, 23391973, 23378646; Fax: 23397378, 23397489
	Andhra Pradesh Power Generation Corporation Ltd.	Vidyut Soudhan, Hyderabad–500 082 Tel: 040 3317643, 3702571 Fax: 040 3317643
	Andhra Pradesh Transmiss-ion Corporation Ltd.	Vidyut Sudhan, Hyderabad–82 Tel: 3317657 Fax: 040 3320565
	Andhra Pradesh Pollution Control Board	Paryarana Bhawan, A-3, Industrial Area, Sanathnagar, Hyderbabad–500 018 Andhra Pradesh
	Non-conventional Energy Development Corporation of Andhra Pradesh (NEDCAP) Ltd.	5-8-207/2 Pisgah Complex Nampally Hyderabad–500 001 Tel: 040 23201172 (O) (office) Fax: 040 23201666
	Non-conventional Energy Development Cooperation of Andhra Pradesh Ltd. (NEDCAP) (state nodal agency for energy efficiency)	5-8-207/2, Pisgah Complex Nampally, Hyderabad–500 001 Tel: 23201172 (O)
Arunachal Pradesh	Secretary, Department of Power	Block No. 11, Civil Secretariat, Itanagar–791 111 Tel: 0360 2216485; fax: 2291598
	Arunachal State Pollution Control Board	Government of Arunachal Pradesh, Office of the Principal Chief and Secretary (E&F) Conservator of Forests, Itanagar–79 1111, Arunachal Pradesh
	Arunachal Pradesh Energy Development Agency	Urja Bhawan Tadar Tang Marg Post Box No. 141 Itanagar–791111 Tel: 0360 211160, 216937 (O); fax: 0360 214426
	Arunachal Pradesh Energy Development Agency (APEDA) (state nodal age-ncy for energy efficiency)	Urja Bhawan, TT Marg Post Box No. 141 P.O. Itanagar–791 111, District Papum Pare Arunachal Pradesh Tel: 0360 2211160; fax: 0360 2214426

Table 1.38. (Continued)

State	Commission/Board/Agency	Contract Details
Assam	Principal Secretary (power)	Energy, Assam Secretariat, Government of Assam, Dispur–781005 Tel: 0361 2261120, 2262674; fax: 0361 2540314
	Assam Electricity Regulatory Commission	ASEB Campus, Dwarandhar G. S. Road, Sixth Mile, Guwahati–781022 Tel: 0361 2234442, Fax: 0361 2234473
	Assam State Electricity Board	Bijulee Bhawan, Paltan Bazar Guwahati–781001 Tel: 540311, 541088, Fax: 0361 41090
	Assam Pollution Control Board	Bamunimaidan, Guwahati–781021, Assam Tel: 91 361 2652774, 2550258 Fax: 91 361 2550259
	Assam Energy Development Agency	Co-operative City Bank Building, U. N. B. Road, Silpukhuri , Guwahati–781 003 Tel: 0361 2662232, 2664415; fax: 0361 2668475
	Chief Electrical Inspector-cum-Adviser (state nodal agency for energy efficiency)	Chief Electrical Inspector-cum-Adviser Government of Assam, Pub-Sarania Road Guwahati–781 003 Assam Tel: 0361 2529611
Bihar	Principle Secretary (power)	Government of Bihar, Patna 800008 Tel: 0612 2225412; fax: 0612 2232852
	Bihar Electricity Regulatory Commission (BERC)	Ground Floor, Vidyut Bhawan-II, B. S. E. B. Campus, Jawahar Lal Nehru Marg (Bailey Road), Patna–800021 Bihar Tel: 0612-5526749, 2205488, 2205489 Fax: 0612-2205488
	Bihar State Electricty Board	Vidyut Bhawan, Bailey Road, Patna–800001 Telefax: 0612 2224534
	Bihar State Pollution Control Board	Beltron Bhawan, 2nd Floor, Lal Bhadur Shastri Nagar, Patna–800 023, Bihar Tel: 0612 2281250; Fax: 0612 2291709
	Bihar Renewable Energy Development Agency	1st Floor, Sone Bhawan, Virchand Patel Marg, Patna–800 001 Tel: 0612 2233572; fax: 0612 2228734
	Bihar Renewable Energy Development Agency (BREDA) (state nodal agency for energy efficiency)	1st Floor, Sone Bhawan, Birchand Patel Marg, Patna–800 001 Tel: 0612 2233572
Chhattisgarh	Secretary Energy	Government of Chattisgarh, Raipur Tel: 0771 5080962; fax: 0771 2221960
	Chhattisgarh State Electricity Regulatory Commission	Civil Lines, G. E. Road, Raipur (C.G.) Pin: 492001 Tel: 91 771 4073555; fax: 4073553

Table 1.38. (Continued)

State	Commission/Board/Agency	Contract Details
	Chhattisgarh State Electricity Board	Dangania, C. S. E. B. P.O. Sundar Nagar, Raipur 492013 Tel: 2242345, 4066900; Fax: 4028882
	Chattisgarh Environment Conservation Board	Nanak Nivas, Civil Lines Raipur–492001 Chattisgarh Tel: 0771 2425523; fax: 0771 2425586
	Chhattisgarh State Renewable Energy Development Agency	MIG/A-20 A/1 Sector 1, Shankar Nagar Raipur Tel: 0771-2426446; fax: 5066770
	Chhattisgarh State Renewable Energy Development (CREDA) (state nodal agency for energy efficiency)	Department of Energy, Government of Chhattisgarh MIG/A-20/1, Sector-1, Shankar Nagar Raipur (C.G.)–492 007 Tel: 0771 4066770; fax: 0771 4066771
Goa	Secretary (power)	Electricity Department, Government of Goa, Panaji–403001 Tel: 0832 2419416; fax: 0832 2419624
	Office of Chief Electrical Engineer	Electicity Department, Government of Goa, Vidyut Bhawan Third Floor, Panaji, Goa Tel: 0832 2426022, 2426421
	Goa State Pollution Control Board	1st Floor, Dempo Tower EDC Patto Plaza, Panaji, Goa. Pin: 403 001 Tel: +91 0832 2438528, 2438567, 2438550 Fax: 0832 2438528
	Goa Energy Development Agency	DST&E Building, 1st Floor, Saligo Plateau Opp. Seminary Saligao, Bardez, Goa–403511 Tel: 0832 271194
Gujarat	Principal Secretary	Energy Department, Government of Gujarat, Sachivayalay Block No. 5, Gandhinagar 382010 Telefax: 079 23250797
	Gujarat Electricity Regulatory Commission (GERC)	Viniyamak Bhawan, C- Block, Shivalik Malviya Nagar, New Delhi Telefax: +91 11 26673608
	Gujarat Electricity Board	Sardar Patel Vidyut Bhawan, Race Course Vadodara–390 007 Tel : 0265 338299 Fax: 0265 337918
	Gujarat Pollution Control Board	Paryavaran Bhavan, Sector 10A Gandhinagar–382 010, Gujarat Tel: 079 23222095, 23222096, 23222756 Fax: 079 23232156, 23222784, 23232161
	Gujarat Energy Development Agency (GEDA)	4th Floor, Block No. 11 and 12, Udyog Bhawan, Sector 11 Ghandhi Nagar–382017 Tel: 079 23247086/89/90 Fax: 079 23247097
	Gujarat Energy Development Agency (GEDA) (state nodal agency for energy efficiency)	Surajplaza-II, 2nd Floor Sayajigunj, Vadodara–390 005, Gujarat Tel: 0265 2362066; fax: 0265 2363120

Table 1.38. (Continued)

State	Commission/Board/Agency	Contract Details
Haryana	Secretary Power	Government of Haryana, Chandigarh Tel: 0172 2713453: fax: 0172 2745279
	Haryana Electricity Regulatory Commission	Bays 33–36, Sector 4, Panchkula–134112, Haryana Tel: +91 172 2582531; fax:+91 172 2572359 EPABX: 2563052, 2572298, 2582532
	Haryana Vidyut Prasaran Nigam Ltd.	Shakti Bhawan Sector No. 6, Panchkula Tel: 0172 740188 Fax: 5611931–38
	Haryana State Pollution Control Board	C-11, Sector-6, Panchkula Tel: 0172 2581005/006
	Haryana Renewal Energy Development Agency (HAREDA)	SCO 48, Sector 26 Chandigarh–160 019 Tel: 0172 2791917, 2790918, 2790911; fax: 0172 2790928
	Renewable Energy Department, Haryana (state nodal agency for energy efficiency)	S. C. O. No. 48, Sector-26 Madhya Marg, Chandigarh–160 026 Tel: 0172 2791917: fax: 0172 2790928
Himachal Pradesh	Principal Secretary	Department of Power, Government of Himachal Pradesh Shimla–171002 Tel: 0177 262 1859; fax: 0177 2621154
	Himachal Pradesh Electricity Regulatory Commission	Keonthal Commercial Complex, Khalini Shimla–171 002 Himachal Pradesh Tel: + 91 177 2627262, 2627263 Fax: +91 177 2627162
	Himachal Pradesh State Electricity Board	Vidyut Bhawan, Shimla–4 Tel: 0177 213563 Fax: 0177 258984
	Himachal Pradesh State Environment Protection and Pollution Control Board	Paryavaran Bhawan, Phase-III New Shimla–171 009 H. P.
	HIMURJA	HIMURJA, SDA Complex Kasumpti, Shimla–171009 Tel: 0177 2620365 Fax: 0177 2620365
	Himachal Pradesh State Electricity Board (state nodal agency for energy efficiency)	Vidyut Bhawan Shimla-171004 (HP) Tel: (O) 0177 2655007; cell: 9816393156
Jammu and Kashmir	Principal Secretary, Power Department	Government of Jammu Kashmir, New Secretariat Jammu–180 001 Tel: 0191 2546715, 0191 2520864, 0194 2452236 Fax: 0194 2452352, 0191 2545447
	J&K State Electricity Regulatory Commission	PDC Complex, Ashok Nagar Satwari, Jammu Tel: 0191 2457899; fax: 0191 2454420
	Jammu and Kashmir State Pollution Control Board	Sheikhul Alam Campus, behind Government Silk Factory Rajbagh, Srinagar (April–Oct.) 0191 572961 Parivesh Bhawan Forest Complex, Gandhi Transport Nagar (Nawal), Jammu (November–March)

Table 1.38. (Continued)

State	Commission/Board/Agency	Contract Details
	Jammu and Kashmir Energy Development Agency (JAKEDA)	12 BC Road, Jammu–180001 Tel: 0191 546495; fax: 2546495
Jharkhand	Secretary (energy)	Government of Jharkhand, Nepal House, Ranchi Tel: 0651 2490053; fax: 0651 2491002
	Jharkhand State Electricity Regulatory Commission	2nd Floor, Rajendra Jawan Bhawan-cum-Sainik Bazar Main Road, Ranchi–834001 Tel: 0651 2330923, 2330763, 2330761, 2330926
	Jharkhand State Electricity Board	Engineering Building, HEC, DHURWA, Ranchi–834004 Tel: 0651 2403807, 2403809
	Jharkhand State Pollution Control Board	T. A. Building, HEC P.O. Dhurwa Ranchi–834004, Jharkhand Fax: 0651 5004123
	Jharkhand Renewable Energy Development Agency	328 B, Road No. 4, Ashok Nagar, Ranchi–834 002 Tel: 0651 2246970; fax: 0651 2240665
	Chief Engineer-cum-Chief Electrical Inspector (state nodal agency for energy efficiency)	Energy Department, Government of Jharkhand Ranchi–834 001 Tel: 0651 2490053; fax: 0651 2491002
Karnataka	Principal Secretary	Energy Department, Government of Karnataka, Sachivalaya II Bangalore–560001 Tel: 080 22034648; fax: 080 22353952
	Karnataka Electricity Regulatory Commission	6th and 7th Floors, Mahalaxmi Chambers # 9/2, M. G. Road, Bangalore–560 001 Tel: +91 080 25320213, 25320214; fax: 25320338
	Karnataka Power Transmission Corporation Ltd.	Corporate Office, Cauvery Bhawan, Banglore–560 009 Tel: 080 2214234
	Karnataka Power Corp. Ltd.	No. 82, Shakthi Bhawan, Race Course Road, Banglore–560 001 Telefax: 080 2252144
	Karnataka State Pollution Control Board	#49, Parisara Bhavan Church Street, Bangalore-01 Karnataka Tel: 080 25581383, 25589112, 25586520
	Karnataka Renewable Energy Development Agency Ltd.	No. 19, Maj. Gen. A. D. Loganadan, INA Cross, Queen's Road Bangalore–560 052 Tel: (O) 080 22282220; fax: 080 22257399
	Karnataka Renewal Energy Development Limited (KR-EDL) (state nodal agency for energy efficiency)	No. 19, Maj. Gen. A. D. Loganadhan, INA Cross Queen's Road, Bangalore–560 052, Karnataka Tel: (O) 080 22282220, 22208109, 22282221

Table 1.38. (Continued)

State	Commission/Board/Agency	Contract Details
Kerala	Principle Secretary	Government of Kerala, Power Department, Secretariat Thiruvananthapuram Tel: 0471 2327979; fax: 0471 2725482
	Kerala Electricity Regulatory Commission	30, Belheven Gardens, Kawdiar P.O. Thiruvananthapuram–695003 Tel: 0471 2725951, 2725952, 2725964
	Kerala State Electricity Board Engineers Association	Engineers House, TC 26/1300, Panavila, Trivandrum–695001 Tel: 0471 2330696; fax: 0471 2330853
	Kerala State Pollution Control Board	Housing Board Complex, Chakkorathukulam Kozhikode–673 006 Tel: 0495 2300745
	Agency for Non-conventional Energy and Rural Technology (ANERT)	Pattom P.O., Pb no.1094, Kesavadasapuram Thiruvananthapuram–695 004 Tel: 0471 2440121, 2440122, 2440124; fax: 0471 2449853
	Energy Management Center (state nodal agency for energy efficiency)	Thycaud P.O., Thiruvananthapuram–695014 Kerala Tel: 0471 2323329, 2115043, 2323363
Madhya Pradesh	Principal Secretary	Government of Madhya Pradesh, Energy Department Bhopal–462001 Tel: 0755 2442055; fax: 0755 2441462
	Madhya Pradesh Electricity Regulatory Commission	"Metro Plaza," 3rd and 4th Floors, E-5 Arera Colony Bittan Market, Bhopal–462 016 Tel: 0761 2430183
	Madhya Pradesh Electricity Board	Shakti Bhawan, Jabalpur–482 008 Tel: 0761 313251 Fax: 0761 311565
	Madhya Pradesh Pollution Control Board	Madhya Pradesh Pollution Control Board, Bhopal Tel: 0755 2469180; fax: 0755 2463742, 2469180
	MP Urja Vikas Nigam Ltd.	Urja Bhawan, Main Road No. 2 Shivaji Nagar, Bhopal–462016 Tel: 0755 2556245, 2553595; fax: 0755 2556245
	M.P.Urja Vikas Nigam Limited (MPUVNL) (state nodal agency for energy efficiency)	Urja Bhavan, Shivaji Nagar Bhopal, Madhya Pradesh Tel: (O) 0755 2556526, 2553595, 2767270 Fax: 0755 2553122
Maharashtra	Principal Secretary (energy)	Mantralaya, Government of Maharashtra, Mumbai–400001 Tel: 022 22026767; fax: 022 22820474
	Maharashtra Electricity Regulatory Commission	World Trade Centre, Center No. 1, 13th Floor, Cuffe Parade Colaba, Mumbai–400005 Tel: 091 22 22163964/65/69; fax: 022 22163976

Table 1.38. (Continued)

State	Commission/Board/Agency	Contract Details
	Maharashtra State Electricity Board	Plot No. G-9, "Prakashgad" Bandra (East) Mumbai–400 051 Tel: 022 2619400; fax: 022 26443749
	Maharashtra Pollution Control Board	Kalpa Taru Point, 3rd and 4th Floors Opp. Cine Planet, Sion Circle, Mumbai–400 022 Tel: 022 24014701, 24010437 Fax: 022 24024068
	Maharashtra Energy Development Agency (MEDA)	S. No. 191/A, Phase 1, 2nd Floor, MHADA Commercial Complex Opp. Tridal Nagar, Yerawada Pune–411 006 Tel: 020 26615354; fax: 020 26615031
	Maharashtra Energy Development Agency (MEDA) (state nodal agency for energy efficiency)	MHADA Commercial Complex, 2nd Floor, Opp. Tridal Nagar Yerwada, Pune–411 006, Maharashtra Tel: (O) 020 26615354, (D) 020 26614393, 26614403
Manipur	Principal Secretary, Department of Power	Government of Manipur, Manipur Secretariat Imphal–795 001 Tel: 0385 2220964; fax: 0385 222629
	State Electricity Regulatory Commission	Not yet formed
	Chief Engineer (power) Office of the Chief Engineer (power) (generation, transmission, distribution, state nodal agency for energy efficiency)	Secretariat: Electricity Department Government of Manipur, Keisampat, Imphal–795001 Manipur Tel: 0385 2220050; fax: 0385 2220143
	Manipur Renewable Energy Development Agency (MANIREDA)	Department of Science, Technology Minuthong Hafiz Hatta Imphal–795001 Tel: 385 441086; fax: 91 385 224930
	Environment and Ecology Wing	Department of Environment and Forests Government of Manipur Porompat Imphal East–795001 Tel: 0385 221537, 222629
Meghalaya	Secretary (power)	Energy Department, Government of Meghalaya, Shillong Tel: 0364 2222016
	State Electricity Regulatory Commission	Formed but at inception stage
	Meghalaya State Electricity Board	Meghalaya State Electricity Board Lum Jingshai, Short Round Road Shillong, Pin: 793001 Meghalaya Tel: 0364 2590610, 2590742, 2590710, 2591843, 2591259 Fax: 0364 2590355
	Meghalaya Pollution Control Board	ARDEN, Lumpyngndad Meghalaya

Table 1.38. (Continued)

State	Commission/Board/Agency	Contract Details
	Meghalaya Non-conventional and Rural Energy Development Agency	Lower Lachaumiere, Opp. P&T Dispensary, near BSF Camp Mawpat Shillong–793 012 Telefax: 0364 2537343
	Senior Electrical Inspector (state nodal agency for energy efficiency)	Horse Shoe Building, Lower Lachumiere Shillong–793 001, Meghalaya Tel: (O) 25007556, (R) 2537722 (residence); cell: 9863049159
Mizoram	Secretary (power)	Government of Mizoram Aizwal–796 001 Tel: 0389 2325653, 2322776; fax: 0389 2318572
	State Electricity Regulatory Commission	Not yet formed
	Power and Electricity Department (state nodal agency for energy efficiency)	Power and Electricity Department, Government of Mizoram Treasury Square, Aizawl–796001, Mizoram Tel: 0389 2322848; fax: 0389 2320862
	Mizoram State Pollution Control Board	M. G. Road, Khatla, Aizawl–796001, Mizoram Tel: 0389 323439
	Zoram Energy Development Agency	H/No.A/4, Muol Veng, Chaltlang, Aizawl, Mizoram–796007 Tel: 0389-2350664, 2350665; fax: 323185
Nagaland	Secretary (power)	Government of Nagaland, Kohima–797001 Tel: 0370 270110; fax: 0370 2220110
	State Electricity Regulatory Commission	Not yet formed
	Department of Power	"Electricity House," Department of Power Government of Nagaland, Kohima–797001, Nagaland
	Nagaland Pollution Control Board	Office of the Chairman, Signal Point Dimapur–797112, Nagaland Tel: 03862 245726 Fax: 03862 245727
	Nagaland Renewable Energy Devel-opment Agency (NREDA) (renewable energy and state nodal agency for energy efficiency)	NRSE Cell Rural Development Department Nagaland Secretariat, Kohima, Nagaland Telefax: 0370 241408
Orissa	Secretary Power	Department of Power, Government of Orissa Bhubaneswar–751001 Tel: 0674 2536960; fax: 0674 2394950
	Orissa Electricity Regulatory Commission	Bidyut Niyamak Bhavan, Unit-VIII, Bhubaneswar–751 012 Tel: 0674-2396117, 2393097, 2391580, 2393606; Fax: 0674 2393306, 2395781
	Orissa Hydropower Corporation Ltd.	Orissa State Police Housing and Welfare Corp. Building Vanivihar, Square, Bhubaneswar–751 022 Tel: 0674 400050; fax: 0674 415402

Table 1.38. (Continued)

State	Commission/Board/Agency	Contract Details
	Grid Corporation of Orissa	Vidyut Bhawan Janpath, Bhubaneswar–751 007 Tel: 0674 410098, 413396; fax: 0674 41904
	Central Electricity Supply Utility of Orissa	2nd Floor, IDCO Tower, Janpath, Bhubaneswar–751022 Phone: 0674 2545681, 2541727 Fax: 0674 2543125
	Orissa State Pollution Control Board	A-118, Nilakantha Nagar Unit-VIII, Bhubaneswar–751012, Orissa Tel: 0674 2564033 Fax: 0674 2562822, 2560955
	Orissa Renewable Energy Development Agency	S-59, Mancheswar Industrial Estate Bhubaneswar–751 010 Tel: (O) 0674 2580660; fax: 0674 2586368
	Superintending Engineer (electrical) (REPO and projects) (state nodal agency for energy efficiency)	EIC (Elecy)-cum-P. C. E. I., Orissa Unit-V, Bhubaneswar–1, Orissa Tel: 0674 2394873; fax: 0674 2391255, 2391024
Punjab	Secretary of Power	Department of Power, Government of Punjab, Chandigarh Tel: 0172 2741524; fax: 0172 2741554
	Punjab State Electricity Regulatory Commission	SCO: 220-221, Sector 34-A, Chandigarh PABX: 0172 2645164 65 66 Fax: 0172 2664758
	Punjab State Electricity Board	The Mall, Patiala–147 001 Tel: 0175 214927, 212005; fax: 0175 213199
	Punjab Pollution Control Board	Vatavaran Bhawan, Nabha Road, Patiala–147 001 Punjab Tel: 0175 2215793, 2215802
	Punjab Energy Development Agency	Plot No. 1-2, Sector 33-D Chandigarh–160 036 Tel: 0172 663392, 663328, 663382 Fax: 0172 2646384, 2662865
	Punjab Energy Development Agency (state nodal agency for energy efficiency)	Solar Passive Complex Plot No. 1–2, Sector 33-D Chandigarh (U.T.)–160 034 Tel: 0172 2663328, 2663382; fax: 0172 2662865
Rajasthan	Secretary (energy)	Government of Rajasthan, Jaipur–302001 Tel: 0141 2227400; fax: 0141 2227635
	Rajasthan Electricity Regulatory Commission	Shed No. 5, Vidhyut Bhawan, Vidhyut Marg, Jyoti Nagar Jaipur–302 005 Tel: 0141 2741181, 2741016; fax: 0141 2741018
	Rajasthan State Electricity Board	Vidyut Bhawan, R. C. Dave Marg, Jaipur–302 005 Tel: 0141 740118; fax: 0141 740168

Table 1.38. (Continued)

State	Commission/Board/Agency	Contract Details
	Rajasthan Pollution Control Board	Rajasthan Pollution Control Board, 4, Institutional Area Jhalana Doongri, Jaipur EPBX: 0141 2700601, 2701801, 2711263, 2707938, 2704581, 2711329; fax: 0141 2710647, 2709980
	Rajasthan Renewable Energy Corpo-ration Limited	E-166, Yudhister Marg, C-Scheme Jaipur–302 001 Tel: 0141 2225898, 2228198; fax: 0141 2226028
	Rajasthan Renewable Energy Corporation (state nodal agency for energy efficiency)	E-166, Yudhishthar Marg C-Scheme, Jaipur–302 001, Rajasthan Tel: 0141 2225859, 2228198, 2221650; fax: 0141 2226028
Sikkim	Secretary, Department of Power	Government of Sikkim, Gangtok–737101 Tel: 03592 2202028, 2202244 Fax: 03592 222927
	Sikkim State Pollution Control Board/ Department of Forests, Environment and Wildlife	Government of Sikkim, Deorali–737102 Tel: 03592 281778, 281385; fax: 03592 281778
	Sikkim Renewable Energy Development Agency (renewable energy and state nodal agency for energy efficiency)	Department of New and Renewable Energy Sources Government of Sikkim, Tashiling Secretariat, Annex- I Gangtok–737 101 Tel: 03592 22659; fax: 03592 22245
Tamil Nadu	Secretary of Power	Government of Tamil Nadu, Secretariat, Chennai Telefax: 044 25671496
	Tamil Nadu Electricity Regulatory Commission	No. 18, 3rd Main Road, Seethammal Colony, Alwarpet Chennai–600 017 Tel: 044 24359215, 24342037; fax: 044 24354982
	Tamil Nadu Electricity Board	N. P. K. R. R., Maaligai, Electricity Avenue, 800 Anna Salai Chennai–600 002 Tel: 044 8251300, 8544528 Fax: 044 8521210
	Tamil Nadu Pollution Control Board	No. 76, Mount Salai, Guindy, Chennai–600 032 Tel: 044 22353134, 22353141; fax: 22353155
	Tamil Nadu Energy Development Agency (TEDA)	EVK Sampath Building, Maaligal, 5th Floor Chennai–600 006 Tel: 044 28224832 Fax: 044 28236592, 28222971
	Electrical Inspectorate Department, Government of Tamil Nadu (state nodal agency for energy efficiency)	Thiru Vi. Ka. Industrial Estate Guindy, Chennai–600 032 Tel: 044 22342915 (D), 22342227, 22343184, 22342796; Fax: 044 22349036

Table 1.38. (Continued)

State	Commission/Board/Agency	Contract Details
Uttarakhand	Principal Secretary of Energy	Government of Uttarakhand, Secretariat, Dehradun–248001 Tel: 0135 2712018; fax: 0135 2712077
	Uttarakhand Electricity Regulatory Commission	Institution of Engineers (I) Building, 1st Floor Near ISBT, Majra, Dehradun (UA) Tel: 0135 2641119; fax: 2643755
	Uttarakhand Power Corporation Limited	Urja Bhawan, Kanwali Road, Dehradun Uttarakhand–248006 Tel: 0135 2763672–75
	Uttarakhand Jal Vidyut Nigam Ltd.	Maharani Bagh, G. M. S. Road Dehradun–248006 Uttarakhand Tel: 0135 2523100, 2763508, 2763808; fax: 0135 2763507
	Uttaranchal Pollution Control Board	E-115, Nehru Colony, Hardwar Road Dehradun–248 011, Uttarakhand Tel: 0135 2668922 Fax: 0135 2668092
	Uttranchal Renewable Energy Development Agency (UREDA)	Energy Park Campus, Industrial Area, Patel Nagar Dehradun–248001 Tel: 0135 2521387, 2521386; fax: 0135 2521553
	Office of Electrical Inspector, Government of Uttaranchal (state nodal agency for energy efficiency)	Panchayat Ghar, Bari Mukhani Near Heera Convent School Haldwani, Nainitall Tel: (O) 05946 262839; fax: 05946 261913
Tripura	Secretary, Power Department	Government of Tripura, Agartala–799 001 Tel: 0381 2324185
	Chairman, Tripura Electricity Regulatory Commission	Tripura Electricity Regulatory Commission, Agartala Tel: 0381 2326372
	Tripura State Electricity Corporation Ltd.	Bidyut Bhavan, North Banamalipur, Agartala–799001, Tripura
	Tripura State Pollution Control Board	Vigyan Bhawan, Kunjaban Agartala (W)–799 006, Tripura Telefax: 0381 225421
	Tripura Renewable Energy Development Agency	Vigyan Bhawan, 2nd Floor Pandit Nehru Complex West Tripura, Agartala–799 006 Tel: (O) 0381 225421; fax: 0381 225900
	Chief Engineer (electrical) (state nodal agency for energy efficiency)	Chief Engineer (Electrical) Government of Tripura Department of Power Tripura, Agartala
Uttar Pradesh	Principal Secretary (energy)	Government of Uttar Praesh, Bapu Bhawan Lucknow–226001 Tel: 0522 2238244; fax: 0522 2237922
	Uttar Pradesh Electricity Regulatory Commission	IInd Floor, Kisan Mandi Bhawan, Gomti Nagar, Vibhuti Khand Lucknow–226010 Tel: 0522 2720426; fax: 0522 2720423
	UP Power Corporation Limited	Shakti Bhawan, 14 Ashok Marg, Lucknow–226 001 Tel: 0522 226736; fax: 0522 211169

Table 1.38. (Continued)

State	Commission/Board/Agency	Contract Details
	Kanpur Electricity Supply Company Limited	14/71, Civil Lines, KESA House, Kanpur–208001 P. B. No. 141 Telegram: KESCo; tel: 0512 2530890 Fax: 0512 2530010
	Uttar Pradesh Pollution Control Board	IIIrd Floor PICUP Bhavan, Vibhuti Khand, Gomti Nagar Lucknow–226020 UP tel: 0522 2720381, 2720681; fax: 0522 2720764
	Non-conventional Energy Development Agency (NEDA), U. P.	Vibhuti Khand, Gomti Nagar Lucknow–226 010 Tel: 0522 2720652; fax: 0522 2720779, 2720829
	Non-conventional Energy Development Agency (NEDA) (state nodal agency for energy efficiency)	Vibhuthikahand Gomtinagar Lucknow–226 016 Telefax: 0522 2720829, 2235503
West Bengal	Secretary (power)	Government of West Bengal, Kolkata–700001 Tel: 033 22481267; fax: 033 22438379
	West Bengal Electricity Regulatory Commission	Poura Bhavan (3rd Floor), Block-FD, 415-A,Bidhannagar Kolkata–700106 Tel: 033 23592189, 033 23593397; fax: 033 23593397
	West Bengal State Electricity Board	Vidyut Bhawan, DJ Block Sector-II, Salt Lake Calcutta–700 091 Tel: 033 3591915, 3371550 Fax: 033 3591954
	West Bengal Pollution Control Board	Paribesh Bhavan, 10A, Block-L.A., Sector III, Salt Lake City Calcutta–700 098 Tel: 1 800 345 3390 (toll free)
	West Bengal Renewable Energy Development Agency	Bikalap Shakti Bhawan, Plot- J-1/10, EP & GP Block Salt Lake Electronics Complex, Sector- V Kolkata–700091 Tel. 033 3575038, 3575348 (O); fax: 033 3575037, 3575347
	West Bengal State Electri-city Board (state nodal age-ncy for energy efficiency)	Bidyut Bhawan, 7th Floor, Block-DJ, Sector II Bidhanagar (Salt Lake), Kolkata–700 091, West Bengal; Tel: 033 23591915, 23371150
Union Territories		
Andman & Nicobar Island	Commissioner Secretary	Department of Power, Andaman and Nicobar Administration Port Blair–744101 Tel: 03192 232479; fax: 03192 235412
	Superintending Engineer, Electricity Department, A&N Administration (electricity generation, transmission and distribution, and nodal agency for energy efficiency)	Electricity Department, A&N Administration Vidyut Bhawan, Port Blair–744 101 Tel: (O) 03192 232404

Table 1.38. (Continued)

State	Commission/Board/Agency	Contract Details
	The Principal Chief Conservator of Forests	Department of Environment and Forest, Andaman and Nicobar Islands, Van Sadan, Haddo P.O. Port Blair–744102 Tel: +91 3192 233321; fax: +91 3192 230113
Chandigarh	Superintending Engineer (electricity/electrical) (state nodal agency for energy efficiency)	Room No. 523, 5th Floor Deluxe Building, U. T. Sectt. Sector 9-D, Chandigarh–160 009 Tel: (O) 0172 2740475
	Chandigarh Pollution Control Committee	Chandigarh Administration, Additional Town Hall Building IInd Floor, Sector 17-C, Chandigarh–160 017
Delhi	Principal Secretary (power)	Government of NCT of Delhi, I P State, New Delhi Tel: 011 23392047, 23215198; fax: 011 23234640
	Delhi Electricity Regulatory Commission	Viniyamak Bhawan, C- Block, Shivalik Malviya Nagar, New Delhi Telefax: +91 11 26673608
	Delhi Vidyut Board	Shakti Bhawan, Nehru Place, New Delhi–110 019 Tel: 011 6484833, 6484802 Fax: 011-6460942
	BSES Rajdhani	A-1/27, Safdarjung Enclave, New Delhi–110029
	Delhi Pollution Control Committee	4th Floor, I. S. B. T. Building Kashmere Gate Delhi–110006
	Delhi Transco Ltd.	EE & REM Center Delhi Transco Ltd. 2nd Floor, SLDC Building, Minto Road New Delhi–110002 Tel: 011 23234994; fax: 23231886
	CMD, Delhi Transco Limited (state nodal agency for energy efficiency)	Principal Secretary (Power) Shakti Sadan, Kotla Road New Delhi–110 002
Lakshad-weep	Secretary (power)	Union Territory of Lakshadweep, Kavaratti via Cochin–682555 Tel: 04896 262256; fax: 04896 262184
	Executive Engineer (generation, transmission, distribution, renewable sources of energy, and nodal agency for energy efficiency)	Department of Electricity, Kavaratti–Lakshadweep–682555 Telegram: POWERLAK Tel: +91 4896 262127, 262363, 262156 Fax: +91 4896 262936
	Secretary Environment	Union Territory of Lakshadweep Kavaratti–682 555 Tel: +91 4896 262896, 262598, 262592
Puducherry	Principal Secretary (power)	Department of Power, Chief Secretariat, Puducherry–60500 Telefax: 0413 2334448

Table 1.38. (Continued)

State	Commission/Board/Agency	Contract Details
	Superintending Engineer-I (head of department)	Department of Electricity, Government of Puducherry Puducherry Tel: (O) 0413 233 4277; fax: 0413 233 1556
	The Puducherry Power Corporation	10, Second Cross, Jawahar Nagar, T. R. Pattinam Nagore Main Road, Boomianpet, Karaikal–609606 Puducherry–605005 Tel: 0413 2204043, 2204688 Tel: 04368233287, 233988 (PBX) Fax: 0413 2202971
	The Project Director Renewable Energy Agency of Pondicherry (state nodal agency for energy efficiency)	No. 10, Second Main Road Elango Nagar Puducherry–11 Fax: 0413 2337575
	Director/ Member Secretary	Department of Science, Technology and Environment IIIrd Floor, PHB Building, Anna Nagar, Puducherry–5 Tel: 0413 2201256; fax: 0413 2203494

SECTION 2: CLEAN ENERGY TECHNOLOGIES DEFINED

This report covers clean energy technologies (CETs) including renewable energy technologies, energy efficiency, hybrids and cogeneration, and clean transportation technologies. CETs are more environmentally friendly than traditional, fossil fuel-based technologies. CETs can either use natural resources such as sunlight, wind, rain, tides, geothermal heat, and plants, which are naturally replenished, and/or use processes to use energy more efficiently.

CETs include renewable energy, hybrid and cogeneration, and energy efficiency technologies for power generation and alternative fuels and advanced technologies for transportation. This chapter presents an overview of these technologies.

Renewable Energy Technologies

Renewable energy technologies considered in this report include biomass and biofuels, waste-to-energy, solar power, wind power, geothermal, hydropower, and ocean power.

Biomass

Biomass consists of plant and plant-derived material. Sources of biomass include agricultural residues such as rice hulls, straw, bagasse from sugarcane production, wood chips, and coconut shells and energy crops such as sugarcane or switch grass. Biomass can be used directly for energy production or processed into fuels. Examples of biomass fuels are liquid and gel fuels including oil and alcohol and pelletized biomass for gasification and combustion. Liquid biomass–derived fuels can be used as substitutes for or additives to fossil fuels.

Although the conversion of biomass into energy results in the release of carbon into the atmosphere, biomass-based energy is considered to be carbon neutral because of the carbon sequestered by plants during the growth of the biomass material. For biomass resources to be renewable, their cultivation must be managed carefully to ensure sustainable harvesting and land use. The use of biomass for energy production can result in competition with food crops, either directly, when food crops themselves are used for energy production, or indirectly, when land and water that would be used to grow crops is used instead for energy crops.

Biomass technologies include equipment for industrial processes that produce heat and steam; electrical power generation through combustion, liquefaction, or gasification; and transportation fuels such as ethanol and biodiesel. Biomass is converted into energy through one of two pathways: thermochemical and biochemical. Thermochemical conversion occurs by combustion, gasification, or pyrolysis. Biochemical conversion results from anaerobic digestion or fermentation. The energy products produced from these biomass conversion processes are electricity, heat, and biofuels.

Combustion

Direct combustion is a widely used process where biomass is converted into useful power through exposure to high temperatures. Heat from the process can be used to produce steam, which in turn can drive a turbine to generate electricity. Depending on the combustion process, various pre-treatment steps such as sizing (shredding, crushing, and chipping) and drying are required. The heating value and moisture content of the biomass determine the efficiency of the combustion process. Drying prior to the combustion process (e.g., with waste heat) helps to lower the moisture content and raise the heating value to acceptable levels.

BOX 2.1. BIOMASS ENERGY RESOURCES

Solid Biomass: Wood, vegetal waste (including wood waste and crops), conventional crops (oil and starch crops), charcoal, animal wastes, and other wastes (including the biodegradable fraction of municipal solid wastes) used for energy production.

Liquid Biofuels: Biodiesel and bioethanol (also includes biomethanol, bio-oil, and biodimethylether).

(A) **Biodiesel:** Biodiesel can be used in pure form or may be blended with petroleum diesel at any concentration for use in most modern diesel engines. Biodiesel can be produced from a variety of feedstocks, such as oil feedstock (rapeseed, soybean oils, jatropha, palm oil, hemp, algae, canola, flax, and mustard), animal fats, or waste vegetable oil.

(B) **Bioethanol:** The largest single use of ethanol is as a fuel for transportation or as a fuel additive. It can be produced from a variety of feedstocks such as sugarcane, corn, and sugar beet. It can also be produced from cassava, sweet sorghum, sunflower, potatoes, and hemp or cotton seeds or derived from cellulose waste.

Biogas: Methane and carbon dioxide produced by anaerobic digestion or fermentation of biomass, such as landfill gas and digester gas.

Gasification

In the gasification process, biomass is thermochemically converted into gaseous fuel by means of partial oxidation of the biomass at high temperatures. This process requires less oxygen than combustion. In addition to the gaseous fuel, gasifiers produce heat and ash. To maximize the efficiency of gasification-based systems, beneficial uses should be developed for all three products.

The main processes of a gasification plant are fuel feeding, gasification, and gas clean-up. Fuel feeding prepares and introduces the feedstock into the gasifier. The gasifier converts the feedstock into a fuel gas containing carbon monoxide, hydrogen, and methane. In the gas clean-up process, harmful impurities are removed from the fuel gas to allow for safe usage in gasburning engines or turbines.

Pyrolysis

Pyrolysis is also a thermochemical conversion process that converts biomass into liquid, solid, and gaseous substances by heating the biomass to about 500 degrees Celsius in the absence of air. The pyrolysis process includes feedstock preparation and the application of liquid and char for heat production. Alternative technologies include rapid thermal processing and the vacuum pyrolysis process. The latter involves the thermal decomposition of matter under reduced pressure for conversion into fuels and chemicals. Fast pyrolysis refers to the rapid heating of biomass in the absence of oxygen. Feedstocks for the pyrolysis process include forestry residue (sawdust, chips, and bark) and by-products from the agricultural industry (bagasse, wheat straw, and rice hulls).

Fermentation

Anaerobic digestion is a type of fermentation that biochemically converts organic material, especially animal waste, into biogas that consists mainly of methane and carbon dioxide and is comparable to landfill gas. The biomass is converted by bacteria under anaerobic conditions—without oxygen present. Biogas plants consist of two components: a digester (or fermentation tank) and a gas holder. The digester is a cube- or cylinder-shaped waterproof container with an inlet into which the fermentable mixture is introduced in the form of liquid slurry.

Fermentation of sugars is a biochemical process that entails the production of ethanol (alcohols) from sugar crops (sugarcane, beet) or starch crops (maize, wheat). The biomass is ground and the starch is converted by enzymes and bacteria into sugars. Yeast then converts the sugars into ethanol. Pure ethanol can be obtained by distillation; the remaining solids can be used as cattle feed. In the case of sugarcane, the remaining bagasse can also be used as fuel for boilers or electricity generation processes. These multiple applications allow ethanol plants to be self-sufficient and even to sell surplus electricity to utilities.

Bioethanol is primarily produced by fermentation of sugarcane or sugar beet. A more complex and expensive process involves producing bioethanol from wood or straw using acid hydrolysis and enzyme fermentation. Production of bioethanol from corn is a fermentation process, but the initial processing of the corn requires either wet or dry milling. Residues from corn milling can be used or sold as animal feed. Bioethanol from wheat requires an initial milling and malting (hydrolysis) process.

Biofuels

As defined by the United Nation's, "there are various pathways to convert feedstock and raw materials into biofuels. First-generation biofuel technologies, such as the fermentation of plant sugars or the transesterification of plant oils, are well established. Second-generation biofuel technologies include, among others, acid hydrolysis of wood chips or straw for bioethanol. The technology for extracting oil from oilseeds has essentially remained the same for the last 10 to 15 years."[17] Biodiesel production is a relatively simple process. However, economic small-scale production of biodiesel still requires sufficient feedstock, some equipment, capital, and skills.

While many of the above conversion processes are accomplished on a large scale, new and emerging technologies make it possible to produce electricity, heat, and fuels on a smaller scale and with modular systems. These technologies are being developed for off-grid applications and at an economic scale suitable for developing countries. An example of a modular biopower system [50 kilowatts electric (kWe)] is pictured above.[18]

Where biomass is produced in conjunction with agriculture for food production, it represents an additional value stream. Biofuels are produced in many countries, albeit in varying quantities and at different costs. Liquid biofuels have the potential to provide communities in developing countries with multiple energy services such as electricity for lighting, small appliances, and battery charging; income generation and educational activities; and pumping water, cooking, and transportation.

Waste-to-Energy

Waste-to-energy technology produces energy from waste, such as waste from a city's municipal waste system, farms and other agricultural operations, or commercial and industrial operations. Large-scale waste-to-energy systems can supply heat or electricity in utility-scale electric power plants or district heating systems. Small-scale systems can provide heating or cooking fuel and electricity to individual farms, homes, and businesses.

In incineration systems, waste is converted into useful energy through combustion. Modern incineration plants include materials separation processes to remove hazardous or recyclable materials from the waste stream before it is incinerated. Improvement in combustion processes and emissions controls minimizes the emission of particulate matter, heavy metals, dioxins, sulfur dioxide, and hydrochloric acid associated with waste combustion. Incineration plants emit fewer air pollutants than coal-fired plants but more than gas-fired plants. While Denmark and Sweden are leaders in the use of incineration technologies for energy generation, other European countries and Japan use the technology as a primary waste-handling system.

Landfill gas systems collect landfill gas for use in boilers, process heaters, turbines, and internal combustion engines, thereby reducing direct emissions of methane and other gases into the atmosphere or displacing the use of fossil fuels for power generation. Landfill gas contains varying amounts of methane and other gases, depending on the type of deposited waste and the characteristics of the landfill. Landfill gas can be piped directly to nearby buildings and used in boilers for heat or industrial processes or used in on-site electric generation plants that can supply electricity to the landfill itself, nearby industries, or to the electric power grid. The amount and type of waste in a landfill, its size, extent of landfill operating activity, and proximity to energy users are all factors that affect a landfill gas project's viability. Environmental precautions to minimize the emission of air pollutants are necessary to meet environmental regulations.

Anaerobic digester systems convert animal and human waste into methane and carbon dioxide, which can be used in turbines and internal combustion engines in electric power plants. Municipal waste treatment plants and confined animal feeding operations can be sources of waste for the digesters. Converting the waste into electricity reduces air and water pollution and the costs associated with processing the waste.

Other new and emerging waste-to-energy technologies use thermal and chemical conversion processes to convert solid waste into fuels.

Solar Power

Solar power is energy from the sun. Solar technologies convert light and heat from the sun into useful energy. Photovoltaic (PV) systems convert sunlight into electricity. Thermal systems collect and store solar heat for air and water heating applications. Concentrating solar power systems concentrate solar energy to drive large-scale electric power plants. Solar power systems produce little or no emissions and have a minimal impact on the environment.

Photovoltaics

PV power systems convert light from the sun into electricity. PV cells are devices made of semiconducting materials similar to those used in computer chips. When these devices are connected to an electrical circuit and exposed to light, they release electrons that flow through the circuit, creating an electric current. PV panels, shown above,[19] are devices that contain a varying number of PV cells and convert sunlight into direct current (DC) electricity. PV panels are typically incorporated into systems that combine batteries and electronic control equipment to provide fulltime DC and/or alternating current (AC) power. Typical applications include lighting, electronics, telecommunications, and small-scale water pumping.

Solar Thermal

Solar thermal technology uses flat and concentrating absorbers that collect heat energy from the sun for such processes as crop drying, food processing, water and space heating, industrial process heat, and electricity generation.

Solar water heating systems, such as the ones pictured in China's Yunnan Province,[20] consist of a solar collector and a storage tank. The collector is typically a rectangular box with a transparent cover, through which pipes run, carrying water that is heated by the sun. The pipes are attached to an absorber plate, which is painted black to absorb the heat. As the sun's heat warms the collector, the water is heated and passed to the storage tank, which stores the hot water heated for domestic use. As explained by the National Renewable Energy Laboratories, "Solar water heating systems can be either active or passive. Active systems rely on pumps to move the liquid between the collector and the storage tank, while passive systems rely on gravity and the tendency for water to naturally circulate as it is heated. Simpler versions of this system are used to heat swimming pools."[21]

Solar heating systems to dry food and other crops can improve the quality of the product while reducing waste. Solar driers outclass traditional open-air drying and have lower operating costs than mechanized fuel-based driers. The three types of solar driers are natural convection, forced convection, and tent driers. In natural convection driers, air is drawn through the dryer and heated as it passes through the collector, then partially cooled as it picks up moisture from the product drying. The flow of air is caused by the lighter warm air inside the dryer moving toward the cooler outside air. In forced convection, a fan is used to create the airflow, reducing drying time by a factor of 3 and the area of collector required by up to 50 percent. A photovoltaic panel can be used to generate electricity for the fan. Tent driers combine the drying chamber and collector and allow for a lower initial cost. Drying times are not much lower than for open-air drying, but the main purpose is to provide protection from dust, dirt, rain, wind, and predators; tent driers are usually used for fruit, fish, coffee, or other products for which wastage is otherwise high.

Passive Solar

Passive solar systems integrate solar air heating technologies into a building's design. Buildings are designed with materials that absorb or reflect solar energy to maintain comfortable indoor air temperatures and provide natural daylight. Floors and walls can be designed to absorb and retain heat during warm days and release it during cool evenings. Sunspaces operate like greenhouses and capture solar heat that can be circulated throughout a building. Trombe walls are thick walls that are painted black and made of a material that absorbs heat, which is stored during the day and released at night. Passive solar designs can also cool buildings, using vents, towers, window overhangs, and other approaches to keep buildings cool in warm climates.

Other Solar Technologies

Solar technologies can be used for residential, commercial, and industrial applications. Commercial and industrial applications can include air preheating for commercial ventilation systems, solar process heating, and solar cooling. A solar ventilation system can preheat the air before it enters a conventional furnace, reducing fuel consumption. Solar process heat systems provide large quantities of hot water or space heating for industrial applications. A typical system includes solar collectors that work with a pump, a heat exchanger, and one or more large storage tanks. Heat from a solar collector can also be used for commercial and industrial cooling of buildings, much like an air conditioner but with more complex technology.

Concentrated solar power systems focus sunlight on collectors that serve as a heat source to produce steam that drives a turbine and electricity generator. Concentrating solar power systems include parabolic-trough, dish-engine, and power tower technologies. Parabolic-trough systems concentrate the sun's energy through long rectangular, u-shaped mirrors, which are tilted toward the sun and focus sunlight on a pipe, heating the oil in the pipe and then using it in a conventional steam generator to produce electricity. Dish-engine systems use a mirrored dish similar to a satellite dish, which collects and concentrates the sun's heat onto a receiver, which in turn absorbs the heat and transfers it to fluid within the engine. The heat causes the fluid to expand against a piston or turbine to produce mechanical power, which is then used to run a generator to produce electricity. Power tower systems use a large field of mirrors to concentrate sunlight onto the top of a tower, where molten salt is heated and flows through a receiver. The salt's heat is used to generate electricity through a conventional steam generator. Because molten salt effi ciently retains heat, it can be stored for days before being converted into electricity and ensures power production on cloudy days and after the sun has set.

Wind Power

Wind power technology converts energy in the wind into useful power. Historically, wind power technology was used for mechanical applications such as grain milling and water pumping and is still used for such purposes. Today, the primary market for wind power technology is for wind turbines, which convert wind energy into electricity.

Wind power for electricity generation is the fastest growing segment of the power sector, driven by the low cost of electricity generation, short project development and construction times, and government policiesfavoring clean and renewable energy technologies. The world's approximately 74,000 megawatts (MW) of installed wind capacity meet about 1 percent of the total global electricity demand. In the United States, as of December 2007, total installed wind capacity was approximately 14,000 MW, with an additional 5.7 MW under construction. Wind power accounts for about 20 percent of Denmark's electricity production, 9 percent of Spain's, and 7 percent of Germany's.

According to a recent study,[22] India and China alone are expected to add 36,000 MW of wind power capacity by 2015, representing over 80 percent of the Asian wind market during that period. Market growth in those countries is being driven by the growth of independent power producers (IPP) in India and by electric utilities in China. Major wind turbine manufacturers, including Vestas, GE, Suzlon, Gamesa, and Nordex, are establishing manufacturing facilities in India and China on the basis of strong market growth for their products in those countries. Suzlon, an Indian wind manufacturing company, is also active in the global wind market, including Europe and North America, as both an equipment supplier and project developer.

Large wind power generating plants, often called wind farms, can be integrated into agricultural and other land uses; a wind farm in Hawaii is shown at right.[23] Wind farms typically use tens to hundreds of wind turbines rated between 600 kilowatts (kW) and 5 MW and produce between 50 and hundreds of megawatts of electric power. In some countries, especially Denmark, Germany, and the United Kingdom, interest in offshore projects is increasing. In these projects, turbines are installed in the shallow waters of coastal areas, where they are exposed to the strong prevailing coastal winds and can be located close to large load centers.

Medium-sized turbines, between 10 and 600 kW, are used in distributed energy applications, supplementing or replacing grid power on farms and other commercial or industrial sites. Small wind turbines, in the 100 watt (W) to 10 kW range, are suitable for household, water pumping, or village power applications.

Conventional horizontal-axis wind turbines for electricity generation consist of a rotor, nacelle, tower, and foundation. The rotor consists of wind-spun blades that drive a gearbox and electric generator in the nacelle, which is located at the top of the tower. (Some turbine designs do not include a gearbox.) The tower and foundation support the nacelle and rotor at a height above the ground where winds are strong. Other wind turbine designs include vertical-axis turbines and small turbines designed for urban use.

Geothermal

Geothermal power is generated using thermal energy from underground sources. Different technologies are used to generate electricity using geothermal resources, which include steam, hot water, and heat stored in rock formations. Dry steam power plants use geothermal steam directly to drive a turbine and electric generator. Water condensed from the process is pumped underground and turned back into steam. Flash steam plants generate power by releasing hot water from underground pressurized reservoirs to drive turbines in an electric power plant. Both types of steam power plants release small amounts of gases and steam into the atmosphere.

Binary-cycle plants have no gas emissions and operate by passing hot water from a geothermal source through a heat exchanger, where heat from the water is transferred into a fluid that drives a turbine for electricity generation. Binary-cycle plants are more efficient than dry steam or flash steam systems and are the preferred technology for projects currently in the planning phase.

Geothermal energy was first used for electric power in Italy in the early 18th century. Geothermal resources are found worldwide in areas where geothermal energy is accessible at shallow levels. Areas with usable geothermal resources include the western United States, the southwestern coast of South America, a few areas in Europe and East Africa, and a significant portion of the Asia–Pacific region. New developments in geothermal power technology will use heat from hot, dry rock formations in and beneath the earth's crust.

Hydropower

Hydropower is the conversion of energy embodied in moving water into useful power. People have been harnessing the power of water for thousands of years for irrigation and operation of mechanical equipment and more recently for electricity generation. In fact, hydroelectric power now supplies about 19 percent of the world's electricity. In the United States, hydropower accounts for only 7 percent of the total electricity production, but over 70 percent of the total installed renewable energy capacity. Most industrialized nations have developed their hydropower potential, but undeveloped resources remain in countries such as China, India, Brazil, and regions of Africa and Latin America. In some countries with access to large untapped hydro resources, the resources are located far from electric load centers, posing a problem for transmission of electricity over long distances. Solving this technological problem and providing efficient transmission of electric power from off-grid hydropower plants is a major opportunity for investment and leadership in many countries around the world.

Hydropower plants are a clean, emission-free source of electricity. The natural hydrological cycle replenishes the resource, but also making it vulnerable to droughts. Competition for scarce water resources for agriculture, recreation, and fishing can affect the availability of water for power production. However, the potential for small hydro project development for rural electrification remains high in countries with concentrations of rural populations living near rivers and streams.

Large hydropower plants with capacities in the tens of megawatts are typically impoundment systems and require a dam that stops or reduces a river's flow to store water in a reservoir. Penstocks carry water from the reservoir to water turbines, which in turn drive electric generators. Impoundment systems offer the advantage of controlled power output and other benefits such as water recreation associated with reservoirs, irrigation, and flood control. However, dams negatively impact fish populations by interfering with migration patterns. Water quality both in the reservoir and downstream of the dam can be affected by changes in water flow and dissolved oxygen levels. Large new hydropower projects often require planning to remove communities from areas that will be flooded after a dam is built and other measures to manage environmental impact. Recent research has also raised concern about the possible effect of large reservoirs on atmospheric concentrations of greenhouse.

Small hydropower plants, such as the one shown at right,[24] with capacities ranging from a few kilowatts to several megawatts, are typically diversion systems, which divert some water from a river through a canal or penstock to a turbine. Small hydropower plants can provide electricity for isolated rural populations. These systems range in size from household-sized systems to ones that can supply power to entire villages and commercial or industrial loads. Diversion systems, also called run-of-river systems, do not require dams or reservoirs, are suitable for small hydropower projects, and have less impact on the environment. Small hydropower projects are being aggressively developed as part of rural electrification programs; in some cases innovative financing approaches are used in countries such as India, Sri Lanka, and Nepal.

Pumped storage systems require two reservoirs at different heights. They pump water during periods of low electric demand between the two heights and release water from the upper reservoir during periods of high demand.

Ocean Power Technology

Ocean power technology makes use of energy embodied in the ocean by converting it into electricity. Some systems convert the energy in moving ocean water into electricity, using either the vertical motion of waves or the horizontal motion of ocean currents. Other systems use temperature differences at different levels of the ocean to generate electricity.

Ocean power technology is in the research and development stage, with several commercial prototypes being tested.

Tidal power technology converts the energy in tidal motion caused by the gravitational forces of the sun and moon on ocean water into electricity. Tidal stream systems operate similarly to wind turbines, using tidal turbines to convert energy in ocean currents into a rotational motion to drive turbines and power generators. Like wind turbines, tidal turbines can use horizontal-axis or verticalaxis machines. These systems rely on currents caused by ocean tides moving through and around obstructions such as entrances to bays and other geographical features. Tidal barrage systems are similar to hydropower dams, using differences in height of water on either side of a dam to generate electricity. Barrage systems use a dam-like structure and gates to store and release water as tides cause water levels to rise and fall.

Wave power technology extracts energy from the vertical motion of ocean water caused by waves. Wave power systems can be built offshore, in deep water typically far from coastlines or onshore in shallower water along the coast. Onshore systems show more promise because of their potential proximity to large load centers. Oscillating water column systems use rising and falling water caused by waves to compress and expand an air column in a vertical steel or concrete structure. The oscillating air pressure levels cause a turbine to spin, which drives an electric generator. Tapered channel systems use wave power to fill a raised reservoir with water, which is then allowed to flow through turbines. Pendulor wave systems consist of a rectangular structure with a hinged door that swings with the motion of waves. The swinging door operates a hydraulic pump that drives a turbine.

Ocean thermal energy conversion systems use temperature differences between warm surface water and cool deep water to convert a liquid into gas. The expanding gas drives a steam turbine and electric power generator. Closed-cycle systems circulate warm surface water through a heat exchanger where a fluid with a low boiling point is vaporized. A second heat exchanger condenses the vapor using cool deep water. Open-cycle systems use ocean water itself as the heat transfer fluid, boiling warm surface water in a low-pressure chamber. Water vapor drives a turbine and is condensed back into liquid using cool deep water. Hybrid systems use a combination of open- and closed-cycle arrangements. A by-product of ocean thermal energy systems is cold water, which can be used in building cooling systems, agriculture, and fisheries applications. Open- and hybrid-cycle systems desalinate ocean water in the vaporization process and could also be a source of fresh water. Ocean thermal energy conversion systems work in areas where the difference between the surface of the ocean and deeper water is about 20 degrees Celsius, which is often the case in tropical coastal areas.

As with other renewable energy technologies, ocean power technology projects are capital intensive, but typically have lower operating costs than fuel-based power technologies.

It should be noted that ocean power systems can impact migration patterns in ocean species and cause other environmentally troubling consequences. Systems employing barrages can cause silt buildup that affects tidewater and coastal ecosystems. These consequences can however be mitigated by careful selection of project sites.

Energy Efficiency

The efficiency of an energy conversion process is the ratio of the useful energy produced by the process to the amount of energy that goes into it. Primary energy is fossil fuel, nuclear, hydroelectric, or renewable energy extracted for use in an energy conversion process. Secondary energy is a high-quality form of energy such as electricity or refined fuel that can be used to provide energy services. An energy service is an end use provided by a process or device that requires secondary energy. Useful energy is the energy that goes toward providing an intended energy service. For example, the light produced by a lighting application is useful energy, whereas the heat produced by the application is not. Energy efficiency can be measured at different points in the process of converting a fuel or other energy resource into an end-use energy service. Efficiency points include the following:

- Extraction efficiency is a measure of the amount of primary energy delivered to a power plant or refinery per unit of energy contained by the energy resource in the ground or atmosphere and required by the extraction process.
- Power plant or refinery conversion efficiency is the ratio of the quantity of secondary energy produced by a power plant, refinery, or other conversion facility to the quantity of primary energy required by the process.
- Transmission and distribution effi ciency is the ratio of secondary energy delivered to an end-use facility to the quantity of that energy produced by the power plant or refinery.

- End-use efficiency is a measure of the quantity of useful energy provided by a device or process per unit of energy delivered to the device or process.

Some analyses of energy efficiency also include a measure of the actual need for the energy service. For example, an office building that provides lighting for an unoccupied room or a factory that runs electric machines after the needed process is complete would be less efficient than a building equipped with motion sensors that provide lights only when people are in a room or a factory that shuts down equipment not being used.

Energy efficiency measures involve replacing existing technologies and processes with new ones that provide equivalent or better energy service using less energy. The value of the saved energy typically covers the cost of deploying the new technologies and processes, especially when the increase efficiency occurs downstream in the conversion process. For example, improving the effi ciency of a pumping system in an industrial facility by redesigning the circulation system to minimize friction in pipes will result in the need for a smaller motor to drive pumps, which in turn consumes less energy. The reduced electricity demand will result in reduced losses in the entire chain, from the generation plant through the distribution system.

Energy efficiency results in savings at the time the energy service is provided. Energy service providers can also use load management to change the time that an energy service is delivered in order to reduce peak loads on an energy distribution system. Demand-side management (DSM) uses both load management and energy efficiency to save the amount of primary energy required to deliver the energy service.

Energy savings provide several benefits. For energy consumers, benefits include reduced costs and reduced emissions; for energy service providers, efficiency reduces the need for (and cost of) fuel; and for governments and communities alike, efficiency reduces CO_2 emissions and can help meet targets for global warming pollutants. Energy efficiency programs can reduce future investment requirements, enhance competitiveness by lowering input and operating costs, free up capital for other social and economic development priorities, and contribute to environmental stewardship objectives. It can also contribute to long-term resource planning and management, hedge fuel risks, and reduce operation and maintenance (O&M) costs. Energy efficiency programs promote improvement and investment in energy generation, delivery, end-use equipment, facilities, buildings, and infrastructure that increase useful energy output or services.

Combining energy efficiency and renewable energy policies maximizes the impact of energy policy on emission reductions. Reducing growth of energy demand allows low- or no-emission renewables to keep up with electric demand. Without coordination, new renewable capacity would be outstripped by increased demand, requiring increased fossil fuel capacity to meet the growth. A combined policy also takes advantage of the temporal synergy of the two approaches: Energy efficiency programs can meet shorter-term goals because efficiency measures can be implemented quickly and at relatively low cost. Renewable energy programs can meet longerterm goals, with new capacity coming on line as the efficiency programs achieve their goals.

Demand Side Management (DSM) is the practice of changing energy consumption patterns to reduce the need for new energy generation capacity. DSM can include energy efficiency programs, peak load reduction programs, real-time and time-of-use energy pricing, interruptible load tariffs, direct load control, and shifting demand from peak to off-peak periods.

Building codes provide guidelines for the construction industry to achieve energy-saving goals through improvements in lighting, heating, and cooling. Special programs promote the development of zero-energy buildings, which combine energy efficiency with energy production technologies to maximize the amount of a building's energy that it generates on site.

In the transportation sector, vehicle efficiency standards, public transportation programs, and urban planning minimize the consumption of transportation fuels while maintaining adequate levels of transportation services.

Industrial efficiency measures the decrease in energy use and pollution in the industrial sector. Investment in efficient motor and pumping systems, combined heat and power, and distributed on-site energy generation results in long-term energy savings and can help industries compete while meeting environmental regulations.

Energy efficiency measures require capacity-building efforts to empower institutions and individuals to implement energy-saving programs and make energy-saving decisions. Examples of capacity building include establishing energy audit procedures and auditor training programs, developing systems to track energy consumption patterns and establish benchmarks, establishing energy management systems, creating certification systems for energy practitioners, developing energy management guidelines, and facilitating technology transfer.

Hybrids and Co-Generation

Hybrid and co-generation power systems take advantage of the benefits of multiple technologies in a single, integrated system. Hybrid power systems use combinations of power generating technologies to generate electricity. Co-generation systems, also called combined heat and power (CHP) systems, generate both electricity and useful heat.

Hybrid Power System Technology
Renewable-based hybrid power systems use combinations of wind turbines, photovoltaic panels, and small hydropower generators to generate electricity. Hybrid power systems typically include a diesel or other fuelbased generator and may include batteries or other storage technology. A completely renewable hybrid power system might use a biofuel-based generator in place of a diesel or other fossil fuel generator. Hybrid power system applications are typically small to medium in scale (producing between 100 watt-hours and tens of megawatt-hours per day) and generate electricity for distributed power generation applications, in remote areas for village power, and for communications and military installations around the world.

Hybrid power system designers select technologies on the basis of the renewable resource available at a particular location to take advantage of resource complementarity. For example, a wind–solar hybrid system can make use of both solar and wind power in areas that experience windy periods at night after the sun has set. A solar–hydropower hybrid system would be appropriate at a location that is near a stream or river and has sunny weather during dry periods of the year when stream flow is low. In some cases, the renewable resource may complement varying availability of fossil fuel resources, such as in areas in the Arctic that experience high winds, when transportation of fuels to remote locations is difficult or impossible due to winter conditions.

Renewable penetration is a measure of the relative contribution of renewable and non-renewable resources in a hybrid power system that includes fossil-fuel-based generation. The simplest and therefore lowest-cost designs are low-penetration systems in which the renewable power components produce sufficient power to save up to 20 percent on fossil fuel consumption. Medium- and high-penetration systems can save up to 40 and 70 percent on fuel consumption, respectively, but are more costly to design and complex to operate because they require additional control equipment to ensure the system's stability.

Advanced hybrid power systems use new technologies for power generation, storage, and system control. New technologies for research and experimental hybrid power systems include natural gas turbines, fuel cells, advanced batteries, flywheels, and other technologies.

Examples of Hybrid Power Systems

Over 400 simple wind–solar–battery hybrid systems provide between 500 and 600 W of electric generation capacity for rural households in Inner Mongolia, China. Each system consists of a 300-W wind turbine and 100- to 200-W photovoltaic array that charges deep-cycle lead acid batteries.

Packaged hybrid power systems, such as the one shown at left,[25] produce power for communications applications, disaster relief, and emergency power and can also provide power for rural electrification and agricultural applications. The SunWize product shown here, can meet continuous loads of 100 to 350 W, equivalent to 2.4 to 8.4 kWh/day.

A final example is a wind–hydro–diesel hybrid system in Coyhaique, Chile, which was designed to provide over 15 percent of the regional capital's electricity needs and to displace about 600,000 liters of diesel fuel annually.

Co-generation System Technology

Conventional fossil-fuel-based electric power plants generate heat as a by-product that is emitted into the environment through gas flues, cooling towers, and by other methods. Co-generation power plants collect this heat for use in thermal applications, thereby converting a higher percentage of the energy in the fuel into useful energy. The most efficient conventional power plants have a typical fuel-to-electricity conversion factor of about 50 percent, while co-generation plants can achieve effi ciencies of over 75 percent. Co-generation plants generate more useful power than conventional plants using the same amount of fuel and also produce less pollution per unit of useful energy.

Co-generation plants are most effective when located near a thermal load center. Examples of thermal loads that can be served by a co-generation plant are district heating systems that provide heat for towns and neighborhoods, industrial processes that require heat such as paper mills, institutions such as prisons and hospitals, and wastewater treatment plants.

Co-generation plants either primarily produce electricity and collect exhaust heat from the electricity generation process (topping cycle plant) or primarily generate heat and use excess thermal energy to drive an electricity generating process (bottoming cycle plant). Co-generation plants can be large (greater than about 25 MW) and based on conventional natural gas turbines, combined-cycle natural gas turbines, or steam turbines. Smaller co-generation plants (25 kW to 25 MW) use reciprocating or Stirling engines to run an electric generator and collect the waste heat from the engine's exhaust system for thermal applications. These smaller plants can be fired by biomass or industrial and municipal waste. Very small co-generation plants (1–25 kW) for distributed energy applications use some of the heat from water or space heating systems to generate electricity for a single household or small business.

Clean Transportation Technologies

Alternative fuels for transportation include biodiesel, ethanol, natural gas, and propane. Biofuels produced from agricultural products are considered renewable fuels because they can be grown annually. Biofuels also produce fewer air pollutants when burned in vehicle engines. Advanced transportation technologies include electric vehicles, hybrid electric vehicles, mobile idle reduction systems, and diesel retrofits.

Biodiesel is a fuel derived from biomass that can be burned in diesel engines, including those in light- and heavy-duty diesel vehicles. Biodiesel can be used in all diesel vehicles and produces fewer emissions than fossil fuel diesel. Because biodiesel is produced from biomass, it can be considered a carbon-neutral fuel from a global warming perspective, although carbon emissions from the production and transportation of biodiesel contribute to its carbon footprint. Biodiesel fuel can easily be distributed through the existing fueling infrastructure.

Ethanol can be mixed with gasoline and used in vehicle engines designed to burn gasoline–ethanol mixtures. E85 fuel consisting of 85 percent ethanol and 15 percent gasoline can reduce air pollutant emissions and be used in vehicles with modified engines or with engines designed for use with ethanol fuel mixtures. Existing fueling stations can be modified to distribute ethanol-based fuels.

Compressed and liquefied natural gas (CNG and LNG) can be used in engines designed or modified for use with the fuels. Natural gas engines produce lower emissions than gasoline engines. Wide-scale use of natural gas as a transportation fuel requires adoption of the specialized vehicles by consumers and transportation companies and development of new fueling infrastructure. Propane (LPG) can be used in passenger and light-duty delivery vehicles and in forklifts and mowers. Propane costs vary from 5 to 40 percent less than gasoline and can result in reductions in air pollutants.

Electric vehicles are appropriate for neighborhood use. Using electricity in electric vehicles represents about a 30 percent reduction in fuel costs over conventional fuels. Using electricity from the conventional grid results in a 50 percent reduction in emissions compared to conventional fossil fuel vehicles.

Hybrid electric vehicle technology can be used in passenger and light-duty vehicles and in buses and trucks. Hybrid electric vehicles are more effi cient than fossil-fuel-only vehicles and offer slight air pollution improvements over average fossil fuel vehicles. Plugin hybrids offer an improvement over hybrid electric vehicles by allowing for some of the vehicle's energy to be supplied by the electric power grid and potentially by renewable energy sources. Because electric power tends to be cleaner than power from internal combustion engines, this approach can result in overall reductions in transportation-related pollution.

Fuel efficiency and air emissions for heavy-duty diesel vehicles can be improved with new technologies. Mobile idle reduction systems provide alternative power sources for use when trucks are idle but still require power for heating and cooling. Diesel engine retrofits including exhaust catalysts and filters reduce the emission of air pollutants.

Summary

This section has presented only a brief summary of the clean energy technologies included in this assessment report. There is a considerable wealth of information on these technologies and on the ongoing research and development of other alternative energy technologies from national laboratories such as the National Renewable Energy Laboratory (NREL) of the U.S. Department of Energy, as well as various renewable energy industry associations. Other resources for U.S. firms are included in Appendix A of this document.

APPENDIX A. RESOURCES FOR U.S. FIRMS

The following table provides a compendium of trade and investment resources for U.S. clean technology firms, with a brief description of each resource. Contact information for individual organizations can be found by at each listed Web site. The provision of this list of resources does not constitute endorsement of any organization.

Organization	Web Site	Description
A. U. S. Government		
U.S. Department of Commerce (DOC), International Trade Administration (ITA)	*www.trade.gov*	DOC/ITA participates in the development of U.S. trade policy, identifies and resolves market access and compliance issues, administers U.S. trade laws, and undertakes a range of trade pro-motion and trade advocacy efforts. ITA has more than 2,000 dedicated individuals posted at U.S. embassies and commercial offices around the world, including in China and India. ITA's lead business unit for trade promotion is the U.S. Commercial Service, which supports U.S. businesses through its global network of offices. The Commercial Service promotes the export of American goods and services world-wide and includes special programs for India and China. A resource guide for U.S. exporters to China, including a listing of legal services for China, is available at www. buyusa. gov/china/ en/contactchina.html. The India site is available at www.buyusa.gov/india/en/. The U.S. Commercial Service offers four ways to grow international sales: world-class market research, trade events that promote products and services to qualified buyers, introductions to qualified buyers and distributors, and counseling through every step of the export process. For more information about how our worldwide network can help your company, call 1-800-USA-TRADE or contact our Export Assistance Centers. ITA's other business units include: Market Access and Compliance, which resolves market access issues, identifies and reduces trade barriers, and ensures that foreign countries are in compliance with trade agreements; Manufacturing and Services, which advocates policies to help U.S. companies be competitive at home and around the world and ensures ind-ustry's voice is reflected in policy development; and Import Administration, which administers various trade laws and monitors subsidies. ITA also has various resources to help in this fight including: the China IPR Advisory Program that provides U.S. companies a one-hour free legal consultation

Appendix A. (Continued)

Organization	Web Site	Description
		with a volunteer attorney experienced in IPR matters; IPR toolkits available online at www.stopfakes. gov containing detailed information on local IP laws and resources, as well as helpful local contact information in key foreign markets; free monthly China IPR Webinar series for U.S. industry; a hotline (1-866-999-HALT) answered by IPR experts to help businesses secure and enforce their IP rights; a Trade Fair IPR Initiative to promote protection of IP at domestic and international trade fairs; domestic outreach programs including a U.S. PTO China Roadshow; as well as a free, web-based IPR Module avail-able at www.stopfakes.gov to help SMEs evalu-ate, protect, and enforce their IP both in the United States and overseas.
Export–Import Bank of the United States (Ex-Im Bank)	*www.exim.gov*	Ex-Im Bank is the official export credit agency of the United States. Ex-Im Bank's mission is to assist in financing the export of U.S. goods and services to international markets. Ex-Im Bank enables U.S. companies—large and small—to turn export opportunities into real sales helping to maintain and create U.S. jobs and contribute to a stronger national economy. Ex-Im Bank does not compete with private-sector lenders but provides export financing products that fill gaps in trade financing. Ex-Im Bank assumes credit and country risks that the private sector is unable or unwilling to accept and helps to level the pla-ying field for U.S. exporters by matching the financing that other governments provide to their exporters. Clean energy is a priority for Ex-Im Bank, and the agency offers its most favorable terms for these technologies.
Overseas Private Investment Corporation (OPIC)	*www.opic.gov*	OPIC helps U.S. businesses invest overseas, fosters economic devel-opment in new and emerg-ing markets, complements the private sector in managing risks associated with foreign direct investment, and supports U.S. foreign policy. Because OPIC charges market-based fees for its products, it operates on a self-sustaining basis at no net cost to taxpayers. OPIC has made clean energy investment a priority and offers favorable terms for these technologies.
U.S. Agency for International Development (USAID)	*www.usaid.gov*	USAID is an independent agency that provides economic, development, and humanitarian assistance around the world in support of the foreign policy goals of the United States. Currently,

Appendix A. (Continued)

Organization	Web Site	Description
		USAID is operational in India (but not China). In India, USAID works with local partners to incre-se viability in the power sector, conserve resources, and promote clean technologies and renewable energy. USAID facilitates sharing of energy and environment best practices between the United States and India and among South Asian countries.
US Department of Agriculture (USDA)	*www.usda.gov*	The Foreign Agricultural Service (FAS) of USDA works to improve foreign market access for U.S. products, build new markets, improve the competitive position of U.S. agriculture in the global marketplace, and provide food aid and technical assistance to foreign countries. FAS has the primary responsibility for USDA's inter-national activities—market development, trade agreements and negotiations, and the collection and analysis of statistics and market information. It also administers USDA's export credit guar-antee programs. USDA helps increase income and food availability in developing nations by mobilizing expertise for agriculturally led econo-mic growth. USDA is also active in bioenergy development, domestically and overseas.
U.S. Department of Energy (USDOE)	*www.energy.gov*	USDOE is committed to reducing America's dependence on foreign oil and developing ener-gy efficient technologies for buildings, homes, transportation, power systems, and industry. The Office of Energy Efficiency and Renewable Energy (EERE) seeks to strengthen America's energy security, environmental quality, and eco-nomic vitality in public–private partnerships that enhance energy efficiency and productivity; br-ing clean, reliable, and affordable energy techno-logies to the marketplace; and make a difference in the everyday lives of Americans by enhancing their energy choices and their quality of life. EERE leads the federal government's research, development, and deployment efforts in energy efficiency. EERE's role is to invest in high-risk, high-value research and development (R&D) that is critical to the nation's energy future and would not be sufficiently con-ducted by the private sector acting on its own. Program activi-ties are con-ducted in partnership with the priv-ate sector, state and local governments, USDOE national laboratories, and universities. EERE offers financial assistance for renewable energy and energy efficiency R&D. EERE also works with stake-holders to develop programs and poli-cies to facilitate the deployment of advanced

Appendix A. (Continued)

Organization	Web Site	Description
		clean energy technologies and practices. EERE has bilateral agreements in clean energy with India and China and participates in the Asia–Pacific Partnership on Clean Development and Climate (APP) (see below).
U.S. Department of State (State)	*www.state.gov*	State is the lead U.S. foreign affairs agency, and the Secretary of State is the president's principal foreign policy adviser. The department advances U.S. objectives and interests in shaping a freer, more secure, and more prosperous world through its primary role in developing and implementing the president's foreign policy. The Bureau of Economic, Energy and Business Affairs (EEB) formu-lates and carries out U.S. foreign econoic policy, integrating U.S. economic interests with our foreign policy goals so that U.S. firms and investors can compete on an equal basis with their counter-parts overseas. It implements U.S. economic policy in cooperation with U.S. com-panies, U.S. Government agencies, and other organizations. State also manages U.S. embass-ies overseas and coordinates U.S. activities under the APP (see below).
U.S. Embassy in China	*http://beijing.usem bassy-china. org.cn*	The embassy provides information on travel, doing business in China, an IPR toolkit (http://beijing.usembassy-china.org.cn/ipr.html), and other useful information for U.S. visitors to China. The U.S. Commercial Service has offices throughout China as well.
U.S. Department of Treasury (Treasury)	*www.treasury.gov*	The Office of Foreign Assets Control (OFAC) of Treasury admin-isters and enforces economic and trade sanctions based on U.S. foreign policy and national security goals against targeted fore-ign countries, terrorists, international narcotics traffickers, and those en-gaged in activities rela-ted to the proliferation of weapons of mass destruction. OFAC acts under presidential war-time and national emergency powers, as well as authority granted by specific legislation, to im-pose controls on transactions and freeze foreign assets under U.S. jurisdiction.
U.S. Small Business Administration (SBA)	*www.sba.gov*	SBA's mission is to aid, counsel, assist, and pro-tect the interests of small-business concerns; to preserve free competitive enterprise; and to maintain and strengthen the overall economy of our nation. SBA also helps small businesses to compete in the global marketplace.

Appendix A. (Continued)

Organization	Web Site	Description
U.S. Trade and Development Agency (USTDA)	*www.tda.gov*	USTDA's mission is to advance economic development and U.S. commercial interests in developing and middle-income countries. To this end, the agency funds various forms of technical assistance, investment analysis, training, orientation visits, and business workshops that support the development of a modern infrastructure and a fair and open trading environment. In carrying out its mis-sion, USTDA gives emphasis to economic sectors that may benefit from U.S. exports of goods and services.
U.S. Trade Representative (USTR)	*www.ustr.gov*	USTR is an agency of over 200 people with specialized experience in trade issues and regions of the world. They negotiate directly with foreign governments to create trade agreements, resolve disputes, and participate in global trade policy organizations. They also meet with governments, business groups, legislators, and public interest groups to gather input on trade issues and explain the president's trade policy positions.
StopFakes	*www.stopfakes.gov*	International Trade Administration of the Department of Commerce manages StopFakes, which provides access to information on promoting trade and investment, strengthening the competetiveness of U.S. industry, and ensuring fair trade and compliance with trade laws and agreements.
B. Non–U.S. Government Organizations		
Alliance to Save Energy (ASE)	*www.ase.org/*	Programs in the United States and abroad (including China and India) conduct research, advise policy-makers, and educate decision-makers on energy efficiency issues. The China program educates manufacturers and government officials on efficient windows and other technologies. In India, ASE is working on municipal water delivery.
Amerex Brokers, LLC	*www.amerexenergy .com/*	A division of the GFI Group that operates markets in electrical power, natural gas, emission allowances, and renewable energy credits. Also provides energy procurement services to large commercial and industrial customers.
American Council for an Energy-Efficient Economy (ACEEE)	*www.aceee.org/*	Non-profit organization provides technical and policy assessments, policy support, business, and public interest collaborations. Organizes conferences and provides information dissemination through publications and education.
American Council on Renewable Energy (ACORE)	*www.acore.org/*	ACORE establishes collaborative research and communication among leaders of financial institutions, government, professional service providers, and others in the wind, solar, geothermal,

Appendix A. (Continued)

Organization	Web Site	Description
		bio-mass and biofuels, hydropower tidal and current energy, and waste energy industries. Organizes an annual international ministerial-level workshop on renewable energy in Washington, D.C.
Asia-Pacific Partnership on Clean Development and Climate (APP)	*www.asiapacificpart nership. org*	The APP is a Presidential initiative to accelerate the development and deployment of clean energy security, reduce harmful air pollution, and green-house gas (GHG) emissions intensity in the con-text of sustained economic growth. The United States, Australia, China, India, Japan, the Repub-lic of Korea, and Canada (accounting for over half of the world's GHG emissions, energy con-sumption, GDP, and population) agreed to work together and the private sector to expand invest-ment and trade in cleaner energy technologies. Led by the State Department, the APP is an industry-focused, technology-driven, results-oriented partnership. Through Activities like the Clean Energy Technologies Trade Mission to China and India, the Department of Commerce seeks to position U.S. companies to make commercial sales while removing obstacles that restrict the ability of U.S. companies to do business in partner countries.
Association of Energy Engineers (AEE)	*www.aeecenter.org/*	Non-profit society of energy professionals in 77 countries promotes interest in sustainable deve-lopment. Publishes industry newsletters for faci-lity managers, renewable energy developers, environmental managers, and energy service providers.
China Embassy in United States	*www.china-embassy.org/eng*	Provides information on China and its economy and trade, ministry information, and some policy documents.
Cultural Savvy	*www.culturalsavvy.c om/*	Provides training and consulting services for international business travelers. Includes some on-line information.
E Source	*www.esource.com/*	For-profit company originally operated as a Rocky Mountain Institute project. E Source pro-vides analysis of retail energy markets, services, and technologies to its members, which include electric and gas utilities, large corporate and institutional energy users, government agencies, energy service companies, manufacturers, consultants, and others in over 20 countries.
Evolution Markets	*new.evomarkets. com/*	Provides financial and brokerage services for the global green market and clean energy sector.

Appendix A. (Continued)

Organization	Web Site	Description
Intergovernmental Panel on Climate Change	www.grida.no/climate/ipcc/tectran/index.htm	This site provides an overview of methodological and technological issues in technology transfer, including financing and partnerships, and sectoral analyses.
International Cultural Enterprises, Inc.	www.businessculture.com	Publishes best-practice reports, audio guides, and Web-based reports on country-specific business practices, customs, negotiating tactics, communi-cation, and other issues. Also provides cross-cultural training and consulting services.
National Association of Energy Service Companies (NAESCO)	www.naesco.org/	The energy service industry trade organization advocates for the delivery of cost-effective energy services, provides industry information and data, and helps establish industry standards.
Organization for Economic Co-operation and Development (OECD) Directorate for Financial and Enterprise Affairs	www.oecd.org/	The OECD Investment Committee provides guidelines for mul-tinational enterprises covering business ethics and sustainable development. Also provides investment statistics and analysis and investment codes.
Organization for International Investment	www.ofii.org/	Represents interests of U.S. subsidiaries of companies headquartered abroad. Educates public and policy-makers about positive role U.S. subsidiaries play in U.S. economy and ensures that U.S. subsidiaries are not discriminated against in state or federal law. Provides peer-to-peer forums for U.S. subsidiaries.
Renewable Energy Access	www.renewableenergyaccess. com	Company directory is a searchable list of companies by function. Searching for financial services companies generates a list of clean energy finance companies worldwide.
RenewableEnergyStocks.com	www.renewableenergystocks. com	Provides information on renewable energy investing and links to renewable energy industry information.
The Association of Energy Services Professionals (AESP)	www.aesp.org/	Membership organization of electric and natural gas utilities, public benefits associations, regulatory and non-profit entities, vendors, manufacturers, and consulting firms provides professional development programs and networking opportunities and promotes knowledge transfer.
The Lett Group	www.lettgroup.com/	Trains executives and professionals in business etiquette, manners, and other skills using international protocol.
UNEP Sustainable Energy Finance Initiative	www.sefi.unep.org/	Provides financiers with tools and access to networks to foster investment in sustainable energy projects.
World Energy Efficiency Association (WEEA)	www.weea.org/	Assists developing and reindustrializing countries in assessing information on energy efficiency. Publications include best practices and case

Appendix A. (Continued)

Organization	Web Site	Description
		studies on energy efficiency projects, financing, and ESCOs. Also publishes directories of international energy organizations and companies.
World Trade Organization	*www.wto.org/*	The WTO site provides information on trade goods, rules, and regulations; intellectual property rights, including trade-related aspects of Intellectual Property Rights (TRIPS); accessions, government procurement, and other commerce and trade topics. Information on China and the WTO is available at www.wto.org /english/ thewto_e/countries_e/china_e.html; information on India and the WTO is available at www.wto.org/english/thewto_e/countries_e/ india_e.htm.

APPENDIX B. SUSTAINABLE ENERGY FINANCE DIRECTORY

This directory is synthesized from the on-line resources available at *www.sef-directory.net/*, which is maintained by the Sustainable Energy Finance Initiative (SEFI), a joint initiative of the United Nations Environment Program and the Basel Agency for Sustainable Energy. It has been updated as of late 2007.

Note that financing for clean energy technologies has increased significantly in the last few years. This directory provides information on a number of these sources based on information from SEFI but is not exhaustive.

Debt Capital

TITLE	FINANCE TYPE	SOURCE OF CAPITAL	TECHNOLOGY TYPES	GEOGRAPHIC FOCUS	
Asian Development Bank (ADB)	Debt, equity, fund development, risk mitigation	Member countries	Energy efciency, bioenergy, geother - mal, small hydropower, solar (PV and thermal), wind Other activities: capacity building, institutional development, policy and regulatory activities, project development, and CDM support. ADB has committed $1 billion per year for renewable energy and energy efciency over the next few years. Of special note are its efforts to catalyze local financing institutions and the private sector to participate in the delivery of clean energy services and to include modern energy access.	West Asia, South Asia, South-east Asia, East Asia	6 ADB Avenue. Mandaluyong City 0401 Metro Manila Philippines Tel: +632 632 4444 Fax: +632 636 2444 information@adb.org www.adb.org
DEG German Investment and Development Company	Debt capital	Public	Energy efciency, bioenergy, Small hydropower	West Asia, East Asia, Southeast Asia, North Africa, Central and Eastern Europe, Central and South America, South Asia, Sub-Saharan Africa	CONTACT—China: DEG Representative Ofce Beijing Beijing Sunfower Tower, Suite 1110 No. 37 Maizidian Street Chaoyang District 100026 Beijing People's Republic of China Tel: +86 10 8527 5168 Fax: +86 10 8527 5170 degbj@public3.bta.net.cn, stb@degchina.com www.deginvest.de/EN_Home/index.jsp
E+Co	Debt capital	Multilateral, Bi-lateral, foundations, private sector	Energy efciency, bioenergy, geother - mal, small hydropower, solar (PV and thermal), wind Also provides business planning support and seed capital	West Asia, North Africa, Central and South America, South Asia, Southeast Asia, East Asia, Sub-Saharan Africa	Hongcheng Plaza Building, Suite 1302 Qingnian Road Kunming 650021 Yunnan, China Tel: +86 871 312 0934 Fax: +86 871 310 0897 EandCo.China@EandCo.net www.energyhouse.com
European Investment Bank (EIB)	Debt capital	Capital markets	Energy efciency, bioenergy, geother - mal, small hydropower, solar (PV and thermal), wind	Southeast Asia, East Asia, West Asia, North Africa, Central and Eastern Europe, Central and South America, North America, Oceania, Western Europe, South Asia, Sub-Saharan Africa	100 Boulevard Konrad Adenauer L-2950 LuxembourgLuxembourg Tel: +35 2 43791 Fax:+35 2 437704 info@eib.org www.eib.org

Organization					Contact
International Finance Corporation	Debt, equity, fund development, risk mitigation	IFC funds, GEF, other	Energy efficiency, bioenergy, geothermal, small hydropower, solar (PV and thermal), wind, among others	Southeast Asia, East Asia, West Asia, North Africa, Central and Eastern Europe, Central and South America, North America, Oceania, Western Europe, South Asia, Sub-Saharan Africa	**CONTACT—China** Michael Ipson, Country Manager 15th Floor, China World Tower 2 China World Trade Center No. 1 Jian Guo Men Wai Avenue Beijing, China 100004 Tel: +86 10 5860 3000 Fax: +86 10 5860 3100 mipson@ifc.org www.ifc.org/ifcext/eastasia.nsf/Content/China Mario Fischel, General Manager Private Enterprise Partnership for China R. 2716, 27th Floor CCB Sichuan Building No. 88, Tidu Street Chengdu, Sichuan Province P. R. China, 610016 Tel: +86 28 8676 6622 Fax: N/A mfischel@ifc.org www.ifc.org/ifcext/eastasia.nsf/Content/China Guwahati–781 005, Assam Tel: +91 361 2463 133 36 Fax: +91 361 2463 152 SouthAsia@ifc.org www.ifc.org/india	**CONTACT—India** New Delhi Paolo Martelli, Director, South Asia or Anil Sinha, General Manager, SEDF 50-M, Shanti Path, Gate No. 3 Niti Marg, Chanakyapuri New Delhi–110 021 Tel: +91 11 4111 1000 Fax: +91 11 4111 1001-02SouthAsia@ifc.org www.ifc.org/ifcext/southasia.nsf/Content/India_overview Mumbai Sujay Bose, Senior Manager Godrej Bhavan, 3rd Floor Murzban Road, Fort Mumbai–400 001, Maharashtra Tel: +91 22 6665 2000 Fax: +91 22 6665 2001 SouthAsia@ifc.org www.ifc.org/ifcext/southasia.nsf/Content/India_overview Chennai Prasad Gopalan, Principal Investment Officer Girguja Enclave, No. 56 2nd Floor, 1st Avenue Shanti Nagar, Adyar Chennai–600 020, Tamil Nadu Tel: +91 44 2446 2570 Fax: +91 44 2446 2571 SouthAsia@ifc.org www.ifc.org/ifcext/India Guwahati Sushanta Kumar Pal, Business Development Officer First Floor, Orion Place Next to Mizoram House Christian Basti, G S Road
Triodos Renewable Energy for Development Fund	Debt capital	Bilaterals, multilaterals, foundations, private sector	Bioenergy, geothermal, small hydropower, solar (PV and thermal), wind	South Asia, Southeast Asia, East Asia, West Asia, North Africa, Sub-Saharan Africa	Utrechtseweg 60, P.O. Box 55 3700 AB Zeist The Netherlands Tel: +31 30 693 6500 Fax: +31 30 693 6566 tref@triodos.com www.triodos.com Team members Bob Assenberg Tel: +31 30 693 65 60 bob.assenberg@triodos.nl	Gerrit-Jan Brunink Tel: +31 30 693 65 78 gerrit-jan.brunink@triodos.nl Helena Korhonen Tel: +31 30 693 65 41 helena.korhonen@triodos.nl Martijn Woudstra Tel: +31 30 694 26 91 martijn.woudstra@triodos.nl

TITLE	FINANCE TYPE	SOURCE OF CAPITAL	TECHNOLOGY TYPES	GEOGRAPHIC FOCUS	CONTACT
Verde Ventures, Conservation International	Debt capital		Energy efficiency	Southeast Asia, Central and South America, Oceania, Sub-Saharan Africa	2011 Crystal Drive, Suite 500 Arlington, Virginia 22201 USA Tel: +1 703 341 2400, +1 800 406 2306 Fax: +1 703 553 0721 verdeventures@conservation.org www.conservation.org/sp/verdeventures/
World Bank	Loans, guarantees, analytic and advisory services to developing countries	Member countries	Energy efficiency, bioenergy, geothermal, small hydropower, solar (PV and thermal), wind	West Asia, South Asia, South-east Asia, East Asia	CONTACT—India Hema Balasubramanian hbalasubramanian@worldbank.org Sunita Malhotra smalhotra@worldbank.org Tel: +91 11 24617241 / CONTACT—Washington, D.C. Junhui Wu 1818 H Street, N.W. Washington, D.C. 20433 USA Tel: +1 202 458 1405 Fax: +1 202 522 1648 jwu@worldbank.org

Private Equities

TITLE	FINANCE TYPE	SOURCE OF CAPITAL	TECHNOLOGY TYPES	GEOGRAPHIC FOCUS	CONTACT
Actis Energy Fund	Private equities		Energy efficiency, cleaner fuels, bioenergy, geothermal, small hydropower, solar (PV and thermal), wind, fuel cells	South Asia, Southeast Asia, East Asia, West Asia, North Africa, Central and South America, Sub-Saharan Africa	CONTACT—China Benjamin Cheng, Investment Principle 712 China World Tower 2 No. 1 Jianguomenwai Street Chaoyang District Beijing 100004 People's Republic of China Tel: +86 10 6505 6655 Fax: N/A bcheng@act.is www.act.is CONTACT—India Bangalore Subba Rao Telidevara, Partner 15 Rest House Crescent Bangalore–560001 India Tel: +91 80 2555 0651 Fax: +91 80 2555 0592 stelidevara@act.is www.act.is Delhi Steven Enderby, Partner NBCC Place, 1st Floor, East Tower Bhisham Pitamah Marg Pragati Vihar New Delhi–110003 India Tel: +91 11 4366 7000 Fax: +91 11 4366 7070 senderby@act.is www.act.is Mumbai JM Trivedi, Partner 704, 7 Floor Dalamal House Jamnala Bajaj Road Nariman Point Mumbai–400021 India Tel: +91 22 2281 6430 Fax: +91 22 2282 0737 jtrivedi@act.is www.act.is
Al Tayyar Energy	Private equities		Bioenergy, small hydropower, solar (PV and thermal), wind	South Asia, Southeast Asia, East Asia, West Asia, North Africa, Central and Eastern Europe, Sub-Saharan Africa	Granville (Pete) Smith P.O. Box 757 Abu Dhabi United Arab Emirates Tel: +971-2-681-4004 Fax: +971 2 681 4005 petes@altayyarenergy.com www.altayyarenergy.com
Battery Ventures	Private equities	Limited partners	Energy efficiency, cleaner fuels, solar (PV and thermal), wind, fuel cells	South Asia, Southeast Asia, West Asia, North America, Western Europe	Ramneek Gupta rgupta@battery.com Mark Sherman mark@battery.com

Name	Type	Technologies	Investor type	Geographic regions	Contact	Additional contact
CDC Group PLC	Private equities	Energy efficiency, bioenergy, geothermal, small hydropower, solar (PV and thermal), Wind	Private	South Asia, Southeast Asia, East Asia, West Asia, North Africa, Central and South America, Sub-Saharan Africa	6 Duke Street, St. James's, London SW1Y 6BN, United Kingdom, Tel: +44 0 20 7484 7700, Fax: +44 0 20 7484 7750, enquiries@cdcgroup.com, www.cdcgroup.com	930 Winter Street, Suite 2500, Waltham, Massachusetts 02341, USA, Tel: +1 781 478 6600, Fax: +1 781 478 6601, www.battery.com
E+Co	Debt capital	Energy efficiency, bioenergy, geothermal, small hydropower, solar (PV and thermal), wind	Multilateral, bilateral, foundations, private sector	South Asia, Southeast Asia, East Asia, West Asia, North Africa, Central and South America, Sub-Saharan Africa	CONTACT—China, Wu Jing, Investment Officer, Laura Colbert, Communications Officer, Zhu Xiaonan, Office Manager, Hongcheng Plaza Building, Suite 1302, Qingmian Road, Kunming 650021 Yunnan, China, Tel: +86 871 312 0934, Fax: +86 871 310 0897, EandCo.China@EandCo.net, www.energyhouse.com	CONTACT—Main Office, Christine Eibs Singer, 383 Franklin Street, Bloomfield, New Jersey, USA, Tel: +1 973 680 9100, Fax: +1 973 680 8066, christine@energyhouse.com, www.energyhouse.com
EnviroTech Financial, Inc.	Private equities	Energy efficiency, bioenergy, geothermal, small hydropower, solar (PV and thermal), wind, fuel cells		South Asia, Southeast Asia, East Asia, West Asia, North Africa, Central and Eastern Europe, Central and South America, North America, Oceania, Western Europe, Sub-Saharan Africa	Gene Beck, President, EnviroTech Financial, Inc., 333 City Boulevard West, 17th Floor, Orange, California 92868-5905, USA, Tel: +1 714 532 2731, Fax: +1 714 459 7492, gbeck@etffinancial.com, www.etffinancial.com	
Global Environment Fund	Private equities	Bioenergy, geothermal, small hydropower, solar (PV and thermal), wind		South Asia, Southeast Asia, East Asia, West Asia, North Africa, Central and Eastern Europe, Central and South America, North America, Sub-Saharan Africa	1225 Eye Street N.W., Suite 900, Washington, D.C. 20005, USA, Tel: +1 (02) 789 4500, Fax: +1 202 789 4508, info@globalenvironmentfund.com, www.globalenvironmentfund.com	
Good Energies Inc.	Private equities	Solar (PV and thermal), wind	Private	South Asia, Southeast Asia, East Asia, West Asia, North Africa, Central and South America, Central and Eastern Europe, North America, Oceania, Western Europe, Sub-Saharan Africa	Michael Ware, 1250 24th Street, N.W., Suite 300, Washington, D.C. 20037, USA, Tel: +1 202 466 0582, Fax: +1 202 466 0564, www.goodenergies.com	
Jane Capital Partners LLC	Private equities	Energy efficiency, cleaner fuels, bioenergy, geothermal, small hydropower, solar (PV and thermal), wind, fuel cells		South Asia, Southeast Asia, East Asia, North America, Oceania	Neal Dikeman, 505 Montgomery, 2nd Floor, San Francisco, California 94111, USA, Tel: +1 415 277 0180, Fax: +1 415 277 8173, dikeman@jmsecapital.com, www.janecapital.com	
New Energies Invest AG (Bank Sarasin + Cie)	Private equities	Energy efficiency, bioenergy, small hydropower, solar (PV and thermal), wind, fuel cells	Rights offering	South Asia, Southeast Asia, East Asia, West Asia, North Africa, Central and Eastern Europe, Central and South America, North America, Oceania, Western Europe, Sub-Saharan Africa	Andreas Knörzer, Elisabethenstrasse 62, CH-4002 Basel, Switzerland, Tel: +41 0 61 277 7477, andreas.knoerzer@sarasin.ch, www.newenergies.ch/index_en.html	

Fund		Investor type	Technology	Region	Contact
OCM/GFI Power Opportunities Fund	Private equities	Corporate pension funds, insurance companies, foundation endowments, etc.	Energy efficiency	South Asia, Southeast Asia, East Asia, West Asia, North Africa, Central and Eastern Europe, Central and South America, North America, Oceania, Western Europe, Sub-Saharan Africa	11611 San Vicente Boulevard, Suite 710 Los Angeles, California 90049 USA Tel: +1 310 442 0542 Fax: +1 310 442 0540 info@gfienergy.com www.gfienergy.com
Private Energy Market Fund LP (PEMF)	Private equities	Private	Bioenergy, wind	South Asia, Southeast Asia, East Asia, West Asia, Central and Eastern Europe, Western Europe.	Gustaf Godenhielm (Tekniikantie 4 D) P.O. Box 92 02151 Espoo Finland Tel: +358 9 469 1208 Fax: +358 9 469 1207 gustaf.godenhielm@pemfund.com www.pemfund.com
Robeco Milieu Technologies	Private equities	Private	Energy efciency, bioenergy, geother-mal, small hydropower, solar (PV and thermal), wind	South Asia, Southeast Asia, East Asia, West Asia, North Africa, Central and Eastern Europe, Central and South America, North America, Oceania, Western Europe, Sub-Saharan Africa	Postbus 973 3000 AZ Rotterdam The Netherlands Tel: +31 10 224 12 24 Fax: +31 10 411 52 88 info@robeco.nl www.robeco.nl
Sigma Capital	Private equities		Energy efciency, bioenergy, small hydro-power, solar (PV and thermal), wind	Southeast Asia, Central and Eastern Europe, Central and South America, North America, Oceania, Western Europe	Bruce Woodry, Chairman and CEO P.O. Box 1002 Harbor Springs, Michigan 49740 USA Tel: +1 231 526 9585 Fax: N/A woodry@sigmacapital.net www.sigmacapital.net/
Triodos International Fund Management BV	Private equities	Institutional and private investors	Bioenergy, geothermal, small hydropower, solar (PV and thermal), wind, fuel cells	South Asia, Southeast Asia, East Asia, West Asia, North Africa, Central and South America, Western Europe, Sub-Saharan Africa	Utrechtseweg 60, P.O. Box 55 3700 AB Zeist The Netherlands Tel: +31 30 693 6500 Fax: +31 30 693 6566 tredf@triodos.nl www.triodos.nl Team members Bob Assenberg Tel: +31 30 693 65 60 bob.assenberg@triodos.nl Gerrit-Jan Brunink Tel: +31 30 693 65 78 gerrit-jan.brunink@triodos.nl Helena Korhonen Tel: +31 30 693 65 41 helena.korhonen@triodos.nl Martijn Woudstra Tel: +31 30 694 26 91 martijn.woudstra@triodos.nl

TITLE	FINANCE TYPE	SOURCE OF CAPITAL	TECHNOLOGY TYPES	GEOGRAPHIC FOCUS	CONTACT
UBS (Lux) Equity Fund Future Energy	Private equities		Energy efficiency, bioenergy, geothermal, small hydropower, solar (PV and thermal), wind	South Asia, Southeast Asia, East Asia, West Asia, North Africa, Central and Eastern Europe, Central and South America, North America, Oceania, Western Europe, Sub-Saharan Africa	CONTACT—Beijing 1609 China World Tower 1 Jian Guo Men Wai Avenue Beijing 100004 People's Republic of China Tel: +86 10-6505 22 13, +86 10-6505 22 14, +86 10-6505 22 15 Fax: +86 10-6505 11 79 CONTACT—Shanghai Room 3407 Citic Square No. 1168 Nanjing Xi Lu Shanghai 200041 People's Republic of China Tel: +86 21 5292 55 55 Fax: +86 21 5292 55 52 CONTACT—India 2/F, Hoechst House Nariman Point Mumbai-400 021 India Tel: +91 22 281 4649, +91 22 281 4676 Fax: +91 22 230 9000, +91-22-281 4673 CONTACT—Main Office Gerhard Wagner, Socially Responsible Investments Analyst Gessnerallee 3 8098 Zurich Switzerland Tel: +41 1 235 55 52 Fax: +411 235 55 30 gerhard.wagner@ubs.com www.ubs.com/swedenfunds.com
Warburg Pincus Investment Consulting Company Ltd.	Private equities	Private	Energy efficiency, bioenergy, geothermal, small hydropower, solar (PV and thermal), wind	South Asia, Southeast Asia, East Asia, West Asia, North Africa, Central and Eastern Europe, Central and South America, North America, Oceania, Western Europe, Sub-Saharan Africa	CONTACT—Beijing Beijing Representative Office 9th Floor, China World Tower 1 1 Jianguomenwai Avenue Beijing 100004 China Tel: +86 10 5923 2533 Fax: +86 10 6505 6683 www.warburgpincus.com CONTACT—Shanghai Shanghai Representative Office Unit 2201; Bund Center Office Tower No. 222 Yanan Road (East) Shanghai, 200002 China Tel: +86 21 6335 0308 Fax: +86 21 6335 0802 www.warburgpincus.com CONTACT—India Mumbai Office 7th Floor, Express Towers Nariman Point Mumbai-400 021 India Tel: +91 22 6650 0000 Fax: +91 22 6650 0001 www.warburgpincus.com CONTACT—Main Office Almack House 28 King Street, St. James's London SW1Y 6QW United Kingdom Tel: +44 207 360 0306 Fax: +44 207 321 0881 www.warburgpincus.com

Public Equities

TITLE	FINANCE TYPE	SOURCE OF CAPITAL	TECHNOLOGY TYPES	GEOGRAPHIC FOCUS	CONTACT
New Alternatives Fund	Public equities	This is an open and mutual fund that seeks shareholders.	Energy efficiency, bioenergy, geothermal, small hydropower, solar (PV and thermal), wind	South Asia, Southeast Asia, East Asia, West Asia, North Africa, Central and Eastern Europe, Central and South America, North America, Oceania, Western Europe, Sub-Saharan Africa	150 Broadhollow Road, Suite 360 Melville, New York 11747 USA Tel: +1 800 423 8383 Fax: N/A info@newalternativesfund.com www.newalternativesfund.com

TITLE	FINANCE TYPE	SOURCE OF CAPITAL	TECHNOLOGY TYPES	GEOGRAPHIC FOCUS	CONTACT
New Energy Fund LP	Public equities	High-net-worth individuals, family offices, foundations, and institutions	Energy efficiency, cleaner fuels, bioenergy, geothermal, small hydropower, solar (PV and thermal), wind, fuel cells	South Asia, Southeast Asia, East Asia, West Asia, North Africa, Central and Eastern Europe, Central and South America, North America, Oceania, Western Europe, Sub-Saharan Africa (This is a global fund, since it is a global phenomenon)	527 Madison Avenue, 6th Floor New York, New York 10022 USA Tel: +1 212 419 3918 Fax: +1 212 419 3971 www.newenergyfundlp.com

Carbon Finance

TITLE	FINANCE TYPE	SOURCE OF CAPITAL	TECHNOLOGY TYPES	GEOGRAPHIC FOCUS	CONTACT
Carboncredits.nl	Carbon finance		Energy efficiency, cleaner fuels, bioenergy, geothermal, small hydropower, solar (PV and thermal), wind, fuel cells	South Asia, Southeast Asia, East Asia, West Asia, North Africa, Central and Eastern Europe, Central and South America, Oceania, Western Europe, Sub-Saharan Africa	Carboncredits.nl Juliana van Stolberglaan 3 The Hague The Netherlands Tel: +31 70 3735 495 Fax: +31 70 3735 000 carboncredits@senternovem.nl www.carboncredits.nl
Climate Change Capital	Carbon finance, equity, venture capital	Public, private	Energy efficiency, renewable energy	Global, active in China and India	CONTACT —London 3 More London Riverside London SE1 2AQ London United Kingdom Tel: +44 0 20 7939 5000 Fax: +44 0 20 7939 5030 / CONTACT—China Climate Change Capital 9/F China Life Tower 16 Chao Wai Da Jie Beijing 100020 Tel: +86 10 85253797 Fax:+86 10 85253197
CO2e	Other	Finance through sale of emissions credits	Energy efficiency, cleaner fuels, bioenergy, geothermal, small hydropower, solar (PV and thermal), wind	West Asia, North Africa, Central and Eastern Europe, Central and South America, North America, Oceania, Western Europe, South Asia, Southeast Asia, East Asia, Sub-Saharan Africa	CONTACT—India CanterCO2e India Private Limited 10th Floor, Raheja Chambers Free Press Journal Marg Nariman Point Mumbai–400 021 India Tel: +91 986 753 1203 Fax: N/A mumbai@cantorco2e.com www.co2e.com / CONTACT—International Office 181 University Avenue, Suite 1500 Toronto, Ontario Canada M5H 3M7 Tel: +1 416 350 2177 Fax: +1 416 350 2985 cdm@cantorco2e.com www.co2e.com

Name	Type	Structure	Focus areas	Regions	Contact
EcoSecurities	Carbon finance	Public, private	Renewable energy, waste management, industrial efficiency.	Global, including China and India	CONTACT—China Unit 708, China Resources Building 8 Jianguomen Bei Avenue Beijing, 100005 Tel: +86 10 6518 1081 Fax: +86 10 6518 1085 china@ecosecurities.com CONTACT—International Office 181 University Avenue, Suite 1500 Toronto, Ontario Canada M5H 3M7 Tel: +1 416 350 2177 Fax: +1 416 350 2985 cdm@cantorco2e.com www.co2e.com
European Carbon Fund	Carbon finance		Energy efficiency, cleaner fuels, geothermal, solar (PV and thermal), wind	South Asia, Southeast Asia, East Asia, West Asia, North Africa, Central and Eastern Europe, Central and South America, North America, Oceania, Western Europe, Sub-Saharan Africa	CONTACT—China Li Chao Beijing Tel: +86 (0)6 655 5735 CONTACT—Asia (w/o China) Anne Dargelos Tel: +33 01 58 55 66 28 CONTACT—Main Office Laurent Segalen Tel: +44 0 207 648 0118 Fax: +33 0 15 855 2965 www.europeancarbonfund.com/
IFC-Netherlands Carbon (CDM) Facility (INCaF)	Carbon finance		Energy efficiency, cleaner fuels, bioenergy, geothermal, small hydropower, wind	South Asia, Southeast Asia, East Asia, West Asia, North Africa, Central and South America, Oceania, Sub-Saharan Africa	2121 Pennsylvania Avenue, N.W. Washington, D.C. 20433 USA Tel: +1 202 473 4194 Fax: +1 202 974 4348 carbonfinance@ifc.org www.ifc.org/carbonfinance
Japan Carbon Finance, Ltd. (JCF)	Carbon finance	Major Japanese private enterprises and policy-lending institutions	Energy efficiency, cleaner fuels, bioenergy, geothermal, small hydropower, solar (PV and thermal), wind, fuel cells	South Asia, Southeast Asia, East Asia, West Asia, North Africa, Central and Eastern Europe, Central and South America, Oceania, Western Europe, Sub-Saharan Africa	1-3, Kudankita 4-chome Chiyoda-ku Tokyo 102-0073 Japan Tel: +81 3 5212 8870 Fax: +81 3 5212 8886 jcf@jcarbon.co.jp www.jcarbon.co.jp/
KfW Carbon Fund	Carbon finance		Energy efficiency, bioenergy, geothermal, small hydropower, solar (PV and thermal), wind, fuel cells	South Asia, Southeast Asia, East Asia, West Asia, North Africa, Central and Eastern Europe, Central and South America, North America, Oceania, Western Europe, Sub-Saharan Africa	Palmengartenstrasse 5-9 60325 Frankfurt Germany Tel: +49 69 7431 4218 Fax: +49 69 7431 4775 carbonfund@kfw.de www.kfw-foerderbank.de
Natsource	Carbon finance	Public, private	Energy efficiency, renewable energy	Global, including China and India	Natsource LLC 100 William Street, Suite 2005 New York, New York 10038 Tel: +1 212 232 5305 Fax: +1 212 232 5353
Prototype Carbon Fund (PCF)	Carbon finance	Trust Fund administered by the World Bank	Energy efficiency, bioenergy, geothermal, small hydropower, solar (PV and thermal), wind	South Asia, Southeast Asia, East Asia, West Asia, North Africa, Central and Eastern Europe, Central and South America, Oceania, Western Europe, Sub-Saharan Africa	1818 H Street, N.W. Washington, D.C. 20433 USA helpdesk@carbonfinance.org prototypecarbonfund.org

TITLE	FINANCE TYPE	SOURCE OF CAPITAL	TECHNOLOGY TYPES	GEOGRAPHIC FOCUS	CONTACT
Swedish International Climate Investment Program (SICLIP)	Carbon finance		Energy efficiency, bioenergy, wind	South Asia, Southeast Asia, Central and East Asia, West Asia, Central and Eastern Europe, Central and South America, Sub-Saharan Africa	Kungsgatan 43 Box 310, SE-631 04 Eskilstuna Sweden Tel: +46 16 544 2241, +46 16 544 2043 Fax: +46 16 544 2090 angela.kallhauge@stem.se, gudrun.knutsson@ energimyndigheten.se www.energimyndigheten.se
Svensk Exportkredit (SEK)– Sweden	Export credits		Bioenergy, geothermal, small hydropower, solar (PV and thermal), wind	West Asia, North Africa, Central and Eastern Europe, Central and South America, North America, Oceania, Western Europe, South Asia, Southeast Asia, East Asia, Sub-Saharan Africa	P.O. Box 16368, SE-103 27 Stockholm Sweden Tel: +45 8 61 38 300 Fax: +46 8 20 38 94 info@sek.se www.sek.se/
World Bank Carbon Finance	Carbon finance	Public, private	Energy efficiency, renewable energy	Global, including China, India	The World Bank Carbon Finance Unit 1818 H Street, N.W. Washington, D.C. Tel: +1 202 473 1000 www.carbonfinance.org

Insurance

TITLE	FINANCE TYPE	SOURCE OF CAPITAL	TECHNOLOGY TYPES	GEOGRAPHIC FOCUS	CONTACT
Aon Global Risk Consultants Ltd.	Insurance			South Asia, Southeast Asia, East Asia, West Asia, North Africa, Central and Eastern Europe, North America, Oceania, Western Europe, Sub-Saharan Africa	CONTACT—China Richard Dong Aon Corporation Beijing Representative Office Room 1206 Capital Tower Beijing 6 Jia Jian Guo Men Wai Avenue Chaoyang District Beijing 100022 The People's Republic of China Tel: +86 10 6563 0671 Fax: +86 10 6563 0672 richard_dong@aon-cofco.com.cn www.aon.com/as/en/china CONTACT—India Prabodh Thakker, Chairman 302 Dalamal House Jamnalal Bajaj Marg Nariman Point Mumbai-400 021 India Tel: +91 22 6656 0505 Fax:+91 22 6656 0506 prabodh_thakker@aon-asia.com www.aon.com/as/en/india CONTACT—Main Office Aon Limited, 8 Devonshire Square London EC3M 4PL United Kingdom Tel: +44 0 20 7623 5500 Fax: +44 0 20 7621 1511 www.aon.co.uk
Miller Insurance Group	Insurance		Wind	South Asia, Southeast Asia, East Asia, West Asia, North Africa, Central and Eastern Europe, North America, Oceania, Western Europe, Sub-Saharan Africa	Susanna Lam, Director Miller Insurance Services (Hong Kong) Ltd. Tel: +852 2525 6982 susanna.lam@miller-insurance.com www.miller-insurance.com/China-Energy David Horne, Director Energy Tel: +44 0 20 7031 2582 david.horne@miller-insurance.com www.miller-insurance.com/China-Energy CONTACT—Main Office Dawron House 5 Jewry Street London EC3N 2PJ United Kingdom Tel: +44 0 20 7488 2345 Fax: N/A info@miller-insurance.com www.aon.co.uk

	FINANCE TYPE	SOURCE OF CAPITAL	TECHNOLOGY TYPES	GEOGRAPHIC FOCUS	CONTACT
Multilateral Investment Guarantee Agency (MIGA)	Insurance		Energy efficiency, bioenergy, geothermal, small hydropower, solar (PV and thermal), wind	South Asia, Southeast Asia, East Asia, West Asia, North Africa, Central and Eastern Europe, Central and South America, North America, Oceania, Western Europe, Sub-Saharan Africa	1818 H Street N.W. Washington, D.C. 20433 USA Tel: +1 202 473 1000 Fax: +1 202 522 0316 migainquiry@worldbank.org www.miga.org
Swiss Re	Insurance		Energy efficiency, bioenergy, geothermal, small hydropower, solar (PV and thermal), wind	South Asia, Southeast Asia, East Asia, West Asia, North Africa, Central and Eastern Europe, Central and South America, North America, Oceania, Western Europe, Sub-Saharan Africa	CONTACT—China Eric Gao, Branch Manager Beijing Branch 23rd Floor, East Tower, Twin Towers No. 812, Jian Guo Men Wai Avenue Chao Yang District Beijing 100022 China Tel: +86 10 6563 8888 Fax: +86 10 6563 8800 Eric_gao@swisre.com www.swisre.com CONTACT—India Dhananjay Date, Managing Director 9th Floor, Essar House 11 K Khadye Marg Mahalaxmi Mumbai-400 034 India Tel: +91 22 6661 2121 Fax: +91 22 6661 2122 Dhananjay_date@swisre.com www.swisre.com CONTACT—Asia-Pacific Headquarters Darryl Pidcock Hong Kong Branch 61/F Central Plaza 18 Harbour Road G.P.O. Box 2221 Wanchai, HK Hong Kong Tel: +852 2827 4345 Fax: +852 2827 6033 Darryl_Pidcock@swisre.com www.swisre.com

Other

TITLE	FINANCE TYPE	SOURCE OF CAPITAL	TECHNOLOGY TYPES	GEOGRAPHIC FOCUS	CONTACT
Capital Equity Partners	Financial engineering and investment banking	Debt capital, private equities, public equities, funds of funds, carbon finance, export credits, insurance, private placements	Energy efficiency, cleaner fuels, bioenergy, geothermal, small hydropower, solar (PV and thermal), wind, fuel cells	West Asia, North Africa, Central and Eastern Europe, Central and South America, North America, Oceania, Western Europe, South Asia, Southeast Asia, East Asia, Sub-Saharan Africa	410 Park Avenue New York, New York 10022 USA Tel: +1 928 436 4212 Fax: +1 270 447 3738 contact@capitalequitypartners.com www.capitalequitypartners.com Aiken Capital Partners +1 212 751 5007 Same address

Organization	Type	Focus	Regions	Contact
The Global Environment Facility (GEF)	Grants to developing countries	Member governments	Energy efficiency, bioenergy, geothermal, small hydropower, solar (PV and thermal), wind	Southeast Asia, East Asia, West Asia, North Africa, Central and Eastern Europe, Central and South America, North America, Oceania, Western Europe, South Asia, Sub-Saharan Africa	CONTACT—China Guangyao Zhu, Director General (Political Focal Point) International Department Ministry of Finance Beijing 100820 People's Republic of China Tel: +86 10 6855 3101 Fax: +86 10 6855 1125 www.gefweb.org Jinkang Wu, Director (Operational Focal Point) Ministry of Finance International Financial Institution Division IV Department of International Affairs Beijing 100820 People's Republic of China Tel: +86 10 6855 3101 Fax: +86 10 6855 1125 jk.wu@mof.gov.cn www.gefweb.org Sudhir Mital, Joint Secretary (Operational Focal Point) Ministry of Environment and Forests Room 414, Paryavaran Bhawan CGO Complex, Lodhi Road New Delhi–110 003 India Tel: +91 11 243 6 3956 Fax: +91 11 24 6 9192 Mital_sudhir@nic.in www.gefweb.org CONTACT—Main Office 1818 H Street, N.W., MSN G6-602 Washington, D.C. 20433 USA Tel: +1 202.473.0508 Fax: +1 202.522.3240, 3245 secretariat@thegef.org www.gefweb.org
Japan Bank for International Cooperation (JBIC)	Other	Japanese government		South Asia, Southeast Asia, East Asia	CONTACT—China 3131 31st Floor China World Trade Center, No. 1 Jian Guo Men Wai Avenue Beijing 100004 People's Republic of China Tel: +86 10 6505 8989, 3825, 3826, 3827, 1196, 1197 Fax: +86 10 6505 3829, 1198 www.jbic.go.jp/english/ CONTACT—India Rajeev Singh, Deputy Secretary (Political Focal Point) Department of Economic Affairs Ministry of Finance Room N. 66-C, North Block New Delhi–110001 India Tel: +91 11 230 93881 Fax: +91 11 230 92477 r_p_singh@nic.in www.gefweb.org CONTACT—India 3rd Floor, DLF Centre Sansad Marg New Delhi–110001 India Tel: +91 11 2371 4362, 4363, 7090, 6200 Fax: +91 11 2371 5066, + 91 11 2373 8389 www.jbic.go.jp/english/ CONTACT—Main Office 4-1, Ohtemachi 1-chome, Chiyoda-ku Tokyo 100-8144 Japan Tel: +03 5218 3101 Fax: +03 5218 3955 www.jbic.go.jp/english/
Kreditanstalt fur Wiederaufbau (KfW Bankengruppe)	Small and medium enterprise (SME), project, and export finance	German government	SMEs, clean energy	South Asia, Southeast Asia, East Asia, West Asia, North Africa, Central and Eastern Europe, Central and South America, North America, Oceania, Western Europe, Sub-Saharan Africa	Charlottenstrasse 33/33a 10117 Berlin Tel: +49 30 20264 0 Fax: +49 30 20264 5188 www.kfw.de/EN

End Notes

[1] International Energy Agency, *World Energy Outlook 2007: China and India Insights* (Paris, France: OCED/IEA, 2007).

[2] Ibid., p. 444.

[3] http://planningcommission.nic.in/plans/planrel/11thf.htm

[4] www.cogen.org/

[5] See http://mnes.nic.in/prog-smallhydro.htm for MNRE's small hydropower programs.

[6] International Energy Agency, *World Energy Outlook 2007: China and India Insights* (OECD/IEA, 2007).

[7] From Ministry of New and Renewable Energy (http://mnes.nic.in/).

[8] http://millenniumindicators.un.org/unsd/mdg/SeriesDetail.aspx?srid=749&crid=

[9] Non-firm power: power or power-producing capacity supplied or available under a commitment having limited or no assured availability.

[10] /www.mnes.nic.in/r&d/om-rnd1006.pdf

[11] *Report of the Working Group on Coal & Lignite for Formulation of Eleventh Five-Year Plan (2007-12)* (Government of India, Ministry of Coal).

[12] http://www.fias.net/ifcext/pressroom/ifcpressroom.nsf/PressRelease?openform&AB056249554C36DF8525731B005BBA3E

[13] http://hdr.undp.org/en/humandev/links/

[14] http://usaid.eco-asia.org/programs/cdcp/reports/annexes/Annex%202_India.pdf

[15] Clean Technology AustralAsia, "Pursuing Clean Energy Business in India," a background paper, , June 2007.

[16] Prepared from *TERI Energy Data Directory and Yearbook 2005/06.*

[17] http://www.un.org/esa/sustdev/csd/csd15/documents/csd15_bp2.pdf

[18] Photo courtesy of U.S. Department of Energy/National Renewable Energy Laboratory (USDOE/NREL) (www.nrel.gov).

[19] Photo courtesy of USDOE/NREL.

[20] Photo courtesy of USDOE/NREL.

[21] http://www.nrel.gov/learning/re_solar_hot_water.html

[22] Emerging Energy Research, Asia Pacific Wind Power Markets & Strategies, 2006–2015 (December 2006). Available from www.emerging-energy.com.

[23] Photo courtesy of USDOE/NREL. (USDOE used to denote United States Department of Energy since DOE has been used already to refer to the Department of Environment)

[24] Photo courtesy of USDOE/NREL.

[25] See www.sunwize.com/.

In: Clean Energy: An Exporter's Guide to India and China   ISBN: 978-1-60741-329-5
Editor: Isaac P. Luttrell   © 2011 Nova Science Publishers, Inc.

Chapter 2

CLEAN ENERGY: AN EXPORTER'S GUIDE TO CHINA

United States Department of Commerce

ACRONYMS

ABS	asset-backed securities
AC	alternating current
ACEEE	American Council for an Energy-efficient Economy
ACORE	American Council on Renewable Energy
ADB	Asian Development Bank
AEE	Association of Energy Engineers
AESP	Association of Energy Services Professionals
AFV	alcohol fuel vehicle
ALM	asset liability management
APM	administered pricing mechanism
APP	Asia–Pacific Partnership on Clean Development and Climate
AQSIQ	Administration of Quality Supervision, Inspection, and Quarantine
ASE	Alliance to Save Energy
ASEAN	Association of Southeast Asian Nations
ASTAE	Asia Alternative and Sustainable Energy
ASTM	American Society for Testing and Materials
bcm	billion cubic meters
BIPV	building-integrated photovoltaics
BOO	build, own, operate
BOOT	build, own, operate, and transfer
BOV	battery-operated vehicle
BPL	below poverty line
BT	billion tons
CATARC	China Automotive Technology and Research Center
CCC	China Compulsory Certification Mark
CDM	Clean Development Mechanism

CE	European Conformity (French acronym)
CEC	China Electricity Council
CER	credits for emission reductions
CET	clean energy technology
CFL	compact fluorescent lighting
CGC	China General Certification Center
CHCP	combined heat, cooling, and power
CH4	methane
CHP	combined heat and power
CLASP	Collaborative Labeling and Appliance Standards Program
CNCA	Certification and Accreditation Administration
CNG	compressed natural gas
CO2	carbon dioxide
CREIA	Chinese Renewable Energy Industries Association
CSC	China Standard Certification Center
CWEA	Chinese Wind Energy Association
DC	direct current
DFI	development financial institution
DME	di-methyl ether
DOC	U.S. Department of Commerce
DRCs	provincial Development and Reform Commissions
DSM	demand-side management
EC	energy conservation
ECB	external commercial borrowing
ECBC	Energy Conservation Building Codes
ECO	Energy Efficiency Commercialization Project
EE	energy efficiency
EEB	Bureau of Economic, Energy and Business Affairs (United States)
EEI	energy efficiency indicator
EERE	Office of Energy Efficiency and Renewable Energy (United States)
EIB	European Investment Bank
EJ	exajoule
EMCO	energy management contract
EOU	export-oriented unit
EPC	equipment procurement and construction
ERI	Energy Research Institute
ESCO	energy service company
ETC	evacuated tube collectors
EV	electric vehicle
EVA	solid phase crystallization of evaporated silicon
Ex-Im	Export–Import Bank of the United States
FAS	Foreign Agricultural Service (United States)
FDI	foreign direct investment
FI	financial institution
FPC	flat plate collector
FYP	Five-Year Plan

GATT	General Agreement on Tariffs and Trade
GB	Guojia Biaozhun
gce	gram of coal equivalent
GDP	gross domestic product
GEF	Global Environment Facility
Gg	gigagram
GHG	greenhouse gas
GNP	gross national product
GPV	gas-powered vehicle
GRP	glass fiber–reinforced plastic
GW	gigawatt
GWe	gigawatt electric
GWp	gigawatt peak
HFC	hydrofluorocarbon
HIT	heterojunction with intrinsic thin layer
HT	high-tension
IBRD	International Bank for Reconstruction and Development
ICB	international competitive bidding
ICBC	Industrial and Commercial Bank of China
IEA	International Energy Agency
IEC	International Electrotechnical Commission
IFC	International Finance Corporation
IFI	international financing institution
IGCC	integrated gasification combined cycle
IIFCL	India Infrastructure Finance Company Limited
INR	Indian National Rupees
IP	intellectual property
IPA	Indian Patent Act
IPP	independent power producer
IPR	intellectual property rights
IREDA	Indian Renewable Energy Development Agency
ITA	U.S. International Trade Administration
JBIC	Japan Bank for International Cooperation
JCF	Japan Carbon Finance, Limited
JV	joint venture
kgce	kilogram of coal equivalent
kha	kilohectare
KP	Kyoto Protocol
kT	kiloton
kV	kilovolt
kW	kilowatt
kWe	kilowatt electric
kWh	kilowatt hour
kWp	kilowatt peak
LC	letter of credit
LED	light-emitting diode

LNG	liquefied natural gas
LOLP	loss of load probability
LPG	liquefied petroleum gas (Propane)
M&A	mergers and acquisitions
mb/d	millions of barrels per day
MIGA	Multilateral Investment Guarantee Agency
MJ	megajoule
MMSCM	million standard cubic meter
MOC	Ministry of Construction
MOF	Ministry of Finance
MOFCOM	Ministry of Commerce
MOFTEC	Ministry of Foreign Trade and Economic Cooperation
MOST	Ministry of Science and Technology
MSIHC	Manufacture, Storage, and Import of Hazardous Chemicals
Mt	million tons
MT	magnetotelluric
mToe	million tons of oil equivalent
MU	million units
MW	megawatt
MWe	megawatt electric
MWeq	megawatt equivalent
MWp	megawatt peak
NAESCO	National Association of Energy Service Companies
NB	national competitive bidding
NBSC	International Center of National Bureau of Statistics of China
NCCCC	National Coordination Committee on Climate Change
NCE	non-conventional energy
NDRC	National Development and Reform Commission
N2O	nitrous oxide
NOx	nitrogen oxide
NPC	National People's Congress
NREL	National Renewable Energy Laboratory of the U.S. Department of Energy
OECD	Organization for Economic Co-operation and Development
OFAC	Office of Foreign Assets Control (United States)
OGL	open general license
O&M	operation and maintenance
OPIC	Overseas Private Investment Corporation (United States)
PCF	Prototype Carbon Fund
PDD	Project Design Documentation
PE	private equity
PECVD	plasma-enhanced chemical vapor deposition
PEMF	Private Energy Market Fund LP
PEMFC	proton exchange membrane fuel cell
PHWR	pressurized heavy water reactor
PPA	power purchase agreement

PPP	public–private partnership
PSU	public–sector undertaking
PV	photovoltaic
R&D	research and development
RE	renewable energy
REDP	World Bank Renewable Energy Development Program
REL	Renewable Energy Law
REPS	renewable energy portfolio standard
RMB	Chinese Yuan Renmimbi
RPS	reserve energy portfolio standard
RSPM	respirable suspended particulate matter
SAC	Standardization Administration of China
SAFE	State Administration of Foreign Exchange
SBA	Small Business Administration (United States)
SDDC	Song Dian Dao Cun (China's National Village Electrification Program)
SDDX	Song Dian Dao Xiang (China's National Township Electrification Program)
SEFI	Sustainable Energy Finance Initiative
SEK	Svensk Exportkredit
SEPA	State Environment Protection Administration
S/F JV	Sino-Foreign Joint Venture
SHP	small hydropower
SHS	solar home system
SI	solar ingot
SICLIP	Swedish International Climate Investment Program
SME	small and medium enterprise
SO2	sulphur dioxide
SOE	state-owned enterprise
SPV	solar PV
SWH	solar water heating
TC-88	Technical Committee 88 of the IEC
tce	tons of coal equivalent
T&D	transmission and distribution
TEDA	Tamil Nadu Energy Development Agency (India)
TERI	Tata Energy Research Institute
toe	tons of oil equivalent
TPES	total primary energy supply
TRIPS	Trade-related Aspects of Intellectual Property Rights
TüV	Technische Überwachungsvereine (Germany standards/testing company)
TWh	terrawatt hour
UCP	Unified Customs and Practice
UL	Underwriters Laboratories
UNDP	United Nations Development Program
UNICITRAL	United Nations Commission on International Trade
UPS	uninterruptible power supply

URIF	Urban Reform Incentive Fund
USAID	U.S. Agency for International Development
USDA	U.S. Department of Agriculture
USDOC	U.S. Department of Commerce
USDOE	U.S. Department of Energy
USTDA	U.S. Trade and Development Agency
USTR	U.S. Trade Representative
VAT	value-added tax
VER	Verified Emission Reduction
VSD	variable-speed drive
W	watt
WEEA	World Energy Efficiency Association
WOFE	wholly-owned foreign enterprise
Wp	watt peak
WTG	wind turbine generator
WTO	World Trade Organization

EXECUTIVE SUMMARY

Introduction

This report is intended as a clean energy technology market overview for China, with two primary objectives: (1) to analyze the clean energy markets in China and (2) to identify opportunities for trade and investment through 2020. The report provides the following:

- analysis of the existing infrastructure of clean energy technologies and market opportunities in China through 2020 including market forecasts, market drivers, cost data, and market segment analysis.
- review of government policies for clean energy development in China.
- detailed analysis of barriers and obstacles to clean energy technologies trade and investment in China.
- definition of clean energy technologies for China.
- review of resources available to U.S. businesses that wish to enter Chinese clean energy markets.

After a short introduction, Section 1 addresses clean energy technologies for China, including information on China's overall energy status, both current and projected; a market overview; identification of clean energy policies; trade and investment opportunities for U.S. firms; and barriers to clean energy market entry, development, and commercialization. This chapter also includes annexes on Chinese policy-makers with authority over clean energy technologies and information on the renewable energy industry in China. Section 2 provides definitions of the clean energy technologies addressed in the report.

Clean Energy Technology Defined

Clean energy technologies include renewable energy, hybrid and co-generation, and energy efficiency technologies for power generation; alternative fuels; and advanced technologies for transportation. They produce power for a wide range of applications using no fuel or less fuel than fossil-fuel-based technologies, produce no or fewer pollutants than conventional technologies and can use renewable energy sources, which, unlike fossil fuels, are not depleted over time. The renewable energy technologies considered in this report are biomass and biofuels, waste-to-energy, solar power, wind power, geothermal, hydropower, and ocean power.

Biomass consists of plant and plant-derived material. Sources include agricultural residues such as rice hulls, straw, bagasse from sugarcane production, wood chips, and coconut shells and energy crops such as sugarcane or switch grass. Biomass can be used directly for energy production or processed into fuels. Waste-to-energy technology converts energy from a waste source, such as a city's municipal waste system, farms, and other agricultural operations, or waste from commercial and industrial operations. Large-scale waste-to-energy systems can supply heat or electricity in utility-based electric power plants or district heating systems. Small-scale systems can provide heating or cooking fuel and electricity to individual farms, homes, and businesses.

Solar technologies convert light and heat from the sun into useful energy. Photovoltaic (PV) systems convert sunlight into electricity, and thermal systems collect and store solar heat for air and water heating applications. *Wind* power technology converts energy in the wind into useful power; the primary market for wind power technology is for wind turbines, which convert wind energy into electricity. *Geothermal* power is generated using thermal energy from underground sources, including steam, hot water, and heat stored in rock formations; various technologies are used to generate electricity. *Hydropower* is the conversion of energy embodied in moving water into useful power. Today, hydropower supplies about 19 percent of the world's electricity. Finally, *ocean power* – sometimes referred to as tidal – technology makes use of energy in the ocean by converting it into electricity

Hybrid and co-generation power systems take advantage of the benefits of multiple technologies in a single, integrated system for power generation. Renewable-based hybrid power systems use combinations of wind turbines, PV panels, and small hydropower generators to generate electricity. Hybrid power systems typically include a diesel or other fuel-based generator (including biofuels) and may include batteries or other storage technology.

Co-generation systems, also called combined heat and power (CHP) systems, generate both electricity and useful heat. Conventional fossil-fuel-based electric power plants generate heat as a byproduct that is emitted into the environment; co-generation power plants collect this heat for use in thermal applications, thereby converting a higher percentage of the energy in the fuel into useful energy. The most efficient conventional power plants have a typical fuel-to-electricity conversion factor of about 50 percent, while co-generation plants can achieve efficiencies of over 75 percent. Examples of thermal loads that can be served by a co-generation plant are: district heating systems that provide heat for towns and neighborhoods; industrial processes that require heat, such as paper mills; institutions such as prisons and hospitals; and wastewater treatment plants.

Energy efficiency (EE) involves replacing existing technologies and processes with new ones that provide equivalent or better service using less energy. EE results in energy savings at the time that the energy service is provided. Energy service providers can also use load management to change the time that an energy service is delivered in order to reduce peak loads on an energy distribution system. Demand-side management uses both load management and EE to save the amount of primary energy required to deliver the energy service.

Almost half a billion vehicles on the world's roads contribute to half of the global oil consumption and generate about 20 percent of the world's greenhouse gases, including carbon monoxide, nitrous oxides, and particulates. *Transportation technologies* can help address these issues through the use of alternative fuels and advanced technologies. Alternative fuels for transportation include biodiesel, ethanol, natural gas, and propane. Advanced vehicle technologies include electric vehicles and hybrid electric vehicles, which offer air pollution improvements over average fossil fuel vehicles. Finally, mobile idle reduction systems and diesel engine retrofits can reduce the emissions of heavy-duty vehicles.

China: Energy Overview

Since the start of the open-door and reform policies in 1978, China has experienced consistent economic growth on the order of 9.5 percent per year. While on average energy demand grew at about 5 percent per year prior to 2001, the past seven years have seen a tremendous surge in energy-intensive heavy industries, which has dramatically accelerated energy demand. According to the National Bureau of Statistics of China, China's current energy consumption increase stands at a rate of 9.3 percent, and this rapid growth is expected to continue. In fact, China is predicted to surpass the United States as the largest energy consumer soon after 2010.

Although China's energy resources are substantial, the country's self-sufficiency is decreasing as the overall energy demand has grown much faster than its domestic output. In 2005, foreign supply accounted for 7.7 percent of the total energy consumption in China, and in 2007 the country became a net coal importer for the first time. China has become increasingly dependent on oil imports and liquid natural gas imports, the latter of which were seen for the first time in 2006. Coal is China's predominant energy source; however, with the rapid increase in energy demand and the urgency of energy and environmental security issues, the shift away from conventional energy toward clean energy has become an interesting strategic option for China.

Exploration for the use of renewable energy technologies in China began in the 1980s, but government support for these options did not officially begin until the 8th Five-Year Plan in 1991. In the late 1990s, China launched its ambitious rural electrification program, which has helped China's renewable energy consumption increase to 7.5 percent of the country's total primary energy consumption as of 2005. However, although the markets for hydropower and solar water heating technologies are mature, the use and development of most other renewable energies has lagged because of high investment costs, specific primary resource shortages, dependence on foreign technology, and small-scale production.

Renewable Resources, Capacity and Potential

China has a large untapped potential for wind energy, perhaps as high as 750 gigawatts (GW) of potentially utilizable onshore resources (250–300 GW of which are considered commercially feasible) and over 1,000 GW of offshore resources. In recent years, Chinese wind generation technology has matured with the help of technology transfer from foreign countries and a national concession policy that stipulates 70 percent of wind turbines in developer tenders must be sourced from domestic manufacturers—which has helped the domestic industry substantially. Still, as of 2006, China's total installed wind power generation capacity was only 2.6 GW, indicating substantial growth opportunities going forward.

The resource potential for solar power in China is equally promising. China receives the equivalent energy potential of 1.7 trillion tons of coal in the form of solar radiation. By the end of 2006, the cumulative installed capacity of solar cells in China had reached 80 megawatts peaks (MWp), with rural electrification, communications, and industry accounting for the majority of the market share. Currently, China is the third-largest PV panel manufacturing country in the world behind Germany and Japan, developing 370 MWp of solar PV cell modules in 2006 – however, only 10 MWp were consumed domestically. Consequently, solar power production remains much lower than actual capacity. While policy support and government subsidy programs can be credited with 46.2 percent of China's developed capacity, high investment costs, undefined feed-in tariffs, and the lack of fiscal incentives means a significant on-grid solar PV market has yet to materialize.

Solar thermal energy for water heating is one of the most advanced renewable energy technologies in China with a mature commercial domestic market. China has a cumulative installed capacity of solar water heaters (SWHs) that surpasses 90 million square meters (m^2) of collector area—roughly 60 percent of the world's total. In fact, nearly one in ten Chinese households owns an SWH. Notably, China has over 1,000 solar water heating manufacturers, and 95 percent of the intellectual property rights for solar thermal technologies used in China are domestically owned. In 2006, the domestic production capacity stood at 6 million m^2, but the domestic market lags behind this capacity—the excess production is currently exported to Europe and Southeast Asia. China has recently developed national testing centers and a national certification center for SWH technologies based on international best practices, and this has led to improved product quality and domestic consumer confidence. Building integrated SWHs is in the early stages. Low aesthetic quality and lack of support from building developers remain challenges for the industry.

China has a vast bioenergy potential with recent average biomass resource utilization above 500 million tons of coal equivalent (tce). The majority of the resource potential comes from wood (300 million tce), followed by straw and stalk resources (150 million tce), waste water (57 million tce), and urban garbage (23 million tce). The key technologies for biomass include combined heat and power combustion (CHP), biogas, landfill, and other waste gasification. In 2006, power production from CHP amounted to 1.7 GW; biogas amounted to 500 megawatts (MW) minus rural use; and 30 MW was produced from landfill and other gasification. Biogas development is backed by the central government through strong fiscal incentives as well as investment subsidies. By the end of 2006, 17 million household biogas digesters, 140,000 municipal waste treatment facilities, and 4,000 industry sewage biogas facilities providing 1.9 million cubic meters (m^3) of biogas per year had been installed. It is estimated that the current biogas potential in China from industry could be used to generate

3.8 GW of base load electricity with 23 terawatt hours (TWh) of electricity potential by 2010. The estimate is considerably higher for 2020 projections.

Compared to biogas, liquid biofuel technology development is still in an early stage. China has important bioethanol potential based on sugarcane, cassava, corn, and broomcorn cultures. The 10th Five-Year Plan saw the beginning of a national program aimed at developing technologies for making bioethanol from broomcorn and similar cellulose waste such as corn stalk. Biodiesel development is also included in the 11th Five-Year Plan but is still at the research stage. Its commercialization will depend on production cost reductions and increased conversion rates.

The total potential for small hydropower (SHP) in China is estimated at 71.87 GW and is concentrated among more than 1,600 mountain counties in the middle and western regions. However, as of the end of 2004, only 2.1 percent of the total potential had been developed in western China, where the majority of the unelectrified poor are located. SHP is now one of the mature renewable energy technologies in China, with a significant domestic manufacturing capacity and competitive export potential in Asia. This is the result of strong fiscal support from the central government. By 2004, there were over 100 SHP manufacturers in China, with an annual production capacity of around 6.3 GW.

Energy Efficiency, Co-Generation and Transportation

In general, production and operation energy efficiency is low in China. Recently, energy efficiency (EE) has decreased due to the growing industry sector, which has the lowest EE level. Operational efficiency for end-use equipment in China is generally 20 percent lower than the international average for advanced countries, which is mainly due to obsolete and poorly maintained production equipment. Nonetheless, the 11th Five-Year Plan includes an ambitious target to decrease energy intensity by 20 percent through 2010, which is being pursued through 10 key government programs. The challenges facing increased EE include a lack of expertise in demand-side management and energy-auditing services and a lack of capacity for innovative high-efficiency technology development.

Co-generation, or combined heat and power (CHP), remained the major heat supply source in China until recently, covering 82 percent of total heat demand and 27 percent of the total water heating demand in 2004. Mixed political signals from the provincial and central government, as well as sustained growth of coal utilization and inconsistent electricity tariff increases, have caused 90 percent of China's domestic CHP operators to take heavy losses over the last five years. The situation is similar for foreign operators. In fact, CHP installations make up almost 50 percent of the power plants closed since the beginning of 2007. Nonetheless, co-generation was identified as an important energy conservation technology for reducing coal consumption in the 11th Five-Year Plan, with ambitious targets set for its development.

China has been actively involved in the demonstration and development of large-scale clean transportation technologies since the launch of the "Clean Vehicles Action" Program in 1999. Gas-powered vehicles (GPVs) are now in operation, and those on the market are third-generation products. As of end-2006, the GPV fleet numbered 265,000 vehicles. Compressed natural gas vehicles are rapidly growing, with a fleet of 174,170 in 2006. Alcohol fuel vehicles are found in the eastern portion of the country, and the planned production level for ethanol fuel was recently set at about 1 million tons per year. There has been a considerable amount of government investment in fuel cell technology research, and a demonstration program is underway in Beijing for fuel cell bus commercialization. Finally, electric vehicle technology is under development, but applications are still limited by low power capacity as well as high production costs. Nonetheless, there is a vibrant market for electric bicycles in China, with about 10 million units produced in 2005 alone.

Market Analysis

Projections for 2010 and 2020 from government planning documents indicate that the clean technology market will increase to $186 billion (based on an exchange rate of $1 = 7.208 RMB) in 2010 and to $555 billion in 2020. Policy objectives for the five key renewable energy (RE) technologies are shown in Table A below. Market development for some renewable energy technologies has already surpassed the targets established by the government, such as wind; others like SWH, will easily reach the targets established if not overtake them. Although the domestic market for solar PV generation is not as developed as the wind and SWH markets, plans have been made for the construction of large-scale on-grid PV and concentrated solar power plants in desert areas of Inner Mongolia, Gansu, and Xinjiang provinces. Two government-led rooftop PV programs will also stimulate the PV market.

The targets for co-generation are equally ambitious. Based on the installed production capacity and the current 6.5 percent average annual growth for CHP generation in China, the total CHP generation capacity will reach 47 GW in 2010 and 87.5 GW in 2020, corresponding respectively to 37 percent and 68.5 percent of the total CHP potential.

The current cost of investment in wind energy is in the range of $1,110–1,387/kW. It is expected that with increasing domestic manufacturing capacity and technology transfer, the investment costs can be brought down to the range of $832–971/kWh by 2010. Similarly, significant future cost reductions are expected for solar PV. Other technologies, however, have less scope for cost reduction as these are already fairly mature in China and worldwide.

Table A. Policy Objectives for Key RE Technologies

Re	Utilization	Objectives by 2010	Objectives by 2020
Hydropower	Large scale	140 GW	225 GW
	Small scale	50 GW	75 GW
Bioenergy	Generation	5.5 GW	30 GW
	Solid biofuel	10 bil. tons	50 bil. tons
	Biogas	19 bil. m^3	44 bil. m^3
	Bioethanol	2 mil. tons	10 mil. tons
	Biodiesel	0.2 mil. tons	2 mil. tons
Wind	Generation	5 GW	30 GW
Solar *	On-grid solar PV	150 MW	1.5 GW
	Off-grid solar PV	150 MW	0.3 GW
	Solar thermal	150 mil. m^2	300 mil. m^2
Geothermal		4 mil. tce	12 mil. tce

Source: NDRC, 2006 Mid- and Long-term Renewable Energy Development Plan.

   * Total solar PV installation includes both on-grid and off-grid generation capacity.

In China, there are currently over 80 wind turbine generator manufacturers and 200 wind developers. Domestic companies occupy over 75 percent of the market. China's solar industry has matured in recent years, with booming investments providing an important opportunity. Over 80 percent of the domestic manufacturers produce monoingot. Two companies— Suntech and Ningbo Solar— dominated the market prior to 2006; in that year the size of the market grew with new companies entering the scene. In total, there are over 3,500 SWH system manufacturers in China, the top ten of which are able to provide highquality products and good after-sales services. Small hydropower technologies are mature in China, with over 100 manufacturers. Finally, as a result of energy efficiency policy and goals set forth in the 11th Five-Year Plan, the energy efficiency market is booming as numerous companies and organizations have developed operations in various fields.

The largest market drivers for energy demand are urbanization and economic growth, the latter of which is a direct result of the country's booming and energyintensive industrial exports. In 2006, according to China's National Bureau of Statistics, China's gross domestic product (GDP) increased by 10.7 percent, while the primary domestic energy consumption rose by 8.4 percent. Not surprisingly, China is dependent increasingly on energy imports to keep up with the demand.

Dependence on costly imports, and the related issue of energy security, represents another market driver. Oil imports alone reached 169 million tons in 2006, and the dependence on exports accounted for 47 percent of the oil balance. Environmental concerns are an additional market driver, specifically in response to the high polluting Chinese coal industry. The International Energy Agency (IEA) concluded that China overtook the United States as the world's biggest carbon dioxide (CO_2) emitter in 2007. The World Bank estimates the total cost of air and water pollution in China is roughly \$50.22 billion, or about 2.68 percent of GDP. Acid rain is estimated to cost \$4.16 billion in crop damage and \$138.73 million in material damage annually. Moreover, about 54 percent of surface water resources in China have been deemed unsafe for human consumption. The Chinese Government considers these issues to be very serious, and the ambitious targets, state investment, and policy seen in recent years can be considered an important result of the country's high priority on sustainable (and sustained) development.

Energy Policy

The development of a more robust clean energy policy is accelerating in response to China's mounting energy pressures. The strategic position of renewable energy was confirmed with the passage of the Renewable Energy Law (REL), which was approved by the National People's Congress in February 2005 and took effect on January 1, 2006. The REL is a framework law that creates targets for renewable energy development and stipulates a number of broadly defined instruments to reach these targets. The targets are shown above in Table A; the overall renewable energy target as a percentage of energy consumption is 10 percent by 2010 and 15 percent by 2020. The REL mandates the establishment of priority grid access for renewable electricity generators, a feed-in tariff for renewable electricity delivered to the grid, a national and regional cost-sharing mechanism for renewable energy subsidies, a special fund for renewable energy, and favorable loan conditions and tax treatment for renewable energy.

The successful implementation of the REL depends on its implementation regulations, which further elaborate upon the policy instruments defined in the REL. Ten such regulations have been issued so far, including the Mid-and Long-term Renewable Energy Development Plan, which stipulates that renewable energy utilization should reach 300 million tce by 2010 and 600 million tce by 2020. Another is the Guidance Catalogue of the Renewable Energy Industry, which was released by the National Development and Reform Commission (NDRC) in November 2006 and aims to guide provincial decision-making on the direction for technological research and innovation and renewable energy investment. Finally, a special fund for renewable energy development supports the key fields of fossil fuel alternatives, building heating and cooling, and renewable energy electricity generation through no-interest and discount loans. An application guidebook for the funds is drafted annually and published by the NDRC and the financial department of the State Council.

China's new Energy Conservation (EC) Law was approved by the 10th State Congress on October 28, 2007, and entered into effect on April 1, 2008. The Law identifies key policy instruments, which includes setting targets, developing procedures for product standardization and efficiency labeling, and establishing incentives for EC technologies, as well as demand-side management including preferential tax policies and subsidy funds. Indeed, many preferential tax policies have been implemented to support clean energy research, development, and production. For example, since 2001 waste-to-energy projects have been value-added tax (VAT) exempt, and a 50 percent VAT discount applies for the use of energysaving materials in buildings, for wind power projects, and for coal bed methane projects.

A draft of China's integrated Energy Law was recently published. The forthcoming law provides a framework law for overall national energy development and will include guiding principles for legislation on energy structure, energy efficiency, energy security, energy development and utilization, and energy and environmental coordination. One of the most important changes in the new Energy Law is the proposed establishment of an Energy Ministry directly under the State Council. The Energy Ministry would be responsible for overseeing energy management in China, including monitoring energy-intensive exports, approving energy and mining activities, promoting energy efficiency and inter-regional energy infrastructure, and establishing market-driven price mechanisms as well as incentive policies. The law also mandates that a 20–30 year energy strategy will be developed every five years, along with five-year energy plans. Industry Analysts anticipate that the Energy Law will be enacted in the years to come. In the meantime, the National Energy Bureau under the National Development and Reform Commission will continue to administer energy policy.

Opportunities for U.S. Clean Technology Firms in China

The opportunities for U.S firms entering the Chinese clean energy market have grown tremendously during recent years. The development of a market economy, increasing concerns about energy security, and the mounting environmental pressures have all incentivized clean technologies and facilitated their entry into the market. Yet the rapidly growing government push and resulting market pull for clean energy development presents special challenges for China due to the technological requirements necessary to reach the aggressive government goals. The commercial market for clean energy technologies in China at this time should be considered embryonic at best. As the demand for clean energy technology increases, it can be expected that there will be an increasing demand for proven, high-quality products and services—which provides an opening in the market for qualified international companies with sustainable business operations.

To fulfill the objective of a 20 percent decrease in energy intensity by 2010 (relative to 2000 levels), the Chinese Government has recognized that major developments in technology and energy management must be achieved across industrial, commercial, and residential sectors. According to China's Energy Research Institute, the investment potential for energy efficiency in China from 2007 to 2010 will be about $120–160 billion. In general, there is a lack of expertise in China in energy efficiency technologies and innovation, energy auditing, and energy management. Areas such as operation and maintenance for renewable energy (RE) generation, energy auditing and advisory services, consulting on energy management and RE integration, and standard energy services are all potentially profitable business opportunities.

Technological needs in the clean energy industry include remote monitoring and control systems for wind farms, technology for large-scale wind turbines (over 2 MW), and software for resource assessment and grid integration. In solar power, opportunities include aesthetic building integration for SWHs, improved technology in thin film, interface technology for building-integrated PV and for power plants, and high-quality converters. In bioenergy, needs include research and development (R&D) on the production of ethanol from cellulosic feedstock, high-efficient fermentation technology for higher biogas yield, demonstration of new building material and technology for digester construction and biogas storage, and biogas processing for feed-in to the natural gas grid.

Barriers for U.S. Firms

Despite the significant opportunities that the Chinese clean energy technology market presents, important barriers need to be carefully considered in developing business in China. These include lack of a transparent and consistent body of laws and regulations, lack of a supervisory mechanism for renewable energy implementation, customs regulations and a phasing out of favorable tariffs for foreign investment, and restrictions on foreign direct investment that include biofuels manufacturing. Lack of transparency in government procurement, including instances of corruption, can also present challenges as well as intellectual property rights and contract enforcement. Finally, other considerations like understanding Chinese business culture, identifying local partners, and building good government relationships are also important nonpolicy related barriers that must be considered.

Conclusion

In summary, China presents both unprecedented opportunities and challenges for clean energy technologies, due to the sheer scale of the market, the demand, and the projected future energy scenario. Over the last decade, China faced serious difficulties related to energy shortages and heavy pollution, both of which have been brought on by rapid economic development. In response, the government of China has actively promoted the development and deployment of renewable energy with ambitious policies and targets.

China will likely be a major net exporter of renewable energy equipment in the near term, as the country produces far more equipment than it can install domestically. However, as the demand for higher product quality and after-sales service increases, and as Chinese consumers become more conscious of efficiency and environmental concerns, this situation is likely to change. The Renewable Energy Law (REL) has already had a major impact on accelerating China's clean energy market and resulted in an increase of new renewable energy projects, particularly in the areas of wind, solar, and biomass. Ambitious targets are included in the REL for the next 10–15 years, which, when paired with the industry outlook, are likely to be even higher. Therefore, U.S. firms should anticipate a growing demand for proven, high-quality products and services in key areas such as energy service companies, energy efficiency auditing, wind farm operation and management, technological innovation of large-scale turbines, aesthetic building integration of SWHs, and improved thin-film PV technology.

INTRODUCTION

Purpose

The report's objectives are twofold: (1) to analyze the clean energy markets in China and (2) to identify opportunities for trade and investment through 2020.

Approach

The report provides the following:

- An analysis of the existing infrastructure of clean energy technologies and market opportunities in China through 2020. This includes market forecasts, market drivers, cost data, and market segment analysis.
- review of government policies for clean energy development in China.
- detailed analysis of barriers and obstacles to clean energy technologies trade and investment in China.
- definition of clean energy technologies for China.
- review of resources available to U.S. businesses that wish to engage in clean energy trade and investment in China.

Methodology

Both primary and secondary data sources were used in the preparation of this report. These included:

China Resources

- Annual reports from relevant ministries at the national level and, where available, at the provincial levels;
- List of relevant agencies, areas of operation, and contact details;
- Policy documents (e.g., China's Renewable Energy Promotion Law 2006 China's Guidance Catalogue of Renewable Energy Industry) as well as documents stating quotas, tax requirements, procurement requirements, foreign investment policy, and master plans for technology development in different sectors;
- Statistical documents containing installed capacity, energy balance, consumption, etc.;
- Five-Year Plans and ministerial long-term development plans; Annual Reports of relevant corporations;
- Data related to financial markets in China.

U.S. Government Sources

- U.S. Department of Commerce;
- U.S. Department of Energy, including the National Renewable Energy Laboratory, Energy Information Agency, and Office of Energy Efficiency and Renewable Energy;
- U.S. Trade and Development Administration;
- Export–Import Bank of the United States;
- Asia–Pacific Partnership on Clean Development and Climate.

International Institutions

- Asian Development Bank;
- World Bank;
- International Energy Agency.

Trade, Industry, and Sector Associations; Business Counsels

- Interviews conducted with key trade associations, including the Chinese Renewable Energy Industries Association (CREIA)
- Documents from the American Council on Renewable Energy (ACORE).

Transmission and Distribution Agencies, Manufacturers, Generators

- Annual Reports from various industry leaders operating in China;
- Annual Reports of major electricity generators in China.

Organization of the Report

The remainder of this report is organized as follows:

- **Section 1 provides a market overview for China.** This chapter includes information on China's overall energy status, both current and projected; a market overview; identification of clean energy policies; trade and investment opportunities for U.S. firms; and barriers to clean energy market entry, development, and commercialization. The chapter also includes annexes on Chinese policy-makers with authority over clean energy technologies and information on the renewable energy industry in China.

- **Section 2 provides a definition of clean energy technologies addressed in the report.** This chapter includes energy efficiency, distributed generation, combined heat and power, wind, solar photovoltaics, solar thermal, small hydropower, biomass, biofuels, waste-toenergy, geothermal, and ocean energy technologies.

- **Appendix A provides a compendium of trade and investment resources for U.S. clean technology firms.** Contact information for individual organizations is also included.

- Appendix B provides a directory of sustainable energy financing sources. This directory is synthesized from the on-line resource available at www.sef-directory. net/, which is maintained by the Sustainable Energy Finance Initiative, a joint initiative of the United Nations Environment Program and the Basel Agency for Sustainable Energy.

SECTION 1: CHINA

1. China's Energy Status

Since the start of China's open-door and reform policies in 1978, China has experienced consistent economic growth on the order of 9.5 percent per year.[1] During that time, energy demand grew roughly 5 percent per year, but has grown significantly more than that in the last seven years.[2] Historically, China's industrial development was laborintensive and heavily dependent on manufacturing with relatively low energy intensity, but since 2001, China has seen a surge in energy-intensive heavy industry.

Energy Supply and Demand

At the beginning of the new millennium, both the Chinese Government and the International Energy Agency (IEA) predicted a 3–4 percent growth in energy demand for China between 2000 and 2010. These scenarios were based on expectations of a structural shift away from heavy industry and toward light industry, as well as a projected economic growth rate of 7–8 percent.[3] These forecasts reflected trends in energy consumption from around the year 2000 and were established following the scaling back of the centrally orchestrated conglomerate-building ambitions in China that followed the Asian financial crisis.[4] They also reflected a continuous increase in energy intensity efficiency since 1978.

However, the shift away from heavy industry failed to materialize and the trend toward greater energy efficiency reversed around 2002. As a result, according to China's National Bureau of Statistics, the rate of increase for energy consumption in China currently stands at 9.3 percent.[5] The most recent IEA forecast predicts that China's average increase in energy consumption will be up to 3.2 percent per year from 2005 to 2030 with a 5.1 percent annual growth rate from 2005 to 2015 (see Figure 1.1 below). In comparison, the Chinese Government's new forecast for the average annual growth in energy consumption is 4 percent.[6] These new scenarios are based on the expectation that China's heavy-industry sector will continue to expand and depend on the stability of the national energy policy environment.

Currently, China is the world's second-largest energy consumer after the United States. According to recent scenarios from the IEA, China will surpass the United States as the largest energy consumer soon after 2010. China's energy demand will rise from 1,742 million tons of oil equivalent (mToe) in 2005 to 2,851 mToe in 2015 and 3,819 mToe in 2030.[7] Such an increase will significantly affect international energy consumption patterns, as shown in Figure 1.2.

Although China's energy resources are substantial, the country's self-sufficiency is decreasing. Since 2004, China's overall energy demand has grown much faster than the domestic output. In 2005, foreign supply accounted for 7.7 percent of the total energy consumption in China, as shown in Figure 1.3.

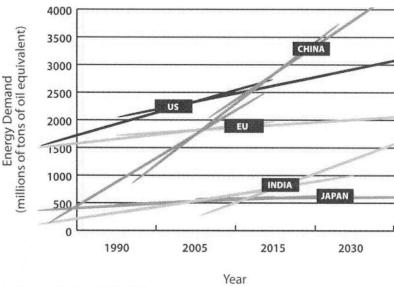

Source: World Energy Outlook 2007, IEA

Figure 1.1. China Energy Consumption in the Future (mToe)

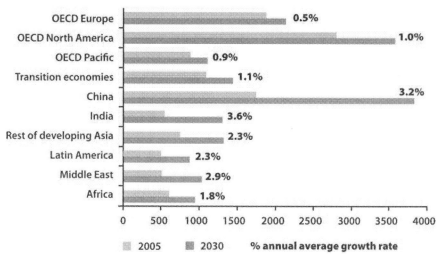

Source: International Energy Agency, World Energy Outlook 2007: China and India Insights (Paris, France: OCED/IEA, 2007).

Figure 1.2. Primary Energy Demand by Region

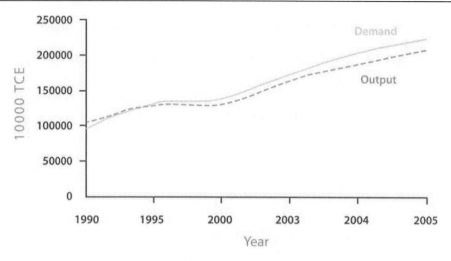

Figure 1.3. China's Overall Eneargy Demanad and Output

Coal is China's predominant energy source. In 2005, coal accounted for 69 percent of China's total energy consumption, but domestic coal production is no longer sufficient to meet China's increasing demand. China became a net coal *importer* for the first time in 2007. In 2030, net imports are expected to reach 3 percent of China's coal demand and 7 percent of global coal trade.[8]

China's oil balance deficit has been increasing rapidly for more than a decade. The country became a net importer of petroleum in 1993. In 2006, China imported 3.7 million barrels of oil per day (mb/d); nearly half its domestic petroleum consumption (see Figure 1.4 below). Such a trend is likely to continue in the future as China will become increasingly dependent on oil to power its growing automotive fleet and emerging industrial capacity. The IEA predicts China's oil consumption will reach 13.1 mb/d in 2030, while the share of imports will rise from 50 to 80 percent.

In addition, liquefied natural gas (LNG) imports are also increasing rapidly. China imported LNG for the first time in 2006. The imports amounted to 0.9 billion cubic meters (bcm) and originated mainly in Australia. China's LNG imports are expected to increase sharply to 12 bcm in 2010 to 28 bcm in 2015 and to 128 bcm in 2030.[9]

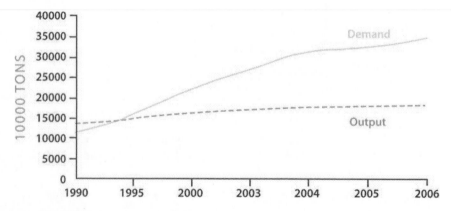

Figure 1.4. China's Petroleum Output and Demand

Current Status of Chinese Clean Energy Technology

Chinese research on the develoment of Clean Energy technologies started in the 1980s, but the dissemination of related technologies to domestic suppliers has remained relatively slow. However, with the rapid increase in energy demand and the recent rise of energy and environmental security issues, the shift away from conventional energy has become an important strategic option for China and an area of potential market penetration from American companies.

Renewable Energy

Government policy recognized the importance of sustainable, renewable energy, and energy efficiency only after the 1991 application of the 8th Five-Year Plan. Renewable energies emerged as a promising alternative to coal and other fossil fuels due to accelerated economic growth and the serious environmental degradation caused by the rapid increase in energy demand.

As a major plank in China's energy strategy, renewable energies now play a significant role in meeting the country's energy demand, structuring the energy industry's development patterns, reducing environmental pollution, and promoting economic development.

In 2005, China's renewable energy consumption rose to 116 mToe and amounted to 7.5 percent of the country's total primary energy consumption.[10] However, while the market for hydropower and solar water heating technologies is mature, the use and development of most other renewable energies have lagged behind thanks to high investment costs, specific primary resource shortages, dependence on foreign technology, and small-scale production.

Wind

Several studies indicate China has 750 gigawatts (GW) of potentially utilizable onshore wind resources (250 to 300 GW of which is commercially feasible) and over 1,000 GW of offshore resources. The development of wind energy in China began in the 1980s with rural electrification in coastal region, but since 2005 Renewable Energy Law (REL), the wind energy sector has been rapidly expanding. Under the new policy set forth in the REL, 15 provinces and municipalities have installed 1,226 megawatts (MW) of wind energy capacity, a 65.6 percent increase installed wind power in that year alone.[11] As of 2006, the total wind power generation capacity installed in 16 provinces had reached 2,599 MW, doubling the amount for 2005.[12] Figure 1.5 below shows the historical development of installed wind power capacity in China.[13]

In addition to the adoption of the REL, other factors have contributed to the current boom in wind energy development, including:

- In recent years, Chinese wind generation technology has matured with the help of technology transfer from foreign countries;
- China's wind turbine manufacturers are locally developing technology adapted to Chinese weather conditions, with the goal of reducing the purchase price for wind turbines as well as investment costs for wind farms;
- National policy for national and provincial concessions stipulates that 70 percent of wind turbines in developer tenders must be sourced from domestic wind turbine manufacturers;

- Most of the wind developers engage in wind farm development with no profit margin or at a loss, possibly to obtain additional wind development projects from the authorities and avoid being barred from future developments.

To establish a viable commercial market in wind energy production, experts have suggested additional tax reductions and feed-in tariffs.

Solar PV and Hybrid Systems

The potential for solar power in China is equally promising. Compared with other countries at the same latitude, China has significant solar resources, amounting to 1.7 trillion tons of coal received in the form of solar radiation. In the period 1971–2000, total radiation ranged from 1050–2450 kWh/m^2; areas with over 1050 kWh/m^2 accounted for more than 96 percent of the country, and areas with over 1400 kWh/m^2 accounted for more than 60 percent. The areas with the strongest resources are found in the western and central portions of the country.[14]

By the end of 2006, the cumulative installed capacity of solar cells in China had reached 80 megawatt peaks (MWp) (see Figure 1.6 below). The largest share of this capacity was found in rural electrification (43.1 percent), followed by communication and industrial uses. The market for photovoltaic (PV) power generation in China is mainly composed of communications, industrial applications, rural off-grid supply, grid-connected systems, and small solar products. Among these applications, rural electrification and grid-connected generation require support from the government.

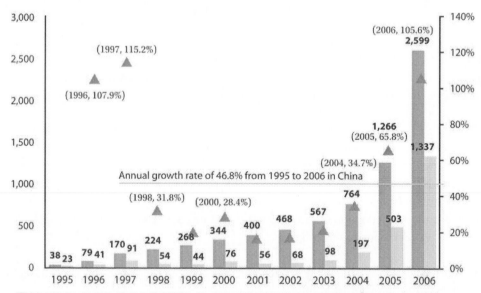

Source: Li Junfeng and Gao Hu, China Wind Power Report 2007 Z(China Environmental Science Press). www.gwec.net/uploads/media/wind-power-report.pdf

Figure 1.5. Cumulative Capacity of Wind Power Installed in China, 1995–2006

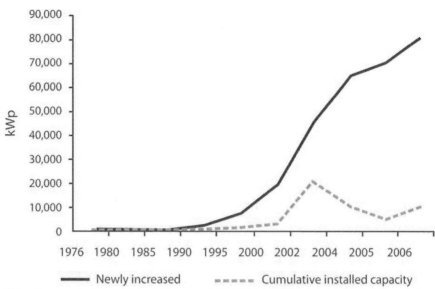

Source: Li Junfeng et *al.*, *China Solar PV Report 2007* (China Environmental Science Press).

Figure 1.6. Cumulative Installed PV Capacity in China.

China has developed an important PV panel production capacity. Currently, China is the third-largest PV panel manufacturing country in the world behind Germany and Japan. China's production capacity increased over two distinct periods. First, solar panel production capacity increased from 200 kilowatt peaks (kWp) before 1984 to 4.5 MWp in 1988 as a result of technology transfer from the United States and Canada, which enabled China to start operating seven solar panel production lines.[15]

The second hike in Chinese PV production capacity stems from the expansion of the international demand around 2002. In 2004, PV production in China reached 50 MW, quadrupling the 2003 production. In 2005 and 2006, PV production continued to increase from 130 to 369.5 MWp. The actual production capacity is much higher than the current production level, which is restrained by silicon shortages. By the end of 2006, the total PV production capacity distributed among 39 manufacturers amounted to 1.6 gigawatt peaks (GWp).[16]

Ninety percent of China's PV panel production is exported to foreign countries.[17] The export of solar panels reached $1.2 billion in 2006.[18] Domestic solar PV applications are mainly used in solar/wind or solar/diesel hybrid systems as well as solar home system (SHS) packages for rural electrification and off-grid generation in northwestern China. Good marketing has made SHS especially popular in plateau regions under the name of "sun on horseback." Due to various factors such as high investment costs, undefined feed-in tariffs, and lack of fiscal incentives, a significant on-grid solar PV market has yet to materialize.

Policy support and government subsidy programs have had an important impact on the development of domestic solar PV production capacity. In fact, 46.2 percent of the current production capacity results from such programs.[19] From 1998 to 2001, the Brightness Program, backed by the World Bank and the Global Environment Facility (GEF) through the Renewable Energy Development Program (REDP), promoted the installation of SHS in seven remote rural northwestern provinces of China—Xinjiang, Qinghai, Gansu, Inner Mongolia,

Shaanxi, Sichuan, and Tibet. In 2001, the Chinese Government launched *Song Dian Dao Xiang* (the National Township Electrification Program [SDDX]), a continuation of the Brightness Program and an ambitious large-scale rural electrification program targeting the same provinces. SDDX resulted in the development of 721 solar or solar/wind hybrid offgrid power generation systems for a total capacity of 19 MW.[20] The program, which ended in June 2003, has provided 1.3 million people in 1,000 townships with access to electricity. Under SDDX, total capital investment reached $600 million.21 SDDX will be followed by a further phase, *Song Dian Dao Cun*, or the National Village Electrification Program (SDDC), which was in the final design stages as of near end-2007.

The Chinese Government is promoting domestic PV development from the following aspects:[22]

- Following the Brightness Program and SDDX, SDDC will electrify another 1 million households in 20,000 villages by installing 100 MW of off-grid solar systems in remote rural and pastoral areas of Tibet, Qinghai, Inner Mongolia, Xinjiang, Ningxia, Gansu, and Yunnan, where grid extension is not feasible. The strategic scheme and the programs are being designed by China's government and a related program of the World Bank.

- The government is constructing large-scale on-grid PV power plants and solar thermal power plants in less developed areas in Inner Mongolia, Gansu, and Xinjiang, which will start from Dunhuang in Gansu and Lasha or Ali in Tibet during the period of the 11th Five-Year Plan. In fact, China planned to start up the biggest solar PV power station in the desert in 2003. A pre-feasibility study had been conducted, and the results were reported to the industry in Dunhuang, Gansu, in September 2003.

- The Start-up Roof PV Program involves constructing on-grid rooftop solar PV power generation in economically booming areas, such as Beijing, Shanghai, Jiangsu, Guangdong, and Shandong. At present, there are more than 10 pilot rooftop PV power stations in Shanghai with a total capacity around 2,000 kW and an annual yield of 2 million kWh. The feasibility study on the 100,000 Roof PV Program is being conducted by Shanghai Jiaotong University. The program aims to install 10,000 rooftop PV on-grid systems by the end of 2010 and another 90,000 systems by 2015.[23] This attempt indicates a direction for China's on-grid PV development.

Solar Water Heating

Solar thermal energy for water heating is one of the most advanced renewable energy technologies in China with a mature commercial market. Notably, China has over 1,000 solar water heating manufacturers, and 95 percent of the intellectual property rights (IPR) for solar thermal technologies used in China are domestically owned.[24] In the past 10 years, the growth rate for solar water heating has reached 15 percent per year, as shown in Figure 1.7. is currently China's solar water heating production surface around 90 million m², or 60 percent of the world's total.[25] In fact, nearly one in 10 Chinese households owns an SWH. In 2006 alone, China installed 20 million m2 of solar thermal production. However, the increase in installed solar thermal surface lags behind the equipment production capacity, which has an annual increase rate of 28 percent.[26] In 2006, the domestic production capacity stood at 6 million m². The excess production is currently exported to Europe and Southeast Asia.

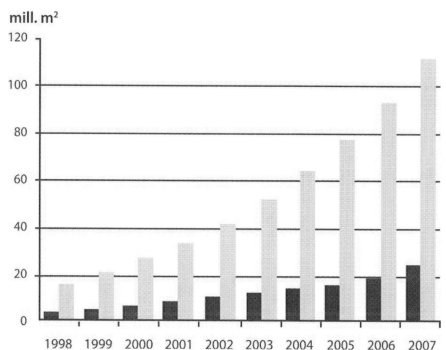

mill. m²

Data: Signifficient effect of solar thermal in energy conservation and emission reduction.
Source: Luo Zhentao and Huo Zhenchen, *Outstanding Effect of SWH in Energy Conservation*. (Solar Thermal Utilization Association of China Rural Energy Industry Association, November 2007); Solar Energy, November 2007. www.tynzz.com

Figure 1.7. Total Installed Capacity of SWH in China Accumulate solar thermal installed areas

Manufacturing standards and product quality for SWH systems are increasingly rigorous with newly developed national testing centers and a national certification center for SWH technologies. Although solar thermal use has increased in developing cities, such as Kunming and Qingdao, market expansion is constrained by the following factors: deficient techniques to integrate SWH technology into buildings; lack of installation support by commercial residence developers in major cities such as Shanghai and Guangdong; and low aesthetic quality, which reduces the appeal of SWH systems for some customers.

Bioenergy

China has a vast bioenergy potential with recent average biomass resource utilization above 500 million tce.[27] Table 1.1 displays the country's bioenergy potential per biomass and provides the key production technologies.

As of 2006, 39 biomass combustion facilities, with a total generation capacity of 1284 MW, have been approved by the National Development and Reform Commission (NDRC) and local provincial Development and Reform Commissions (DRCs). These new projects have a combined investment of about $1.39 billion. In 2006, the planned investments resulted in the installation of 54 MW of power generation capacity with no clear deadline for the installation of the total approved capacity. Table 1.2 displays the key technologies in biomass production in China and their current status of deployment.

Table 1.1. Biomass Potential in China by Source

Resources	Annual Potential (Tce)	Remarks
Straw & stalk	150 million	
Waste water	57 million	80 billion m³ biogas
Wood	300 million	
Urban garbage	13 million	120 billion tons

Source: NDRC, Mid- and Long-term Renewable Energy Development Plan, August 2006.

Table 1.2. Key Technologies in Biomass Production and Current Status

Utilization	Technologies	Status in 2006	Remarks
Power generation	Combustion (CHP)	1700 MW	
	Biogas	500 MW	
	Landfill & gasification	30 MW	
Clean fuel	Biogas	9 billion m³	For rural life
Clean biofuel	Biodiesel Bioethanol	Research	Key project in Program 863 from 11th FYP

Source: NDRC, Mid- and Long-term Renewable Energy Development Plan, August 2006.

Biogas utilization began in rural China during the 1970s and has made considerable progress since then. Biogas is now widely used in small-scale household production (8–10 m³ tanks). Biogas development is backed by the central government through strong fiscal incentives as well as investment subsidies to rural households amounting to about $763.04 million between 2003 and 2006.[28] Under the government subsidies program, households in northwestern and northeastern China receive $166.5 toward the purchase of a system; households in southwestern China receive $138.7: and households in other areas receive $111.[29] As a result, by end-2006, 17 million household biogas digesters,[30] 140,000 municipal waste treatment facilities, and 4,000 industry sewage biogas facilities providing 1.9 million m³ of biogas per year[31] had been installed.

Biogas production amounted to 500 MW in 2006, but the potential exists for substantially more. The estimated resource potential, according to a 2002 estimate of feedstock, includes 2.5 billion tons of wastewater from industry and 49 million tons of solid excrement from feed lots. There is an estimated potential of 14.5 billion m³ per year of industrial-scale biogas, of which 10.6 billion m³ come from industry, 2.7 billion m³ come from large feedlots, and 1.2 billion m³ come from small livestock farms. It is estimated that the above could be used to generate 3.8 GW of base load electricity with 23 TWh of electricity potential or could be used like natural gas for supporting peak load periods. The estimated potential in 2020 is vastly higher, including 41.5 billion m³ of industrial-scale biogas, comprising 21.5 billion m³ from industry and 20 billion m³ from livestock farms. This would amount to an installed capacity potential of 13.8 GW, assuming an efficiency-of-conversion increase. Only 1.2 billion m³ out of the current 14 billion m³ industrial-scale biogas potential is currently being used; most of the gas produced is vented, since the industry is focus on waste treatment and not energy production. Therefore, the potential for the industrial biogas industry is huge and, with only about 10 percent being exploited, largely untapped.

The government aims to increase biogas utilization by improving rural liming conditions and by promoting the livestock and poultry industries, industry waste biogas, and city sewage treatment.

Liquid biofuel technology is also in an early stage of development. China does however have important bioethanol potential based on sugarcane, cassava, corn, and broomcorn cultures. In accordance with the 10th Five-Year Plan, national Program 863 targeted developing technologies for making bioethanol from broomcorn and similar cellulose waste such as corn stalk. Biodiesel development is also included in Program 863 as of the 11th Five-Year Plan, but is still at the research stage. Its commercialization will depend on production cost reductions and increased conversion rates. Several demonstrations of biofuel have begun in Guangxi, Chongqing, and Sichuan, with cassava as the resource; demonstration stations in the Northeast and Shandong are being constructed with broomcorn.

Small Hydro

According to Chinese domestic regulations, small hydropower (SHP) refers to a power generation capacity lower than 50 MW. The total potential for SHP stations in China is estimated at 71.87 GW and is distributed among more than 1,600 mountain counties in middle and western China (see Figure 1.8 below). The potential for SHP is especially important in western China, where 70 percent of the unelectrified rural population is located.

China began utilizing small hydro for rural electrification in the early 1960s. So far, around 800 counties have been electrified with SHP stations connected to local transmission grids. By the end of 2004, however, only 2.1 percent of the total SHP potential had been developed in western China.[32] By the end of 2006, there were more than 40,000 SHP stations installed in rural China with a total power generation capacity of 50 GW and an annual yield of over 150 terrawatt hours (TWh).[33] Figure 1.9 below shows the developed and remaining potentials for SHP power generation per region.

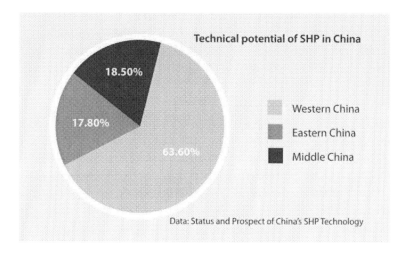

Figure 1.8. Total Potential for SHP in China

Source: "Current Status and Prospect of China's SHP," presentation of International Workshop on China Renewable Energy Strategy Development, August 16, 2006. http://newenergy.com.cn/html/2006-8/2006816_11456_1.html

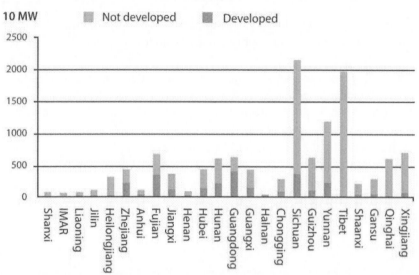

Source: "Current Status and Prospect of China's SHP," presentation of International Workshop on China Renewable Energy Strategy Development, August 16, 2006. http://newenergy.com.cn/html/ 2006-8/2006816_11456_1.html

Figure 1.9. Development Potential for SHP in China

SHP is one of the mature renewable energy technologies in China, with a significant domestic manufacturing capacity and competitive export potential in Asia. This is the result of strong fiscal support from the central government. SHP manufacturers benefit from significantly lower value-added taxes–currently at 6 percent, compared to 17 percent for other sectors. By 2004, there were over 100 SHP manufacturers in China, with an annual production capacity of around 6.3 GW.

Development of hydropower is focused on the areas of the Jinshajiang River, the Yanpanjiang River, the Daduhe River, upstream of the Huanghe River, and the Nujiang River basin. To accelerate the development of SHP, the Chinese Government is combining rural electrification with the SHP Generation Fuel Program, as well as exporting electricity from Tibet.

Energy Efficiency

In general, production and operation energy efficiency is low in China. Recently, energy efficiency (EE) has decreased due to the growing industry sector, which has the lowest energy efficiency level. Seventy-five percent of the total energy consumption increase comes from the industrial sector.[34] In the past six years, energy efficiency has further decreased as a result of the shift away from light industry toward heavy industry, which has a comparatively lower end-product value for higher energy consumption. Figure 1.10 shows China's energy consumption by sector over the past six years.

Table 1.3 compares China's energy efficiency to the international average for major industrial products.

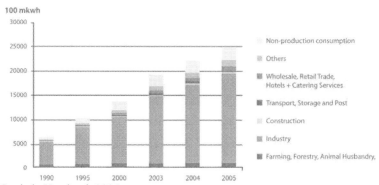

Data: NBSC, Statistic Yearbook 2006

Figure 1.10. China's Energy Consumption by Sector from 1990 to 2005

Table 1.3. Comparison of Energy Efficiencies for Major Products between Chinese Domestic and International Averages

Product Type	Energy Efficiency					
	China			Inter-national	Discrepancy in 2004	
	1990	2000	2004	Average*	Absolute	%
Power plant electric supply coal consumption (gce/kwh)	392	363	349	299.4	49.6	16.57
Thermal power generation coal consumption (gce/kwh)	427	392	376	312	64	20.51
Alternating current consumption for electrolytic aluminum (kwh/t)	16233	15480	15080	14100	980	7.00
Steel (large plants) (kgce/ton)	997	784	705	610	95	15.57
Cement (kgce/ton)	201.1	181	157	127.3	29.7	23.33
Crude oil refining (kgce/ton)	102.5	118.4	112	73	39	53.42
Ethene (kgce/ton)	1580	1125	1004	629	375	59.62
Synthetic ammonia (large-scale production) (kgce/ton)	1343	1327	1314	970	344	35.46
Paper and cardboard (kgce/ton)	1550	1540	1500	640	860	134.38

Source: Qinyi Wang, International Petroleum Economics, 2006, No.2.
  * Data are for the advanced counties in 2003.

The level of energy efficiency for all industrial products is included in Table 1.3 and is much lower than the overall international average. This is especially obvious for crude oil refining, as well as ethane and paper and cardboard production. Operation efficiency for end-use equipment in China is generally 20 percent lower than the international average for advanced countries, as shown in Table 1.4 below.

Table 1.4. Discrepancy in Operational Efficiency of End-Use Equipment between China and The International Average

End-Use Equipment	Operational Efficiency %	Discrepancy with International Average, %
Boilers in industry	65	15–20
Middle and small-size motors	87 (design)	20 (operation)
Fans and pumps	75 (design)	20 (operation)
Vehicles	9.5 L/100 km	25 (European)
Trucks	7.6 L/100 ton km	100
Fluvial navigation	—	10–20

Source: Yu Cong, China's Successful Case of Energy Efficiency in Industry (Energy Research Institute, NDRC, April 3, 2007).

The discrepancy in EE between China and the international average is mainly due to obsolete production equipment installed several decades ago, which has received little or no maintenance and has been poorly managed for the last 20 year

To improve energy performance, the Chinese Government set an ambitious target to decrease energy intensity by 20 percent in the 11th Five-Year Plan period, which spans from 2006 to 2010. Ten key programs in eight intensive industries are planned by the NDRC and provincial governments to achieve the target (details are provided in the EE market forecast section), including the annual publication of each province's energy intensity.

Co-Generation

In China, the use of combined heat and power (CHP) generation for heat supply began in the 1950s. At its maximum development in the 1980s and 1990s, CHP generation made an important contribution to national energy savings. Despite a relative decline, CHP remains a major heat supply source in China.

Political constraints often hamper the development of CHP generation. Heat generation from CHP falls within provincial or local jurisdiction, whereas electricity generation is subject to central government feed-in policies. Because of its clean power generation process and high efficiency, CHP receives support from local and provincial authorities. However, because of its low electricity yield, CHP has not received central government support through feed-in tariffs. In addition, up until 2005, CHP was categorized as small-scale thermal power generation with no grid connection possibility.

As a result of the mixed political signals from local/provincial and central governmental levels, as well as sustained growth of coal utilization and inconsistent electricity tariff increases, CHP has faced extra difficulties. Since 2002, 90 percent of China's domestic CHP operators have faced losses.[35] The situation is similar for foreign operators as French and American investors have retreated from China's CHP market since 2004. According to recent data from NDRC, CHP installations make up almost 50 percent of the power plants closed since the beginning of 2007.[36] Figure 1.11 displays the status of CHP generation in China as of 1998.

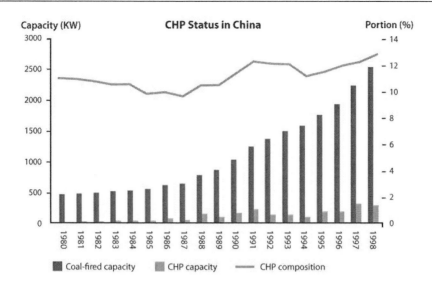

Data: Wang Zhenming, Potential Analysis on CHP China

Figure 1.11. Status of CHP in China

Clean Transportation Technology

Before 1993, China's national energy output in liquid fuel was higher than domestic consumption. Incentives for the development of clean fuel transportation technology were small, and research was not significant. Research on clean fuel transportation technology really began in the second half of the 1990s, with governmental support to universities but without private-sector involvement. The turning point occurred in 1999, when China's Ministry of Science and Technology (MOST) launched the Clean Vehicles Action Program, a demonstration and development program for large-scale clean transport technology that is currently in operation. Figure 1.12 below displays the program's operational organization chart.

Gas-Powered Vehicles

Gas-powered vehicles (GPVs) have come into operation since related technologies (e.g., gas storage systems) have matured – the GPVs presently on the market are thirdgeneration products. GPV technologies have now been introduced in 17 large cities and two provinces (Sichuan and Hainan—see Figure 1.13), and total a 265,000 unit vehicle fleet. GPV technology is expected to go into largescale production in the near future.

Fleet growth is faster for CNG vehicles than LPG vehicles. Recently, the CNG fleet grew at an average of 30,000 cars per year, from 22,300 in 2001 to 174,170 in 2006; reaching 66 percent of the GPV fleet (see Figure 1.14).

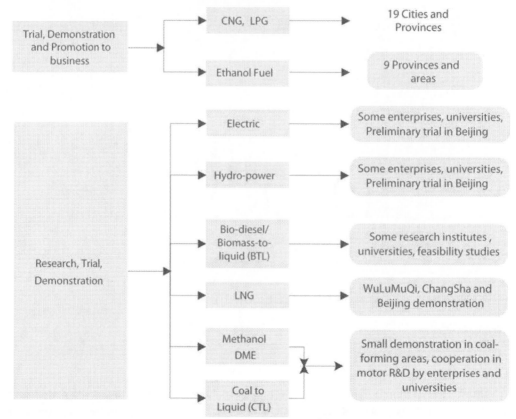

Source: China Automotive Technology and Research Center, CATRC

Figure 1.12. Organizational Chart for Clean Vehicles Action Program

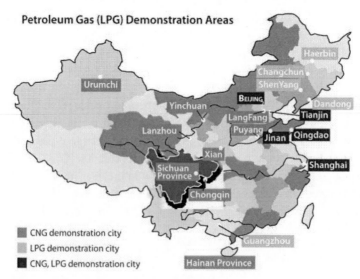

Source: database of China Automotive Technology and Research Center, CATRC

Figure 1.13. Compressed Natural Gas (CNG) and Liquefied Petroleum Gas (LPG) Demonstration Areas

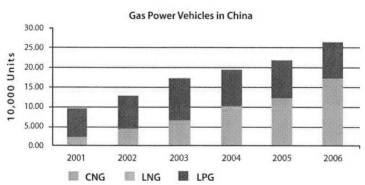

Source: database of China Automotive Technology and Research Center, CATRC

Figure 1.14. Breakdown of GPVs in China

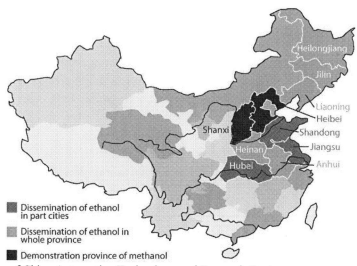

Source: database of China Automotive Technology and Research Center,

Figure 1.15. Distribution of AFV Development

China began its alcohol fuel vehicles (AFVs) development about 30 years ago. Initially, ethanol fuel vehicle pilots were formally launched in five cities (Nanyang, Zhengzhou, and Lyoyang Nanyang in the province of Henan; Ha'erbin and Zhaodong in the province of Heilongjiang) to be later extended to five provinces (Jilin, Liaoning, Heilongjiang, Henan, and Anhui) and parts of other provinces (Jiangsu, Hebei, Shandong, and Hubei—see Figure 1.15). Recently, the planned production level for ethanol fuel was set at about 1 million tons per year. Methanol gasoline fuel was primarily applied in Shanxi Province. Research on di-methyl ether (DME) fuel produced through clean coal technology is only beginning.

Electric Vehicles

Government support for electric vehicle (EV) research and development started early in the 1990s. The many research projects conducted since that time have not gone past the experimental stage with manufacturing trials, as EV technology applications are still limited by low power capacity and autonomy as well as high production costs.

Nonetheless, market growth for electric bicycles has been impressive. There were over 1,200 electric bicycle manufacturers and 3,000 parts suppliers in 2005, for a total production of about 10 million units. This dramatic growth is largely due to legislation banning gasoline-fueled scooters in several major Chinese cities, including Beijing and Shanghai.

Fuel Cell Electric Vehicles

Many of China's research institutions have invested in proton exchange membrane fuel cell (PEMFC) research and development since the 1990s, with the main research projects conducted in:

- Dalian Institute of Chemical Physics;
- Beijing FuYuan Pioneer New Energy Material Co., Ltd.;
- Shanghai Sun Li High Technology Co., Ltd;
- Beijing Lu Neng Power Sources Co., Ltd.

From 2001 to 2005, MOST approved a RMB 880 million ($122 million) research and development program to develop advanced hybrid electric fuel cell vehicles. Private sector investment is expected to bring in another $200–300 million from 2005 to 2010.

In March 2003, the Chinese Government launched a demonstration program in Beijing for fuel cell bus commercialization. This program is backed by the United Nations Development Program (UNDP) and the Global Environment Facility (GEF) as part of a demonstration project for 46 Daimler Chrysler–manufactured Citaro buses involving five countries and six cities over 2003–2008. The MOST and the municipal authorities signed the supply contract for three fuel cell buses with Daimler Chrysler in May 2004.

Chapter 2: Market Analysis

China's clean energy technology market is booming, with significant domestic production capacity. There are currently over 80 wind turbine manufacturers and 200 wind developers in China; domestic companies occupy over 75 percent of the domestic market. China's solar industry is growing rapidly, with a current capacity of 2,500 tons per year in solar ingot production. Significantly, there are over 3,500 solar water heating (SWH) system manufacturers in China, representative of the fact that China has the largest SWH market in the world. Finally, China's energy efficiency market is booming as a result of the goals set forth in the 11th Five-Year Plan. The major Chinese market players in wind, solar PV, SWH, hydropower, and energy efficiency are given in Annex 1.

Renewable Energy

Presently, total renewable energy utilization reaches only 7.5 percent of China's energy consumption. However, the potential renewable energy market is vast. As a component of China's energy strategy, the development of renewable energy receives support from the central government through a Mid- and Long-term Renewable Energy Development Plan, which has been released to implement the REL.

The Mid- and Long-term Renewable Energy Development Plan draws an ambitious blueprint for China's renewable energy development. The plan emphasizes renewable energy development for hydropower, biogas, solar thermal, and geothermal technologies as mature technologies with high potential for economic benefits. Wind, biomass, and solar PV power generation are also earmarked for accelerated development. According to the plan, renewable energy utilization should reach 300 million tce by 2010 and 600 million tce by 2020, as shown in Tables 1.5 and 1.6 below. The mid- and long-term projections from the plan indicate that the clean technology market will increase to $185.9 million in 2010 and approximately to $554.94 million in 2020 (see Table 1.7 below).

Market development for some of the renewable energy technologies has surpassed the targets established by the Mid- and Long-term Renewable Energy Development Plan. China's wind power generation capacity has experienced a steady increase since 2000. Between 2002 and 2007, the average annual growth rate was 97 percent. As a result, the total installed capacity for wind power generation reached 5 GW in 2007, three years ahead of the goal set forth in the plan.[37]

The solar water heating market is also rapidly expanding. Based on the recent annual surface installation increase of 15 percent, the objective for 2010 of 150 million m^2 production surface (as established in the Mid- and Long-term Renewable Energy Development Plan) should be attained easily, as shown in Figure 1.16 below.

Table 1.5. Goals for RE Utilization in RE Development Plan

Timeline	Utilization	Proportion of Energy Consumption
2010	300 million tce	10%
2020	600 million tce	15%

Data: NDRC, Mid- and Long-term Renewable Energy Development Plan, August 2006.

Table 1.6. Objectives for Key RE Technologies.

Re	Utilization	Objectives By	Objectives By 2020
Hydropower	Large scale	140 GW	225 GW
	Small scale	50 GW	75 GW
Bioenergy	Generation	5.5 GW	30 GW
	Solid biofuel	10 bil. tons	50 bil. tons
	Biogas	19 bil. m3	44 bil. m3
	Bioethanol	2 mil. tons	10 mil. tons
	Biodiesel	0.2 mil. tons	2 mil. tons
Wind	Generation	5 GW	30 GW
Solar *	On-grid solar PV	150 MW	1.5 GW
	Off-grid solar PV	150 MW	0.3 GW
	Solar thermal	150 mil. m2	300 mil. m2
Geothermal		4 mil. tce	12 mil. tce

Data: NDRC, Mid- and Long-term Renewable Energy Development Plan, August 2006.

* Total solar PV installation includes both on-grid and off-grid generation capacity.

Table 1.7. Government Objectives for Renewable Energy Market Potential

Resources	Market Potential Until 2010*	Market Potential Until 2020*	Estimated Investment Costs
Hydropower	$76.3 billion	$180.36 billion	$971.14/kW
Biomass generation	$3.47 billion	$27.75 billion	$971.14/kW
Wind	$1.09 billion	$23.86 billion	$901.78/kW
Biogas	$11.38 billion	$26.36 billion	$416.2/hh
Solar	$240 million	$18.04 billion	$10,405/kW
Others	$92.95 million	$277.47 million	

Source: Data are from Mid- and Long-term Renewable Energy Development Plan.

* Data for 2020 are from NDRC, Mid- and Long-term Renewable Energy Development Plan, August 2006. Data for 2010 are calculated on the basis of estimated investment cost and estimated generation capacity from 2006 to 2010.

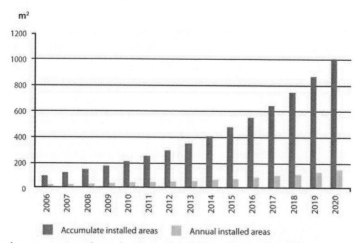

Data: Based on scheme on promoting solar thermal in China, International Energy Net

Figure 1.16. Solar Water Heating Forecast Through 2020 Based on an Estimated Annual Growth Rate of 15 percent

The domestic market for solar PV generation is relatively undeveloped compared to the markets for wind and solar water heating. China's government however is making efforts to promote a domestic solar PV generation market including the following programs:

- Government subsidy programs: Although the Brightness Program and SDDX have significantly improved rural electrification through solar PV generation, 3 million households in target areas remain without electricity. It is expected that 1.5 million households will be electrified through grid extensions as well as small and mini-hydro installations, but the remaining 1.5 million households will need to be electrified through solar PV and solar/wind hybrid systems.[38] The Village Electrification Program (SDDC) was to originally electrify 1 million households in 20,000 villages by installing off-grid solar systems with a 100-MW total generation capacity in remote rural areas of Tibet, Qinghai, Inner Mongolia, Xinjiang, Ningxia,

Gansu, and Yunnan;[39] however, the final plan and design for this program has yet to be confirmed.

- Construction of PV power stations: Plans have been made for the construction of large-scale on-grid PV power plants and solar thermal power plants in desert areas of Inner Mongolia, Gansu, and Xinjiang Provinces. The first plants will be constructed before the end of the 11th Five-Year Plan period in Dunhuang in the province of Gansu and in Lasha in the province of Tibet. The construction of the world's biggest solar PV power station has been actively planned since 2003.

- Start-up Roof PV Program and 100,000 Roof PV Program: the Start-up Roof PV Program promotes the construction of on-grid roof solar PV power generation in areas with dynamic economies such as Beijing, Shanghai, Jiangsu, Guangdong and Shandong. At present, there are more than 10 pilot roof PV power stations in Shanghai with a total generation capacity of 2,000 kW and an annual yield of 2 million kWh. Feasibility studies for the 100,000 Roof PV Program are currently being conducted by Shanghai Jiaotong University. The objective of this program is to install 10,000 rooftop PV on-grid systems by the end of 2010 and another 90,000 systems by 2015.[40] According to industry experts, one of the bottlenecks for large-scale on-grid application of solar PV generation is related difficulties in establishing the appropriate feed-in tariffs to stimulate the market. The Shanghai Roof PV Program provides the opportunity to fine-tune feed-in tariff policies for solar PV on-grid generation.

According to Tsing Capital in Beijing,[41] when combined with the environmental protection field, the market value of the clean tech industry totals over $200 billion. In the renewable energy sector, $2.8 billion has been invested in wind, $8.1 billion in solar thermal energy, $1.7 billion in solar PV, $3.1 billion in ethanol, and $1.3 billion in biodiesel. An additional $172 billion has been spent on environmental protection. Tsing Capital predicts energy generation will become the most popular segment of clean tech venture capital in the 2007–2008 period, followed by water and energy efficiency.

Energy Efficiency

In October 2005, Premier Wen Jiabao announced that China's energy intensity over the national GDP must decline by 20 percent between 2005 and 2010. The key policy initiatives toward reaching this goal were an emphasis on domestic technological innovations with planned leaps in key areas, close monitoring of current global technological developments, and leadership initiatives in emerging strategic sectors.

The new energy efficiency targets were included in the 11th Five-Year Plan. Planned reductions in energy intensity for the industrial sector account for 80 percent of total reduction targets. Reductions in industrial energy intensity will depend on the GDP growth level, with the planned reduction in energy intensity at 24 percent for a 7.5 percent GDP annual growth and a 26 percent reduction for a 9 percent GDP annual growth. The energy efficiency reduction targets are ambitious, and the challenge is to define appropriate measures and policies to reach the objectives. At present, China's central government has taken or will take the following operational measures:

- Put forward a series of structural adjustment policies in various industrial sectors and sub-sectors;
- Lower or cancel tax rebates on high-energy-intensity production exports;
- Implement the Top-1,000 Enterprises Energy Efficiency Program, which plans for the 1,000 highest energyconsuming enterprises in China to reduce their energy consumption by 100 million tce from 2005 to 2010;
- Promote the application of mature high-energyefficiency technologies;
- Eliminate inefficient processes and appliances.

According to the energy efficiency targets, the environmental impact of key energy-consuming sectors and unit energy consumption indicators for China's main products should reach the international average in the first quarter of this century. According to the plan, the energy efficiency of mass-market products with high-energy consumption should reach the mid-1990s' international average for developed countries. Targets are more ambitious for some products such as automobiles and specific electric appliances for household use, whose energy efficiency should now be almost on par with the current international average for advanced countries.

Table 1.8. Unit Energy Consumption Indicator for Main Products

Products	Unit	2000	2005	2010 (Planned)
Coal consumption for thermal power supply	tce/kwh	$3.92 \times 10-4$	$3.70 \times *10-4$	$3.55 \times *10-4$
Energy consumption per ton of steel	tce/t	0.906	0.760	0.730
Comparable energy consumption per ton of steel	tce/t	0.784	0.700	0.685
Specific energy consumption of 10 kinds of nonferrous metal	tce/t	4.809	4.665	4.595
Specific energy consumption for aluminum	tce/t	9.923	9.595	9.471
Specific energy consumption for copper	tce/t	4.707	4.388	4.256
Oil refining unit energy factor	tce/t.factor	0.014	0.013	0.012
Specific energy consumption of ethylene plant	tce/t	1.296	1.070	0.993
Specific energy consumption by synthetic ammonia	tce/t	1.372	1.210	1.140
Specific energy consumption by soda	tce/t	1.553	1.503	1.400
Specific energy consumption by cement	tce/t	0.181	0.159	0.148
Specific energy consumption by construction ceramics	tce/m2	0.01004	0.0099	0.0092
Specific energy consumption by railway transportation	tce/mt km	0.01041	0.00965	0.0094

Data from NDRC, 11th Five-Year Energy Plan.

Table 1.9. Energy Efficiency Indicators for Main Energy Consumption Equipment

Products	Unit	2000	2010 (Planned)
Coal-fired industrial boilers (operational)	%	65	70–80
Small and medium-size generators (design)	%	87	90–92
Wind turbines (design)	%	70–80	80–85
Pumps (design)	%	75–80	83–87
Air compressors (design)	%	75	80–84
Room air conditioners (energy efficiency rate)		2.4	3.2–4
Refrigerator energy efficiency indicator (EEI)	%	80	62–50
Cookstove for household use (heat efficiency)	%	55	60–65
Gas water heater for household use (heat efficiency)	%	80	90–95
Economic status of average automobile (fuel burning)	L/100 km	9.5	8.2–6.7

Data from NDRC, 11th Five-Year Energy Plan.

Table 1.10. The 10 Key EE Programs Put Forward by NDRC

Projects	Focus
Coal-fired industrial boiler alteration	Low-efficiency industrial boilers: alteration or replacement
Regional CHP projects	Heating CHP, industrial CHP, distributed CHP, CHCP, integrated utilization thermal power plants
Surplus heat and pressure utilization projects	Equipment alterations for surplus heat, pressure, and energy utilization in building materials as well as in steel and chemical sectors
Petroleum conservation and alteration projects	Electricity, petroleum, petrochemical, building material, chemical, and transportation; promoting biodiesel and bioethanol
Energy conservation (EC) on motor systems	Alteration of low-efficiency motors, EC alteration on drag equipment of motor systems, timing alteration on large and mid-sized variable motor systems
Energy system optimization	Systematic EC alteration in oil refining, ethylene, synthesis ammonia, and steel factories
EC in buildings	Improving the EE of buildings by 50%, EC restructuring for the existing buildings, integrating RE in buildings construction, promoting EC in wall materials, and industrializing the EC building material
Green lighting	Improving product quality, reducing costs, promoting innovations on EC lamp
EC for govt. organizations	EC restructuring of existing buildings, EE alterations on electrification, supervision for new building
EC monitoring and technology service systems	Alteration of EC monitoring equipment; energy audits for energy-intensive enterprises

Data from NDRC, 11th Five-Year Energy Plan.

Table 1.10 shows the 10 energy consumption programs put forward by the NDRC to reach the energy efficiency targets. These programs have been identified by the central government as the most effective means by which to reduce energy consumption as technology becomes mature within these areas.

The 20 percent energy savings targets established for the next five years seem difficult to achieve, but there is substantial potential to conserve energy throughout China's well developed supply chain, including energy extraction, conversion, transport, storage, distribution, and end use. On the other hand, it is an ambitious target that will require much capital, suitable market mechanisms, subsidies, and the cooperation of energy-intensive industries to curb demand. Currently the national energy reduction rate stands at only 1.23 percent, and only Beijing met the projected energy consumption reduction in 2006 out of all 34 provinces and municipalities.

Since then, China's central government has placed greater attention on energy saving and places it as an equal priority with economic development when assessing the leadership of the governors of provinces and municipalities. Since 2006 more and more measures have been successively issued by NDRC to guarantee the planned savings target, and more capital was invested in the energy efficiency field in 2007. At the end of 2007, China had achieved a 3 percent reduction in energy consumption. 2008 will most likely be an important year for the energy-saving target, since the benefits of many big energy efficiency projects will begin to be seen. It is also the middle of the 11th Five-Year Plan.

Co-Generation

With the development of the 10 key energy conservation programs put forward by the NDRC (under the 11th Five-Year Plan as shown in Table 1.10 above), cogeneration has been identified as an important energy conservation technology for reducing coal consumption. One expert estimates that CHP can save 48 million tce per year in China.[42]

According to China's CHP development plan, the installed CHP generation capacity should reach 120 GW by 2010, 15 percent of the total electricity generation capacity, and 200 GW in 2020, 22 percent of the total electricity generation capacity. To achieve these objectives, the average capacity installed annually must be around 9 GW through 2020.[43]

Based on the currently installed production capacity and the current 6.5 percent average annual growth for CHP generation in China, the total CHP generation capacity will reach 47 GW in 2010 and 87.5 GW in 2020, corresponding, respectively, to 37 percent and 68.5 percent of the total CHP potential.

Clean Transportation Technology

In 2006, China's vehicle fleet totaled roughly 40 million units — it is expected to reach 140 million in 2020 (see Figure 1.17). This increase is caused by a reduction in car prices, due to lower tariffs since China joined the World Trade Organization (WTO). Car price reductions are expected to continue as China develops a significant domestic production capacity, with the government identifying the car industry as a "pillar industry." Another important driver for the expansion of the domestic vehicle fleet will be the increase in consumer purchasing power.

The rapid expansion of the vehicle fleet will undoubtedly increase demand for oil. Based on reference scenarios, oil consumption for transportation is expected to exceed 50 percent of the total domestic oil demand by 2020. The Chinese Government has set targets to limit the oil demand to 125 million tons in 2020, with plans to reduce the oil demand by 20 percent through use of clean transportation technology, as shown in Figure 1.18.

China (in tens of thousands)

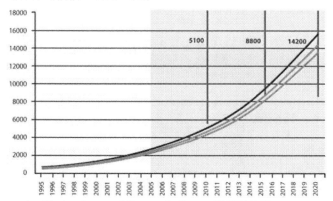

Source: China Automotive Technology and Research Center (CATARC).

Figure 1.17. Projections for the Number of Vehicles in China (in tens of thousands)

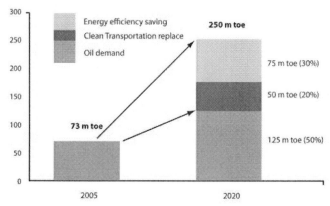

Data from CATARC, 2006.

Figure 1.18. Vehicle Fuel in 2020

Market Drivers

According to the most recent "BP-Statistical Review of World Energy," China is now the world's second largest energy consumer behind only the United States. Their energy consumption accounts for an astounding 15.6 percent of world's entire energy total. Since 2001, China's elasticity ratio for energy consumption averaged around 1, meaning any rise in GDP depends on a rise in energy consumption. As a result, China's 2006 GDP increase of 10.7 percent caused energy consumption to rise by 8.4 percent, while the global increase was only 2.4 percent.[44] This is in large part due to the increasing demand China's energy consumption due to urbanization and economic growth.

Figure 1.19 demonstrates, steel, aluminum, cement, and chemicals manufacturers have been the beneficiaries of the growing demand for heavy industries and energy intensive products.[45]

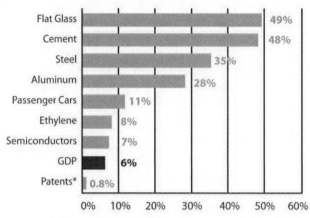

Source: Daniel H. Rosen and Trevor Houser, China Energy: A Guide for the Perplexed (Peterson Institute for International Economics, May 2007).

Figure 1.19. China's Share of Global Production (2006)

Table 1.11. Trends in Industrial Energy Demand (mToe)

	1990	2005	2015	2030	2005–2015*	2005–2030*
Total energy	242	478	833	1046	5.7%	3.2%
Iron and steel	42	132	260	273	7.0%	2.9%
Non-metallic minerals	56	109	157	142	3.7%	1.1%
Chemicals and petrochemicals	38	74	119	127	4.9%	2.2%
Other	106	163	298	504	6.2%	4.6%
CO_2 emissions (Mt)	800	1430	2186	2373	4.3%	2.0%

Source: IEA, World Energy Outlook 2007.

The industrial production capacity however far exceeds domestic demand as the Chinese Government has turned to exports to sustain economic growth and maintain profit margins. This "workshop of the world" mentality has led industrial energy demand to grow to 70 percent of total domestic energy consumption.

These drivers will continue to impact China's energy demand going forward. The huge urban market demand and booming investment in energy-intensive heavy industries together ensure a sustained energy consumption increase over the long term, as shown in Table 1.11.

Shortage of Liquid Fuel and High Dependency on Imports

In 2006, China consumed 350 million tons of crude oil, up 6.7 percent from 2005, while its oil output rose 1.6 percent to 183.7 million tons. Oil imports for 2006 reached 169 million tons, indicating a dependence on imports of 47 percent.[46]

According to the IEA, the share of oil imports will account for 70 percent of the total oil consumption in China by 2020, with the trend continuing until 2030. In 2020, China's crude oil production will reach its peak at approximately 200 million tons. As Figure 1.20 shows, after 2020, production will decrease, and the gap between the domestic oil demand and production will expand rapidly.

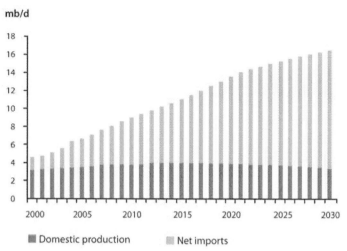

Source: IEA, *World Energy Outlook 2007.*

Figure 1.20. China's Oil Balance

Environmental Concerns

Coal dominates China's energy supply, creating severe pollution. Sulphur dioxide (SO_2) discharge exceeded 25 million tons in 2005. In 2007, SO_2 and dust discharge exceeded 80 percent of the gross discharge total resulting mainly from energy consumption and domestic energy production.[47] According to the World Bank, SO_2 and nitrogen oxide (NOx) emissions could reach 40 mt and 35 mt, respectively, in 2020 if no additional control measures are taken. Figures 1.21 and 1.22 display the areas affected by SO_2 discharge in China and the expected coal consumption to 2020, respectively.

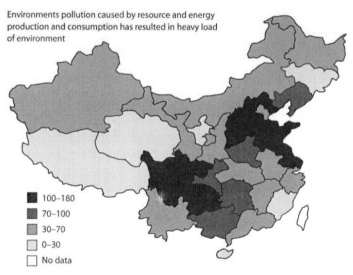

Source: Yande Dai, *China Energy Supply and Demand Situation and Energy Conservation Policy* (ERI, NDRC, March 2007).

Figure 1.21: SO_2 Discharge in China

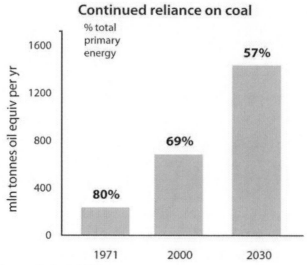

Source: IEA *World Energy Outlook 2005*

Figure 1.22. Continued Reliance on Coal

The World Bank estimates the total cost of air and water pollution in China in 2003 was $50.22 billion, or about 2.68 percent of the GDP. According to conservative estimates, the economic burden of premature mortality and morbidity associated with air pollution was $21.82 billion in 2003, or 1.16 percent of the national GDP. Another evaluation of the health losses due to ambient air pollution using willingness-to-pay measures estimates the cost at 3.8 percent of the GDP.[48]

Acid rain areas occupy over one-third of the country's soil surface. Acid rain is estimated to cost $4.16 billion in crop damage and $971.14 million in material damage annually.[49] More than 90 percent of the coal-burning plants are not equipped with desulphurization units. Coal exploitation has caused land collapse of over 988,421 acres. Annual sewage discharge from coal exploitation amounts to 3 billion m^3. Mine exhaust emissions amount to 9–12 billion m^3.[50]

Water pollution is also a cause for serious concern. Between 2001 and 2005, 54 percent of surface water resources were deemed unsafe for human consumption.[51] Estimates suggest the cost of groundwater depletion is around $6.94 billion per year. Cost estimates for polluted water usage by industry are comparable in magnitude, bringing the overall cost of water scarcity associated with water pollution to $20.4 billion, or about 1 percent of GDP.

Important Greenhouse Gas (GHG) Emissions
According to the IEA, China overtook the United States as the world's largest carbon dioxide (CO_2) emitter in 2007 (Figure 1.23), though its per capita emissions will reach only 60 percent of those of the OECD countries in 2030. Since the Kyoto Protocol came into force in 2005, China has become one of the largest Clean Development Mechanism (CDM) markets in the world. Currently, 2,701 CDM projects are in the pipeline.

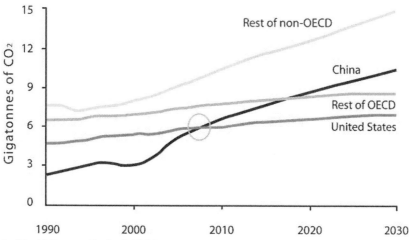

Figure 1.23. World CO_2 Emissions

The Clean Development Mechanism (CDM) is one of China's most important avenues for clean energy and advanced technology transfer. It provides not only additional venture capital, but also incentivizes other nations to invest in Chinese power generation and increase Chinese efficiency. In October 2005, the National Coordination Committee on Climate Change (NCCCC) released their "Measures for Operation and Management of Clean Development Mechanism Projects in China" program, which highlights the special rules for regulation of CDM developments in China, as follows:

a.   Priority areas for CDM development in China are:
     Energy efficiency improvement projects;
     Development and utilization of new and renewable energy;
     Methane recovery and utilization.
b.   If no foreign buyer has been determined when a project is submitted to NDRC for approval, which implies that the price of credits for emission reductions (CERs) is not fixed, the Project Design Documentation (PDD) must indicate the emissions reductions for the project will be transferred into China's national account in the CDM registry and can be transferred back out only with the authorization of China's National Designated Authority.
c.   Only Chinese-funded projects or Chinese-holding enterprises are qualified to become the owner of CDM projects. To ensure the technology transfers to China, the joint ventures seeking approval from NDRC must conform to the "51/49" ownership rule.
d.   Because CERs are owned by the Chinese Government and the emissions reductions generated by specific CDM projects belong to the project owners, revenues from the transfer of CERs shall be owned jointly by the Government of China and the project owners.

Table 1.12. Investment Cost and per kWh Cost for Existing Technologies in China

	Wind Energy	Solar Pv	Solar Thermal	Waste CHP	Geothermal	Biogas
Investment	$1,109.88–1,387.35	$8,324.1–11,098.78 per kWp	$277.47 per m^2	$6,936.74 per kWe	$32.68–52.72 per m^2	$166.48–277.47 /hh
Operation and maintenance	$0.012 per kWh	$0.006 per kWh	$2.77 per m^2	$0.003 per kWe	$2.5–4.16 per m^2	$8.32–13.87/a
Electricity production costs	$0.06–0.1 per kWh	$0.5–0.7 per kWh	N/A	N/A	N/A	N/A
Expected cost reduction	Small	Prices of $5 per Wp (2010) to $20 per Wp (2020)	Small	None	The price is decreasing.	Small

Source: Azure International, proprietary research.

Cost Analysis

Current Investment Cost and Cost Forecast through 2020

The current cost of investment in wind energy is in the range of $1,109.88–1,387.35/kW. It is expected that with increasing domestic manufacturing capacity and technology transfer, the investment costs can be lowered to the range of $832.41–971.14/kWh by 2010. Similarly, significant future cost reductions are expected for solar PV. Other more mature technologies, however, have less scope for cost reduction both in China and worldwide. The scenario for investment costs in renewable technologies is shown in Table 1.12.

2. Clean Energy Policies

The policy environment in China is a determining factor for the development of clean energy technology. Moreover, clean energy policy development is currently accelerating in response to China's mounting energy pressures. This section provides an overview of the key existing and planned policies.

Renewable Energy Law

The strategic position of renewable energy in China's energy policy was first affirmed through the Renewable Energy Law (REL) approved by the National People's Congress in February 2005. The REL is a framework law, which went into effect January 1, 2006. It set targets for renewable energy development and stipulates a number of broadly defined instruments to reach these targets.

The REL mandates the establishment of priority grid access for renewable electricity generators, a feed-in tariff for renewable electricity delivered to the grid, a national and regional cost-sharing mechanism for renewable energy subsidies, a special fund for renewable energy, and favorable loan conditions and tax treatment for renewable energy. See Table 1.13: Instruments in REL.

However, the general policy directions set out within this framework law are often vague and need to be further elaborated in implementing regulations in order to give clear signals for renewable energy development to the market. Development of such implementing regulations is underway.

Table 1.13. Instruments in REL

Instruments OF Rel	Specification
National renewable energy target	• Establishes the strategic position of renewable energy. • Identifies the scale of market development and plans for each step of renewable energy development. • Identifies the types of technologies. • Identifies the priority key locations for development.
Grid connection priorities	o Assurance that renewable energy power generation is a priority for grid connection. o Grid companies must accept all the power generated by renewable energy with the price fixed by the government. o Grid companies are required to invest in and construct transmission systems and the connection components for renewable energy integration to the grid.
Classifying tariffs for RE power	o The government determines the price based on the average cost or cost with advanced technologies or bidding price. o The price, application period, adjustment measures and appeal procedures are not yet clearly determined in REL.
Sharing costs at national level	o Costs for on-grid renewable energy electricity and off-grid generators in rural areas are shared by grid consumers in the whole country. o Costs for biofuel are to be shared regionally. It is not mentioned in which region in REL.
Renewable energy special fund	**Special fund covers:** o Technology research, standards development, and pilot projects; o Household renewable energy utilization projects in rural and pastoral areas; o Off-grid electrification projects in remote areas; o Renewable energy resource assessments and evaluation, as well as establishment of information systems; o Establishment of the localized renewable energy manufacturing industry; o Special fund comes from central and local finance as well as the balance of cost sharing.
Policies on favorable credit treatment	o Financial institutions may offer preferential loans with national financial interest subsidies to eligible renewable energy development and utilization projects that are listed in the national guidance catalogue for renewable energy industry development. o National policy banks, national banks, bilateral aid funds, and international multilateral aid banks or financial organizations are able to supply favorable loans.
Policies on favorable tax treatment	o A preferential tax will be given to renewable energy projects listed in the guidance catalogue for renewable energy industry development. o Detailed implementation measures should be issued by the taxing authority.

Source: Renewable Energy Law

Implementing Regulations of the Renewable Energy Law

The successful implementation of the REL depends on the implementation of regulations, which remain general and leave substantial room for interpretation. By the end of 2007, 10 implementing regulations had been issued regarding the development of renewable energy.

Mid- and Long-term Renewable Energy Development Plan

The Mid- and Long-term Renewable Energy Development Plan was published in August 2006. It sets goals for the development of each renewable energy technology for both 2010 (10 percent) and 2020 (15 percent).

Management Regulations for Electricity Generation from Renewable Energy

The National Development and Reform Commission released the Management Regulations for Electricity Generation from Renewable Energy in February 2006. The regulations establish the authority for approval of renewable energy projects, the eligibility rules for renewable electricity for policy and fiscal support, and a system for managing grid access.

Hydro projects on major rivers over 250 MW and wind projects over 50 MW are to be approved by the NDRC. Other projects are approved by the provinciallevel DRCs with notification provided to NDRC. Biomass, geothermal, wave, and solar PV are declared eligible for policy and fiscal support.

Grid companies are required to grant priority access to renewable energy generators, both from the large national power groups and from independent power producers. Furthermore, grid companies are responsible for the construction, expansion, and adaptation of the grid to facilitate access for medium- and large-scale renewable energy projects.

The China Electricity Council (CEC) is to supervise the operation of renewable electricity generators, the settlement of feed-in tariffs, and the relationship between renewable electricity generators and the grid companies.

Tentative Management Measures for Price and Sharing of Expenses for Electricity Generation from Renewable Energy

The Tentative Management Measures for Price and Sharing of Expenses for Electricity Generation from Renewable Energy were published in January 2006. The measures stipulate two mechanisms for determining the feed-in price for renewable electricity:

- The State Council sets the price;
- The price is determined by a competitive bidding round for a project development concession. The concession and bidding process exists at both the national and the provincial levels.

In addition to the above two pricing mechanisms, the management measures determine the feed-in tariff for biomass generation, which consists of the benchmarking price of desulferized coal-fired units plus a 0.03 $/kWh premium. For new projects, this premium will be decreased by 2 percent each year.

To finance the cost of the feed-in tariffs, the Notice on Adjusting the Local Grid Feed-in Tariff, was released in June 2006 and instituted a national surcharge of 0.0001 $/kWh[52] on electricity sales.

Guidance Catalogue of the Renewable Energy Industry

The "Guidance Catalogue of the Renewable Energy Industry" was released by the NDRC in November 2006. This guidance catalogue specifies the key renewable energy technologies supported by the government, the utilization of these technologies, and their development status (see Annex 3 for details). The aim of the catalogue is to guide decision-making on the direction of technological research and innovation, as well as the direction of renewable energy investment. Based on the catalogue, each province and municipality is to develop plans for supporting renewable energy technological development, pilot projects, and renewable energy investment that fit the local context.

Interim Measures on a Special Fund for Renewable Energy Development

The REL mandated the establishment of a special fund for renewable energy development. To ensure efficient use of the special fund, the Interim Measures on a Special Fund for Renewable Energy Development were released by the Ministry of Finance (MOF) in May 2006.

The special fund, through no-interest and discount loans, supports the key fields of fossil fuel alternatives, building heating and cooling, and renewable energy electricity generation (see Table 1.14). The amount of special funds for each year is published by the MOF and NDRC at the end of each previous year. According to the *China Reform Newspaper* of the NDRC, the special funds increased to $2.96 billion for energy conservation and emissions reduction in 2007, of which $1.25 billion was to be used to support the 10 key projects in energy conservation and capacity building. This amount is 13 times greater than in 2006.[53]

An application guidebook for the funds is drafted annually and published by the NDRC and the financial department of the State Council, in which the conditions for application are stipulated, as well as the fields and technologies supported by the special funds. Corresponding training is held by the Application Steering Committee of the National Energy Foundation Project and China Project Application Net to explain the details of the application. To date, two application guidebooks have been published, including:

- Special Funds Application Guidebook for RE Integrated in Buildings,[54] published by the MOF and Ministry of Construction (MOC). It stipulates the technologies for RE uilding integration, especially for:
  Building-integrated solar water heating, solar thermal air conditioners, and solar PV;
  Heat pumps with sources of ground, aquifer, fresh water, sea water, and sewage.
- 2007 Technology Innovation Fund Guidelines for a Number of Key Projects,[55] published by the Ministry of Science and Technology (MOST). It stipulates that private small and medium enterprises (SMEs) and joint ventures obeying "51/49" rules that have RE-related technological innovation are eligible to apply for innovation funds up to $140,000 as interest-free or discount loans. In addition, the innovation funds support technology transfer through fiscal support in the form of $100,000–$280,000 interest-free loans.[56]

Based on this application guidebook, companies can apply for the special funds support through the Energy Bureau of provincial DRCs and the provincial Department of Finance under the Ministry of Finance.

Table 1.14. Key Fields Supported by Special Funds

Key Fields	Technologies	Remarks
Fossil fuel alternatives	Biodiesel	Made from sugarcane, cassava, and broomcorn.
	Bioethanol	Made from oil crops, oil fruit, and oil aquatic plants.
Building heating and cooling systems	Solar	Integration in building.
	Geothermal	
Electricity generation	Wind	
	Solar PV	
	Ocean energy	

Source: NDRC, Interim Measures on Special Fund for Renewable Energy Development.

Other Implementing Regulations

The effectiveness of the REL depends on carrying out its implementing regulations, many of which must still be developed. One regulation is of special importance: preferential financing and taxation, which would significantly reduce the gap between the market competitiveness of renewable technologies and existing power generators. Industry experts have been appealing for several years to make progress on this regulation, but thus far have remained unsuccessful.

Energy Conservation Policies

The Chinese Government is increasingly focused on energy efficiency and conservation. In this section the key energy conservation policies are outlined.

Energy Conservation Law

The new Energy Conservation Law was approved by the 10th State Congress on October 28, 2007, and will enter into effect April 1, 2008.[57] The law revises the existing Energy Conservation Law (EC Law) of 1998 and identifies five key policy instruments, which are shown in Table 1.15. Like the REL, the EC Law sets broad targets, but lacks the regulatory muscle to implement many of the changes it hopes to make.

Incentive Policy for Energy Conservation

Enterprises can apply for a subsidy for energy efficiency improvements to the NDRC and provincial DRCs at the beginning of each year. The subsidies are disbursed to the enterprises in batches. Applications that fall under the Top-1,000 Enterprises Energy Efficiency Program and the NDRC's key 10 energy efficiency programs in the 11th Five-Year Plan get priority in subsidy allocation. The local provincial governments annually gather the proposals from industry and submit them to NDRC for final approval. MOF then transfers the subsidies to the provincial Departments of Finance, which in turn transfer the subsidies to the enterprises.

In addition to this incentive scheme, a new fiscal incentive for energy efficiency projects was recently established under the Tentative Management Measures for Fiscal Subsidy Funds on Energy Conservation Technological Innovation (August 2007). The implementation period for this new incentive spans from August 2007 through December 2010. The policy awards an investment subsidy of $27.75 per tce saved for investments in energy conservation measures. The subsidy is disbursed on the basis of the actual amount of energy saved. The energy savings are audited by a third party and verified by a qualified certification organization such as the China General Certification Center (CGC). The government budget for this incentive is open-ended and separate from the existing incentive policy budget.

Tax Incentives

Many special preferential tax policies have been implemented to support clean energy research, development, and production. For example, since 2001 waste-to-energy projects have been value-added tax (VAT) exempt. A 50 percent VAT discount applies for the use of energy-saving materials in buildings, for wind power projects, and for coal bed methane projects. Furthermore, since 2005 small-scale hydro has had a reduced VAT rate of 6 percent, and both large-scale hydro production and ethanol production have been VAT exempt -- ethanol is also exempt from the consumption tax.

Moreover, there are income tax deductions for various energy-saving and environmental technologies for both domestic and foreign firms.

Table 1.15. Instruments in the EC Law

Instruments of EC Law	Specifications
National energy conservation target	• Energy conservation is a key strategic policy objective. • Technologies are identified for energy conservation. • The reporting process is identified, as well as the mechanism for assigning responsibility, approvals, and appraising.
Management of energy conservation	• Develops a procedure for product standardization, industrial process standardization, and energy-saving labels for appliances. • Identifies an energy-saving assessment and appraisal system for fixed asset investment projects. • Phases out energy-intensive equipment and production processes. • Calls for improved public awareness on energy conservation through industry associations.
Key industries targeted for energy conservation	• Energy-intensive industry. • Building energy savings. • Public facilities energy savings. • Enterprises with annual energy consumption over 10,000 tce.
Technological advances	• Identify energy conservation technologies. • Draft guidance catalogues of energy conservation technologies.
Incentive measures	• Special funds for technology innovation, pilot projects, and the 10 key energy efficiency programs of the NDRC. • Preferential tax for EC technologies and products. • Preferential loans for research on EC technologies, EC products, and technology innovation. • Preferential tax for demand-side management (DSM), energy management contracts (EM-COs), and voluntary agreements.

Source: Energy Conservation Law

Government Procurement Policies

There are a number of Chinese government procurement laws, including the Government Procurement Law, Contract Law, Public Bidding Law, and Law against Unfair Competition, all of which are important to American firms looking to enter the Chinese market. There are also a number of regulations regarding the financing of government procurement, supervision of government procurement agents, and registration of suppliers. Most procurements are conducted in one of the following ways:

- Public invitation;
- Invited bidding;
- Competitive negotiation;
- Single-source procurement;
- Request for quotation;
- Other methods confirmed by the department of government procurement under the State Council.

"The Government Procurement Law was enacted for the purpose of regulating government procurement activities, including improving efficiency in the use of government funds, safeguarding the interests of the state and the public, and promoting transparency in governance. The law establishes the principles for government procurement, including openness and transparency, fair competition, impartiality, honesty, and good faith."[58] Government procurement information not involving commercial secrets is published in the *China Financial and Economic News, China Government Procurement Net, and China Government Procurement Journal.*

If government procurement occurs through public bidding, relevant information is to be published by media selected by related government agencies. Experts who evaluate the bids are to be randomly selected, and must make evaluations in accordance with pre-set procedures.[59]

With the rapid growth of procurement and increasing concern over energy efficiency, Chinese policy-makers are beginning to realize their actions can lead the rest of the market, both through the direct buying and the setting of examples. It should be noted however that although the government procurement process is becoming more transparent, there are still significant biases toward domestic products.

In December 2004, China's Ministry of Finance (MOF), in tandem with the NDRC, announced a new policy for government energy efficiency procurement. The program started in 2005 and was rolled out to all levels of government, including central, provincial, and local governments; schools; and hospitals. In 2006, the total amount of government purchasing for energy and water conservation products increased to about $1.297 billion.[60]

The Chinese Government's "List of Energy Efficient Products for Government Procurement" specifies the products all provincial governments should seek to procure. The MOF and NDRC have the responsibility to develop and update this energy efficiency list. The efficiency specifications for each product are those underlying China's current energy efficiency labeling program run by the China Standard Certification Center (CSC, formerly the China Certification Center for Energy Conservation Products). Qualified procurement models must receive CSC certification, which can present a problem for U.S. firms and their products.

Standards and Quality System

China requires strict conformity with assessment licenses, quality and safety licenses, testing, and labeling verifications for many products. The Administration of Quality Supervision, Inspection, and Quarantine (AQSIQ) is responsible for China's standards development and conformity assessment policies. Two independent agencies under AQSIQ, the Standardization Administration of China (SAC) and the Certification and Accreditation Administration (CNCA), play the dominant role in standards development and conformity assessment policies, respectively.

In general, exporters to China should be aware of three broad regulatory requirements in the standards and testing area. First, AQSIQ maintains approximately 20,000 national standards, of which about 2,800 are mandatory. The mandatory standards are known as *Guojia Biaozhun* or GB standards. Compliance with these standards, generally related to safety or quality, is mandatory for both domestic and imported products.

Second, numerous government agencies in China mandate industry-specific standards or testing requirements for products under their jurisdiction, in addition to the GB standards and the China Compulsory Certification (CCC) Mark. The CCC Mark is a compulsory safety Certification and combines China's previous two inspection systems—one to check the contents of products for import and export and the other for quality control. Although China already has some standards related to clean energy technology, most notably for solar water heating systems, these standards still need to be harmonized with international standards, such as the standards of the International Electrotechnical Commission (IEC).

Furthermore, an appropriate Chinese certification scheme based on international standards must be developed for type certification and project certification (postinstallation). For example, development of international standards for wind turbines takes place in the Technical Committee 88 (TC-88) of the IEC. Often national standards are based on these IEC recommendations, as was the case with China's standards for wind turbines. Recent scientific and technical developments however may lead to additional standards that can meet the special requirements of the Chinese market.

With respect to PV, the existing Chinese standards for PV are being assessed. Two Chinese standards became Reference Standards for IEC. In addition, China changed its Module Standard to correspond with IEC 61215.

Forthcoming Energy Law

To date, several laws regarding coal, electric power, energy conservation, and renewable energy development have been released, but often these lack the strong integrated approach a complex energy portfolio requires. China's increasing dependence on imports, its rapid demand increase, and severe environmental damage has caused traditional energy sources to become outdated from an investment perspective.

A draft of China's integrated Energy Law was recently published. The Energy Law is an integrated framework law for overall national energy development and will include guiding principles for legislation on energy structure, energy efficiency, energy security, energy development and utilization, and energy and environmental coordination. Table 1.16 provides an outline of the main instruments included in the new Energy Law. One of the most important changes is the proposed establishment of an Energy Ministry directly under the State Council.

Table 1.16. Instruments of China's Forthcoming Energy Law

Instruments	Specifications
Energy management	• Establishes an Energy Ministry under the State Council, to oversee energy management in China. • Clarifies the role of industry associations in providing information on industry statistics, standardization, technologies, market development, and consultancy for policy decision-making and to enterprises. • Enhances the management of exports of energy-intensive products. • Establishes an energy statistics and forecasting system.
Energy strategy and plan	• A 20–30-year energy strategy will be published and revised by the State Council once every five years. • A five-year energy plan will be published one year after the publication of the economic plan and social development plan. • The provinces are to develop provincial energy plans according to their specific needs and report to the State Council energy department.
Energy development and conversion	• Property of energy resources belongs to the state. • Development of mining, renewable energy, and energy production and conversion should be approved by the State Council energy department. • Establishment of environmental compensation mechanism for energy production and conversion.
Energy supply and service	• Business on energy supply should be approved by the State Council energy department. • Construction of an inter-regional energy infrastructure is encouraged. • Establishment of energy universal service compensation mechanism.
Energy conservation	• Allows the government to encourage energy conservation for optimizing industry and consumption structures and to support energy conservation technology as well as energy management and conservation in key industries. • Establishes energy conservation market mechanisms and perfect consultancy and service system. • Promotes energy efficiency labeling, EMCOs, voluntary agreement, and DSM.
Energy reserve	• Increases strategic reserves of petroleum, natural gas, uranium, and high-quality coal.
Energy emergency	• Emergency back-up capacity is to be constructed. • Basic supply of energy for emergency conditions is determined by order of importance from essential national institutions, national defense facilities, emergency command agencies, the communication and transporttation hub, and emergency medical treatment.
Rural energy	• Develops a preferential tax, financial, and price policy encouraging investment in rural energy. • Promotes utilization of new and renewable energy such as CHP, biomass, wind, and solar energy. • Increases the proportion of rural grid coverage. • Promotes rural energy conservation system and services.
Energy tariff and tax	• Establishes market-driven energy price mechanism. • Allows the government to determine or guide tariffs for the use of

Table 1.16. (Continued)

Instruments	Specifications
	• pipelines and grids of strategic public importance. • Implements incentive tariff policy for new and renewable energy development. • Allows the government to guide the energy price for energy-intensive and polluting industries. • Establishes a national and provincial expenditure budget system. • Establishes government investment for environmental protection in mine areas, rural energy development, energy technology research and development, energy conservation, and development and utilization of renewable energy.
Energy technology	• Promotes energy technology development for innovation and research on energy resource exploration; energy conversion and transportation technology; comprehensive utilization of clean energy technologies; energy conservation and emission reduction technologies; and energy security production technologies. • Increases budget for energy technology development at national and provincial government levels. • Promotes enhancing public awareness.
Energy international cooperation	• Establishes a mechanism for international energy cooperation, management, and coordination. • Establishes publication of "Industry Guidance Catalogue for Foreign Investment on Energy Sector" and relevant policy.
	• Promotes international cooperation in energy trade, energy transportation, capacity building, and energy security.
Supervision and inspection	• Proposes three supervision methods: State Congress, administration, and society. • Promotes energy performance site checking. • Calls for publication of energy performance of high-intensity enterprises.
Liability	• Assigns liability to different government officials, energy enterprises, and energy end-users as well as to the public at large.

The draft of the Energy Law has been posted on the Web site of the Office of the National Energy Leading Group,[61] only available in Chinese. It is anticipated that passage of the bill will be achieved in 2009 after being approved by the National People's Congress.

4. Opportunities for U.S. Firms in China

Since China's entry into the WTO in 2001, the opportunities for U.S. firms to enter the Chinese market are accelerating. This potential is often extremely attractive to foreign manufacturers, investors, and other firms. The opportunities for U.S firms entering the Chinese clean energy market have likewise grown tremendously over the last few years thanks to increasing energy security concerns and mounting environmental pressures. In this section, two key enablers are considered:

- New and emerging Chinese Government energy policies;
- Lag in the current Chinese CET market relative to those in the European Union and North America.

Ambitious objectives for China's renewable energy development are evident from government policies. According to China's Energy Research Institute, the investment potential for energy efficiency in China from 2007 to 2010 is $120–160 billion.[62] For renewable energy, the main technologies promoted are hydro, wind, solar PV, solar thermal, biomass electric power generation, and biofuels. The areas of geothermal and ocean energy are also mentioned in these policies.

To fulfill the objective of a 20 percent decrease in energy intensity by 2010 (relative to 2000 levels), the Chinese Government has recognized that major developments in technology and energy management must be achieved across industrial, commercial, and residential sectors. Furthermore, evolution of the energy infrastructure provides avenues for broader adoption of renewable energy technologies.

Personal and materials transportation is likewise a core factor in China's energy demand policy. Given the rapid urbanization of China, the demand for intra-city and inter-city transportation is growing rapidly. It can be expected that more fuel-efficient and lower-emission vehicles will be increasingly popular in China. The booming personal transport sector is especially driving a need for alternative liquid fuels and more efficient personal and mass transit solutions.

The rapidly growing government push, and resulting market pull, for clean energy development presents special challenges for China due to the technological requirements necessary to reach the aggressive government goals. These challenges are elaborated upon below.

Need for High-quality Equipment, Products, and Services

The commercial market for clean energy technologies in China is developing. As CET demand picks up, increasing demand for proven, high-quality products and services can be expected, providing an opening in the market for qualified international companies with sustainable business operations.

Expanding Market for High- quality Equipment

To succeed in the competition, more and more RE manufacturers are eager to increase their product quality by introducing process line or purchasing production licenses from international top manufacturers as well as cooperating with them through technology transfer.

To successfully achieve China's energy efficiency target (a 20 percent decrease in energy intensity by 2010), along with targeted improvements in public awareness and new building improvements, more and more small and medium enterprises (SMEs) are looking to improve their energy performance by introducing effective energy management and importing high-quality and efficient proven equipment.

Professional Clean Energy Technology Services

The development of CET service companies has not been well established in China. In fact, the entire concept of energy service companies (ESCOs) is generally unknown to many

Chinese companies. Some key areas of opportunity for professional ESCOs include: operation and maintenance for renewable energy generation, energy auditing and advisory services, consultancy on energy management and RE integration, and ongoing energy efficiency services within a large business. There will be a growing market for all of these services for international and domestic businesses operating in China.

Proven Energy Conservation Technology

Increasing energy efficiency performance is one of China's key energy strategies. Except for the 10 EC programs and Top-1000 Enterprises Program being used by the government to achieve the objective, there is a need to improve public awareness, as well as technology and advisory services to help SMEs improve their energy performance. However, there is a lack of expertise in China regarding energy efficiency technologies and innovation, energy auditing, and energy management. As a result, there is a need for qualified consultancy companies in these areas.

Table 1.17. Key Areas of Opportunity for U.S. Clean Tech Firms

Technology	Opportunity
Wind energy	• Dedicated O&M service companies. • Remote monitoring systems and control systems. • Wind turbine design and testing. • Technologies for large-scale wind turbines (capacity over 2 MW). • Software for wind resource assessment, grid integration, and wind power prediction.
Solar thermal	• Aesthetic building integration. • High-quality installation. • After-sales service.
Solar PV	• Improved technology in thin-film solar panels. • Cooperation for technology transfer to increase the quality of solar PV products and decrease the cost. • Technology on high-quality converters to increase the conversion efficiency. • Interface technology for building-integrated PV (BIPV) and for power plants. • High-quality crystalline silicon technology. • Technology/software for optimizing PV systems. • Ultra-thin stainless steel bands for soft solar PV panels used in BIPV.
Biofuels	• R&D cooperation on the production of ethanol from cellulosic feedstock.
Biogas	• Training on technology, equipment, and service;, development of high-efficient fermentation technology for higher biogas yield. • Demonstration of new building material and technology for digester construction and biogas storage; high-pressure biogas storage. • Reliable (more than 7,000 hours/year) biogas heat and power co-generation. • Efficient post-treatment technology for water and solids after fermentation. • Biogas fuel cell development cooperation. • Biogas purification with air intake (biological sulfur removal). • Biogas processing for feed-in natural gas grid and as transport biofuel.
Geothermal	• Technology and equipment for geological exploration and project development.

Source: Guidance Catalogue of the Renewable Energy Industry and interviews

At present, SMEs have to find energy-savings solutions themselves, but information on which technologies are suitable for particular kinds of energy efficiency improvement is not readily available. There is also a lack of proven energy efficiency technologies, providing an important opportunity for U.S. firms to provide expert consultancy and technology services.

Energy Technology Development Opportunities

China can benefit greatly from firms that offer key technology solutions. Table 1.17 below provides an overview of the areas of technology development where foreign companies provide unique solutions that China currently does not have.

Given the ambitious near-term targets set by the Chinese Government for deployment of renewable energy technologies and energy efficiency improvements, as well as the increased investment in industry, there is currently substantial opportunity for U.S. firms in China.

5. Investment and Financing of Renewable Energy and Energy Efficiency

By the year 2020, China plans to develop 120,000 MW of renewable energy. This would account for 12 percent of China's total installed energy-producing capacity. China's growth target for renewable energy production will require an investment of approximately $100 billion by 2020. The challenges involved in attracting this investment are significant and will depend on the enabling policy and regulatory frameworks being developed to entice energy investors. Financing needs include:

Project Equity

Equity capital in China is typically sourced from the government, strategic investors and joint ventures, private equity funds, utilities, or capital markets (i.e., public equities or bonds). oint ventures in particular are one of the main sources of project equity in China. Of late, the number of new renewable energy private equity funds and investors has increased to include both pure equity and quasi-equity funding.

Project Debt

The bulk of the financing provided to a project is usually in the form of senior debt. A significant amount of innovation in debt-financing instruments is currently in progress in China by organizations such as the World Bank, export credit agencies, and other development finance institutions to reduce risks and improve access to long-term financing.

End-User Finance

As renewable energy markets continue to grow in China, end-user finance will become important.

Small and Medium Enterprise Finance

SMEs will play an increasingly important role in providing technologies and services in China; however, these markets are rarely served by bank financing. Niche organizations such as E&Co, which is active in China, provide business planning and advisory services as well as critical seed capital, but additional funding sources are needed in this area.

Financing Sources for Clean Energy

Clean energy financing sources in China include:

Government Agencies

Government agencies, at the national and local levels, will continue to be a key source of funding for clean energy investments in China. China's renewable energy program has made significant achievements in small hydropower, biogas plants, solar hot water systems, and recently PV and wind systems due in large part to government support. For instance, the Ministry of Science and Technology and the National Development and Reform Commission jointly launched the International Science and Technology Cooperation on New and Renewable Energy on November 12, 2007. Special funds will be earmarked for the launch of the program.

Multilateral and Bilateral Organizations

Both the World Bank and the Asian Development Bank have made significant lending commitments to renewable energy and energy efficiency in the Asia region, with particular emphasis on China. For example, the World Bank has committed $86 million of a total $132 million project for follow-up to the China Renewable Energy Scale-up Project. This project hopes to demonstrate early success in large-scale renewable energy investments with participating local developers. The project comprises two components: a 100-MW wind farm at Huitengxile in Inner Mongolia and a bundle of small hydro construction and rehabilitation projects in Zhejiang Province. The World Bank also has a dedicated program for promoting clean energy in Asia—the Asia Alternative and Sustainable Energy (ASTAE) Program, which seeks to mainstream investment in renewable energy and energy efficiency in the region.

The Asian Development Bank (ADB) recently approved $35 million in funding for the Gansu Clean Energy Development Project and $600,000 in support for establishing a Clean Development Mechanism Fund and has a number of energy efficiency projects being considered for approval. GEF has supported over 28 projects under the climate change focal area in China, valued at over $376 million. Bilateral organizations providing financing and technical assistance include GTZ and KfW of Germany, Triodos Bank of the Netherlands, and export credit agencies from a number of countries including the United States, Japan, and Europe.

International and Local Finance Institutions

International and local financial institutions have been active in supporting clean energy in China. International investors include entities such as Citigroup, Actis, and Credit Suisse, while local financial institutions include China Merchants Bank, China Development Bank, and the Industrial and Commercial Bank of China (ICBC).

Besides long-term loans, short-term bonds are an important way to expand financing channels and reduce costs. In May 2005, the People's Bank of China sold the first short-term bond; since then, 364 shortterm bonds have been issued with a total of approximately $67.8 billion.[63]

Trust funds are another financing channel to reduce costs. The bank commission trust company operates as the client's capital, the enterprises act as the main body of the loan, and the capital received from the trust company is used to meet medium and long-term requirements.

The All-China Federation of Industry & Commerce, together with the New Energy Chamber and some membership enterprises, has recently proposed to the NDRC to set up so-called Industry Investment Funds for New Energy, which will benefit new energy enterprises.

Grants/Soft Loans

Such loans refer to financing or credit support from a government institution or multilateral institution. Government financing sources have special criteria or non-commercial objectives.

Public Offering

Renewable energy enterprises can access capital through public offerings. China GoldWind, for instance, a wind turbine manufacturer in Xinjiang Province, received approximately $260.4 million by public offering in December 2007.[64]

Carbon Finance

Both the CDM and the emerging voluntary carbon markets are providing a revenue stream to increase the financial viability of clean energy projects in China. In 2006, the global carbon market amounted to $30 billion, up from $11 billion in 2005. CDM accounted 88 percent of this market. As noted in Figure 1.24 below, China received 61 percent of the market's volume.

According to national policy, joint CDM ventures must abide by the"51/49" rule , in which case the profit from the carbon market is logically allocated in accordance with the share.

The easiest way to enter China's carbon market is to purchase Verified Emission Reductions (VERs) on the voluntary market. Compared to CDM trade, VER is a flexible mechanism for joint ventures with foreign shares over 50 percent. According to ICF International predictions,[65] global VER requirements will reach 0.4 billion tonnes of CO_2 by 2010, of which three-quarters come from group buys and the remainder from private buyers. Based on the current VER price of $5.5/ton, the potential of the VER market is $2.2 billion, 40 percent of which is in China.[66] VERs are applicable to wind projects, small hydropower projects, biogas utilization, landfill projects, and hydrofluorocarbon (HFC) and N_2O decomposition projects, the latter of which is favored by the Chinese government.

Venture Capital and Private Equity Investment

U.S. investment in clean technology companies worldwide has increased steadily from around $590 million in 2000 to $2.6 billion in 2007.[67] The implementation of China's Renewable Energy Law and the 11th Five-Year Plan are the main policy drivers in China's clean tech industry and will continue to stimulate the market going forward. In the first quarter of 2007, $154 million was invested in six deals – almost 14 times the amount invested in the first quarter of 2006. This investment expected to expand the Chinese clean tech markets to around $700 million in 2008.[68] Figure 1.25 displays the number of deals by quarter.

Private equity funds will also continue to seek opportunities in the Chinese market. Note that China will likely be more selective in bringing in overseas investors as the total amount of foreign investment continues to grow. Therefore, the major problems faced by private equity investors in China are no-exit mechanisms and political risks.

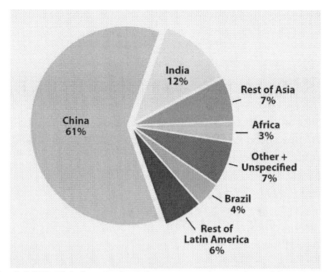

Source: Viakatta Putti, "CDM Market Outlook," a presentation at the Africa Lighting Carbon Finance
   Workshop, October 2007.

Figure 1.24. Carbon Sellers in 2006

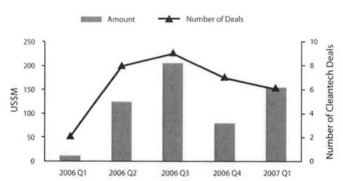

Source: Cleantech Group LLC, "China Cleantech Venture Capital Investment Report," .2006–2007.

Figure 1.25. Clean Tech Venture Investments by Quarter

Table 1.18. Selected Private Equity and Venture Capital Investment Firms in China

Name of Firm	Company Invested
Sino-Belgium Direct Equity Investment Company	Goldwind
HSBC Infrastructure Fund Management	Canadian Solar
London Asia Capital	China New Energy
DragonTech Venture Management	Suntech Power
Actis Capital LLP	Suntech Power
Natexis Private Equity	Suntech Power
Prax Capital	Suntech Power

Source: Azure-international

Table 1.18 shows the main private equity and venture capital firms in the Chinese clean technology market.[69]

6. Barriers to Clean Energy Trade and Investment for U.S. Firms

Despite the significant opportunities the Chinese clean energy market presents, important barriers remain that must be considered before developing a successful Chinese business strategy. These barriers are addressed below:

Intellectual Property Rights Enforcement

Although China's leadership has recognized the importance of improving the protection of intellectual property (IP), IP theft remains a major challenge to U.S. companies. The latest U.S. trade losses due to counterfeiting and piracy in China remain unacceptably high. Copyright industry losses were estimated at over $2.9 billion in 2007. In FY2007, 80 percent of the fake products seized at the U.S. border, valued at $158 million, came from China. This $158 million figure represents a 25 percent increase compared to the value of FY2006 seizures. Taking steps to protect your U.S. intellectual property in China is a critical part of doing business with China.

Because U.S. registered patents and trademarks provide no protection outside the United States, securing your IP rights in China and other countries is essential. If, for example, you enter the Chinese market without having registered your trademark in China (in English, and ideally, in Chinese as well), one of your competitors, distributors or partners could register before you and bar you from selling or manufacturing products bearing your trademark in China. This practice, commonly known as "trademark squatting," is among one of the most frequent problems faced by U.S. industry. Additionally, mandatory technology transfer requirements and "patent squatting" have become problems for U.S. industry in China.

China has three tracks for seeking enforcement of IP rights – civil, criminal and administrative. However, the lack of effective and deterrent enforcement of IP rights remains a serious problem. Enforcement efforts, particularly at the local level, are restricted by poor coordination among Chinese Government ministries and agencies, local protectionism and corruption, high thresholds for initiating investigations and prosecuting criminal cases, lack of training, and inadequate and non-transparent processes. If a company does not register its IP rights in China, China's three enforcement tracks not only are not available to you but also may be used against you. Sophisticated counterfeiters manipulate the loopholes in the Chinese system to prevent market access for foreign technology.

The United States has consistently made the protection and enforcement of IP a top priority and recently launched the Strategy Targeting Organized Piracy (STOP!), a U.S. Government initiative to fight global counterfeiting and piracy. The Department of Commerce plays a critical role in this effort by providing U.S. businesses, including SMEs, specific IP resources to educate and assisting them with protecting and enforcing their IPR. See Appendix A for a list of resources.

Legal and Regulatory Environment

Chinese laws and regulations for clean technology tend to be broadly defined and lack specific implementing rules and measures. This can make it difficult for U.S firms to determine precisely whether their activities match or contradict a particular regulation.

While the Energy Conservation Law has played an important role in improving energy efficiency, it is widely recognized that the law's incentives and enforcement regulations are too weak. It is expected that more incentives will be provided and a more restrictive management system adopted in the amended Energy Conservation Law currently under review by the National People's Congress.

Several much needed regulations are also not yet in place under the Renewable Energy Law. A governmental guiding price has not been implemented for wind power generation. And while competitive tendering is effective for large wind power projects, no mechanism exists to price small wind projects and improvements of existing wind farms. Feed-in tariffs are also not fixed nationwide, increasing the risk for project developers and capital investors.

The overlapping responsibilities and areas of authority among government organizations often cause additional confusion to foreign companies. China lacks an open system that disseminates planning information, project approval, and pricing to the public. As a result, foreign companies often face ad hoc decision-making and an often cryptic response from the government to their questions. It is therefore advised that U.S firms carry out due diligence and seek professional advice before entering the Chinese market.

Clean Energy Technology–Related Customs Regulations and Trade Tariffs

Foreign companies operating in China are required to pay an income tax, which is calculated differently according to the percentage of ownership a foreign firm has in a joint venture. China intends to eventually phase out its two-tier income tax system for domestic and foreign enterprises, because domestic enterprises have long resented rebates and other tax benefits enjoyed by foreign-invested firms. The move toward national treatment will mean the gradual elimination of special tax breaks enjoyed by foreign investors. According to the framework of corporate income tax reform, the corporate income tax will be unified to domestic and foreign direct investment (FDI) companies, meaning FDI companies will no longer have advantages in terms of favorable tariffs.

A comprehensive guide to China's customs regulations is available in the *Customs Clearance Handbook* compiled by China's General Administration of Customs. It contains the tariff schedule, national customs rules, and appropriate regulations. This guide can be purchased at bookshops in China.

Restrictions on Foreign Direct Investment

Although the Chinese Government encourages foreign investment in the clean energy industry, the "Catalogue for the Guidance of Foreign Investment Industries (2007 revised),"70 does limit foreign firms to some degree. In the catalogue, which came into force December 1, 2007, foreign industries are divided into "encouraged," "restricted," and "prohibited." The items related to clean energy technologies are summarized below:

Encouraged Sectors

Development and utilization of cleancoal technologies; construction and operation of hydropower stations with the main purpose of generating power; construction and management of nuclear power plants (Chinese partner shall hold the majority of shares); and construction and management of new energy power plants (solar, wind, magnetic, geothermal, tide, and biomass energy). New energy power equipment is however limited to equity joint ventures and cooperative joint ventures.

Restricted Sectors

Manufacturing of biofuels; construction and management of conventional coal-fired condensing steam power plants whose unit installed capacity is less than 300,000 kW within the small grids of Tibet, Xinjiang, and Hainan Provinces; and coal-fired condensing-extraction steam power plants with dual use unit co-generation.

Prohibited Sectors

Construction and management of conventional coal-fired condensing steam power plants whose unit installed capacity is less than 300,000 kW outside the small grids of Tibet, Xinjiang, and Hainan Provinces.

The National Development and Reform Commission and Ministry of Commerce jointly issued a new "Industrial Catalog for Foreign Investment." It is recommended that U.S. firms look through the related special laws and regulations carefully before investing or pursuing business in China.

Lack of Government Relations

In China, *Guangxi* (relationship) is a complicated matter. Building quality government relationships should be a primary business development focus for many U.S firms, especially for those firms entering the Chinese market for the first time. There will be unpredictable challenges and it is important for U.S. firms to coordinate with the Chinese Government when dealing with issues of foreign trade and economic cooperation. Lack of a government relationship will create unnecessary difficulties and delays in acquiring government approvals. A good relationship can pave the way. In addition, the Chinese Government tends to protect local firms, especially state-owned firms, from imports, while encouraging exports. Although WTO accession is certainly helping in this area, progress is being made only gradually.

There are resources available to help U.S. firms develop relationships with the Chinese Government. The U.S. Commercial Service in Beijing also offers a wide range of services to assist U.S. companies in finding Chinese partners. See Appendix A for a list of additional resources.

Low Awareness of Intercultural Issues

There is a large culture gap between the United States and China, which is too often ignored. Intercultural sensitivity is critical, and should be considered a core focus for any company working in China. Between the two countries the ideas of law, profit, decision-making, market orientation, business relationships, and technical standards are quite different.

Low awareness of how to navigate these differences will cause misunderstandings and miscommunication and can cause conflicts of interest as time goes on.

A good way to prevent cultural conflict is to visit China in order to gain a better perspective and understanding, which can provide a company great insight into the country, the culture, the business climate, and its people. Chinese companies prefer and respect face-to-face meetings, which demonstrate a U.S. company's commitment to working in China. Note that China has many different regions and that each province is unique both economically and socially.

Relative Higher Product Prices

Generally U.S. production costs and product prices are higher than Chinese production costs and prices. Most Chinese consumers are very sensitive to price and will usually choose the less expensive product unless better after-sales service or clearly better product quality is available.

Government Procurement

The transparency of government procurement is a concern for foreign companies. Local relationships and networking of domestic companies play a very important role in procurement, which may lead to unfair competition and may put U.S firms in a weak position.

Corruption in government departments remains widespread, though the government continues to call for improved self-discipline and anti-corruption efforts at all levels. For competitive procurement contracts, there is little direct evidence that corrupt practices have influenced awards or resulted in a failure to enforce competitive measures. However, competitive procedures are not followed for the bulk of procurement in China.

Contract Enforcement

The Contract Law came into force on October 1, 1999, and contains both general and specific provisions. Technology Contract Regulations were published in 2002. There are some other laws and regulations regarding contract enforcement, such as:

- Administration of Technology Import and Export;
- Administrative Measures on Prohibited and Restricted Technology Exports;
- Administrative Measures on Prohibited and Restricted Technology Imports;
- "Catalogue of Technologies Prohibited and Restricted for Import";
- Circular (Ministry of Foreign Trade and Economic Cooperation & State Administration of Foreign Exchange) Administration of Foreign Exchange Sale and Payment Related to Technology Import Contracts (February 20, 2002).

Technology contract regulation is divided between domestic technology contracts ruled by the Contract Law of 1999, and technology contracts with at least one foreign party, ruled by the Technology Regulations of 1985 and a long string of closely related legislation. The greatest problem for technology contracts remains dual regulations and unfair restrictions. The technology transfer sub-section has many parallel articles to the regulations and leaves additional room for maneuvering to the contract parties themselves.

One of the problems in contract enforcement is that China does not enforce foreign judgments, in particular U.S. judgments. Problems caused by improper interpretation of contract documents may therefore lead to ineffective enforcement. It is unclear who will interpret the Contract Law since the National People's Congress (NPC) Standing Committee has jurisdiction but has not yet fulfilled its role. Instead the Supreme Court has created a series of suggested interpretations. There is also the possibility that other ministries of the State Council will claim the right to implement the new law in the absence of NPC interpretation.

Payment Security

Letters of credit and documentary collection are common methods for payment, under which foreign exchange is allocated by the central government for an approved import. Although the Bank of China dominates China's trade-finance business, most Chinese commercial banks, such as the China Construction Bank, Industrial and Commercial Bank of China, and the Agricultural Bank of China, have the authority to issue letters of credit for imports. Foreign banks with branches or representative offices in China can also issue letters of credit.

China has been a member of the International Chamber of Commerce since 1995 and is subject to the Unified Customs and Practice (UCP) 500 Code regarding international trade payments. Nevertheless, terms and conditions are generally negotiable in practice and determined on a transaction-bytransaction basis in the form of a "silent" confirmation.

Documentary collection is less formal and more flexible. The exporter submits a full set of trade documents for payment collection to the bank designated in the contract. The Chinese bank sends the documents to the home office for examination and in some cases passes them on to the buyer for further examination. Payment is made after the documents have met the approval of all parties. This method of payment provides less coverage against default and should be used with caution. It is the responsibility of the exporter to determine the specific instructions to be used in the collection letter.

E-commerce in China has great potential. However, Internet security needs to be taken into account. In April 2005, the Law on Electronic Signatures took effect and enhanced the safety of on-line transactions.

Conclusion

China presents both unprecedented opportunities and challenges for clean energy technologies, due to the sheer scale of the market, the demand, and the projected future energy scenario. Over the last decade, the country has faced serious challenges related to energy shortages and heavy pollution, both of which have been brought on by rapid economic development. In response, the government of China has actively promoted the development and deployment of renewable energy with progressive and ambitious policies and targets. This combination of factors represents a host of opportunities for U.S. firms. While some technologies, such as solar water heating and hydropower, are mature and their markets relatively stable, others—such as large-scale wind power, buildingintegrated PV, and energy efficiency—lag behind in global competitiveness due to resource shortages, lack of expertise, and/or dependence on foreign technology.

Though China's clean energy market is clearly growing, it lags behind the more rapid development of heavy industry. China will therefore likely be a major net exporter of renewable energy equipment in the near term, as the country produces far more equipment than it can install domestically. However, as the demand for higher product quality and after-sales service increases, and as Chinese consumers become more conscious of efficiency and environmental responsibility, this situation will change. The Renewable Energy Law has already had a demonstrable effect on China's clean energy market and resulted in an increase of new renewable energy projects, particularly in the areas of wind, solar, and biomass. Ambitious targets were included in the REL for the next 10–15 years, which when paired with the industry outlook are likely to be even higher. Therefore, U.S. firms should anticipate a growing demand for proven, highquality products and services in key areas such as energy service companies, energy efficiency auditing, wind farm operation and management, technological innovation of large-scale turbines, aesthetic building integration of SWH, and improved thin-film PV technology.

ANNEX 1. MAJOR MARKET PLAYERS IN CHINA

Wind Power

In China, there are currently over 80 wind turbine generator (WTG) manufacturers and 200 wind developers. Domestic companies occupy over 75 percent of the domestic market. The top seven WTG manufacturers and top 10 developers share 80 percent of the market (see Table 1.19).

Table 1.19. Wind Market Shares by Developers and WTG Companies in the First Half of 2007

1H07 Installations Share by Developer (Total: 1,094MW, Est. Equity Weighted Cap.)		
Company	**Market Share for The Year**	**% of Market**
Longyuan	292,390	27
Ningxia Power	131,775	12
CPI	123,525	11.3
Shenhua	138,763	12.7
Keshiketeng County Huifeng New Energy Co. Ltd.	48,510	4.4
Datang	47,750	4.4
IMAR Wind Power	45,000	4.1
Beijing Energy Investment	47,250	4.3
Huaneng	34,538	3.1
CECIC	31,500	3.0
Huadian	28,900	2.6
CWIC	23,250	2.1
Shandong Luneng	21,650	2.0
13 cos (<1% each)	79,550	0.1

Table 1.19. (Continued).

1H07 Wtg Market Shares by Company (Total: 1,094MW)		
Manufacturer Name (Yw)	**Market Share for The Year**	**% of Market**
Goldwind	392,250	36
Sinovel	156,000	14
Dongfang Electric Machinery	121,500	11
Vestas	101,350	9
GE Wind	115,500	11
Gamesa	110,500	10
Nordex	19,500	2
Suzlon Energy Ltd.	62,500	6
Windey	8,250	0.75
ENGGA	1,500	0.14
China Creative	3,000	0.27
Shanghai Electric	2,500	0.23

Source: Azure International

Table 1.20. Leading Companies in WTG Technology in China

Company	Type of Company	Tech/ License	Units Cap.
Gamesa	Wholly owned foreign enterprise (WOFE)	Gamesa	0.85 MW
GE	WOFE	GE	1.5 MW
NCWA-Acciona	Sino–foreign joint venture (S/F JV)	Acciona	1.5 MW
NCWA-Acciona-Wandian (Beijing) Ltd.	S/F JV	Own/Wandian	0.6 MW
Nordex-Xian Weide	S/F JV	Nordex	0.6 MW
Nordex-Ningxia	S/F JV	Repower	1.3 MW
Suzlon Energy Ltd.	WOFE	Suzlon	1.25 MW, 2.1 MW
Vestas (850)	WOFE	Vestas	0.85 MW
Vestas (2 MW)	WOFE	Vestas	2 MW
Sinovel-Dalian Heavy Industry	State-owned enterprise (SOE)	Fuhrlaender	1.5 MW
Dongfang Electric Machinery	SOE	Repower	1.5 MW
Goldwind Science & Technology Co., Ltd. (750 kW)	SOE	Repower	0.75 MW
Huayi (Zhejiang) Wind Power Co., Ltd.	Domestic private	Own	0.78 MW
Windey (Zhejiang) Wind Generating Engineering Co., Ltd.	SOE	Own/Windey/ Garrad Hassan	0.75 MW

Source: Azure International

To date, Chinese WTG technology lags behind, and key technology and licenses still belong to European and U.S. companies. Narrowing the technological gap will require important investments in WTG technical development from Chinese companies. The leading Chinese WTG companies are shown in Table 1.20.

China has developed a mature solar industry market in recent years, with booming investments at the international level providing an important opportunity. The capacity of the solar industry feedstock production lines increased sharply in 2007 and now surpasses 2,500 tons per year, as shown in Table 1.21.

Table 1.21. Solar Ingot Feedstock Production Lines

Company	Capacity (Tons/Year)	Beginning of Exploitation
Sichuan E'Mei SIi feedstock pilot line	100	1999
Sichuan E'Mei Si Feed Stock Production	200	2006
Luo Yang Zhong Gui (First Phase)	300	2005
Luo Yang Zhong Gui (First Phase)	700	2007
Luo Yang Zhong Gui (Third Phase)	2000	2008
Sichuan Leshan Xingguang Si	1260	2007

Source: Kong Li, *The Development of PV Technology in China* (Institute of Electrical Engineering, Chinese Academy of Sciences, November 2006).

In 2005, the total production capacity for solar industrial ingot reached 5,842 tons while the actual production stood at 2,386 tons. Over 80 percent of the domestic manufacturers produce mono-ingot, as shown in Table 1.22.

Table 1.22. Manufacturers of Solar Ingot (2005)

Manufacturer	Type	Capacity (Tons)	Production (Tons)
Ling Long	Mono-ingot	2250	1126
Jinzhou Huari	Mono-ingot	800	400
Trina Solar	Mono-ingot	180	60
New Energy Research Institute of Qinghai	Mono-ingot	270	0
Tianwei Yingli	Cast	770	260
Ningbo Jingyuan	Cast	90	40
Jingsu Sunda	Mono-ingot	350	100
Jinggong	Cast	132	0
Others	Mono-Ingot	1000	400
	Total	5,842: 4,850 Mono Si; 992 Poly Si	2,386: 2,086 Mono Si; 300 Poly Si

Source: Kong Li, *The Development of PV Technology in China* (Institute of Electrical Engineering, Chinese Academy of Sciences, November 2006).

In 2005, the market for solar cells was dominated by two companies, Suntech and Ningbo Solar. In 2006, the size of the solar cell market multiplied by 11, and new companies rushed into this sector. Table 1.23 below identifies the current players.

Table 1.23. Solar Cell Manufacturers

Company	Production In 2005 (MWP/Year)	Capacity By 2006 (MWP/Year)
Suntech	82	300
Ningbo Solar Power	20	100
Nanjing PV-Tech	5	200
Tianwei Yingli	3	60
Yunnan Tianda PV	3	50
Jiangsu Linyang Solarfun	1	100
Shenzhen Topry	9.6 (monosilicon: 3, amorphous silicon: 6.6)	68 (monosilicon: 38, amorphous silicon: 30)
Shenzhen Riyuehuan	2 (amorphous silicon)	2 (amorphous silicon)
Shanghaijiaoda	7	25
Jinneng	2.1 (amorphous silicon)	7.5 (amorphous silicon)
Shenzhen Trony	2 (amorphous silicon)	5 (amorphous silicon)
Total	145.7 (crystalline: 133, amorphous silicon: 12.7)	1673.5 (crystalline: 1629, amorphous silicon: 44.5)

Source: Kong Li, *The Development of PV Technology in China* (Institute of Electrical Engineering, Chinese Academy of Sciences, November 2006).

In 2005, the production capacity for solar modules was 858 MWp, with an actual production of 284 MWp, as shown in Table 1.24.

Table 1.24. Manufacturers of Solar Modules

Company	Certification	Capacity (MWP)	2005 Production (MWP)
SunTech (Wuxi)	TüV	120	78
Solar Energy-Tech (Shanghai)	TüV	100	45
Tianwei Yingli (Baoding)	TüV	50	13
BP Jiayang	TüV	50	8
Solar Energy (Ningbo)	TüV/CE/UL	50	15
Jiangsu Linyang	TüV	50	6
Trinar Solar (Changzhou)	TüV	50	10
Others		388	109
	Total	**858**	**284**

Source: Kong Li, *The Development of PV Technology in China* (Institute of Electrical Engineering, Chinese Academy of Sciences, November 2006)

Solar Water Heating

In total there are over 3,500 solar water heating (SWH) system manufacturers in China, the top 10 of which are able to provide high-quality products and good after-sales services. These top 10, listed in Table 1.25, share less than 20 percent of the market.[71]

Table 1.25. The Top 10 SWH Manufacturers in China

Manufacturer	Collector Type
Himin	Evacuated tube
Tsinghua Sunshine	All-glass evacuated tube
Huayang	All-glass evacuated tube and evacuated tube
Aucma	Evacuated tube
Sijimicoe	All-glass evacuated tube
Guangpu	All-glass evacuated tube
Gomang	Matel superconducting heat pipe
Szlinuo	Evacuated tube
Sangle	U-type evacuated tube
Sunpu	All-glass evacuated tube and evacuated tube

Source: 2007 China Renewable Energy Industry Blue List, http://www.in-en.com/data/html/energy_ 1556155694129395.html_

Small Hydropower

Small hydropower technologies are mature in China. Of over 100 manufacturers, 10 qualified manufacturers were published in the 2007 China Renewable Energy Industry Blue List, and they are listed in Table 1.26. The Web sites of these manufacturers are also provided.

Energy Efficiency

The energy efficiency market is booming as a result of the policy and goals set forth in the 11th Five-Year Plan. Numerous companies and organizations have developed energy efficiency operations in various fields. Many of the top 500 companies, such as GE, ABB, Siemens, Schneider, and Panasonic, have expanded their energy efficiency businesses all over China. Some of them sell energy efficiency products such as energy-saving lamps and high-efficiency motors directly to the consumer or provide technical solutions and services for plants and buildings. Table 1.27 shows the top 10 energy efficiency consulting companies in China. Table 1.28 displays the main products produced by the top energy efficiency players in China.

Table 1.26. China's Top 10 Small Hydropower Manufacturers

Manufacturers	Web Sites
Zhejiang Jinlun Electro-mechanical Co. Ltd.	*www.zjjl.com/*
Hangzhou Electric Equipment Works	*www.chinaheew.com/index_c.php*
Kunming Electric Machinery Co., Ltd.	*/http://cn.5095.cnele.com/*
Sichuan Dongfeng Elec-tric Machinery Co., Ltd.	*www.dongfengem.com/disp.asp?xh=493*
Zhejiang Linhai Electric Machinery Co. Ltd.	*www.lhemc.com/about.htm*
Zhejiang Yueqing Electric Machinery Works	*www.yueqing.org/zjyq/content/scqy/gdqy/corpora tion/yqjijei.htm*
Nanning Generating Equipment General Works	*www.ngegw.com/*
Henan Xixia Hydropower Equipment Co. Ltd.	*www.xxsd.net/*
Sichuan Hongya Hydro Turbine Works	*www.hyslj.com/about.asp*
Hangzhou Nanwang Automatic Technologies Co. Ltd.	*www.hznwauto.com/*

Source: Beijing Development and Reform Commission, http://www.bjpc.gov.cn/tztg/200704/ t155937.htm (Chinese version)

Table 1.27. Top 10 Consulting Companies in the EE Field in China

Company	Expertise	Web Site
China IPPR Engineering Corporation	Construction, industry, infrastructure	www.ippr.com.cn/
Wuzhou Engineering Design Research Institute	Construction, industry	www.wuzhou.com.cn/
China Electronic Engineering Design Institute	Construction, industry, consulting	www.ceedi.com.cn/
Institute of Architecture Design & Research Institute of Chinese Academy of Sciences	Construction, infrastructure	www.adcas.cn/ (Chinese Web site)
China Architecture Design & Research Group	Construction	www.cadreg.com.cn/
China Enfi Engineering Technology Co. Ltd.	Construction	www.enfi.com.cn
Sinothru Construction Consultants Co. Ltd.	Construction, infrastructure	http://ztcec.cn
CECIC Blue-Sky Consulting Management Co. Ltd.	Industry	www.cecic-consulting.com.cn/english/
China Coal Research Institute	Industry	www.ccri.com.cn/
China Machinery International Engineering Design & Research Institute	Industry	www.cmiei.com
Fifth Survey & Design Institute of Railway	Infrastructure	www.t5y.cn/

Source: Azure-international

Table 1.28. Main EE Products and Players

Company	Product	Web site
GE	Green electric products, high-efficiency motors, energy conservation switches, electricity control systems, etc.	www.ge.com.cn
ABB	High-efficiency motors, energy conservation switches, electricity control systems, etc.	www.abb.com.cn/
Schneider Electric	Energy conservation switches, electricity control systems, etc.	www.schneider-electric.com.cn
Siemens	High-efficiency motors, energy conservation switches, electricity control systems, etc.	www.siemens.com.cn
Fuji Electric	Electric meters, clean energy, UPS, monitoring systems, etc.	www.fujielectric.com.cn
Mitsubishi Electric in China	Industry control systems, high-efficiency motors, energy conservation switches, electricity control systems, etc.	www.mitsubishielectric.com.cn
Delta Electronics, Inc.	VSD motors, energy conservation power source, etc.	www.delta.com.tw/
Panasonic China	Industry control systems, high-efficiency motors, energy conservation switches, electricity control systems, etc.	www.panasonic.com.cn
Moeller	Low-voltage electric appliances	www.moeller.cn

Source: Azure-international

ANNEX 2. CHINESE POLICY-MAKERS WITH AUTHORITY OVER CLEAN ENERGY TECHNOLOGIES

National-level Decision-making Authorities and Procedure

The Constitution accords the National People's Congress (NPC) the highest position in China. Its main functions are:

- To enact and revise basic laws in China;
- To examine and approve the plan for national economic and social development.

The State Council of the People's Republic of China, namely, the Central People's Government, is the highest executive entity of state power, as well as the highest body of state administration. It is responsible for:

- Carrying out the principles and policies of the Communist Party as well as the regulations and laws adopted by the NPC;
- Dealing with such affairs as China's internal politics, diplomacy, national defense, finance, economy, culture, and education.

The State Council is composed of the General Affairs Office, 28 ministries and commissions, 17 directly affiliated entities, and seven working offices, in addition to a number of directly administered institutions.

Main Responsibilities and Functions of Individual Institutions

National Development and Reform Commission

After merging with the State Council Office for Restructuring the Economic System and part of the State Economic and Trade Commission in 2003, the State Planning Commission was restructured into the NDRC, which is a macroeconomic management agency under the State Council. The NDRC studies and formulates policies for economic and social development, maintains a balance of economic aggregates, and oversees the overall economic system.

One of NDRC's roles is to coordinate China's forward strategy and policy implementation in the energy and environmental fields. NDRC's missions in these fields are as follows:

- Advancement of China's sustainable development strategy;
- Research and preparation of drafts on the comprehensive utilization and conservation of resources;
- The establishment and coordination China's ecology rebuilding plan;
- Policy creation for the comprehensive utilization and conservation of resources;
- Coordination of the environmental protection industry.

The Energy Bureau of the NDRC is responsible for studying energy development and utilization both at home and abroad and putting forward energy development strategies and major policies; formulating development plans and making recommendations on energy sector reform; administering oil, natural gas, coal, power, and other parts of the energy sector and national oil reserves; and formulating policy measures for energy conservation and renewable energy development.

The NDRC coordinates its activities with other governmental agencies as follows:

Ministry of Commerce (MOFCOM):

- Is in charge of domestic and international trade and economic cooperation;
- Formulates policies and regulations for standardizing market operation and circulation order;
- Promotes the establishment and improvement of the market system; deepens the reform of the circulation system;
- Monitors and analyzes market operation, commodity supply and demand, and conducts international economic operation;
- Coordinates state support matters; investigates the harm that subsidies and other government interventions can bring to industries.

Ministry of Environmental Protection (MEP):

- Is in charge of natural ecological conservation and environmental pollution prevention;
- Strengthens supervision on nuclear safety; enforces environmental regulations;
- Improves supervision and administration;
- Safeguards the environmental rights and interests of the public; promotes the sustainable development of the society, economy, and environment.

Ministry of Science and Technology (MOST):

- Proposes macro-strategy for scientific and technological development, including policies, guidelines, and regulations for promoting economic and social development in line with science and technology;
- Studies major issues of promoting economic and social development with science and technology;
- Formulates plans and priority areas for scientific and technological development;
- Promotes national science and technology development, including capacity building and compiling annual plans for the development of civil-use science and technology;
- Proposes policies, guidelines, and measures to adapt science and technology system to the socialist market economy.

Ministry of Land and Resources

- Investigates and plans management, protection, and rational utilization of such natural resources as land, mineral reserves, and marine resources;
- Drafts related laws, policies, and regulations on the management, protection, and utilization of such natural resources;
- Formulates technical standards, specifications, and methods for the management of such resources;
- Compiles and implements national plans for land use;
- Supervises land resource administrative departments in enforcing laws and plans on land, mineral, and marine resources; oversees protection of land owner rights as
- well as settling disputes;
- Manages the State Oceanic Administration and State Bureau of Mapping and Surveying.

Ministry of Construction

- Formulates policies, guidelines, regulations, and related development strategies, as well as long- and medium-term plans, for urban planning, village and town planning, engineering construction, urban construction, village and town construction, the construction and building industry, and the housing and real estate industry;
- Consults with industry on survey and design; oversees the undertakings of urban utilities; and conducts industrial administration;

- Provides guidance for the planning of cities, villages, and towns; urban surveying; and municipal engineering surveying;
- Standardizes the building market; supervises engineering bidding; and oversees engineering quality and safety.

Ministry of Transportation

- Formulates development strategies, policies, guidelines, regulations, and long- and medium-term development plans for highway and waterway industries; supervises their implementation;
- Oversees data analysis and information synthesis of the transport industry; controls the transportation of the country's key materials, cargo, and passengers; and organizes construction of key national highways and waterway transportation;
- Guides the reform of the transportation system; maintains fair competition in the highway and waterway transportation industry;
- Formulates scientific and technological policies, technical standards, and specifications for the transport industry; promotes the technical progress of the transport industry.

Ministry of Water Resources

- Formulates water-related policies, legislation, development strategies, and medium- and long-term development plans, including water conservation and demand management policies;
- Ensures integrated management of water resources, including atmospheric water, surface water, and groundwater;
- Formulates water resource protection plans in accordance with related national laws, regulations, and standards concerning resource and environment protection;
- Formulates economic regulatory measures for the water sector; conducts macro-economic regulation of the utilization of funds within the water industry; and provides recommendations on water pricing, taxation, credit, and financial affairs;
- Reviews proposals and feasibility study reports on largeand medium-sized capital construction projects in the water sector;
- Drafts and maintains technical standards for the water sector as well as specifications and codes for water works;
- Organizes the protection of hydraulic facilities, water areas, dykes, and coast lines and the regulation, reclamation, and development of major water bodies;
- Guides activities related to rural water resources;
- Organizes water and soil conservation nationwide.

Ministry of Finance

- Formulates strategies, policies, guidelines, medium- and long-term development plans, and reform programs for public finance and taxation; participates in macroeconomic policy making;

- Drafts laws and regulations on public finance and financial and accounting management; organizes negotiations concerning external finance and debts; and signs related agreements/accords;

- Prepares the draft annual budget of the central government and its final accounts; organizes budget implementation;

- Proposes tax legislation plans; reviews proposals on tax legislation and tax collection regulations with the State Tax Administration before reporting to the State Council;

- Administers the central expenditures; formulates government procurement policies; and manages the budgetary non-trade-related foreign exchange of government agencies;

- Supervises central government expenditures for economic development, the appropriation of funds for central government financed projects, and funds for technological innovation and new product testing;

- Monitors the implementation of fiscal and tax policies, laws, and regulations.

Figure 1.28 displays the organizational structure of the Chinese Government.

Contact Information of Main National-Level Decisionmaking Authorities in Clean Energy Technology

Table 1.29 below provides the contact information for key personnel in the clean energy technology sector in China.

Local-level Decision-making Authorities and Procedure

In accordance with the existing administrative divisions of the country, there are People's Congresses in the provinces (autonomous regions and municipalities directly under the Central Government), counties (cities), and townships (towns), and those at or above the county level have standing committees. There is government representation at all levels.

Local People's Congresses are the local organs of state power. They have the power to decide on important local affairs in their respective administrative areas. The People's Congresses of provinces, autonomous regions, and municipalities directly under the Central Government have the power to formulate local laws and regulations.

Local people's governments are local administrative organs of the state. Working under the unified leadership of the State Council, they report on their work to the People's Congresses at the corresponding levels and their standing committees and to the organs of state administration at the next highest level. They have overall responsibility for the administrative work within their respective administrative areas.[73]

There are altogether 23 provinces, five autonomous regions, and four municipalities (the last group includes Beijing, Shanghai, Tianjin, and Chongqing) under direct central government control, as well as two special Administrative Regions (Hong Kong and Macau).

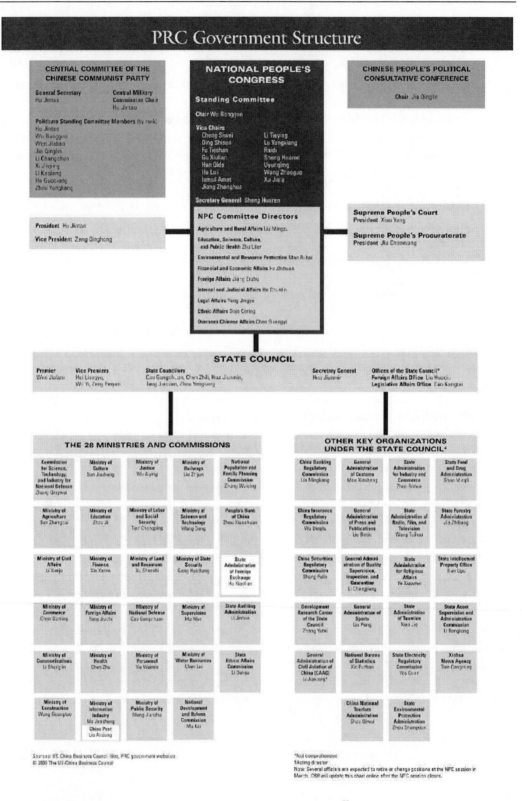

Figure 1.28. Government Structure of the People's Republic of China[72]

Table 1.29. Contact Information for Key Personnel in China's CET Sector

National Development and Reform Commission	38 South Yuetan Street, Beijing, 100824	+86 10 6850 2872	Minister: Ma Kai	www.sdpc.gov.cn	ndrc@ndrc.gov.cn
Ministry of Commerce	2 Dong Chang An Street, Beijing 100731	+86 10 6512 1919	Minister: Chen Deming	www.mofcom.gov.cn/	http://gzly.mofcom.gov.cn/website/pubmail/send_mail_en.jsp
State Environmental Protection Administration	115 Nan Xiao Street, Xi Zhi Men Nei, Beijing, 100035	+86 10 6711 6801	Minister: Zhou Shengxian	http://english.sepa.gov.cn/	mailbox@sepa.gov.cn
Ministry of Science and Technology	15 B Fuxing Road, Beijing	+86 10 5888 1521, 5888 1527	Minister: Wan Gang	www.most.gov.cn/eng/index.htm	http://appweblogic.most.gov.cn/eng/guestbook/guestbook.htm
Ministry of Land and Resources	No. 64 Funei Street,100812 Beijng,China	+86 10 6655 8407/08/20	Minister: Xu Shaoshi	www.mlr.gov.cn	www.mlr.gov.cn/hdpt/zxpt/
Ministry of Construction	No. 9 Sanlihe Lu, Xicheng District, Beijing, 100835	+86 10 6839 4114	Minister: Wang Guangtao	www.cin.gov.cn/	cin@mail.cin.gov.cn
Ministry of Communication	11 Jianguomennei Dajie, Dongcheng District, Beijing 100736	+86 10 6529 2114	Minister: Li Shenglin	www.moc.gov.cn	jtbweb@moc.gov.cn
Ministry of Water Resources	No. 2 Tiao Baiguang Road, Beijing, 100053	+86 10 6320 2114	Minister: Chen Lei	www.mwr.gov.cn	webmaster@mwr.gov.cn
Ministry of Finance	3 Nansanxiang Sanlihe, Beijing 100820	+86 10 6855 1114	Minister: Xie Xu	/www.mof.gov.cn/	webmaster@mof.gov.cn

ANNEX 3. GUIDANCE CATALOGUE OF THE RENEWABLE ENERGY INDUSTRY[74]

Serial Number	Project	Instruction and Technical Indicator	Status Quo of Development
I. Wind energy			
Wind energy power generation			
1	Off-grid wind power generation	It is used for rural electrification where the grid fails to cover, including two kinds of electricity generation/ supply, individual household plant and concentrated village plant.	Basic commercialization
2	On-grid wind power generation	It is used for grid-connected electrification, including land and offshore network-forming wind power electricity generation, which can generate electricity through single machine networking and multi-machines networking electricity generation.	Land networking wind power electricity generation: offshore networking electricity generation; technological research and development
Equipment/fitting manufacture			
3	Wind resources evaluation and analysis software	It is used for undertaking technological and economic evaluation upon regional wind energy resources so as to select the correct wind field. Its main functions include: measurement of treatment and statistical analysis of wind, formation of wind map, wind resource evaluation, wind generating set and annual electricity yield by wind field and etc.	Technology research, development or introduction
4	Wind field design and optimization software	It is used for optimized design of electricity field (i.e. micro-location selection and arrangement plan design and optimization of wind generating set). Its main functions include: confirming the influence of wake flow of wind generating set and adjusting the distributing distance between wind generating sets, undertaking analysis and prediction upon noise of wind generating set and wind field, eliminating the section failing to meet the requirement of technology, land quality and environment; optimizing the location-selection of wind generating set automatically, providing visualized interface of the design process, undertaking technical and economic analysis and etc.	Technology research and development

Annex 3. (Continued)

Serial Number	Project	Instruction and Technical Indicator	Status Quo of Development
5	Wind concentrated and remote monitoring system	It is used for concentrated and remote monitoring of wind generating set and wind field operation. Its main functions include: timely collecting, analyzing and reporting the wind situation and set and supervision data of wind field operation by means of modern information and communication technology, undertaking efficiency optimization and safety guarantee system automatically or via the feedback of instruction.	Technology research and development
6	Construction of wind field and maintenance of exclusive equipment	It is used for transport of land and off-shore wind generating set, on-the-spot lift and maintenance.	Technology research and development
7	Off-grid wind turbines generating system	It is used for independent system and concentrated village electricity genera-tion, including wind power independent electricity generation and wind-solar photovoltaic hybrid generate electricity system to ensure its system safety, eco-nomic and continuous and reliable electricity supply.	Basically commercialized
8	Wind power generating set of network-forming	It is used for networking wind power generation, including land and offshore generating set. Offshore wind generating set shall be adapted to oceanic geology, hydrologic condition and climate.	Land wind genera-ting set: above-sea wind generating set of the primary stage of commercialize-tion; technology research and development
9	Total design software of wind generating set	It is used for the total design of structural dynamics modeling and analysis, limit load and fatigue load calculation, and win generating set dynamic emulation.	Technology research, development or introduction
10	Wind mill blade	It is used for supporting large scale wind mill set with its capacity no less than 1,000 kw.	Technology research and development
11	Wind mill blade design software	It is used for designing large scale Wind mill blade pneumatic shape and its construction technique	Technology research and development
12	Wind mill blade material	It is used for manufacturing of high strength, low-mass, large-volume blade, including GRP and carbon fiber rein-forced plastics	Technology research and development

Annex 3. (Continued)

Serial Number	Project	Instruction and Technical Indicator	Status Quo of Development
13	Wind mill wheel hub	It is used for supporting wind generating set with its capacity no less than 1,000 kw.	Technology research and development
14	Wind mill driving system	It is used for supporting wind generating set with its capacity no less than 1,000 kw.	Technology research and development
15	Wind mill deviation system	It is used for supporting wind generating set with its capacity no less than 1,000 kw.	Technology research and development
16	Wind mill braking system/mechanic braking	It is used for supporting wind generating set with its capacity no less than 1,000 kw.	Technology research and development
17	Wind mill generator	It is used for supporting wind generating set with its capacity no less than 1,000 kw, including double-fed generator and permanent magnet generator.	At the beginning of commercialization, technology research and development (permanent magnet generator)
18	Wind generating operation control system and converter	It is used for supporting wind generating set with its capacity no less than 1,000 kw, including: off-grid wind generating controller; speed-loss wind generating controller; variable-speed constant-frequency wind-power generating controller and converter.	Technology research and development
19	Wind mill generating set safety guarantee system	It is used for ensuring the safety of wind generating set on occasion of extreme weather, system failure and grid failure	Technology research and development
20	Testing equipment for compatibility between electricity and magnet in wind mill generating set, lighting impulse	It is used for testing the compatibility between electricity and magnet in wind mill generating set and lighting impulse in order to make the set adaptable to natural environment.	Technology research and development
21	Design of Integration between Wind Power and Power Grid and grid stability analysis software	It is used for evaluating the large-scale wind field integration system and stability of the grid	Technology research and development

Annex 3. (Continued)

Serial Number	Project	Instruction and Technical Indicator	Status Quo of Development
22	Wind field electricity generating capacity prediction and grid scheduling and matching software	It is used for monitoring and collecting information about the performance and generating capacity upon the wind generating capacity, analyzing and estimating the variation of the wind field in the second day and its generating output, making scheduling plan for grid enterprise and promoting large-scale wind field development and operation.	Technology research and development
23	Wind field smooth transition and controlling system	It is used for providing support for the smooth transition of large-scale wind field in case of grid integration failure.	Technology research and development
II. Solar energy			
Utilization of solar energy and heat utilization			
24	Off-grid solar energy photovoltaic electricity generation	It is used for supplying electricity to the resident area where the grid fails to cover, including independent household system and concentrated village.	Basic commercialization
25	Networking solar energy photovoltaic electricity generation	It is used for supplying grid with electricity, including building integrated solar energy photovoltaic electricity generation	Technology research and development and project model
26	Solar energy for electricity generation	It is used for supplying electricity to the resident area where the grid fails to cover, including tower solar energy electricity generator, trough-shaped solar energy electricity generator, disk-shaped solar energy electricity generator and instant focal solar energy electricity generator	Technology development
27	Industrial photovoltaic electricity resources	It is used for supplying electricity to scattered meteorological station, seismic station, highway station, broadcast and television, satellite ground station, hydrometry, solar energy navigation mark, highway and railway signal and solar energy cathodic protection system.	Commercialization
28	Solar energy lighting system	Including solar energy street lamp, yard lamp, lawn lamp, billboard, solar energy LED cityscape lamp and etc.	Commercialization
29	Solar energy vehicle	Including: solar energy-driven automobile, solar energy motor-assisted bicycle and etc.	Technology research and development, project model

Annex 3. (Continued)

Serial Number	Project	Instruction and Technical Indicator	Status Quo of Development
30	Solar energy photovoltaic sea water desalination system	It is used for providing fresh water to remote island resident area where fresh water is in scarcity.	Technology research and development, project model
31	Photovoltaic Pump	It is used for providing fresh water to the western drought-hit area, and remote and population-scattered area, to the construction and amelioration of grassland and reforestation in the desert.	Commercialization
32	Solar energy water heater for household	It is used for providing life heat water to the residents, including flat-type solar energy water heater, vacuum solar energy water heater and etc.	Commercialization
33	Solar energy concentrated heating system	It is used for providing heat water or heating to the residents or industry and commerce, including solar energy concentrated	Technology research and development, extension and application
34	Solar energy air-conditioner system	It is used for realizing heat and cold convertibility and providing cooling and air-conditioner service (via solar energy collector and absorption refrigerating machine.	Technology research and development and model project
35	Zero solar energy building complex	It is used for meeting the demand of energy in building via integrating solar energy collector (realizing solar energy collecting system and air-conditioner system) in the building (roof and external wall) and solar energy photovoltaic Cell.	Technology research and development
Equipment/ outfit manufacture			
36	Off-grid solar energy photovoltaic electricity generating system	It is used in independent household system and concentrated village plant	Commercialization
37	Networking solar energy photovoltaic electricity generating system	It is used for supplying energy to grid, including building integrated solar energy photovoltaic electricity generating system.	Technology research and development, project model
38	Solar energy electricity generating system	Including: tower solar energy light and heat electricity generating system, trough shaped solar energy light and heat electricity generating system, disk-shaped solar energy light and heat electricity generating system and instant focal solar energy generating system.	Technology development

Annex 3. (Continued)

Serial Number	Project	Instruction and Technical Indicator	Status Quo of Development
39	Crystal silicon solar energy cell	Including: Single crystal silicon solar energy cell and multi-crystal silicon solar energy cell	Commercialization and technology amelioration
40	Membrane solar energy cell	Including: multi-junction amorphous thin-film solar cell, polycrystalline thin-film solar energy cell, compound thin-film solar energy cell	Technology research and development
41	Other new type solar energy cell	Including: flexible underlay solar energy cell, spot light solar energy cell, HIT heterojunction solar energy cell, organic solar energy cell, nanometer noncrystal solar energy cell, mechanic stacking solar energy cell, thin-film noncrystal silicon/ minicrystal stacking solar energy cell and etc.	Technology research and development
42	Architectural solar energy arrays	It is used in architectural integrated solar energy photovoltaic electricity generating system, including semitranslucidus photovoltaic electricity generating system, photovoltaic that can be interchanged with building units, photovoltaic glass curtain wall, photovoltaic sun-shield and etc.	Technology research and development
43	Solar energy cell and its component parts manufacture equipment	It is used for manufacturing solar energy cell and its component parts, including: solar energy silicon furnace charge outfit manufacture, multicrystal ingot casting, wire cutting machine, saw squarer, silicon slice polishing equipment, silicon slice cleaner, diffusion equipment, PECVD, hard coat equipment, screen printing, drying and sinter equipment, wafer scriber, automatic welding, component part layer press and etc.	Technology research and development or introduction
44	Solar energy cell test equipment	Including: solar energy cell separation equipment, solar analog meter, high voltage insulation test equipment and etc.	Technology research and development
45	Solar cell auxiliary material for production use	Including: low low-iron toughened glass, EVA, solar cell back packaging composite membrane, silver plasm and aluminum plasm, weld and etc.	Technology research and development
46	Photovoltaic electricity generating system, controller of electricity use and discharging	It is used for controlling intellectually the process of electricity charging and discharging	Technology research and development

Annex 3. (Continued)

Serial Number	Project	Instruction and Technical Indicator	Status Quo of Development
47	Ac/dc inverter for photovoltaic electricity generating system,	It is used for off-grid and networking ac/dc inverter, the latter needs the function of networking invert, maximum power tracking, protection for the prevention of island effect and etc.	Technology research and development
48	Household photovoltaic and wind/ light complementary control/ inverter	It is used for photovoltaic and wind/light complementary electricity generating system with its volume less than 1 kw.	Technology research and development
49	(exclusive) storage cell	It is used for independent photovoltaic and wind electricity generating system, with the endurance capacity for excessive charging and discharging performance and long service life.	Technology research and development
50	Redox liquid storage cell	It is used in independent photovoltaic electricity generation and wind power electricity generation system; its storage capacity shall reach one hundred mega-watts when its power is ranged from dozes to several hundred kw.	Technology research and development and project model
51	Photovoltaic silicon material	It is used for the production of solar cell crystal silicon.	Technology research and development or introduction
52	Concentrated and remote control system for the use of photo-voltaic electricity generating system	It is used in the operation data in collecting, transmitting solar radiation, environmental parameters and photo-voltaic electricity generation and realizing concentrated or remote control monitoring.	Technology research and development
53	Reflector for the use of solar energy heat and light electricity generation	It is used for supporting various solar energy light and heat electricity generating system.	Technology research and development
54	Automatic tracking equipment for light and heat generating reflector	It is used for supporting various solar energy light and heat electricity generating system so as to automatically track solar radiation, adjust the angle of the reflector and absorb the maximum solar energy.	Technology research and development

Annex 3. (Continued)

Serial Number	Project	Instruction and Technical Indicator	Status Quo of Development
55	Light and heat collector	It is used for supporting various solar energy light and heat electricity generating system to absorb solar radiation from the reflector, i.e. "solar boiler" within small volume and high conversion efficiency.	Technology research and development
56	Light and heat electricity generating and heat storage equipment	It is used for supporting various solar energy light and heat electricity generating system, ensuring the relative stability of light and heat electricity generation via the heat energy absorbed by the storage collector.	Technology research and development
57	Instant light and heat electricity generating equipment	It is used for supporting instant solar energy light and heat electricity generating system, including alkali metal thermo-electric converter, Semiconductor electricity generator, thermion electricity generator and photovoltaic electricity generator.	Technology research and development
58	Solar energy light and heat system, architectural application design, optimization, measurement and evaluation software.	It is used for the design and emulation of optimized architectural heating equipment geared to the applied solar energy light and heat system in different regions, different lighting conditions in China; for measurement and evaluation upon the solar energy light and heat system used in the processing of building.	Technology research and development and extension and application
III. Biomass energy			
Biomass energy and biological fuel production			
59	Gas supply and electricity generation by large and medium-sized methane project	Including large scale livestock and poultry farm, Breeding area, urban sewage project	Commercialization, extension and application
60	Instant Electricity by Biomass fuel	Electricity generation by utilizing crop straw, and wood	Technology update and project model
61	Biomass liquefied gas supply and electricity generation	Liquefied gas supply and electricity generation by utilizing crop straw, and wood	Technology research and development, extension and application

Annex 3. (Continued)

Serial Number	Project	Instruction and Technical Indicator	Status Quo of Development
62	Electricity generation by utilizing urban solid refuse	Electricity generation by utilizing urban solid refuse, including fuel and methane.	Basic commercialization
63	Biological liquefied fuel	Production of liquefied fuel by utilizing non-grain crop and wood biomass.	Technology research and development
64	Biomass solid fuel	Transforming crop straw and wood to solid fuel as the alternative of coal.	Project model
Equipment/component parts manufacture and raw material production			
65	Biomass direct-fired boiler	It is used for supporting biomass direct-fired boiler system, for which technological performance and specification shall be used.	Technology update
66	Biomass fuel gas combustion engine	It is used for supporting electricity generation via liquefied biomass. Its performance and specification shall be used in liquefied biomass electricity generation system.	Technology research and development
67	Liquefied biomass tar catalyzing and cracking equipment	It is used for cracking tar arisen in the process of gasification to available and disposable gas.	Technology research and development
68	Liquefied biomass fuel production outfit	It is used for producing the aforesaid various liquefied biomass fuel.	Technology research and development and project model
69	Plantation of energy plant	It is used for providing various biological fuel production with non-crop biomass material such as sweet sorghum, cassava, purging-nut tree, sugar cane.	Project model, extension and application
70	Breeding of energy plant	It is used for breeding and cultivating energy crop which boasts stable and high yield and, innocuity to ecological environment and adaptability to barren mountains and waste, sandlot and alkali land.	Technology research and development and project model
71	High-efficiency, wide-range methane strain improvement	It is used for improving the yield of methane project and its usage in relatively low temperature.	Technology research and development
IV. Geothermal energy			
Electricity generation by utilizing geothermal energy and heat utilization			
72	Electricity generation by	Including electricity generation by utilizing geothermal steam, double-circulation	Technology research and

Annex 3. (Continued)

Serial Number	Project	Instruction and Technical Indicator	Status Quo of Development
	utilizing geothermal energy	geothermal electricity generating system and flash geothermal electricity generating system (the latter two is adaptable to middle and low geothermal resources.	development
73	Heat supply by utilizing geothermal energy	Including single circulation direct heating and double-circulation indirect heating.	Project model, extension and application
74	Geothermal source heat pump heating and/or air conditioner	Including underground water source, river and lake water source, sea water source, sewage sources (including urban sewage, industrial sewage, hospital sewage) and soil geothermal source heat pump.	Project model
75	Underground thermoenergy storage system	The storage types include such energies as solar energy, and the cool and heat set off by air conditioners in the buildings.	Technology research and development
Equipment/outfit manufacture			
76	Drilling equipment exclusively for geothermal well use	It is used for drilling geothermal well, which shall be adapted to its geological structure, high temperature and corrosion hydraulic conditions and the requirement for making the well.	Technology research and development
77	Geothermal well pump	It is used for supporting geothermal heating and geothermal source heat pump system, which shall be adapted to its high temperature and corrosion.	Technology research and development
78	Water source thermal pump assembly	It shall be adapted to the temperature of underground water or sea water as well as their temperature.	Technology research and development and project model
79	Geothermal Energy design, optimization and evaluation system	It is used for undertaking measurement and evaluation upon the building adaptable to the geothermal energy in different regions and with different types.	Technology research and development, extension and application
80	Utilization of water heat source	The temperature difference of water is utilized to cool and heat the building, including utilizing such water sources as underground water, sewage in urban treatment sewage treatment factory.	Project model, extension and application
V. Ocean energy			
Ocean power generation			
81	Ocean power generation	Including: tidal power generation, wave power generation, marine thermoelectric power generation and ocean current power generation.	Technology research and development and project model

Annex 3. (Continued)

Serial Number	Project	Instruction and Technical Indicator	Status Quo of Development
Equipment/ outfit manufacture			
82	Ocean power generation outfit	Including: the outfit of wave power generation, marine thermoelectric power generation and ocean current power generation.	Technology research and development
VI. Hydropower			
Waterpower			
83	Networking Waterpower	Various waterpower in line with the requirement of watershed development, and environmental protection	Commercialization
84	Small-scale off-grid waterpower	It is used for electricity and energy usage in in-place development, neighborhood electricity supply and solving the problems in remote area for electricity and energy use.	Commercialization
Equipment/outfit manufacture			
85	Water turbine-typed spectrum	It is used for manufacture and type selection of water turbine, improvement of the efficiency and quality of water turbine, reduction of construction cost and standardization of the equipment market.	Technology research and development
86	Automatic hydroelectric technology	It is used for the automatic management of hydroelectric operation, the improvement of its performance and the reduction of its operational cost.	Technology update
87	Large-scale and high-efficiency water turbine generating set	It is used for improving the capacity, performance and efficiency of water turbine generating set.	Technology research and development
88	Integration technology of small plant	It is used in small waterpower with its capacity less than 1,000 kw for realizing the control and integration of such auxiliary equipments as petroleum, water and gas and such supervision integration as speed regulation, excitation, protection and measurement, improving its credibility and reducing its equipment construction cost.	Technology update

SECTION 2: CLEAN ENERGY TECHNOLOGIES DEFINED

This report covers clean energy technologies (CETs) including renewable energy technologies, energy efficiency, hybrids and cogeneration, and clean transportation technologies. CETs are more environmentally friendly than traditional, fossil fuel-based technologies. CETs can either use natural resources such as sunlight, wind, rain, tides, geothermal heat, and plants, which are naturally replenished, and/or use processes to use energy more efficiently.

CETs include renewable energy, hybrid and cogeneration, and energy efficiency technologies for power generation and alternative fuels and advanced technologies for transportation. This chapter presents an overview of these technologies.

Renewable Energy Technologies

Renewable energy technologies considered in this report include biomass and biofuels, waste-to-energy, solar power, wind power, geothermal, hydropower, and ocean power.

Biomass
Biomass consists of plant and plant-derived material. Sources of biomass include agricultural residues such as rice hulls, straw, bagasse from sugarcane production, wood chips, and coconut shells and energy crops such as sugarcane or switch grass. Biomass can be used directly for energy production or processed into fuels. Examples of biomass fuels are liquid and gel fuels including oil and alcohol and pelletized biomass for gasification and combustion. Liquid biomass–derived fuels can be used as substitutes for or additives to fossil fuels.

Although the conversion of biomass into energy results in the release of carbon into the atmosphere, biomass-based energy is considered to be carbon neutral because of the carbon sequestered by plants during the growth of the biomass material. For biomass resources to be renewable, their cultivation must be managed carefully to ensure sustainable harvesting and land use. The use of biomass for energy production can result in competition with food crops, either directly, when food crops themselves are used for energy production, or indirectly, when land and water that would be used to grow crops is used instead for energy crops.

Biomass technologies include equipment for industrial processes that produce heat and steam; electrical power generation through combustion, liquefaction, or gasification; and transportation fuels such as ethanol and biodiesel. Biomass is converted into energy through one of two pathways: thermochemical and biochemical. Thermochemical conversion occurs by combustion, gasification, or pyrolysis. Biochemical conversion results from anaerobic digestion or fermentation. The energy products produced from these biomass conversion processes are electricity, heat, and biofuels.

Combustion
Direct combustion is a widely used process where biomass is converted into useful power through exposure to high temperatures. Heat from the process can be used to produce steam, which in turn can drive a turbine to generate electricity. Depending on the combustion

process, various pre-treatment steps such as sizing (shredding, crushing, and chipping) and drying are required. The heating value and moisture content of the biomass determine the efficiency of the combustion process. Drying prior to the combustion process (e.g., with waste heat) helps to lower the moisture content and raise the heating value to acceptable levels.

Gasification

In the gasification process, biomass is thermochemically converted into gaseous fuel by means of partial oxidation of the biomass at high temperatures. This process requires less oxygen than combustion. In addition to the gaseous fuel, gasifiers produce heat and ash. To maximize the efficiency of gasification-based systems, beneficial uses should be developed for all three products.

TEXTBOX 2.1: BIOMASS ENERGY RESOURCES

Solid biomass: Wood, vegetal waste (including wood waste and crops), conventional crops (oil and starch crops), charcoal, animal wastes, and other wastes (including the biodegradable fraction of municipal solid wastes) used for energy production.

Liquid biofuels: Biodiesel and bioethanol (also includes biomethanol, bio-oil, and biodimethylether).

A) **Biodiesel:** Biodiesel can be used in pure form or may be blended with petroleum diesel at any concentration for use in most modern diesel engines. Biodiesel can be produced from a variety of feedstocks, such as oil feedstock (rapeseed, soybean oils, jatropha, palm oil, hemp, algae, canola, flax, and mustard), animal fats, or waste vegetable oil.

B) **Bioethanol:** The largest single use of ethanol is as a fuel for transportation or as a fuel additive. It can be produced from a variety of feedstocks such as sugarcane, corn, and sugar beet. It can also be produced from cassava, sweet sorghum, sunflower, potatoes, and hemp or cotton seeds or derived from cellulose waste.

Biogas: Methane and carbon dioxide produced by anaerobic digestion or fermentation of biomass, such as landfill gas and digester gas.

The main processes of a gasification plant are fuel feeding, gasification, and gas clean-up. Fuel feeding prepares and introduces the feedstock into the gasifier. The gasifier converts the feedstock into a fuel gas containing carbon monoxide, hydrogen, and methane. In the gas clean-up process, harmful impurities are removed from the fuel gas to allow for safe usage in gasburning engines or turbines.

Pyrolysis

Pyrolysis is also a thermochemical conversion process that converts biomass into liquid, solid, and gaseous substances by heating the biomass to about 500 degrees Celsius in the absence of air. The pyrolysis process includes feedstock preparation and the application of liquid and char for heat production. Alternative technologies include rapid thermal processing and the vacuum pyrolysis process. The latter involves the thermal decomposition of matter under reduced pressure for conversion into fuels and chemicals. Fast pyrolysis refers to the rapid heating of biomass in the absence of oxygen. Feedstocks for the pyrolysis process include forestry residue (sawdust, chips, and bark) and by-products from the agricultural industry (bagasse, wheat straw, and rice hulls).

Fermentation

Anaerobic digestion is a type of fermentation that biochemically converts organic material, especially animal waste, into biogas that consists mainly of methane and carbon dioxide and is comparable to landfill gas. The biomass is converted by bacteria under anaerobic conditions—without oxygen present. Biogas plants consist of two components: a digester (or fermentation tank) and a gas holder. The digester is a cube- or cylinder-shaped waterproof container with an inlet into which the fermentable mixture is introduced in the form of liquid slurry.

Fermentation of sugars is a biochemical process that entails the production of ethanol (alcohols) from sugar crops (sugarcane, beet) or starch crops (maize, wheat). The biomass is ground and the starch is converted by enzymes and bacteria into sugars. Yeast then converts the sugars into ethanol. Pure ethanol can be obtained by distillation; the remaining solids can be used as cattle feed. In the case of sugarcane, the remaining bagasse can also be used as fuel for boilers or electricity generation processes. These multiple applications allow ethanol plants to be self-sufficient and even to sell surplus electricity to utilities.

Bioethanol is primarily produced by fermentation of sugarcane or sugar beet. A more complex and expensive process involves producing bioethanol from wood or straw using acid hydrolysis and enzyme fermentation. Production of bioethanol from corn is a fermentation process, but the initial processing of the corn requires either wet or dry milling. Residues from corn milling can be used or sold as animal feed. Bioethanol from wheat requires an initial milling and malting (hydrolysis) process.

Biofuels

As defined by the United Nation's, "there are various pathways to convert feedstock and raw materials into biofuels. First-generation biofuel technologies, such as the fermentation of plant sugars or the transesterification of plant oils, are well established. Second-generation biofuel technologies include, among others, acid hydrolysis of wood chips or straw for bioethanol. The technology for extracting oil from oilseeds has essentially remained the same for the last 10 to 15 years."[75] Biodiesel production is a relatively simple process. However, economic small-scale production of biodiesel still requires sufficient feedstock, some equipment, capital, and skills.

While many of the above conversion processes are accomplished on a large scale, new and emerging technologies make it possible to produce electricity, heat, and fuels on a smaller scale and with modular systems. These technologies are being developed for off-grid applications and at an economic scale suitable for developing countries. An example of a modular biopower system [50 kilowatts electric (kWe)] is pictured above.[76]

Where biomass is produced in conjunction with agriculture for food production, it represents an additional value stream. Biofuels are produced in many countries, albeit in varying quantities and at different costs. Liquid biofuels have the potential to provide communities in developing countries with multiple energy services such as electricity for lighting, small appliances, and battery charging; income generation and educational activities; and pumping water, cooking, and transportation.

Waste-to-Energy

Waste-to-energy technology produces energy from waste, such as waste from a city's municipal waste system, farms and other agricultural operations, or commercial and industrial operations. Large-scale waste-to-energy systems can supply heat or electricity in utility-scale electric power plants or district heating systems. Small-scale systems can provide heating or cooking fuel and electricity to individual farms, homes, and businesses.

In incineration systems, waste is converted into useful energy through combustion. Modern incineration plants include materials separation processes to remove hazardous or recyclable materials from the waste stream before it is incinerated. Improvement in combustion processes and emissions controls minimizes the emission of particulate matter, heavy metals, dioxins, sulfur dioxide, and hydrochloric acid associated with waste combustion. Incineration plants emit fewer air pollutants than coal-fired plants but more than gas-fired plants. While Denmark and Sweden are leaders in the use of incineration technologies for energy generation, other European countries and Japan use the technology as a primary waste-handling system.

Landfill gas systems collect landfill gas for use in boilers, process heaters, turbines, and internal combustion engines, thereby reducing direct emissions of methane and other gases into the atmosphere or displacing the use of fossil fuels for power generation. Landfill gas contains varying amounts of methane and other gases, depending on the type of deposited waste and the characteristics of the landfill. Landfill gas can be piped directly to nearby buildings and used in boilers for heat or industrial processes or used in on-site electric generation plants that can supply electricity to the landfill itself, nearby industries, or to the electric power grid. The amount and type of waste in a landfill, its size, extent of landfill operating activity, and proximity to energy users are all factors that affect a landfill gas project's viability. Environmental precautions to minimize the emission of air pollutants are necessary to meet environmental regulations.

Anaerobic digester systems convert animal and human waste into methane and carbon dioxide, which can be used in turbines and internal combustion engines in electric power plants. Municipal waste treatment plants and confined animal feeding operations can be sources of waste for the digesters. Converting the waste into electricity reduces air and water pollution and the costs associated with processing the waste.

Other new and emerging waste-to-energy technologies use thermal and chemical conversion processes to convert solid waste into fuels.

Solar Power

Solar power is energy from the sun. Solar technologies convert light and heat from the sun into useful energy. Photovoltaic (PV) systems convert sunlight into electricity. Thermal systems collect and store solar heat for air and water heating applications. Concentrating solar power systems concentrate solar energy to drive large-scale electric power plants. Solar power systems produce little or no emissions and have a minimal impact on the environment.

Photovoltaics

PV power systems convert light from the sun into electricity. PV cells are devices made of semiconducting materials similar to those used in computer chips. When these devices are connected to an electrical circuit and exposed to light, they release electrons that flow through the circuit, creating an electric current. PV panels, shown above,[77] are devices that contain a varying number of PV cells and convert sunlight into direct current (DC) electricity. PV panels are typically incorporated into systems that combine batteries and electronic control equipment to provide fulltime DC and/or alternating current (AC) power. Typical applications include lighting, electronics, telecommunications, and small-scale water pumping.

Solar Thermal

Solar thermal technology uses flat and concentrating absorbers that collect heat energy from the sun for such processes as crop drying, food processing, water and space heating, industrial process heat, and electricity generation.

Solar water heating systems, such as the ones pictured in China's Yunnan Province,[78] consist of a solar collector and a storage tank. The collector is typically a rectangular box with a transparent cover, through which pipes run, carrying water that is heated by the sun. The pipes are attached to an absorber plate, which is painted black to absorb the heat. As the sun's heat warms the collector, the water is heated and passed to the storage tank, which stores the hot water heated for domestic use. As explained by the National Renewable Energy Laboratories, "Solar water heating systems can be either active or passive. Active systems rely on pumps to move the liquid between the collector and the storage tank, while passive systems rely on gravity and the tendency for water to naturally circulate as it is heated. Simpler versions of this system are used to heat swimming pools."[79]

Solar heating systems to dry food and other crops can improve the quality of the product while reducing waste. Solar driers outclass traditional open-air drying and have lower operating costs than mechanized fuel-based driers. The three types of solar driers are natural convection, forced convection, and tent driers. In natural convection driers, air is drawn through the dryer and heated as it passes through the collector, then partially cooled as it picks up moisture from the product drying. The flow of air is caused by the lighter warm air inside the dryer moving toward the cooler outside air. In forced convection, a fan is used to create the airflow, reducing drying time by a factor of 3 and the area of collector required by up to 50 percent. A photovoltaic panel can be used to generate electricity for the fan. Tent driers combine the drying chamber and collector and allow for a lower initial cost. Drying times are not much lower than for open-air drying, but the main purpose is to provide protection from dust, dirt, rain, wind, and predators; tent driers are usually used for fruit, fish, coffee, or other products for which wastage is otherwise high.

Passive Solar

Passive solar systems integrate solar air heating technologies into a building's design. Buildings are designed with materials that absorb or reflect solar energy to maintain comfortable indoor air temperatures and provide natural daylight. Floors and walls can be designed to absorb and retain heat during warm days and release it during cool evenings. Sunspaces operate like greenhouses and capture solar heat that can be circulated throughout a building. Trombe walls are thick walls that are painted black and made of a material that absorbs heat, which is stored during the day and released at night. Passive solar designs can also cool buildings, using vents, towers, window overhangs, and other approaches to keep buildings cool in warm climates.

Other Solar Technologies

Solar technologies can be used for residential, commercial, and industrial applications. Commercial and industrial applications can include air preheating for commercial ventilation systems, solar process heating, and solar cooling. A solar ventilation system can preheat the air before it enters a conventional furnace, reducing fuel consumption. Solar process heat systems provide large quantities of hot water or space heating for industrial applications. A typical system includes solar collectors that work with a pump, a heat exchanger, and one or more large storage tanks. Heat from a solar collector can also be used for commercial and industrial cooling of buildings, much like an air conditioner but with more complex technology.

Concentrated solar power systems focus sunlight on collectors that serve as a heat source to produce steam that drives a turbine and electricity generator. Concentrating solar power systems include parabolic-trough, dish-engine, and power tower technologies. Parabolic-trough systems concentrate the sun's energy through long rectangular, u-shaped mirrors, which are tilted toward the sun and focus sunlight on a pipe, heating the oil in the pipe and then using it in a conventional steam generator to produce electricity. Dish-engine systems use a mirrored dish similar to a satellite dish, which collects and concentrates the sun's heat onto a receiver, which in turn absorbs the heat and transfers it to fluid within the engine. The heat causes the fluid to expand against a piston or turbine to produce mechanical power, which is then used to run a generator to produce electricity. Power tower systems use a large field of mirrors to concentrate sunlight onto the top of a tower, where molten salt is heated and flows through a receiver. The salt's heat is used to generate electricity through a conventional steam generator. Because molten salt efficiently retains heat, it can be stored for days before being converted into electricity and ensures power production on cloudy days and after the sun has set.

Wind Power

Wind power technology converts energy in the wind into useful power. Historically, wind power technology was used for mechanical applications such as grain milling and water pumping and is still used for such purposes. Today, the primary market for wind power technology is for wind turbines, which convert wind energy into electricity.

Wind power for electricity generation is the fastest growing segment of the power sector, driven by the low cost of electricity generation, short project development and construction times, and government policies favoring clean and renewable energy technologies. The world's approximately 74,000 megawatts (MW) of installed wind capacity meet about 1 percent of the total global electricity demand. In the United States, as of December 2007, total installed wind capacity was approximately 14,000 MW, with an additional 5.7 MW under construction. Wind power accounts for about 20 percent of Denmark's electricity production, 9 percent of Spain's, and 7 percent of Germany's.

According to a recent study,[80] India and China alone are expected to add 36,000 MW of wind power capacity by 2015, representing over 80 percent of the Asian wind market during that period. Market growth in those countries is being driven by the growth of independent power producers (IPP) in India and by electric utilities in China. Major wind turbine manufacturers, including Vestas, GE, Suzlon, Gamesa, and Nordex, are establishing manufacturing facilities in India and China on the basis of strong market growth for their products in those countries. Suzlon, an Indian wind manufacturing company, is also active in the global wind market, including Europe and North America, as both an equipment supplier and project developer.

Large wind power generating plants, often called wind farms, can be integrated into agricultural and other land uses; a wind farm in Hawaii is shown at right.[81] Wind farms typically use tens to hundreds of wind turbines rated between 600 kilowatts (kW) and 5 MW and produce between 50 and hundreds of megawatts of electric power. In some countries, especially Denmark, Germany, and the United Kingdom, interest in offshore projects is increasing. In these projects, turbines are installed in the shallow waters of coastal areas, where they are exposed to the strong prevailing coastal winds and can be located close to large load centers.

Medium-sized turbines, between 10 and 600 kW, are used in distributed energy applications, supplementing or replacing grid power on farms and other commercial or industrial sites. Small wind turbines, in the 100 watt (W) to 10 kW range, are suitable for household, water pumping, or village power applications.

Conventional horizontal-axis wind turbines for electricity generation consist of a rotor, nacelle, tower, and foundation. The rotor consists of wind-spun blades that drive a gearbox and electric generator in the nacelle, which is located at the top of the tower. (Some turbine designs do not include a gearbox.) The tower and foundation support the nacelle and rotor at a height above the ground where winds are strong. Other wind turbine designs include vertical-axis turbines and small turbines designed for urban use.

Geothermal

Geothermal power is generated using thermal energy from underground sources. Different technologies are used to generate electricity using geothermal resources, which include steam, hot water, and heat stored in rock formations. Dry steam power plants use geothermal steam directly to drive a turbine and electric generator. Water condensed from the process is pumped underground and turned back into steam. Flash steam plants generate power by releasing hot water from underground pressurized reservoirs to drive turbines in an electric power plant. Both types of steam power plants release small amounts of gases and steam into the atmosphere.

Binary-cycle plants have no gas emissions and operate by passing hot water from a geothermal source through a heat exchanger, where heat from the water is transferred into a fluid that drives a turbine for electricity generation. Binary-cycle plants are more efficient than dry steam or flash steam systems and are the preferred technology for projects currently in the planning phase.

Geothermal energy was first used for electric power in Italy in the early 18th century. Geothermal resources are found worldwide in areas where geothermal energy is accessible at shallow levels. Areas with usable geothermal resources include the western United States, the southwestern coast of South America, a few areas in Europe and East Africa, and a significant portion of the Asia–Pacific region. New developments in geothermal power technology will use heat from hot, dry rock formations in and beneath the earth's crust.

Hydropower

Hydropower is the conversion of energy embodied in moving water into useful power. People have been harnessing the power of water for thousands of years for irrigation and operation of mechanical equipment and more recently for electricity generation. In fact, hydroelectric power now supplies about 19 percent of the world's electricity. In the United States, hydropower accounts for only 7 percent of the total electricity production, but over 70 percent of the total installed renewable energy capacity. Most industrialized nations have developed their hydropower potential, but undeveloped resources remain in countries such as China, India, Brazil, and regions of Africa and Latin America. In some countries with access to large untapped hydro resources, the resources are located far from electric load centers, posing a problem for transmission of electricity over long distances. Solving this technological problem and providing efficient transmission of electric power from off-grid hydropower plants is a major opportunity for investment and leadership in many countries around the world.

Hydropower plants are a clean, emission-free source of electricity. The natural hydrological cycle replenishes the resource, but also making it vulnerable to droughts. Competition for scarce water resources for agriculture, recreation, and fishing can affect the availability of water for power production. However, the potential for small hydro project development for rural electrification remains high in countries with concentrations of rural populations living near rivers and streams.

Large hydropower plants with capacities in the tens of megawatts are typically impoundment systems and require a dam that stops or reduces a river's flow to store water in a reservoir. Penstocks carry water from the reservoir to water turbines, which in turn drive electric generators. Impoundment systems offer the advantage of controlled power output and other benefits such as water recreation associated with reservoirs, irrigation, and flood control. However, dams negatively impact fish populations by interfering with migration patterns. Water quality both in the reservoir and downstream of the dam can be affected by changes in water flow and dissolved oxygen levels. Large new hydropower projects often require planning to remove communities from areas that will be flooded after a dam is built and other measures to manage environmental impact. Recent research has also raised concern about the possible effect of large reservoirs on atmospheric concentrations of greenhouse.

Small hydropower plants, such as the one shown at right,[82] with capacities ranging from a few kilowatts to several megawatts, are typically diversion systems, which divert some water from a river through a canal or penstock to a turbine. Small hydropower plants can provide electricity for isolated rural populations. These systems range in size from household-sized systems to ones that can supply power to entire villages and commercial or industrial loads. Diversion systems, also called run-of-river systems, do not require dams or reservoirs, are suitable for small hydropower projects, and have less impact on the environment. Small hydropower projects are being aggressively developed as part of rural electrification programs; in some cases innovative financing approaches are used in countries such as India, Sri Lanka, and Nepal.

Pumped storage systems require two reservoirs at different heights. They pump water during periods of low electric demand between the two heights and release water from the upper reservoir during periods of high demand.

Ocean Power Technology

Ocean power technology makes use of energy embodied in the ocean by converting it into electricity. Some systems convert the energy in moving ocean water into electricity, using either the vertical motion of waves or the horizontal motion of ocean currents. Other systems use temperature differences at different levels of the ocean to generate electricity. Ocean power technology is in the research and development stage, with several commercial prototypes being tested.

Tidal power technology converts the energy in tidal motion caused by the gravitational forces of the sun and moon on ocean water into electricity. Tidal stream systems operate similarly to wind turbines, using tidal turbines to convert energy in ocean currents into a rotational motion to drive turbines and power generators. Like wind turbines, tidal turbines can use horizontal-axis or verticalaxis machines. These systems rely on currents caused by ocean tides moving through and around obstructions such as entrances to bays and other geographical features. Tidal barrage systems are similar to hydropower dams, using differences in height of water on either side of a dam to generate electricity. Barrage systems use a dam-like structure and gates to store and release water as tides cause water levels to rise and fall.

Wave power technology extracts energy from the vertical motion of ocean water caused by waves. Wave power systems can be built offshore, in deep water typically far from coastlines or onshore in shallower water along the coast. Onshore systems show more promise because of their potential proximity to large load centers. Oscillating water column systems use rising and falling water caused by waves to compress and expand an air column in a vertical steel or concrete structure. The oscillating air pressure levels cause a turbine to spin, which drives an electric generator. Tapered channel systems use wave power to fill a raised reservoir with water, which is then allowed to flow through turbines. Pendulor wave systems consist of a rectangular structure with a hinged door that swings with the motion of waves. The swinging door operates a hydraulic pump that drives a turbine.

Ocean thermal energy conversion systems use temperature differences between warm surface water and cool deep water to convert a liquid into gas. The expanding gas drives a steam turbine and electric power generator. Closed-cycle systems circulate warm surface water through a heat exchanger where a fluid with a low boiling point is vaporized. A second heat exchanger condenses the vapor using cool deep water. Open-cycle systems use ocean water itself as the heat transfer fluid, boiling warm surface water in a low-pressure chamber. Water vapor drives a turbine and is condensed back into liquid using cool deep water. Hybrid systems use a combination of open- and closed-cycle arrangements. A by-product of ocean thermal energy systems is cold water, which can be used in building cooling systems, agriculture, and fisheries applications. Open- and hybrid-cycle systems desalinate ocean water in the vaporization process and could also be a source of fresh water. Ocean thermal energy conversion systems work in areas where the difference between the surface of the ocean and deeper water is about 20 degrees Celsius, which is often the case in tropical coastal areas.

As with other renewable energy technologies, ocean power technology projects are capital intensive, but typically have lower operating costs than fuel-based power technologies.

It should be noted that ocean power systems can impact migration patterns in ocean species and cause other environmentally troubling consequences. Systems employing barrages can cause silt buildup that affects tidewater and coastal ecosystems. These consequences can however be mitigated by careful selection of project sites.

Energy Efficiency

The efficiency of an energy conversion process is the ratio of the useful energy produced by the process to the amount of energy that goes into it. Primary energy is fossil fuel, nuclear, hydroelectric, or renewable energy extracted for use in an energy conversion process. Secondary energy is a high-quality form of energy such as electricity or refined fuel that can be used to provide energy services. An energy service is an end use provided by a process or device that requires secondary energy. Useful energy is the energy that goes toward providing an intended energy service. For example, the light produced by a lighting application is useful energy, whereas the heat produced by the application is not. Energy efficiency can be measured at different points in the process of converting a fuel or other energy resource into an end-use energy service. Efficiency points include the following:

- Extraction efficiency is a measure of the amount of primary energy delivered to a power plant or refinery per unit of energy contained by the energy resource in the ground or atmosphere and required by the extraction process.
- Power plant or refinery conversion efficiency is the ratio of the quantity of secondary energy produced by a power plant, refinery, or other conversion facility to the quantity of primary energy required by the process.

- Transmission and distribution efficiency is the ratio of secondary energy delivered to an end-use facility to the quantity of that energy produced by the power plant or refinery.
- End-use efficiency is a measure of the quantity of useful energy provided by a device or process per unit of energy delivered to the device or process.

Some analyses of energy efficiency also include a measure of the actual need for the energy service. For example, an office building that provides lighting for an unoccupied room or a factory that runs electric machines after the needed process is complete would be less efficient than a building equipped with motion sensors that provide lights only when people are in a room or a factory that shuts down equipment not being used.

Energy efficiency measures involve replacing existing technologies and processes with new ones that provide equivalent or better energy service using less energy. The value of the saved energy typically covers the cost of deploying the new technologies and processes, especially when the increase efficiency occurs downstream in the conversion process. For example, improving the efficiency of a pumping system in an industrial facility by redesigning the circulation system to minimize friction in pipes will result in the need for a smaller motor to drive pumps, which in turn consumes less energy. The reduced electricity demand will result in reduced losses in the entire chain, from the generation plant through the distribution system.

Energy efficiency results in savings at the time the energy service is provided. Energy service providers can also use load management to change the time that an energy service is delivered in order to reduce peak loads on an energy distribution system. Demand-side management (DSM) uses both load management and energy efficiency to save the amount of primary energy required to deliver the energy service.

Energy savings provide several benefits. For energy consumers, benefits include reduced costs and reduced emissions; for energy service providers, efficiency reduces the need for (and cost of) fuel; and for governments and communities alike, efficiency reduces CO_2 emissions and can help meet targets for global warming pollutants. Energy efficiency programs can reduce future investment requirements, enhance competitiveness by lowering input and operating costs, free up capital for other social and economic development priorities, and contribute to environmental stewardship objectives. It can also contribute to long-term resource planning and management, hedge fuel risks, and reduce operation and maintenance (O&M) costs. Energy efficiency programs promote improvement and investment in energy generation, delivery, end-use equipment, facilities, buildings, and infrastructure that increase useful energy output or services.

Combining energy efficiency and renewable energy policies maximizes the impact of energy policy on emission reductions. Reducing growth of energy demand allows low- or no-emission renewables to keep up with electric demand. Without coordination, new renewable capacity would be outstripped by increased demand, requiring increased fossil fuel capacity to meet the growth. A combined policy also takes advantage of the temporal synergy of the two approaches: Energy efficiency programs can meet shorter-term goals because efficiency measures can be implemented quickly and at relatively low cost. Renewable energy programs can meet longerterm goals, with new capacity coming on line as the efficiency programs achieve their goals.

Demand Side Management (DSM) is the practice of changing energy consumption patterns to reduce the need for new energy generation capacity. DSM can include energy efficiency programs, peak load reduction programs, real-time and time-of-use energy pricing, interruptible load tariffs, direct load control, and shifting demand from peak to off-peak periods.

Building codes provide guidelines for the construction industry to achieve energy-saving goals through improvements in lighting, heating, and cooling. Special programs promote the development of zero-energy buildings, which combine energy efficiency with energy production technologies to maximize the amount of a building's energy that it generates on site.

In the transportation sector, vehicle efficiency standards, public transportation programs, and urban planning minimize the consumption of transportation fuels while maintaining adequate levels of transportation services.

Industrial efficiency measures the decrease in energy use and pollution in the industrial sector. Investment in efficient motor and pumping systems, combined heat and power, and distributed on-site energy generation results in long-term energy savings and can help industries compete while meeting environmental regulations.

Energy efficiency measures require capacity-building efforts to empower institutions and individuals to implement energy-saving programs and make energy-saving decisions. Examples of capacity building include establishing energy audit procedures and auditor training programs, developing systems to track energy consumption patterns and establish benchmarks, establishing energy management systems, creating certification systems for energy practitioners, developing energy management guidelines, and facilitating technology transfer.

Hybrids and Co-generation

Hybrid and co-generation power systems take advantage of the benefits of multiple technologies in a single, integrated system. Hybrid power systems use combinations of power generating technologies to generate electricity. Co-generation systems, also called combined heat and power (CHP) systems, generate both electricity and useful heat.

Hybrid Power System Technology

Renewable-based hybrid power systems use combinations of wind turbines, photovoltaic panels, and small hydropower generators to generate electricity. Hybrid power systems typically include a diesel or other fuel-based generator and may include batteries or other storage technology. A completely renewable hybrid power system might use a biofuel-based generator in place of a diesel or other fossil fuel generator. Hybrid power system applications are typically small to medium in scale (producing between 100 watt-hours and tens of megawatt-hours per day) and generate electricity for distributed power generation applications, in remote areas for village power, and for communications and military installations around the world.

Hybrid power system designers select technologies on the basis of the renewable resource available at a particular location to take advantage of resource complementarity. For example, a wind–solar hybrid system can make use of both solar and wind power in areas that experience windy periods at night after the sun has set. A solar–hydropower hybrid system would be appropriate at a location that is near a stream or river and has sunny weather during dry periods of the year when stream flow is low. In some cases, the renewable resource may complement varying availability of fossil fuel resources, such as in areas in the Arctic that experience high winds, when transportation of fuels to remote locations is difficult or impossible due to winter conditions.

Renewable penetration is a measure of the relative contribution of renewable and non-renewable resources in a hybrid power system that includes fossil-fuel-based generation. The simplest and therefore lowest-cost designs are low-penetration systems in which the renewable power components produce sufficient power to save up to 20 percent on fossil fuel consumption. Medium- and high-penetration systems can save up to 40 and 70 percent on fuel consumption, respectively, but are more costly to design and complex to operate because they require additional control equipment to ensure the system's stability.

Advanced hybrid power systems use new technologies for power generation, storage, and system control. New technologies for research and experimental hybrid power systems include natural gas turbines, fuel cells, advanced batteries, flywheels, and other technologies.

Examples of Hybrid Power Systems

Over 400 simple wind–solar–battery hybrid systems provide between 500 and 600 W of electric generation capacity for rural households in Inner Mongolia, China. Each system consists of a 300-W wind turbine and 100- to 200-W photovoltaic array that charges deep-cycle lead acid batteries.

Co-generation System Technology

Conventional fossil-fuel-based electric power plants generate heat as a by-product that is emitted into the environment through gas flues, cooling towers, and by other methods. Co-generation power plants collect this heat for use in thermal applications, thereby converting a higher percentage of the energy in the fuel into useful energy. The most efficient conventional power plants have a typical fuel-to-electricity conversion factor of about 50 percent, while co-generation plants can achieve efficiencies of over 75 percent. Co-generation plants generate more useful power than conventional plants using the same amount of fuel and also produce less pollution per unit of useful energy.

Co-generation plants are most effective when located near a thermal load center. Examples of thermal loads that can be served by a co-generation plant are district heating systems that provide heat for towns and neighborhoods, industrial processes that require heat such as paper mills, institutions such as prisons and hospitals, and wastewater treatment plants.

Co-generation plants either primarily produce electricity and collect exhaust heat from the electricity generation process (topping cycle plant) or primarily generate heat and use excess thermal energy to drive an electricity generating process (bottoming cycle plant). Co-generation plants can be large (greater than about 25 MW) and based on conventional natural gas turbines, combined-cycle natural gas turbines, or steam turbines. Smaller co-generation plants (25 kW to 25 MW) use reciprocating or Stirling engines to run an electric generator and collect the waste heat from the engine's exhaust system for thermal applications. These smaller plants can be fired by biomass or industrial and municipal waste. Very small co-generation plants (1–25 kW) for distributed energy applications use some of the heat from water or space heating systems to generate electricity for a single household or small business.

Clean Transportation Technologies

Alternative fuels for transportation include biodiesel, ethanol, natural gas, and propane. Biofuels produced from agricultural products are considered renewable fuels because they can be grown annually. Biofuels also produce fewer air pollutants when burned in vehicle engines. Advanced transportation technologies include electric vehicles, hybrid electric vehicles, mobile idle reduction systems, and diesel retrofits.

Biodiesel is a fuel derived from biomass that can be burned in diesel engines, including those in light- and heavy-duty diesel vehicles. Biodiesel can be used in all diesel vehicles and produces fewer emissions than fossil fuel diesel. Because biodiesel is produced from biomass, it can be considered a carbon-neutral fuel from a global warming perspective, although carbon emissions from the production and transportation of biodiesel contribute to its carbon footprint. Biodiesel fuel can easily be distributed through the existing fueling infrastructure.

Ethanol can be mixed with gasoline and used in vehicle engines designed to burn gasoline–ethanol mixtures. E85 fuel consisting of 85 percent ethanol and 15 percent gasoline can reduce air pollutant emissions and be used in vehicles with modified engines or with engines designed for use with ethanol fuel mixtures. Existing fueling stations can be modified to distribute ethanol-based fuels.

Compressed and liquefied natural gas (CNG and LNG) can be used in engines designed or modified for use with the fuels. Natural gas engines produce lower emissions than gasoline engines. Wide-scale use of natural gas as a transportation fuel requires adoption of the specialized vehicles by consumers and transportation companies and development of new fueling infrastructure. Propane (LPG) can be used in passenger and light-duty delivery vehicles and in forklifts and mowers. Propane costs vary from 5 to 40 percent less than gasoline and can result in reductions in air pollutants.

Electric vehicles are appropriate for neighborhood use. Using electricity in electric vehicles represents about a 30 percent reduction in fuel costs over conventional fuels. Using electricity from the conventional grid results in a 50 percent reduction in emissions compared to conventional fossil fuel vehicles.

Hybrid electric vehicle technology can be used in passenger and light-duty vehicles and in buses and trucks. Hybrid electric vehicles are more efficient than fossil-fuel-only vehicles and offer slight air pollution improvements over average fossil fuel vehicles. Plugin hybrids offer an improvement over hybrid electric vehicles by allowing for some of the vehicle's energy to be supplied by the electric power grid and potentially by renewable energy sources. Because electric power tends to be cleaner than power from internal combustion engines, this approach can result in overall reductions in transportation-related pollution.

Fuel efficiency and air emissions for heavy-duty diesel vehicles can be improved with new technologies. Mobile idle reduction systems provide alternative power sources for use when trucks are idle but still require power for heating and cooling. Diesel engine retrofits including exhaust catalysts and filters reduce the emission of air pollutants.

Summary

This section has presented only a brief summary of the clean energy technologies included in this assessment report. There is a considerable wealth of information on these technologies and on the ongoing research and development of other alternative energy technologies from national laboratories such as the National Renewable Energy Laboratory (NREL) of the U.S. Department of Energy, as well as various renewable energy industry associations. Other resources for U.S. firms are included in Appendix A of this document.

Appendix A. Resources for U.S. Firms

The following table provides a compendium of trade and investment resources for U.S. clean technology firms, with a brief description of each resource. Contact information for individual organizations can be found by at each listed Web site. The provision of this list of resources does not constitute endorsement of any organization.

Organization	Web Site	Description
A. U. S. Government		
U.S. Department of Commerce (DOC), International Trade Administration (ITA)	*www.trade.gov*	DOC/ITA participates in the development of U.S. trade policy, identifies and resolves market access and compliance issues, administers U.S. trade laws, and undertakes a range of trade promotion and trade advocacy efforts. ITA has more than 2,000 dedicated individuals posted at U.S. embassies and commercial offices around the world, including in China and India. ITA's lead business unit for trade promotion is the U.S. Commercial Service, which supports U.S. businesses through its global network of offices. The Commercial Service promotes the export of American goods and services worldwide and includes special programs for India and China. A resource guide for U.S. exporters to China, including a listing of legal services for China, is available at *www. buyusa.gov/china/en/ contactchina.html.* The India site is available at *www.buyusa.gov/india/en/.* The U.S. Commercial Service offers four ways to grow international sales: world-class market research, trade events that promote products and services to qualified buyers, introductions to qualified buyers and distributors, and counseling through every step of the export process. For more information about how our worldwide network can help your company, call 1-800-USA-TRADE or contact our Export Assistance Centers. ITA's other business units include: Market Access and Compliance, which resolves market access issues, identifies and reduces trade barriers, and ensures that foreign countries are in compliance with trade agreements; Manufacturing and Services, which advocates policies to help U.S. companies be competitive at home and around the world and ensures industry's voice is reflected in policy development; and Import Administration, which administers

Appendix A. (Continued)

Organization	Web Site	Description
		various trade laws and monitors subsidies. ITA also has various resour-ces to help in this fight including: one-on-one consultat-ions with IPR trade specia-lists; IP attaches in China, Brazil, India, Russia, Thailand and Egypt to assist American businesses and actively engage with local IP agencies; the China IPR Advisory Program that provides U.S. companies a one-hour free legal consultation with a volunteer attorney experienced in IPR matters; IPR toolkits available online at *www.stopfakes.gov* containing detailed information on local IP laws and resources, as well as helpful local contact information in key foreign markets; free monthly China IPR Webinar series for U.S. industry; a hotline (1-866-999-HALT) answered by IPR experts to help businesses secure and enforce their IP rights; a Trade Fair IPR Initiative to promote protection of IP at domestic and international trade fairs; domestic outreach programs including a U.S. PTO China Roadshow; as well as a free, web-based IPR Module available at *www.stopfakes.gov* to help SMEs evaluate, protect, and enforce their IP both in the United States and overseas.
Export–Import Bank of the United States (Ex-Im Bank)	*www.exim.gov*	Ex-Im Bank is the official export credit agency of the United States. Ex-Im Bank's mission is to assist in financing the export of U.S. goods and services to international markets. Ex-Im Bank enables U.S. compa-nies—large and small—to turn export opp-ortunities into real sales helping to main-tain and create U.S. jobs and contribute to a stronger national economy. Ex-Im Bank does not compete with private-sector lend-ers but provides export financing products that fill gaps in trade financing. Ex-Im Bank assumes credit and country risks that the private sector is unable or unwilling to accept and helps to level the playing field for U.S. exporters by matching the finance-ing that other governments provide to their exporters. Clean energy is a priority for Ex-Im Bank, and the agency offers its most favorable terms for these technologies.
Overseas Private Investment Corporation (OPIC)	*www.opic.gov*	OPIC helps U.S. businesses invest over-seas, fosters economic development in new and emerging markets, complements the

Appendix A. (Continued)

Organization	Web Site	Description
		private sector in managing risks associated with foreign direct investment, and supports U.S. foreign policy. Because OPIC charges market-based fees for its products, it operates on a self-sustaining basis at no net cost to taxpayers. OPIC has made clean energy investment a priority and offers favorable terms for these technologies.
U.S. Agency for International Development (USAID)	*www.usaid.gov*	USAID is an independent agency that provides economic, development, and humanitarian assistance around the world in support of the foreign policy goals of the United States. Currently, USAID is operational in India (but not China). In India, USAID works with local partners to increase viability in the power sector, conserve resources, and promote clean technologies and renewable energy. USAID facilitates sharing of energy and environment best practices between the United States and India and among South Asian countries.
US Department of Agriculture (USDA)	*www.usda.gov*	The Foreign Agricultural Service (FAS) of USDA works to improve foreign market access for U.S. products, build new markets, improve the competitive position of U.S. agriculture in the global marketplace, and provide food aid and technical assistance to foreign countries. FAS has the primary responsibility for USDA's international activities—market development, trade agreements and negotiations, and the collection and analysis of statistics and market information. It also administers USDA's export credit guarantee programs. USDA helps increase income and food availability in developing nations by mobilizing expertise for agriculturally led economic growth. USDA is also active in bioenergy development, domestically and overseas.
U.S. Department of Energy (USDOE)	*www.energy.gov*	USDOE is committed to reducing America's dependence on foreign oil and developing energy efficient technologies for buildings, homes, transportation, power systems, and industry. The Office of Energy Efficiency and Renewable Energy (EERE) seeks to strengthen America's energy security, environmental quality, and economic vitality in public–private partnerships that enhance energy efficiency and productivity; bring clean, reliable, and

Appendix A. (Continued)

Organization	Web Site	Description
		affordable energy technologies to the marketplace; and make a difference in the everyday lives of Americans by enhancing their energy choices and their quality of life. EERE leads the federal government's research, development, and deployment efforts in energy efficiency. EERE's role is to invest in high-risk, high-value research and development (R&D) that is critical to the nation's energy future and would not be sufficiently conducted by the private sector acting on its own. Program activities are conducted in partnership with the private sector, state and local governments, USDOE national laboratories, and universities. EERE offers financial assistance for renewable energy and energy efficiency R&D. EERE also works with stakeholders to develop programs and policies to facilitate the deployment of advanced clean energy technologies and practices. EERE has bilateral agreements in clean energy with India and China and participates in the Asia–Pacific Partnership on Clean Development and Climate (APP) (see below).
U.S. Department of State (State)	*www.state.gov*	State is the lead U.S. foreign affairs agency, and the Secretary of State is the president's principal foreign policy adviser. The department advances U.S. objectives and interests in shaping a freer, more secure, and more prosperous world through its primary role in developing and implementting the president's foreign policy. The Bureau of Economic, Energy and Business Affairs (EEB) formulates and carries out U.S. foreign economic policy, integrating U.S. economic interests with our foreign policy goals so that U.S. firms and investors can compete on an equal basis with their counterparts overseas. It implements U.S. economic policy in cooperation with U.S. companies, U.S. Government agencies, and other organizations. State also manages U.S. embassies overseas and coordinates U.S. activities under the APP (see below).
U.S. Embassy in China	*http://beijing.usembassy-china. org.cn*	The embassy provides information on travel, doing business in China, an IPR toolkit (*http://beijing.usembassy-china.org.cn/ipr.html*), and other useful

Appendix A. (Continued)

Organization	Web Site	Description
		information for U.S. visitors to China. The U.S. Commercial Service has offices throughout China as well.
U.S. Department of Treasury (Treasury)	*www.treasury.gov*	The Office of Foreign Assets Control (OFAC) of Treasury administers and enforces economic and trade sanctions based on U.S. foreign policy and national security goals against targeted foreign countries, terrorists, international narcotics traffickers, and those engaged in activities related to the proliferation of weapons of mass destruction. OFAC acts under presidential wartime and national emergency powers, as well as authority granted by specific legislation, to impose controls on transacttions and freeze foreign assets under U.S. jurisdiction.
U.S. Small Business Administration (SBA)	*www.sba.gov*	SBA's mission is to aid, counsel, assist, and protect the interests of small-business concerns; to preserve free competitive enterprise; and to maintain and strengthen the overall economy of our nation. SBA also helps small businesses to compete in the global marketplace.
U.S. Trade and Development Agency (USTDA)	*www.tda.gov*	USTDA's mission is to advance economic development and U.S. commercial interests in developing and middle-income countries. To this end, the agency funds various forms of technical assistance, investment analysis, training, orientation visits, and business workshops that support the development of a modern infrastructure and a fair and open trading environment. In carrying out its mission, USTDA gives emphasis to economic sectors that may benefit from U.S. exports of goods and services.
U.S. Trade Representative (USTR)	*www.ustr.gov*	USTR is an agency of over 200 people with specialized experience in trade issues and regions of the world. They negotiate directly with foreign governments to create trade agreements, resolve disputes, and participate in global trade policy organizations. They also meet with governments, business groups, legislators, and public interest groups to gather input on trade issues and explain the president's trade policy positions.

Appendix A. (Continued)

Organization	Web Site	Description
StopFakes	*www.stopfakes.gov*	International Trade Administration of the Department of Commerce manages Stop-Fakes, which provides access to information on promoting trade and investment, strengthening the competitiveness of U.S. industry, and ensuring fair trade and compliance with trade laws and agreements.
B. Non–U.S. Government Organizations		
Alliance to Save Energy (ASE)	*www.ase.org/*	Programs in the United States and abroad (including China and India) conduct research, advise policy-makers, and educate decision-makers on energy efficiency issues. The China program educates manufacturers and government officials on efficient windows and other technologies. In India, ASE is working on municipal water delivery.
Amerex Brokers, LLC	*www.amerexenergy.com /*	A division of the GFI Group that operates markets in electrical power, natural gas, emission allowances, and renewable energy credits. Also provides energy procurement services to large commercial and industrial customers.
American Council for an Energy-Efficient Economy (ACEEE)	*www.aceee.org/*	Non-profit organization provides technical and policy assessments, policy support, business, and public interest collaborations. Organizes conferences and provides information dissemination through publications and education.
American Council on Renewable Energy (ACORE)	*www.acore.org/*	ACORE establishes collaborative research and communication among leaders of financial institutions, government, professional service providers, and others in the wind, solar, geothermal, biomass and biofuels, hydropower tidal and current energy, and waste energy industries. Organizes an annual international ministerial-level workshop on renewable energy in Washington, D.C.
Asia-Pacific Partnership on Clean Development and Climate (APP)	*www.asiapacificpartners hip. org*	The APP is a Presidential initiative to acelerate the development and deployment of clean energy security, reduce harmful air pollution, and greenhouse gas (GHG) emissions intensity in the context of sustained economic growth. The United States, Australia, China, India, Japan, the Republic of Korea, and Canada (accounting for over half of the world's GHG emissions, energy consumption, GDP, and population) agreed to work together and

Appendix A. (Continued)

Organization	Web Site	Description
		the private sector to expand investment and trade in cleaner energy technologies. Led by the State Department, the APP is an industry-focused, technology-driven, results-oriented partnership. Through Activities like the Clean Energy Technologies Trade Mission to China and India, the Department of Commerce seeks to position U.S. companies to make comercial sales while removing obstacles that restrict the ability of U.S. companies to do business in partner countries.
Association of Energy Engineers (AEE)	www.aeecenter.org/	Non-profit society of energy professionals in 77 countries promotes interest in sustainable development. Publishes industry newsletters for facility managers, renewable energy developers, environmental managers, and energy service providers.
China Embassy in United States	www.china-embassy.org/eng	Provides information on China and its economy and trade, ministry information, and some policy documents.
Cultural Savvy	www.culturalsavvy.com/	Provides training and consulting services for international business travelers. Includes some on-line information.
E Source	www.esource.com/	For-profit company originally operated as a Rocky Mountain Institute project. E Source provides analysis of retail energy markets, services, and technologies to its members, which include electric and gas utilities, large corporate and institutional energy users, government agencies, energy service companies, manufacturers, consultants, and others in over 20 countries.
Evolution Markets	new.evomarkets.com/	Provides financial and brokerage services for the global green market and clean energy sector.
Intergovernmental Panel on Climate Change	www.grida.no/climate/ipcc/tectran/index.htm	This site provides an overview of methodological and technological issues in technology transfer, including financing and partnerships, and sectoral analyses.
International Cultural Enterprises, Inc.	www.businessculture.com	Publishes best-practice reports, audio guides, and Web-based reports on country-specific business practices, customs, negotiating tactics, communication, and other issues. Also provides cross-cultural training and consulting services.
National Association of Energy Service	www.naesco.org/	The energy service industry trade organization advocates for the delivery of cost-effective energy services, provides industry

Appendix A. (Continued)

Organization	Web Site	Description
Companies (NAESCO)		information and data, and helps establish industry standards.
Organization for Economic Co-operation and Development (OECD) Directorate for Financial and Enterprise Affairs	*www.oecd.org/*	The OECD Investment Committee provides guidelines for multinational enterprises covering business ethics and sustainable development. Also provides investment statistics and analysis and investment codes.
Organization for International Investment	*www.ofii.org/*	Represents interests of U.S. subsidiaries of companies headquartered abroad. Educates public and policy-makers about positive role U.S. subsidiaries play in U.S. economy and ensures that U.S. subsidiaries are not discriminated against in state or federal law. Provides peer-to-peer forums for U.S. subsidiaries.
Renewable Energy Access	*www.renewableenergyaccess. com*	Company directory is a searchable list of companies by function. Searching for financial services companies generates a list of clean energy finance companies worldwide.
RenewableEnergyStocks.com	*www.renewablenergystocks. com*	Provides information on renewable energy investing and links to renewable energy industry information.
The Association of Energy Services Professionals (AESP)	*www.aesp.org/*	Membership organization of electric and natural gas utilities, public benefits associations, regulatory and non-profit entities, vendors, manufacturers, and consulting firms provides professional development programs and networking opportunities and promotes knowledge transfer.
The Lett Group	*www.lettgroup.com/*	Trains executives and professionals in business etiquette, manners, and other skills using international protocol.
UNEP Sustainable Energy Finance Initiative	*www.sefi.unep.org/*	Provides financiers with tools and access to networks to foster investment in sustainable energy projects.
World Energy Efficiency Association (WEEA)	*www.weea.org/*	Assists developing and reindustrializing countries in assessing information on energy efficiency. Publications include best practices and case studies on energy efficiency projects, financing, and ESCOs. Also publishes directories of international energy organizations and companies.
World Trade Organization	*www.wto.org/*	The WTO site provides information on trade goods, rules, and regulations; intellectual property rights, including trade-related

Appendix A. (Continued)

Organization	Web Site	Description
		aspects of Intellectual Property Rights (TRIPS); accessions, government procurement, and other commerce and trade topics. Information on China and the WTO is available at *www.wto.org/english/thewto_e/ countries_e/china_e.html*; information on India and the WTO is available at *www.wto.org/english/thewto_e/countries_e /india_e.htm*.

APPENDIX B. SUSTAINABLE ENERGY FINANCE DIRECTORY

This directory is synthesized from the on-line resources available at *www.sef-directory.net/*, which is maintained by the Sustainable Energy Finance Initiative (SEFI), a joint initiative of the United Nations Environment Program and the Basel Agency for Sustainable Energy. It has been updated as of late 2007.

Note that financing for clean energy technologies has increased significantly in the last few years. This directory provides information on a number of these sources based on information from SEFI but is not exhaustive.

TITLE	FINANCE TYPE	SOURCE OF CAPITAL	TECHNOLOGY TYPES	GEOGRAPHIC FOCUS	CONTACT
Swedish International Climate Investment Program (SICLIP)	Carbon finance		Energy efficiency, bioenergy, wind	South Asia, Southeast Asia, East Asia, West Asia, Central and Eastern Europe, Central and South America, Sub-Saharan Africa	Kungsgatan 43 Box 310, SE-631 04 Eskilstuna Sweden Tel: +46 16 544 2241; +46 16 544 2043 Fax: +46 16 544 2099 angska.kallhaugpelstrom.se, gudrun.knutssong energimyndigheten.se www.energimyndigheten.se
Svensk Exportkredit (SEK)– Sweden	Export credits		Bioenergy, geothermal, small hydropower, solar (PV and thermal), wind	West Asia, North Africa, Central and Eastern Europe, Central and South America, North America, Oceania, Western Europe, South Asia, Southeast Asia, East Asia, Sub-Saharan Africa	P.O. Box 16368, SE 103 27 Västra Trädgårdsgatan 11 B Stockholm Sweden Tel: +46 8 61 38 300 Fax: +46 8 20 38 94 info@sek.se www.sek.se/
World Bank Carbon Finance	Carbon finance	Public, private	Energy efficiency, renewable energy	Global, including China, India	The World Bank Carbon Finance Unit 1818 H Street, N.W. Washington, D.C. Tel: +1 202 473 1000 www.carbonfinance.org

Insurance

TITLE	FINANCE TYPE	SOURCE OF CAPITAL	TECHNOLOGY TYPES	GEOGRAPHIC FOCUS	CONTACT
Aon Global Risk Consultants Ltd.	Insurance		Bioenergy, geothermal, small hydropower, solar (PV and thermal), wind	South Asia, Southeast Asia, East Asia, West Asia, North Africa, Central and South America, Central and Eastern Europe, North America, Oceania, Western Europe, Sub-Saharan Africa	CONTACT—China Richard Dong Aon Corporation Beijing Representative Office Room 1206 Capital Tower Beijing 6 Jia Jian Guo Men Wai Avenue Chaoyang District Beijing 100022 The People's Republic of China Tel: +86 10 6563 0671 Fax: +86 10 6563 0672 richard_dong@aon-cofco.com.cn www.aon.com/us/en/china CONTACT—India Prabodh Thakker, Chairman 302 Dalamal House Jamnalal Bajaj Marg Nariman Point Mumbai–400 021 India Tel: +91 22 6656 0505 Fax: +91 22 6656 0506 prabodh_thakker@aon-asia.com www.aon.com/cn/en/india CONTACT—Main Office Aon Limited, 8 Devonshire Square London EC2M 4PL United Kingdom Tel: +44 0 20 7623 5500 Fax: +44 0 20 7621 1511 www.aon.co.uk
Miller Insurance Group	Insurance		Wind	South Asia, Southeast Asia, East Asia, West Asia, North Africa, Central and Eastern Europe, Central and South America, North America, Oceania, Western Europe, Sub-Saharan Africa	Suzanna Lam, Director Miller Insurance Services (Hong Kong) Ltd. Tel: +852 2525 6982 suzanna.lam@miller-insurance.com www.miller-insurance.com/China-Energy David Horne, Director Energy Tel: +44 0 20 7031 2582 david.horne@miller-insurance.com www.miller-insurance.com/China-Energy CONTACT—Main Office Dawson House 5 Jewry Street London EC3N 2PJ United Kingdom Tel: +44 0 20 7488 2345 Fax: N/A info@miller-insurance.com www.aon.co.uk

(Continued)

Organization				Contact
International Finance Corporation	Debt, equity, fund development, risk mitigation	IFC funds, GEF, other	Energy efficiency, bioenergy, geothermal, small hydropower, solar (PV and thermal), wind, among others	Southeast Asia, East Asia, West Asia, North Africa, Central and Eastern Europe, Central and South America, North America, Oceania, Western Europe, South Asia, Sub-Saharan Africa	CONTACT—China Michael Ipson, Country Manager 19th Floor, China World Tower 2 China World Trade Center No. 1 Jian Guo Men Wai Avenue Beijing, China 100004 Tel: +86 10 5860 3000 Fax: +86 10 5860 3100 mipson@ifc.org www.ifc.org/ifcext/eastasia.nsf/Content/China Mario Fischel, General Manager Private Enterprise Partnership for China R 2716, 27th Floor CCB Sichuan Building No. 86 Tidu Street Chengdu, Sichuan Province P.R. China, 610015 Tel: +86 28 8676 6622 Fax: N/A mfischel@ifc.org www.ifc.org/ifcext/eastasia.nsf/Content/China Guwahati–781 005, Assam Tel: +91 361 2463 133 36 Fax: +91 361 2463 132 SouthAsia@ifc.org www.ifc.org/india CONTACT—India New Delhi Paolo Martelli, Director, South Asia or Anil Sinha, General Manager, SEDF 50-M, Shanti Path, Gate No. 3 Niti Marg, Chanakyapuri New Delhi–110 021 Tel: +91 11 4111 1000 Fax: +91 11 4111 1001/025SouthAsia@ifc.org www.ifc.org/ifcext/southasia.nsf/Content/India_overview Mumbai Sujoy Bose, Senior Manager Godrej Bhavan, 3rd Floor Murzban Road, Fort Mumbai–400 001, Maharashtra Tel: +91 22 6665 2000 Fax: +91 22 6665 2061 SouthAsia@ifc.org www.ifc.org/ifcext/southasia.nsf/Content/India_overview Chennai Prasad Gopalan, Principal Investment Officer Girijapur Enclave, No. 56 2nd Floor, 1st Avenue Shastri Nagar, Adyar Chennai–600 020, Tamil Nadu Tel: +91 44 2446 2570 Fax: +91 44 2446 2571 SouthAsia@ifc.org www.ifc.org/ifcext/india Guwahati Sushanta Kumar Pal, Business Development Officer First Floor, Orion Place Next to Mizoram House Christian Basti, G S Road
Triodos Renewable Energy for Development Fund	Debt capital	Bilaterals, multilaterals, foundations, private sector	Bioenergy, geothermal, small hydropower, solar (PV and thermal), wind	South Asia, Southeast Asia, East Asia, West Asia, North Africa, Sub-Saharan Africa	Utrechtseweg 60, P.O. Box 55 3700 AB Zeist The Netherlands Tel: +31 30 693 6500 Fax: +31 30 693 6566 benff@triodos.nl www.triodos.com Team members Bob Assenberg Tel: +31 30 693 65 63 bob.assenberg@triodos.nl Gerrit-Jan Brunink Tel: +31 30 693 65 78 gerrit-jan.brunink@triodos.nl Helena Korhonen Tel: +31 30 693 65 41 helena.korhonen@triodos.nl Martijn Woudstra Tel: +31 30 094 26 91 martijn.woudstra@triodos.nl

Verde Ventures, Conservation International	Debt capital		Energy efficiency	Southeast Asia, Central and South America, Oceania, Sub-Saharan Africa	2011 Crystal Drive, Suite 500 Arlington, Virginia 22201 USA Tel: +1 703 341 2400, +1 800 406 2306 Fax: +1 703 553 0721 verdeventure@conservation.org www.conservation.org/sp/verdeventures/
World Bank		Member countries	Loans, guarantees, analytic, and advisory services to developing countries	West Asia, South Asia, South-east Asia, East Asia	CONTACT—Washington, D.C. Junhui Wu 1818 H Street, N.W. Washington, D.C. 20433 USA Tel: +1 202 458 1405 Fax: +1 202 522 1648 Jwu@world.org CONTACT—India Hema Balasubramanian hbalasubramanian@worldbank.org Sunita Malhotra smalhotra@worldbank.org Tel: +91 11 24617241

Private Equities

TITLE	FINANCE TYPE	SOURCE OF CAPITAL	TECHNOLOGY TYPES	GEOGRAPHIC FOCUS	CONTACT
Actis Energy Fund	Private equities		Energy efficiency, cleaner fuels, bioenergy, geothermal, small hydropower, solar (PV and thermal), wind, fuel cells	South Asia, Southeast Asia, East Asia, West Asia, North Africa, Central and South America, Sub-Saharan Africa	CONTACT—China Benjamin Cheng, Investment Principle 712 China World Tower 2 No.1 Jianguomenwai Street Chaoyang District Beijing 100004 People's Republic of China Tel: +86 10 6505 6655 Fax: N/A bcheng@act.is www.act.is CONTACT—India Bangalore Subba Rao Telidevara, Partner 15 Rest House Crescent Bangalore–560001 India Tel: +91 80 2555 0651 Fax: +91 80 2555 0592 stelidevara@act.is www.act.is Delhi Steven Enderby, Partner NBCC Place, 1st Floor, East Tower Bhisham Pitamah Marg Pragati Vihar New Delhi–110003 India Tel: +91 11 4366 7000 Fax: +91 11 4366 7070 senderby@act.is www.act.is Mumbai JM Trivedi, Partner 704, 7 Floor Dalamal House Jamnala Bajaj Road Nariman Point Mumbai–400021 India Tel: +91 22 2281 6430 Fax: +91 22 2282 0737 jtrivedi@act.is www.act.is
Al Tayyar Energy	Private equities		Bioenergy, small hydropower, solar (PV and thermal), wind	South Asia, Southeast Asia, East Asia, West Asia, North Africa, Central and Eastern Europe, Sub-Saharan Africa	Granville (Pete) Smith P.O. Box 757 Abu Dhabi United Arab Emirates Tel: +971-2-681-4004 Fax: +971 2 681 4005 pete@altayyarenergy.com www.altayyarenergy.com
Battery Ventures	Private equities	Limited partners	Energy efficiency, cleaner fuels, solar (PV and thermal), wind, fuel cells	South Asia, Southeast Asia, West Asia, North America, Western Europe	Ramneek Gupta rgupta@battery.com Mark Sherman mark@battery.com

(Continued)

Name	Category	Type	Technology focus	Regions	Contact
CDC Group PLC	Private equities	Private	Energy efficiency, bioenergy, geothermal, small hydropower, solar (PV and thermal), Wind	South Asia, Southeast Asia, East Asia, West Asia, North Africa, Central and South America, Sub-Saharan Africa	6 Duke Street, St. James's London SW1Y 6BN United Kingdom Tel: +44 0 20 7484 7700 Fax: +44 0 20 7484 7750 enquiries@cdcgroup.com www.cdcgroup.com · 930 Winter Street, Suite 2500 Waltham, Massachusetts 02541 USA Tel: +1 781 478 6600 Fax: +1 781 478 6601 www.battery.com
E+Co	Debt capital	Multilateral, bi-lateral, foundations, private sector	Energy efficiency, bioenergy, geothermal, small hydropower, solar (PV and thermal), wind	South Asia, Southeast Asia, East Asia, West Asia, North Africa, Central and South America, Sub-Saharan Africa	CONTACT—China Wu Jing, Investment Officer Laura Colbert, Communications Officer Zhu Xiaonan, Office Manager Hongcheng Plaza Building, Suite 1302 Qingnian Road Kunming 650021 Yunnan, China Tel: +86 871 312 0934 Fax: +86 871 310 0897 EandCo.China@EandCo.net www.energyhouse.com · CONTACT—Main Office Christine Eibs Singer 383 Franklin Street Bloomfield, New Jersey USA Tel: +1 973 680 9100 Fax: +1 973 680 8066 chris@energyhouse.com www.energyhouse.com
EnviroTech Financial, Inc.	Private equities		Energy efficiency, bioenergy, geothermal, small hydropower, solar (PV and thermal), wind fuel cells	South Asia, Southeast Asia, East Asia, West Asia, North Africa, Central and Eastern Europe, Central and South America, North America, Oceania, Western Europe, Sub-Saharan Africa	Gene Beck, President EnviroTech Financial, Inc. 333 City Boulevard West, 17th Floor Orange, California 92868-5905 USA Tel: +1 714 532 2731 Fax: +1 714 459 7492 gbeck@etffinancial.com www.etffinancial.com
Global Environment Fund	Private equities		Bioenergy, geothermal, small hydropower solar (PV and thermal), wind	South Asia, Southeast Asia, East Asia, West Asia, North Africa, Central and Eastern Europe, Central and South America, North America, Sub-Saharan Africa	1225 Eye Street N.W., Suite 900 Washington, D.C. 20005 USA Tel: +1 202 789 4500 Fax: +1 202 789 4508 info@globalenvironmentfund.com www.globalenvironmentfund.com
Good Energies Inc.	Private equities	Private	Solar (PV and thermal), wind	South Asia, Southeast Asia, East Asia, West Asia, North Africa, Central and Eastern Europe, Central and South America, North America, Oceania, Western Europe, Sub-Saharan Africa	Michael Ware 1250 24th Street, N.W., Suite 300 Washington, D.C. 29037, USA Tel: +1 202 466 0582 Fax: +1 202 466 0564 www.goodenergies.com
Jane Capital Partners LLC	Private equities		Energy efficiency, cleaner fuels, bioenergy geothermal, small hydropower, solar (PV and thermal), wind, fuel cells	South Asia, Southeast Asia, East Asia, North America, Oceania	Neal Dikeman 505 Montgomery, 2nd Floor San Francisco, California 94111 USA Tel: +1 415 277 0180 Fax: +1 415 277 0173 dikeman@janecapital.com www.janecapital.com
New Energies Invest AG (Bank Sarasin + Cie)	Private equities	Rights offering	Energy efficiency, bioenergy, small hydropower, solar (PV and thermal), wind fuel cells	South Asia, Southeast Asia, East Asia, West Asia, North Africa, Central and Eastern Europe, Central and South America, North America, Oceania, Western Europe, Sub-Saharan Africa	Andreas Knörzer Elisabethenstrasse 62 CH-4002 Basel Switzerland Tel: +41 0 61 277 7477 andreas.knoerzer@sarasin.ch www.newenergies.ch/index_e.html

(Continued)

Name	Investment type	Investors	Technology	Region	Contact
OCM/GFI Power Opportunities Fund	Private equities	Corporate pension funds, insurance companies, foundation endowments, etc.	Energy efficiency	South Asia, Southeast Asia, East Asia, West Asia, North Africa, Central and Eastern Europe, Central and South America, North America, Oceania, Western Europe, Sub-Saharan Africa	11611 San Vicente Boulevard, Suite 710 Los Angeles, California 90049 USA Tel: +1 310 442 0542 Fax: +1 310 442 0540 info@gfienergy.com www.gfienergy.com
Private Energy Market Fund LP (PEMF)	Private equities	Private	Bioenergy, wind	South Asia, Southeast Asia, East Asia, West Asia, Central and Eastern Europe, Western Europe.	Gustaf Godenhielm (Tekniikantie 4 D) P.O. Box 92 02151 Espoo Finland Tel: +358 9 469 1208 Fax: +358 9 469 1207 gustaf.godenhielm@pemfund.com www.pemfund.com
Robeco Milieu Technologies	Private equities	Private	Energy efficiency, bioenergy, geothermal, small hydropower, solar (PV and thermal), wind	South Asia, Southeast Asia, East Asia, West Asia, North Africa, Central and Eastern Europe, Central and South America, North America, Oceania, Western Europe, Sub-Saharan Africa	Postbus 973 3000 AZ Rotterdam The Netherlands Tel: +31 10 224 12 24 Fax: +31 10 411 52 88 info@robeco.nl www.robeco.nl
Sigma Capital	Private equities		Energy efficiency, bioenergy, small hydropower, solar (PV and thermal), wind	Southeast Asia, Central and Eastern Europe, Central and South America, North America, Oceania, Western Europe	Bruce Woodry, Chairman and CEO P.O. Box 1002 Harbor Springs, Michigan 49740 USA Tel: +1 231 526 9585 Fax: N/A woodry@sigmacapital.net www.sigmacapital.net/
Triodos International Fund Management BV	Private equities	Institutional and private investors	Bioenergy, geothermal, small hydropower, solar (PV and thermal), wind, fuel cells	South Asia, Southeast Asia, East Asia, West Asia, North Africa, Central and South America, Western Europe, Sub-Saharan Africa	Utrechtseweg 60, P.O. Box 55 3700 AB Zeist The Netherlands Tel: +31 30 693 6500 Fax: +31 30 693 6566 tredf@triodos.nl www.triodos.nl Team members Bob Assenberg Tel: +31 30 693 65 60 bob.assenberg@triodos.nl Gerrit-Jan Brunink Tel: +31 30 693 65 78 gerrit-jan.brunink@triodos.nl Helena Korhonen Tel: +31 30 693 65 41 helena.korhonen@triodos.nl Martijn Woudstra Tel: +31 30 694 26 91 martijn.woudstra@triodos.nl

TITLE	FINANCE TYPE	SOURCE OF CAPITAL	TECHNOLOGY TYPES	GEOGRAPHIC FOCUS	CONTACT
UBS (Lux) Equity Fund Future Energy	Private equities		Energy efficiency, bioenergy, geothermal, small hydropower, solar (PV and thermal), wind	South Asia, Southeast Asia, East Asia, West Asia, North Africa, Central and Eastern Europe, Central and South America, North America, Oceania, Western Europe, Sub-Saharan Africa	CONTACT—Beijing 1609 China World Tower 1 Jian Guo Men Wai Avenue Beijing 100004 People's Republic of China Tel: +86 10-6505 22 13,+86 10-6505 22 14, +86 10-6505 22 15 Fax: +86 10-6505 11 79 CONTACT—Shanghai Room 3407 Citic Square No. 1168 Nanjing Xi Lu Shanghai 200041 People's Republic of China Tel: +86 21 5292 55 55 Fax: +86 21 5292 55 52 CONTACT—India 2/F, Hoechst House Nariman Point Mumbai-400 021 India Tel: +91 22 281 4649, +91 22 281 4676 Fax: +91 22 230 9000, +91-22-281 4673 CONTACT—Main Office Gerhard Wagner, Socially Responsible Investments Analyst Gessneralllee 3 8098 Zurich Switzerland Tel: +41 1 235 55 52 Fax: +41 1 235 55 30 gerhard.wagner@ubs.com www.ubs.com/swedenfunds.com
Warburg Pincus Investment Consulting Company Ltd.	Private equities	Private	Energy efficiency, bioenergy, geothermal, small hydropower, solar (PV and thermal), wind	South Asia, Southeast Asia, East Asia, West Asia, North Africa, Central and Eastern Europe, Central and South America, North America, Oceania, Western Europe, Sub-Saharan Africa	CONTACT—Beijing Beijing Representative Office 9th Floor, China World Tower 1 1 Jianguomenwai Avenue Beijing 100004 China Tel: +86 10 5923 2533 Fax: +86 10 6505 6663 www.warburgpincus.com CONTACT—Shanghai Shanghai Representative Office Unit 2201, Bund Center Office Tower No. 222 Yanan Road (East) Shanghai, 200002 China Tel: +86 21 6335 0308 Fax: +86 21 6335 0802 www.warburgpincus.com	CONTACT—India Mumbai Office 7th Floor, Express Towers Nariman Point Mumbai-400 021 India Tel: +91 22 6650 0000 Fax: +91 22 6650 0001 www.warburgpincus.com CONTACT—Main Office Almack House 28 King Street, St. James's London SW1Y 6QW United Kingdom Tel: +44 207 360 0306 Fax: +44 207 321 0881 www.warburgpincus.com

Public Equities

TITLE	FINANCE TYPE	SOURCE OF CAPITAL	TECHNOLOGY TYPES	GEOGRAPHIC FOCUS	CONTACT
New Alternatives Fund	Public equities	This is an open and mutual fund that seeks shareholders.	Energy efficiency, bioenergy, geothermal, small hydropower, solar (PV and thermal), wind	South Asia, Southeast Asia, East Asia, West Asia, North Africa, Central and Eastern Europe, Central and South America, North America, Oceania, Western Europe, Sub-Saharan Africa	150 Broadhollow Road, Suite 360 Melville, New York 11747 USA Tel: +1 800 423 8383 Fax: N/A info@newalternativesfund.com www.newalternativesfund.com

(Continued)

TITLE	FINANCE TYPE	SOURCE OF CAPITAL	TECHNOLOGY TYPES	GEOGRAPHIC FOCUS	CONTACT
New Energy Fund LP	Public equities	High-net-worth individuals, family offices, foundations, and institutions	Energy efficiency, cleaner fuels, bioenergy, geothermal, small hydropower, solar (PV and thermal), wind, fuel cells	South Asia, Southeast Asia, East Asia, West Asia, North Africa, Central and South America, North America, Oceania, Western Europe, Sub-Saharan Africa (This is a global fund, since it is a global phenomenon.)	527 Madison Avenue, 6th Floor New York, New York 10022 USA Tel: +1 212 419 3918 Fax: +1 212 419 3971 www.newenergyfundlp.com

Carbon Finance

TITLE	FINANCE TYPE	SOURCE OF CAPITAL	TECHNOLOGY TYPES	GEOGRAPHIC FOCUS	CONTACT
Carboncredits.nl	Carbon finance		Energy efficiency, cleaner fuels, bioenergy, geothermal, small hydropower, solar (PV and thermal), wind, fuel cells	South Asia, Southeast Asia, East Asia, West Asia, North Africa, Central and Eastern Europe, Central and South America, Oceania, Western Europe, Sub-Saharan Africa	Carboncredits.nl Juliana van Stolberglaan 3 The Hague The Netherlands Tel: +31 70 3735 495 Fax: +31 70 3735 000 carboncredits@senternovem.nl www.carboncredits.nl
Climate Change Capital	Carbon finance, equity, venture capital	Public, private	Energy efficiency, renewable energy	Global, active in China and India	CONTACT—London 3 More London Riverside London SE1 2AQ London United Kingdom Tel: +44 0 20 7939 5000 Fax: +44 0 20 7939 5030 CONTACT—China Climate Change Capital 9/F China Life Tower 16 Chao Wai Da Jie Beijing 100020 Tel: +86 10 85253797 Fax: +86 10 85253197
CO2e	Other	Finance through sale of emissions credits	Energy efficiency, cleaner fuels, bioenergy, geothermal, small hydropower, solar (PV and thermal), wind	West Asia, North Africa, Central and Eastern Europe, Central and South America, North America, Oceania, Western Europe, South Asia, Southeast Asia, East Asia, Sub-Saharan Africa	CONTACT—India CantorCO2e India Private Limited 10th Floor, Raheja Chambers Free Press Journal Marg Nariman Point Mumbai-400 021 India Tel: +91 986 7531203 Fax: N/A mumbai@cantorco2e.com www.co2e.com CONTACT—International Office 181 University Avenue, Suite 1500 Toronto, Ontario Canada M5H 3M7 Tel: +1 416 350 2177 Fax: +1 416 350 2985 cdm@cantorco2e.com www.co2e.com

Name	Type	Participants	Technologies	Regions	Contact
EcoSecurities	Carbon finance	Public, private	Renewable energy, waste management, industrial efficiency.	Global, including China and India	CONTACT—China Unit 708, China Resources Building 8 Jianguomen Bei Avenue Beijing, 100005 Tel: +86 10 6518 1081 Fax: +86 10 6518 1085 china@ecosecurities.com CONTACT—International Office 181 University Avenue, Suite 1500 Toronto, Ontario Canada M5H 3M7 Tel: +1 416 350 2177 Fax: +1 416 350 2985 cdm@ecosecurities.com www.co2e.com
European Carbon Fund	Carbon finance		Energy efficiency, cleaner fuels, geothermal, solar (PV and thermal), wind	South Asia, Southeast Asia, East Asia, West Asia, North Africa, Central and Eastern Europe, Central and South America, North America, Oceania, Western Europe, Sub-Saharan Africa	CONTACT—China Li Chao Beijing Tel: +86 106 655 5735 CONTACT—Asia (w/o China) Anne Dargelos Tel: +33 01 58 55 66 28 CONTACT—Main Office Laurent Segalen Tel: +44 0 207 648 0118 Fax: +33 015 855 2965 www.europeancarbonfund.com/
IFC-Netherlands Carbon (CDM) Facility (INCaF)	Carbon finance		Energy efficiency, cleaner fuels, bioenergy geothermal, small hydropower, wind	South Asia, Southeast Asia, East Asia, West Asia, North Africa, Central and South America, Oceania, Sub-Saharan Africa	2121 Pennsylvania Avenue, N.W. Washington, D.C. 20433 USA Tel: +1 202 473 4194 Fax: +1 202 974 4348 carbonfinance@ifc.org www.ifc.org/carbonfinance
Japan Carbon Finance, Ltd. (JCF)	Carbon finance	Major Japanese private enterprises and policy-lending institutions	Energy efficiency, cleaner fuels, bioenergy geothermal, small hydropower, solar (PV and thermal); wind, fuel cells	South Asia, Southeast Asia, East Asia, West Asia, North Africa, Central and Eastern Europe, Central and South America, Oceania, Western Europe, Sub-Saharan Africa	1-3, Kudankita 4-chome Chiyoda-ku Tokyo 102-0073 Japan Tel: +81 3 5212 8870 Fax: +81 3 5212 8886 jcf@jcarbon.co.jp www.jcarbon.co.jp/
KfW Carbon Fund	Carbon finance		Energy efficiency, bioenergy, geothermal, small hydropower, solar (PV and thermal), wind, fuel cells	South Asia, Southeast Asia, East Asia, West Asia, North Africa, Central and Eastern Europe, Central and South America, North America, Oceania, Western Europe, Sub-Saharan Africa	Palmengartenstrasse 5-9 60325 Frankfurt Germany Tel: +49 69 7431 4218 Fax: +49 69 7431 4775 carbonfund@kfw.de www.kfw-foerderbank.de
Natsource	Carbon finance	Public, private	Energy efficiency, renewable energy	Global, including China and India	Natsource LLC 100 William Street, Suite 2005 New York, New York 10038 Tel: +1 212 232 5305 Fax: +1 212 232 5353
Prototype Carbon Fund (PCF)	Carbon finance	Trust Fund administered by the World Bank	Energy efficiency, bioenergy, geothermal, small hydropower, solar (PV and thermal), wind	South Asia, Southeast Asia, East Asia, West Asia, North Africa, Central and South America, Oceania, Western Europe, Sub-Saharan Africa	1818 H Street, N.W. Washington, D.C. 20433 USA helpdesk@carbonfinance.org prototypecarbonfund.org

(Continued)

TITLE	FINANCE TYPE	SOURCE OF CAPITAL	TECHNOLOGY TYPES	GEOGRAPHIC FOCUS	CONTACT
Swedish International Climate Investment Program (SICLIP)	Carbon finance		Energy efficiency, bioenergy, wind	South Asia, West Asia, Central and Eastern Europe, Central and South America, Sub-Saharan Africa	Kungsgatan 43 Box 310, SE-631 04 Eskilstuna Sweden Tel: +46 16 544 3241; +46 16 544 2043 Fax: +46 16 544 2099 angela.kallhauge@sten.se, gudrun.knutsson@energimyndigheten.se www.energimyndigheten.se
Svensk Exportkredit (SEK)–Sweden	Export credits		Bioenergy, geothermal, small hydropower, solar (PV and thermal), wind	West Asia, North Africa, Central and Eastern Europe, Central and South America, North America, Oceania, Western Europe, South Asia, Southeast Asia, East Asia, Sub-Saharan Africa	P.O. Box 16368, SE-103 27 Västra Trädgårdsgatan 11 B Stockholm Sweden Tel: +46 8 61 38 300 Fax: +46 8 20 38 94 info@sek.se www.sek.se/
World Bank Carbon Finance	Carbon finance	Public, private	Energy efficiency, renewable energy	Global, including China, India	The World Bank Carbon Finance Unit 1818 H Street, N.W. Washington, D.C. Tel: +1 202.473.1000 www.carbonfinance.org

Insurance

TITLE	FINANCE TYPE	SOURCE OF CAPITAL	TECHNOLOGY TYPES	GEOGRAPHIC FOCUS	CONTACT
Aon Global Risk Consultants Ltd.	Insurance		Bioenergy, geothermal, small hydropower, solar (PV and thermal), wind	South Asia, Southeast Asia, East Asia, West Asia, North Africa, Central and Eastern Europe, Central and South America, North America, Oceania, Western Europe, Sub-Saharan Africa	CONTACT—China Richard Dong Aon Corporation Beijing Representative Office Room 1206 Capital Tower Beijing 6 Jia Jian Guo Men Wai Avenue Chaoying District Beijing 100022 The People's Republic of China Tel: +86 10 6563 0671 Fax: +86 10 6563 0672 richard_dong@aon-cofco.com.cn www.aon.com/cn/en/china CONTACT—India Prabodh Thakker, Chairman 302 Dalamal House Jamnalal Bajaj Marg Nariman Point Mumbai-400 021 India Tel: +91 22 6656 0505 Fax: +91 22 6656 0506 prabodh_thakker@aon-asia.com www.aon.com/asia/en/india CONTACT—Main Office Aon Limited, 8 Devonshire Square London EC2M 4PL United Kingdom Tel: +44 0 20 7623 5500 Fax: +44 0 20 7621 1511 www.aon.co.uk
Miller Insurance Group	Insurance		Wind	South Asia, Southeast Asia, East Asia, West Asia, North Africa, Central and Eastern Europe, Central and South America, North America, Oceania, Western Europe, Sub-Saharan Africa	Susanna Lam, Director Miller Insurance Services (Hong Kong) Ltd. Tel: +852 2525 6982 susanna.lam@miller-insurance.com/China-Energy www.miller-insurance.com/China-Energy David Horne, Director Energy Tel: +44 0 20 7031 2582 david.horne@miller-insurance.com/China-Energy www.miller-insurance.com/China-Energy CONTACT—Main Office Dawson House 5 Jewry Street London EC3N 2PJ United Kingdom Tel: +44 0 20 7488 2345 Fax: N/A info@miller-insurance.com www.aon.co.uk

	FINANCE TYPE	SOURCE OF CAPITAL	TECHNOLOGY TYPES	GEOGRAPHIC FOCUS	CONTACT
Multilateral Investment Guarantee Agency (MIGA)	Insurance		Energy efficiency, bioenergy, geothermal, small hydropower, solar (PV and thermal), wind	South Asia, Southeast Asia, East Asia, West Asia, North Africa, Central and Eastern Europe, Central and South America, North America, Oceania, Western Europe, Sub-Saharan Africa	1818 H Street N.W. Washington, D.C. 20433 USA Tel: +1 202 473 1000 Fax: +1 202 522 0316 migainquiry@worldbank.org www.miga.org
Swiss Re	Insurance		Energy efficiency, bioenergy, geothermal, small hydropower, solar (PV and thermal), wind	South Asia, Southeast Asia, East Asia, West Asia, North Africa, Central and Eastern Europe, Central and South America, North America, Oceania, Western Europe, Sub-Saharan Africa	CONTACT—China Eric Gao, Branch Manager Beijing Branch 23rd Floor, East Tower, Twin Towers No. B12, Jian Guo Men Wai Avenue Chao Yang District Beijing 100022 China Tel: +86 10 6563 8888 Fax: +86 10 6563 8800 Eric_gao@swissre.com www.swissre.com CONTACT—India Dhananjay Date, Managing Director 9th Floor, Essar House 11 K Khadye Marg Mahalaxmi Mumbai-400 034 India Tel: +91 22 6661 2121 Fax: +91 22 6661 2122 Dhananjay_date@swissre.com www.swissre.com CONTACT—Asia-Pacific Headquarters Darryl Pidcock Hong Kong Branch 61/F Central Plaza 18 Harbour Road G.P.O. Box 2221 Wanchai, HK Hong Kong Tel: +852 2827 4345 Fax: +852 2827 6033 Darryl_Pidcock@swissre.com www.swissre.com

Other

TITLE	FINANCE TYPE	SOURCE OF CAPITAL	TECHNOLOGY TYPES	GEOGRAPHIC FOCUS	CONTACT
Capital Equity Partners	Financial engineering and investment banking	Debt capital, private equities, public equities, funds of funds, carbon finance, export credits, insurance, private placements	Energy efficiency, cleaner fuels, bioenergy, geothermal, small hydropower, solar (PV and thermal), wind, fuel cells	West Asia, North Africa, Central and Eastern Europe, Central and South America, North America, Oceania, Western Europe, South Asia, Southeast Asia, East Asia, Sub-Saharan Africa	410 Park Avenue New York, New York 10022 USA Tel: +1 928 436 4212 Fax: +1 270 447 3738 contoc@capitalequitypartners.com www.capitalequitypartners.com Aiken Capital Partners +1 212 751 5007 Same address

Organization	Description	Source	Technology	Regions	Contact
The Global Environment Facility (GEF)	Grants to developing countries	Member governments	Energy efficiency, bioenergy, geothermal, small hydropower, solar (PV and thermal), wind	Southeast Asia, East Asia, West Asia, North Africa, Central and Eastern Europe, Central and South America, North America, Oceania, Western Europe, South Asia, Sub-Saharan Africa	CONTACT—China Guangyao Zhu, Director General (Political Focal Point) International Department Ministry of Finance Beijing 100820 People's Republic of China Tel: +86 10 6855 3101 Fax: +86 10 6855 1125 www.gefweb.org Jinkang Wu, Director (Operational Focal Point) Ministry of Finance International Financial Institution Division IV Department of International Affairs Beijing 100820 People's Republic of China Tel: +86 10 6855 3101 Fax: +86 10 6855 1125 jk.wu@mof.gov.cn www.gefweb.org Sudhir Mital, Joint Secretary (Operational Focal Point) Ministry of Environment and Forests Room 414, Paryavaran Bhawan CGO Complex, Lodhi Road New Delhi–110 003 India Tel: +91 11 243 6 3956 Fax: +91 11 24 6 9192 Mital_sudhir@nic.in www.gefweb.org CONTACT—Main Office 1818 H Street, N.W., MSN G6-602 Washington, D.C. 20433 USA Tel: +1 202 473.0508 Fax: +1 202 522.3240, 3245 secretariat@thegef.org www.gefweb.org
Japan Bank for International Cooperation (JBIC)	Other	Japanese government		South Asia, Southeast Asia, East Asia	CONTACT—China 3131 31st Floor China World Trade Center, No. 1 Jian Guo Men Wai Avenue Beijing 100004 People's Republic of China Tel: +86 10 6505 8989, 3825, 3826, 3827, 1196, 1197 Fax: +86 10 6505 3829, 1198 www.jbic.go.jp/english/ CONTACT—India Rajeev Singh, Deputy Secretary (Political Focal Point) Department of Economic Affairs Ministry of Finance Room N. 66-C, North Block New Delhi–110001 India Tel: +91 11 230 93881 Fax: +91 11 230 92477 r_p_singh@nic.in www.gefweb.org CONTACT—India 3rd Floor, DLF Centre Sansad Marg New Delhi–110001 India Tel: +91 11 2371 4362, 4363, 7090, 6200 Fax: +91 11 2371 5066, + 91 11 2373 8389 www.jbic.go.jp/english/ CONTACT—Main Office 4-1, Ohtemachi 1-chome, Chiyoda-ku Tokyo 100-8144 Japan Tel: +03 5218 3101 Fax: +03 5218 3955 www.jbic.go.jp/english/
Kreditanstalt fur Wiederaufbau (KfW Bankengruppe)	Small and medium enterprise (SME); project and export finance	German government	SMEs, clean energy	South Asia, Southeast Asia, East Asia, West Asia, North Africa, Central and Eastern Europe, Central and South America, North America, Oceania, Western Europe, Sub-Saharan Africa	Charlottenstrasse 33/33a 10117 Berlin Tel: +49 30 20264 0 Fax: +49 30 20264 5188 www.kfw.de-EN

End Notes

[1] Yang Jingyin, Zhen Zexiang, and Guo Yimin, *International Status Comparative Study on China's Economy and Social Development in 2006* (International Center of National Bureau of Statistics of China, November 30, 2006). www.stats.gov.cn/tjfx/fxbg/t20061128_402368780.htm

[2] Dai Yande, *China Energy Supply and Demand Situation and Energy Conservation Policy* (ERI of NDRC, March 2007). HYPERLINK "/http://neec.no/uploads/File/Whatsup/whatsupforneec/EM-" /http://neec.no/uploads/File/Whatsup/whatsupforneec/EM-workshop/BJPDF/27-0900-Dai%20Yan%20De.pdf

[3] Daniel H. Rosen and Trevor Houser, *China Energy: A Guide for the Perplexed* (Peterson Institute for International Economics May 2007). HYPERLINK "www.iie.com/publications/papers/rosen0507.pdf" www.iie.com/publications/ papers/rosen0507.pdf

[4] *Ibid.*

[5] National Bureau of Statistics of China. www.stats.gov.cn/english/

[6] China National Development and Reform Commission., "11th Five-Year Energy Plan."

[7] International Energy Agency, World Energy Outlook 2007: China and India Insights (Paris, France: OCED/IEA, 2007)

[8] *Ibid.*

[9] *Ibid.*

[10] NDRC, Mid- and Long-term Renewable Energy Development Plan, August 2006. Note: this figure does not include traditional biomass combustion for cooking and heating in rural households. According to the IEA's 2007 *World Energy* Outlook estimates, which include traditional biomass consumption, China's renewable energy consumption accounted for about 15 percent of China's total primary energy consumption in 2005.

[11] Shi Pengfei, Statistics on *Wind Farms in China*, 2005 (Chinese Wind Energy Association , March 23, 2006). www.cwea.org.cn/download/display_info.asp?cid=2&sid=&id=2

[12] Shi Pengfei, *Statistics on Wind Farms in China*, 2006 (Chinese Wind Energy Association, March 18, 2007). www.cwea.org.cn/download/display_info.asp?cid=2&sid=&id=19

[13] Data on installed wind capacity by province compiled by Azure International Technology Development Ltd. (Beijing) based on proprietary research. Data are not available from the Chinese Government on renewable energy capacities per province.

[14] Li Junfeng et al., *China Solar PV Report 2007* (China Environmental Science Press).

[15] Chen Yingjie and Fu Zhongwen, "Development Tendency and Outlook of Solar PV Industry," July 18, 2006. http://market.ccidnet.com/market/article/content/420/200607/135747.html

[16] "2007–2008 China's Solar PV Industry Development Analysis Report," November 8, 2007.

[17] "2007 Chinese Renewable Energy Weekly Monitoring Report (07/10/13 – 07/10/19),"October 21, 2007. www.ccei.org.cn/shownews.asp?ID=25482

[18] Liu Yanlong, *Analysis of China's Battery Exports* (China Chemical and Physical Power Supply Industry Association, June 19, 2007).www.cibf.org.cn/iec_newsdetail.php?id=78

[19] "2007–2008 China's Solar PV Industry Development Analysis Report," November 8, 2007.

[20] NDRC, Mid- and Long-term Renewable Energy Development Plan, August 2006.

[21] *Wind Energy Country Study* (GTZ, September 2007). (A portion of the $600M capital investment was used for the installation of 268 mini-hydropower facilities with a total generation capacity around 293 MW.)

[22] NDRC, Mid- and Long-term Renewable Energy Development Plan, August 2006.

[23] "Prospect of Roof PV development of China," *International New Energy Net* (April 14, 2006). /www.in-en.com/newenergy/html/newenergy-2006200604145255.html

[24] NDRC, Mid- and Long-term Renewable Energy Development Plan, August 2006.

[25] Han Weiping, *The Concept of Green Building Integrated with Design*, vol 23, no. 6, p. 117. www.gotoread.com/vo/5274/page553552.html

[26] GTZ, "Wind Energy Country Study," September 2007.

[27] NDRC, Mid- and Long-term Renewable Energy Development Plan, August 2006.

[28] Gansu Lintao rural energy office.

[29] Gansu Lintao rural energy office.

[30] "Interesting Times—Focus on Clean Energy Investment Opportunities in China" *New Energy Finance* (September 22, 2006).

[31] Heinz-Peter Mang, *Biogas Investments as a Profitable Business in China* (Chinese Academy of Agricultural Engineering, June 14, 2007).

[32] "Current Status and Prospect of China's SHP," presentation of International Workshop on China Renewable Energy Strategy Development, August 16, 2006. http://newenergy.com.cn/html/2006- 8/2006816_11456_1.html

[33] Li Qidao, "Situation, Data, Analysis and Suggestions to Small Hydro," thesis of China Energy Net, September 7, 2007.

[34] NBSC, Statistic Yearbook 2006

[35] Han Xiaoping, "CIO of China Energy Network," presentation in Briefing Workshop on Current Situation and Prospects of CHP Industry, September 2005.

[36] NDRC, List of small thermal power plants that have been closed from January to September 2007. www.sdpc.gov.cn/zcfb/zcfbgg/2007gonggao/W020071221580581956235.xls

[37] Calculated by the Azure International Research Team, as of December 2007.

[38] Wu Guihui, *Development of Decentralized Energy in China* (July 2007). www.chinainfo.gov.cn/ata/200708/1_20070822_159913.html

[39] NDRC, Mid- and Long-term Renewable Energy Development Plan, August 2006.

[40] Shanghai local government Web site material, August 22, 2006. www.shtong.gov.cn/node2/node4429/node4437/node70463/userobject1ai85052.html

[41] Information presented at the United States–China Clean Energy Forum in January 2008.

[42] Wu Guihui, *Development of Decentralized Energy in China* (July 2007). www.chinainfo.gov.cn/data/200708/1_20070822_159913.html

[43] Ibid.

[44] Data from "BP Statistical Review of World Energy," June 2007.

[45] In 2005 there were 113 cities of more than 1 million people, which means a large domestic market for basic materials and intense pressure on supply—which has grown at breakneck speed since 2001. Data from NBSC, *Statistic Yearbook 2006*.

[46] "BP Statistical Review of World Energy," June 2007.

[47] Yande Dai, *China Energy Supply and Demand Situation and Energy Conservation Policy* (ERI, NDRC, March 2007).

[48] The World Bank and State Environmental Protection Administration of China, *Cost of Pollution in China* (February 2007).

[49] *Ibid.*

[50] Yande Dai, *China Energy Supply and Demand Situation and Energy Conservation Policy* (ERI, NDRC, March 2007).

[51] The World Bank and State Environmental Protection Administration of China, *Cost of Pollution in China* (February 2007).

[52] NDRC, Notice on Adjusting the Local Grid Feed-in Tariff, June 2006.

[53] "21.3 Billion RMB Special Funds on Energy Conservation," *Financial Observer of the China Reform Newspaper*, July 31, 2007./www.crd.net.cn/ShowNews.asp?NewsID=7906

[54] *Special Funds Application Guidebook for RE in Building Integration.* www.cin.gov.cn/zcfg/jswj/jskj/200706/P020070606463375283662.doc

[55] *2007 SME Technology Innovation Fund Guidelines for a Number of Key Projects* (Chinese version). www.innofund.gov.cn/innofile/se_02_t02.asp

[56] "Support Notice for *2007 SME Technology Innovation Fund guidelines for a Number of Key Projects*" (Chinese version). www.innofund.gov.cn/innofile/se_02_t03.asp

[57] Energy Conservation Law, 2007 version.

[58] http://www.gov.cn/english/laws/2005-10/08/content_75023.htm

[59] "Anti-corruption Policies in Asia and the Pacific: Thematic review of provisions and practices to curb corruption in public procurement." www.oecd.org/dataoecd/62/49/35593529.pdf

[60] "China Focus: China Begins Compulsory Procurement of Energy-saving Items," December 2007. http://en.ec.com.cn/article/enindustry/enenergy/eneereport/200712/528299_1.html

[61] The Office of the National Energy Leading Group is a department of the NDRC. http://en.ndrc.gov.cn/

[62] Bai Quan, *Energy Efficiency in China: Strategies and Financing Options* (ERI of NDRC).

[63] Second China New Energy International Forum. www.cnecc.org.cn/ luntan2/kms.htm

[64] Sina Finance News; Haitong Stock Company. finance.sina.com.cn/ stock/s/20080129/20541971337.shtml

[65] www.icfi.com/

[66] *VER and Carbon Neutral in Volunteer Emission Reduction Market* (Azure CDM team material, May 16, 2007).

[67] Thomson Financial/NVCA. www.cvca.com.cn/template/newstemplate. asp?ArticleID=1052

[68] Cleantech Network™ LLC. www.cleantechventure.com69 Thomson Financial/NVCA. www.cvca.com.cn/template/newstemplate.asp?ArticleID=1052

[69] *New Energy Finance.*

[70] The full catalogue is available in English at www.fdi.gov.cn/pub/FDIEN/Laws/law_en_infor.jsp?docid=87372.

[71] China Investment Consulting Web, *2007–2008 Market Analysis and Investment Consulting Report on China SWH*, November 2007. www.ocn.com.cn/reports/2006112tynrsq.htm

[72] Source: United States–China Business Council. www.chinabusinessreview. com/public/0611/prc-government-structure.pdf; PRC Government Web sites.

[73] Source: www.china.org.cn/e-china/politicalsystem/index.htm

[74] NDRC, "Guidance Catalogue of Renewable Energy Industry," November 29, 2005.

[75] http://www.un.org/esa/sustdev/csd/csd15/documents/csd15_bp2.pdf

[76] Photo courtesy of U.S. Department of Energy/National Renewable Energy Laboratory (USDOE/NREL) (www.nrel.gov).

[77] Photo courtesy of USDOE/NREL.

[78] Photo courtesy of USDOE/NREL.

[79] http://www.nrel.gov/learning/re_solar_hot_water.html

[80] Emerging Energy Research, *Asia Pacific Wind Power Markets & Strategies, 2006–2015* (December 2006). Available from www.emerging-energy.com.

[81] Photo courtesy of USDOE/NREL. (USDOE used to denote United States Department of Energy since DOE has been used already to refer to the Department of Environment)

[82] Photo courtesy of USDOE/NREL.

[83] See www.sunwize.com/.

CHAPTER SOURCES

Chapter 1 – This is an edited, reformatted and augmented version of U.S. Department of Commerce, International Trade Administration Contract Number DG1350-07-SE-4516 ESG104 ITA, released July 2008.

Chapter 2 – This is an edited, reformatted and augmented version of U.S. Department of Commerce, International Trade Administration Contract Number G1350-07-SE-4516 ESG104 ITA, released July 2008.

INDEX

A

acid, 109, 110, 111, 121, 237, 238, 248
acquisitions, 67, 148
adaptability, 232
adaptation, 35, 47, 192
additives, 107, 235
advocacy, 124
aesthetic, 153, 158, 159, 169, 211
agencies, 17, 33, 38, 44, 48, 49, 53, 55, 58, 59, 60, 61, 65, 66, 67, 90, 91, 92, 94, 127, 129, 160, 196, 197, 198, 202, 203, 206, 218, 221, 252, 257
agricultural sector, 38
agriculture, 46, 110, 115, 117, 126, 238, 243, 245, 253
air emissions, 122, 250
air pollutants, 111, 122, 123, 238, 239, 249, 250
air quality, 33
air temperature, 113, 240
alcohols, 109, 237
algae, 108, 236
alternative energy, 123, 250
ambient air, 38, 188
ammonia, 173, 182, 183
anaerobic digestion, 108, 235, 236
arbitration, 63
ASEAN, 1, 145
Association of Southeast Asian Nations, 1, 145
atmosphere, 108, 111, 115, 118, 235, 238, 242, 245
atmospheric pressure, 35
207, 210, 255
automobiles, 182
awareness, 209

B

bacteria, 109, 237

barriers, vii, 7, 15, 17, 18, 57, 66, 67, 69, 71, 124, 150, 158, 160, 161, 206, 251
batteries, 8, 112, 120, 121, 151, 239, 248
BEE, 1, 38, 42, 44, 48, 90
benchmarking, 192
benchmarks, 42, 120, 247
benefits, 8, 48, 49, 52, 61, 90, 116, 119, 120, 130, 151, 179, 184, 207, 244, 246, 247, 258
bilateral aid, 191
biodiesel, 8, 10, 15, 36, 39, 45, 47, 48, 59, 91, 108, 110, 122, 152, 181, 183, 235, 238, 249
bioenergy, 14, 36, 126, 153, 158, 169, 253
biofuel, 110, 120, 154, 155, 170, 171, 179, 191, 201, 238, 248
biogas, 36, 38, 47, 66, 109, 153, 154, 158, 170, 171, 179, 201, 203, 204, 237
biological processes, 64
biomass, vii, 7, 9, 10, 12, 13, 14, 16, 18, 19, 24, 25, 26, 29, 30, 35, 36, 40, 47, 49, 51, 52, 57, 60, 61, 62, 71, 107, 108, 109, 110, 122, 151, 153, 159, 161, 169, 179, 192, 200, 208, 211, 232, 235, 236, 237, 238, 249, 256, 271
biopower, 110, 238
boilers, 35, 36, 45, 47, 90, 109, 111, 183, 237, 238
business environment, 52, 58
business ethics, 130, 258
business strategy, 206
business travelers, 129, 257
businesses, 7, 8, 17, 56, 110, 124, 125, 150, 151, 160, 201, 206, 215, 238, 251, 252
by-products, 109, 237

C

cadmium, 35
capacity building, 13, 53, 57, 120, 193, 199, 219, 247
capital intensive, 118, 245

capital markets, 53, 54, 55, 202

carbon, 2, 8, 15, 16, 35, 38, 47, 70, 71, 108, 109, 111, 122, 146, 152, 156, 188, 204, 225, 235, 236, 237, 239, 249

carbon dioxide, 2, 108, 109, 111, 146, 156, 188, 236, 237, 239

carbon emissions, 122, 249

carbon monoxide, 8, 109, 152, 236

carbon neutral, 108, 235

cattle, 36, 47, 109, 237

CEC, 146, 192

cellulose, 108, 154, 171, 236

CGC, 146, 195

chemical, 5, 111, 148, 183, 239

chemical vapor deposition, 5, 148

chemicals, 14, 36, 44, 47, 64, 109, 185, 237

Chinese government, 196, 204

clean coal, 177

clean energy technologies, vii, 7, 17, 18, 33, 37, 40, 52, 66, 70, 107, 123, 127, 131, 150, 157, 158, 160, 161, 199, 200, 207, 210, 235, 250, 254, 259

clean technology, 13, 19, 124, 155, 162, 179, 204, 206, 207, 251

climate(s), 13, 37, 41, 52, 66, 70, 113, 130, 203, 209, 225, 240, 257

climate change, 13, 41, 66, 70, 203

CO2, 2, 20, 45, 119, 146, 156, 186, 188, 189, 204, 246

coal, 3, 4, 6, 9, 10, 19, 20, 24, 30, 31, 38, 43, 45, 51, 57, 58, 69, 90, 111, 147, 149, 152, 153, 154, 156, 157, 164, 165, 166, 173, 174, 177, 184, 187, 188, 192, 195, 197, 198, 208, 218, 232, 238

coastal ecosystems, 118, 245

coastal region, 165

coffee, 113, 240

combustion, 12, 15, 35, 36, 47, 107, 108, 109, 111, 122, 153, 169, 235, 236, 238, 239, 250, 271

combustion processes, 111, 238

commerce, 65, 131, 210, 228, 259

commercial bank, 55, 56, 61, 62, 210

competition, 14, 15, 108, 196, 200, 209, 220, 235

competitiveness, 61, 66, 119, 194, 210, 246, 256

competitors, 206

compliance, 13, 41, 44, 45, 90, 124, 128, 251

computer, 112, 239

Congress, 148, 156, 157, 190, 194, 199, 207, 210, 217

conservation, 2, 11, 13, 31, 38, 39, 44, 91, 146, 154, 169, 183, 184, 193, 194, 195, 196, 197, 198, 199, 217, 218, 219, 220

construction, 2, 11, 31, 35, 38, 44, 63, 90, 114, 120, 146, 155, 158, 181, 182, 192, 201, 203, 208, 219, 220, 225, 234, 242, 247

consumers, 13, 44, 45, 59, 119, 122, 159, 191, 209, 211, 246, 250

consumption, 8, 13, 14, 17, 20, 31, 38, 41, 43, 50, 59, 120, 121, 152, 154, 156, 160, 162, 163, 164, 165, 172, 173, 175, 182, 184, 185, 186, 187, 188, 195, 198, 247, 248, 271

contract enforcement, 158, 209, 210

conversion rate, 154, 171

cooking, 8, 12, 13, 14, 35, 37, 110, 151, 238, 271

cooling, 2, 12, 35, 36, 47, 113, 117, 120, 121, 123, 146, 157, 193, 194, 228, 241, 245, 247, 249, 250

copper, 35, 47, 182

corrosion, 233

corruption, 62, 158, 206, 209, 272

cost, 7, 11, 12, 17, 30, 39, 41, 42, 45, 49, 52, 56, 58, 61, 66, 69, 70, 113, 114, 119, 121, 125, 130, 150, 154, 155, 156, 160, 171, 180, 188, 190, 191, 192, 201, 234, 240, 242, 246, 248, 253, 257

cost accounting, 66

cost saving, 56

cotton, 30, 108, 236

crop, 112, 156, 188, 231, 232, 239

crop drying, 112, 239

crops, 7, 107, 108, 109, 112, 151, 194, 235, 236, 237, 240

crude oil, 58, 173, 186

crust, 115, 243

crystalline, 14, 35, 201, 214

crystallization, 3, 146

cultivation, 10, 14, 37, 39, 108, 235

culture, 158, 208, 209, 217

customers, 68, 128, 169, 256

Customs Regulations, 207

D

Department of Agriculture, 6, 126, 150, 253

Department of Commerce, 129, 206, 256, 257

Department of Energy, 6, 18, 96, 123, 126, 143, 150, 161, 250, 253, 273

deposits, 62

depreciation, 13, 39, 49, 50, 52, 56, 60

deregulation, 59, 70

detoxification, 12, 35

developed countries, 11, 31, 182

developing countries, 11, 32, 56, 110, 238

developing nations, 126, 253

diesel engines, 108, 122, 236, 249

diesel fuel, 121

dissolved oxygen, 116, 244

distillation, 109, 237

distortions, 15, 66, 69

distributed generation (DG), 18, 34, 49, 61, 69, 161

distribution, 2, 8, 10, 13, 30, 31, 38, 39, 42, 43, 44, 46, 56, 67, 68, 91, 100, 105, 106, 118, 119, 149, 152, 184, 246
district heating, 8, 110, 121, 151, 238, 249
DOC, 2, 124, 146, 251
domestic demand, 186
domestic industry, 153
domestic markets, 65
DOP, 2, 91, 92
draft, 13, 43, 93, 157, 197, 199, 221
drought, 228

E

ecology, 218
economic cooperation, 208, 218
economic development, 33, 40, 45, 119, 158, 165, 184, 210, 221, 246, 252, 255
economic evaluation, 224
economic growth, 9, 15, 19, 54, 129, 152, 156, 162, 165, 185, 186, 253, 256
economic growth rate, 162
economic policy, 127, 254
efficiency level, 172
electrons, 112, 239
embassy, 127, 129, 254, 257
emerging markets, 252
emission, 2, 10, 14, 30, 45, 48, 111, 115, 119, 123, 128, 146, 169, 189, 199, 200, 238, 239, 243, 246, 250, 256
energy consumption, 9, 11, 13, 20, 25, 31, 42, 44, 45, 119, 120, 152, 156, 162, 163, 165, 172, 178, 182, 183, 184, 185, 186, 187, 195, 247, 256, 271
energy efficiency, vii, 2, 7, 10, 13, 14, 15, 18, 31, 38, 39, 40, 41, 42, 44, 45, 47, 48, 52, 55, 56, 57, 61, 62, 63, 65, 66, 67, 70, 71, 90, 91, 93, 94, 95, 96, 97, 98, 99, 100, 101, 102, 103, 104, 105, 106, 107, 119, 120, 126, 128, 131, 146, 151, 154, 156, 157, 158, 159,앰161, 162, 165, 172, 173, 178, 181, 182, 183, 184, 194, 195, 196, 197, 198, 200, 201, 202, 203, 207, 210, 211, 215, 235, 246, 247, 253, 254, 256, 258
energy prices, 45
energy supply, 6, 14, 38, 58, 149, 187, 198
enforcement, 15, 63, 67, 68, 70, 206, 207, 210
engineering, 12, 36, 65, 219, 220
environment, 8, 15, 37, 67, 68, 70, 90, 91, 94, 111, 116, 121, 126, 128, 151, 162, 190, 219, 220, 224, 226, 239, 244, 249, 253, 255
environmental degradation, 165
environmental impact, 116, 182, 244
environmental protection, 181, 199, 218, 234
environmental quality, 126, 253

environmental regulations, 111, 120, 219, 239, 247
EPC, 2, 63, 73, 75, 146
ethanol, 8, 10, 39, 59, 108, 109, 122, 152, 154, 158, 177, 181, 195, 201, 235, 236, 237, 249
ethylene, 182, 183
evacuated tube collectors, 2, 146
exchange rate, 155
excitation, 35, 47, 234
expenditures, 53, 221
expertise, 12, 14, 34, 36, 69, 71, 126, 154, 158, 201, 210
exploitation, 188
exporter, 159, 210, 211
exporters, 124, 125, 197, 251, 252
exports, 128, 156, 157, 182, 186, 198, 208, 255
exposure, 56, 108, 235
externalities, 66, 70
extraction, 36, 118, 184, 208, 245
extracts, 117, 244

F

factories, 183
farmers, 10
farming techniques, 64
farms, 8, 110, 114, 151, 170, 238, 242
FAS, 3, 126, 146, 253
FDI, 3, 59, 146, 207, 272
federal government, 126, 254
federal law, 130, 258
feedstock, 108, 109, 110, 158, 170, 201, 213, 236, 237, 238
fermentation, 108, 109, 110, 158, 201, 235, 236, 237, 238
fermentation technology, 158, 201
fertilizers, 11, 30, 31, 71, 91
fiber(s), 3, 30, 147, 225
films, 35, 47
filters, 123, 250
financial, 2, 3, 13, 15, 17, 38, 39, 42, 43, 49, 52, 53, 54, 55, 56, 57, 58, 60, 61, 65, 67, 68, 69, 70, 91, 93, 126, 128, 129, 130, 146, 157, 160, 162, 191, 193, 198, 203, 204, 220, 221, 254, 257, 258
financial crisis, 162
financial incentives, 13, 49, 52, 60
financial institutions, 53, 54, 55, 56, 58, 60, 61, 68, 91, 93, 203
financial intermediaries, 55, 69
financial markets, 17, 56, 160
financial support, 38
fish, 113, 116, 240, 244
fisheries, 117, 245
fishing, 115, 243

fluid, 68, 113, 115, 117, 241, 243, 245
fluidized bed, 14, 35, 36, 47
food, 12, 35, 64, 108, 110, 112, 126, 235, 238, 239, 240, 253
food production, 110, 238
food products, 12, 35
forecasting, 198
foreign affairs, 127, 254
foreign companies, 58, 202, 207, 209
foreign direct investment, 3, 59, 71, 125, 146, 158, 207, 253
foreign exchange, 210, 221
foreign firms, 14, 70, 195, 207
foreign investment, 14, 17, 49, 52, 60, 71, 158, 160, 204, 207
foreign policy, 125, 127, 253, 254, 255
formation, 66, 224
fossil fuels, vii, 7, 11, 12, 33, 66, 69, 70, 107, 111, 151, 165, 235, 238
fuel cell, 5, 11, 33, 121, 148, 154, 178, 201, 248
fuel consumption, 113, 121, 241, 248
fuel efficiency, 32
fuel prices, 63, 70
funding, 48, 53, 55, 58, 68, 91, 202, 203
funds, 48, 53, 54, 55, 56, 57, 65, 69, 91, 128, 157, 191, 193, 195, 202, 203, 204, 220, 221, 255

G

garbage, 67, 153, 170
gasification, 3, 12, 15, 30, 35, 36, 47, 62, 90, 107, 108, 109, 147, 153, 170, 232, 235, 236
GATT, 3, 64, 147
GDP, 3, 11, 13, 20, 24, 42, 54, 55, 129, 147, 156, 181, 185, 188, 256
GDP per capita, 24
gel, 107, 235
General Agreement on Tariffs and Trade, 3, 64, 147
geology, 225
gestation, 55
global trade, 128, 255
global warming, 119, 122, 246, 249
GNP, 3, 147
goods and services, 124, 125, 128, 252, 255
governance, 15, 67, 69, 196
government budget, 195
government expenditure, 221
government funds, 196
government intervention, 218
government policy, 15, 70
government procurement, 131, 158, 196, 209, 221
government securities, 69
grants, 49, 53, 58, 61

grass, 7, 107, 151, 235
gravitational force, 117, 244
gravity, 112, 240
greenhouse, 3, 8, 13, 14, 37, 38, 116, 147, 152, 244, 256
greenhouse gases, 8, 152
greenhouses, 113, 240
grid generation, 155, 167, 179, 181
grids, 10, 14, 27, 36, 38, 46, 47, 171, 199, 208
gross domestic product, 3, 147, 156
gross national product, 3, 147
groundwater, 188, 220
growth, 9, 11, 13, 14, 20, 24, 25, 32, 33, 38, 42, 54, 55, 69, 71, 108, 114, 119, 126, 152, 153, 154, 155, 162, 168, 174, 175, 178, 179, 181, 184, 196, 202, 235, 242, 246
growth rate, 11, 24, 162, 168, 179
guidelines, 41, 42, 44, 52, 58, 59, 62, 67, 90, 93, 120, 130, 219, 220, 247, 258, 272
guiding principles, 157, 197

H

harvesting, 108, 235
heat transfer, 117, 245
heavy metals, 111, 238
hemp, 108, 236
high strength, 225
high winds, 121, 248
highways, 220
homes, 8, 110, 126, 151, 238, 253
House, 78, 79, 88, 98, 99, 101, 105
housing, 219
Housing and Urban Development, 3, 55
hub, 198, 226
hybrid, vii, 7, 8, 11, 33, 61, 107, 117, 120, 121, 122, 151, 152, 167, 168, 178, 180, 225, 235, 245, 248, 249, 250
hydroelectric power, 115, 243
hydrogen, 14, 33, 36, 47, 109, 236
hydrolysis, 109, 110, 237, 238

I

imported products, 197
imports, 9, 12, 20, 24, 50, 152, 156, 164, 186, 197, 208, 210
impurities, 109, 236
income, 13, 53, 110, 126, 128, 195, 207, 238, 253, 255
income tax, 13, 195, 207
Indian law, 65

indium, 35, 47
industrial sectors, 13, 44, 182
infrastructure, 7, 15, 17, 46, 53, 54, 55, 56, 57, 58,
    67, 69, 119, 122, 128, 150, 157, 160, 198, 200,
    216, 246, 249, 250, 255
institutions, 8, 13, 40, 55, 57, 58, 69, 120, 121, 151,
    191, 198, 202, 203, 218, 247, 249, 256
insulation, 229
integration, 14, 15, 36, 47, 54, 66, 158, 159, 191,
    193, 201, 211, 226, 227, 234
intellectual property, 3, 63, 131, 147, 153, 158, 168,
    206
intellectual property rights, 3, 131, 147, 153, 158,
    168
interest rates, 49, 52, 61
International Bank for Reconstruction and
    Development, 3, 57, 147
International Chamber of Commerce, 210
international financial institutions, 38
International Financial Institutions, 56
international standards, 60, 197
international trade, 125, 210, 218, 252
ions, 252
IPR, 3, 124, 125, 127, 147, 168, 206, 252, 254
iron, 30, 229
irrigation, 46, 115, 116, 243, 244
issues, 8, 13, 15, 54, 61, 67, 69, 124, 128, 130, 152,
    156, 165, 208, 251, 255, 256, 257

J

joint ventures, 14, 52, 58, 66, 67, 71, 189, 193, 202,
    204, 208
jurisdiction, 91, 127, 174, 197, 210, 255

K

kerosene, 58, 70

L

labeling, 13, 39, 42, 157, 196, 197, 198
laws, 40, 41, 69, 124, 125, 128, 158, 196, 197, 207,
    208, 209, 217, 219, 220, 221, 251, 252, 256, 272
laws and regulations, 158, 207, 208, 209, 221
lead, 11, 33, 34, 38, 67, 68, 121, 124, 127, 196, 197,
    209, 210, 248, 251, 254
leadership, 115, 181, 184, 206, 221, 243
learning, 143, 273
LED, 4, 147, 227

legislation, 63, 127, 157, 178, 197, 209, 220, 221,
    255
lending, 54, 56, 57, 65, 203
letters of credit, 62, 210
liberalization, 40, 41, 62
lifetime, 70
light, 4, 8, 111, 112, 118, 122, 147, 151, 162, 172,
    228, 229, 230, 231, 239, 245, 249, 250
liquefied natural gas, 4, 59, 122, 148, 164, 250
liquid fuels, 14, 36, 45, 47, 200
liquidity, 54, 69
litigation, 63
livestock, 170, 171, 231
loans, 55, 56, 57, 58, 60, 61, 62, 65, 69, 157, 191,
    193, 195, 203, 204
local authorities, 39
local government, 53, 126, 196, 254, 272
LPG, 4, 45, 58, 70, 90, 122, 148, 175, 176, 250
lysis, 226

M

machinery, 12, 35, 66
macroeconomic management, 218
macroeconomic policy, 220
major issues, 219
majority, 9, 10, 30, 37, 55, 58, 153, 154, 208
manufacturing, 12, 14, 35, 37, 45, 56, 65, 66, 71,
    114, 153, 154, 155, 158, 162, 167, 172, 178, 190,
    191, 206, 225, 229, 242
market access, 124, 126, 206, 251, 253
market economy, 157, 219
market penetration, 165
market position, 16
market segment, 7, 17, 150, 160
market share, 153
marketing, 45, 167
marketplace, 16, 71, 126, 127, 253, 254, 255
mass, 42, 66, 129, 182, 198, 200, 225
materials, 35, 43, 44, 47, 111, 112, 113, 157, 183,
    195, 200, 220, 238, 239, 240, 272
matter, 5, 109, 111, 149, 208, 237, 238
measurement, 13, 224, 231, 233, 234
media, 166, 196
medical, 198
meter, 4, 27, 39, 148, 229
migration, 116, 118, 244, 245
military, 120, 248
miscommunication, 209
mission(s), 98, 100, 125, 127, 128, 218, 252, 255
models, 57, 196
modernization, 45, 66
modifications, 15, 36, 47

modules, 153, 214
moisture, 108, 112, 236, 240
moisture content, 108, 236
Mongolia, 121, 155, 167, 168, 180, 181, 203, 248
monopoly, 70
moratorium, 62
morbidity, 188
mortality, 188
motor system, 183
multilateral aid, 191
multinational enterprises, 258
municipal solid waste, 66, 108, 236

N

nanometer, 229
national emergency, 64, 127, 255
national policy, 41, 43, 204
national security, 127, 255
natural gas, 2, 8, 11, 24, 32, 43, 121, 122, 128, 130, 146, 152, 154, 158, 170, 198, 201, 218, 248, 249, 250, 256, 258
natural resources, 107, 219, 235
networking, 130, 209, 224, 225, 230, 258
neutral, 122, 249
nitrogen, 5, 148, 187
nitrous oxide, 5, 8, 38, 148, 152
non-renewable resources, 121, 248
nuclear power, 24, 208

O

obstacles, 7, 17, 129, 150, 160, 257
officials, 128, 199, 256
oil, 4, 6, 8, 9, 10, 11, 19, 20, 24, 39, 45, 58, 59, 90, 107, 108, 110, 113, 126, 148, 149, 152, 156, 162, 164, 173, 183, 184, 186, 194, 218, 235, 236, 238, 241, 253
oilseed, 10, 39
operating costs, 68, 112, 118, 119, 240, 245, 246
operations, 8, 14, 36, 57, 110, 111, 151, 156, 158, 200, 215, 238, 239
opportunities, vii, 7, 14, 15, 17, 18, 35, 40, 46, 65, 71, 125, 150, 153, 157, 158, 160, 161, 199, 204, 206, 210, 258
optimization, 183, 224, 225, 231
organ, 220, 221
outreach programs, 125, 252
Overseas Private Investment Corporation, 5, 125, 148, 252
ownership, 189, 207
oxidation, 109, 236

oxygen, 109, 236, 237

P

palm oil, 108, 236
patents, 63, 64, 70, 206
pathways, 108, 110, 235, 238
petroleum, 4, 13, 42, 58, 90, 108, 148, 164, 173, 176, 183, 198, 234, 236
pharmaceuticals, 91
PHB, 107
plants, 8, 12, 24, 34, 36, 38, 42, 45, 47, 51, 107, 108, 109, 111, 114, 115, 116, 121, 151, 168, 173, 181, 188, 194, 203, 208, 215, 235, 237, 238, 239, 242, 243, 244, 249
plastics, 225
policy initiative, 40, 67, 181
policy instruments, 156, 157, 194
politics, 217
pollutants, vii, 7, 119, 151, 246
pollution, 8, 11, 13, 32, 36, 41, 45, 65, 90, 91, 94, 111, 120, 121, 122, 129, 152, 156, 158, 165, 187, 188, 210, 219, 239, 247, 249, 250, 256
pools, 112, 240
portfolio, 5, 12, 26, 33, 37, 42, 50, 56, 67, 70, 149, 197
poultry, 37, 171, 231
poverty, 2, 15, 46, 145
poverty alleviation, 46
poverty line, 2, 145
power generation, vii, 7, 8, 10, 12, 13, 14, 15, 24, 27, 30, 33, 35, 37, 42, 47, 51, 52, 53, 56, 57, 60, 61, 65, 66, 71, 107, 108, 111, 120, 121, 151, 153, 165, 166, 168, 169, 171, 173, 174, 179, 181, 189, 191, 200, 207, 224, 225, 233, 234, 235, 238, 248
power plants, 8, 24, 45, 66, 67, 110, 111, 115, 121, 151, 154, 155, 158, 168, 174, 181, 183, 201, 208, 238, 239, 242, 249, 272
PRC, 272
precedent, 33, 70
predators, 113, 240
president, 127, 128, 254, 255
prevention, 219, 230
price mechanism, 157, 198
price stability, 70
prima facie, 65
principles, 36, 47, 63, 196, 217
prisons, 8, 121, 151, 249
private investment, 60
private sector investment, 56, 58
probability, 4, 24, 148
producers, 114, 192, 242
production costs, 155, 178, 190, 209

professional development, 130, 258
professionals, 130, 258
profit, 128, 129, 130, 166, 186, 204, 208, 256, 257, 258
profit margin, 166, 186
project, 11, 14, 15, 16, 30, 33, 37, 44, 47, 49, 52, 53, 55, 57, 58, 59, 60, 61, 62, 63, 66, 68, 69, 70, 71, 90, 111, 114, 115, 118, 129, 170, 178, 189, 192, 197, 201, 202, 203, 207, 227, 228, 230, 231, 232, 233, 239, 242, 243, 245, 257
project sponsors, 61, 63, 69
proliferation, 127, 255
propane, 8, 122, 152, 249
property rights, 258
protection, 113, 125, 181, 206, 219, 220, 227, 230, 234, 240, 252
protectionism, 206
prototypes, 117, 244
public awareness, 195, 199, 200, 201
public finance, 220, 221
public interest, 128, 255, 256
public policy, 57
public sector, 45, 49, 59, 60, 90, 92
publishing, 13
pumps, 112, 119, 174, 193, 240, 246
purchasing power, 184
purification, 12, 35, 201
pyrolysis, 12, 14, 36, 47, 108, 109, 235, 237

Q

quality control, 197
quality of life, 126, 254
quality standards, 38
quotas, 14, 17, 38, 49, 50, 52, 59, 160

R

radiation, 10, 27, 153, 166, 230, 231
raw materials, 65, 110, 238
real estate, 219
recommendations, iv, 197, 218, 220
reconstruction, 55
recovery, 12, 15, 36, 47, 189
recreation, 115, 116, 243, 244
Reform(s), 6, 40, 41, 43, 53, 57, 146, 148, 150, 152, 157, 162, 169, 192, 193, 203, 208, 216, 218, 220, 223, 271, 272
regions of the world, 128, 255
regulations, 44, 69, 90, 131, 156, 158, 171, 190, 192, 194, 196, 207, 209, 217, 218, 219, 220, 221, 258
regulatory framework, 40, 53, 91, 202

regulatory requirements, 54, 197
rehabilitation, 57, 203
reliability, 24
REM, 106
renewable energy, vii, 5, 7, 9, 10, 11, 13, 14, 15, 18, 20, 25, 26, 30, 33, 34, 37, 38, 39, 40, 41, 42, 43, 45, 52, 55, 56, 57, 59, 60, 61, 62, 63, 65, 66, 67, 68, 69, 70, 71, 90, 91, 93, 94, 103, 107, 114, 115, 118, 119, 122, 123, 126, 128, 129, 130, 149, 150, 151, 152, 153, 154, 155, 156, 157, 158, 159, 161, 165, 168, 172, 178, 179, 181, 189, 190, 191, 192, 193, 197, 198, 199, 200, 201, 202, 203, 210, 211, 218, 235, 242, 243, 245, 246, 250, 253, 254, 256, 257, 258, 271
renewable fuel, 122, 249
Renewable Portfolio Standard (RPS), 5, 42, 67, 149
renewables, 11, 19, 52, 66, 119, 246
requirements, 11, 13, 17, 30, 41, 43, 44, 45, 46, 54, 119, 157, 160, 197, 200, 203, 204, 206, 246
RES, 73
research institutions, 178
reserves, 9, 24, 31, 198, 218, 219
residues, 7, 107, 151, 235
resource availability, 61
resource utilization, 153, 169
resources, 7, 9, 13, 14, 17, 19, 24, 25, 31, 37, 38, 42, 43, 57, 108, 115, 121, 123, 124, 125, 126, 131, 150, 152, 153, 160, 162, 163, 165, 166, 198, 206, 208, 218, 219, 224, 227, 233, 235, 242, 243, 248, 250, 251, 252, 259
restrictions, 15, 158, 209
restructuring, 58, 183
retail, 42, 69, 129, 257
revenue, 53, 63, 70, 204
risk management, 69
risk perception, 68
river systems, 116, 244
rules, 44, 90, 131, 189, 192, 193, 207, 258
rural areas, 13, 43, 44, 46, 180, 191
rural development, 46
rural population, 116, 171, 243, 244

S

safety, 44, 197, 210, 219, 220, 225, 226
sanctions, 127, 255
savings, 8, 119, 120, 152, 174, 184, 195, 202, 246, 247
sawdust, 109, 237
scale system, 8, 110, 151, 238
scaling, 162
scarcity, 188, 228
science, 219

SCO, 97, 102
seed, 202
segregation, 49, 61
self-discipline, 209
self-sufficiency, 152, 163
sensitivity, 208
service provider, 8, 119, 129, 152, 246, 256, 257
services, iv, 16, 39, 44, 46, 56, 57, 62, 66, 71, 110, 118, 119, 120, 124, 128, 129, 130, 154, 156, 158, 159, 198, 200, 201, 202, 208, 211, 215, 238, 245, 246, 247, 251, 256, 257, 258
sewage, 54, 153, 170, 171, 188, 193, 231, 233
short supply, 9, 24
silicon, 3, 14, 35, 47, 146, 167, 201, 214, 229, 230
silver, 229
small businesses, 127, 255
social development, 15, 57, 198, 217, 218, 219
social relations, 15, 67
social relationships, 15, 67
solar cells, 153, 166, 214
solar collectors, 113, 241
solar system, 113, 168, 180, 240
solid phase, 3, 146
solid waste, 54, 57, 58, 111, 239
species, 118, 245
stakeholders, 63, 254
standardization, 67, 157, 195, 198, 234
starch, 108, 109, 236, 237
state-owned enterprises, 66
statistics, 126, 130, 198, 253, 258
steel, 11, 30, 31, 71, 91, 117, 182, 183, 185, 186, 201, 245
storage, 8, 11, 33, 44, 112, 113, 116, 120, 121, 151, 158, 175, 184, 201, 230, 231, 233, 239, 241, 244, 248
strain improvement, 232
strategic position, 156, 190, 191
structural adjustment, 182
structure, 40, 52, 54, 55, 61, 70, 90, 91, 117, 157, 197, 221, 233, 244, 245, 272
structuring, 165
subsidy, 33, 34, 49, 52, 60, 61, 70, 153, 157, 167, 180, 194
substitutes, 107, 235
sugar beet, 108, 109, 236, 237
sugar mills, 49, 59, 60
sugarcane, 7, 107, 108, 109, 151, 154, 171, 194, 235, 236, 237
sulfur, 111, 201, 238
sulfur dioxide, 111, 238
sulfuric acid, 30
sulphur, 6, 149
Sun, 80, 82, 86, 178

supplier(s), 15, 35, 37, 45, 47, 61, 63, 114, 165, 178, 196, 242
supply chain, 184
Supreme Court, 210
surplus, 10, 29, 109, 183, 237
sustainable development, 130, 218, 219, 258
sustainable economic growth, 56
sustainable energy, 19, 130, 162
synchronization, 35
synthesis, 183, 220

T

tactics, 130, 257
tanks, 113, 170, 241
tar, 36, 47, 232
target, 11, 31, 34, 38, 154, 156, 174, 180, 184, 191, 195, 200, 202
tariff, 14, 38, 42, 43, 51, 52, 59, 68, 154, 156, 174, 181, 190, 192, 198, 199, 207
tax breaks, 207
tax collection, 221
tax rates, 15, 71
tax reform, 207
tax system, 207
taxation, 194, 220
taxes, 13, 50, 53, 90, 172
taxpayers, 125, 253
technical assistance, 57, 126, 128, 203, 255
technological advances, 35
technological developments, 181
technology transfer, 71, 120, 153, 155, 165, 167, 189, 190, 193, 200, 201, 206, 209, 247
telecommunications, 112, 239
temperature, 35, 47, 116, 117, 232, 233, 244, 245
testing, 6, 33, 34, 149, 153, 169, 197, 201, 221, 226
thermal decomposition, 109, 237
thermal energy, 8, 9, 47, 115, 117, 121, 151, 153, 168, 181, 242, 245, 249
thin films, 35, 47
tides, 107, 117, 235, 244
total energy, 27, 31, 43, 50, 152, 163, 164, 172
total product, 178, 213
trade, vii, 7, 15, 17, 18, 19, 62, 69, 71, 124, 125, 126, 127, 128, 129, 130, 131, 150, 160, 161, 162, 164, 204, 206, 208, 210, 221, 251, 252, 253, 255, 256, 257, 258, 259
trade agreement, 124, 126, 128, 251, 253, 255
trade policy, 124, 128, 251, 255
trademarks, 206
training, 57, 120, 128, 129, 130, 193, 206, 247, 255, 257
training programs, 120, 247

transaction costs, 68
transactions, 54, 127, 210
transesterification, 110, 238
transmission, 31, 38, 39, 42, 56, 68, 91, 105, 106, 115, 149, 171, 191, 243
transparency, 54, 62, 158, 196, 209
transport, 11, 32, 42, 43, 45, 175, 184, 200, 201, 220, 225
transportation, vii, 7, 8, 11, 32, 33, 41, 43, 49, 57, 61, 107, 108, 110, 120, 121, 122, 126, 151, 152, 154, 175, 182, 183, 184, 199, 200, 220, 235, 236, 238, 247, 248, 249, 250, 253
Treasury, 101, 127, 255
treatment, 8, 36, 47, 108, 121, 151, 156, 171, 190, 191, 198, 201, 207, 224, 233, 236, 249
treatment methods, 36, 47

U

U.S. Department of Commerce, vii, 1, 2, 18, 124, 145, 146, 150, 161, 251
U.S. economy, 130, 258
universal access, 41
universities, 126, 175
uranium, 198
urban, 6, 11, 32, 42, 43, 49, 54, 57, 58, 115, 120, 153, 186, 219, 220, 231, 232, 233, 242, 247
urbanization, 156, 185, 200
USDA, 6, 126, 150, 253

V

vacuum, 109, 228, 237
vapor, 117, 245
VAT, 6, 150, 157, 195
vegetable oil, 108, 236
vehicles, 8, 11, 32, 33, 42, 122, 152, 154, 175, 177, 178, 200, 249, 250
ventilation, 38, 113, 241
venture capital, 69, 181, 189, 206
VSD, 6, 150, 217

W

war, 127
Washington, 129, 256
waste, vii, 7, 8, 9, 12, 15, 16, 18, 20, 26, 30, 34, 36, 37, 45, 49, 55, 58, 61, 66, 67, 71, 107, 108, 109, 110, 111, 112, 122, 129, 151, 153, 154, 157, 161, 170, 171, 195, 232, 235, 236, 237, 238, 239, 240, 249, 256
waste heat, 108, 122, 236, 249
waste management, 55
waste treatment, 111, 153, 170, 239
wastewater, 8, 121, 151, 153, 170, 249
water, 5, 6, 8, 10, 12, 14, 27, 30, 35, 38, 44, 49, 54, 56, 57, 61, 108, 110, 111, 112, 113, 114, 115, 116, 117, 122, 128, 143, 148, 149, 151, 152, 153, 154, 156, 165, 168, 170, 178, 179, 180, 181, 183, 188, 193, 196, 197, 201, 203, 210, 215, 220, 228, 233, 234, 235, 238, 239, 241, 242, 243, 244, 245, 249, 256, 273
water heater, 10, 27, 153, 183, 228
water resources, 10, 30, 115, 156, 188, 220, 243
watershed, 234
wave power, 117, 233, 234, 245
weapons of mass destruction, 127, 255
welding, 229
wind farm, 10, 27, 114, 158, 159, 165, 166, 203, 207, 211, 242
wind turbines, 8, 14, 114, 115, 117, 120, 151, 153, 158, 165, 197, 201, 225, 241, 242, 244, 248
wood, 7, 107, 108, 109, 110, 151, 153, 231, 232, 235, 236, 237, 238
wood waste, 108, 236
World Bank, 18, 56, 57, 149, 156, 161, 167, 168, 187, 188, 202, 203, 272
World Trade Organization (WTO), 7, 131, 150, 184, 199, 208, 258, 259
worldwide, 115, 124, 130, 155, 190, 204, 243, 251, 258

Y

yield, 158, 168, 171, 174, 181, 201, 224, 232